# STOCK TRADER'S ALMANAC

## 2 O 2 3

Jeffrey A. Hirsch & Christopher Mistal

WILEY

www.stocktradersalmanac.com

**In memory of Yale Hirsch**
(1923-2021)
Creator and founder of the *Stock Trader's Almanac*—who continues to inspire us.

| | |
|---|---|
| **Editor in Chief** | Jeffrey A. Hirsch |
| **Director of Research** | Christopher Mistal |
| **Graphic Design** | Darlene Dion Design |
| ***Publisher 1966-2000 & Editor 1966-2003*** | Yale Hirsch (1923-2021) |

For general information about our other products and services, please contact our Customer Care Department within the United States at 800-762-2974, outside the United States at 317-572-3993, or fax at 317-572-4002. For bulk or custom orders, please contact Special Sales at specialsales@wiley.com.

Wiley also publishes its books in a variety of electronic formats. Some content that appears in print may not be available in electronic formats. For more information about Wiley products, visit our web site at www.wiley.com.

ISBN: 978-1-119-98646-1 (paper)
ISBN: 978-1-119-98687-4 (ePDF)
ISBN: 978-1-119-98686-7 (ePub)

SKY10035806_090622

# THE 2023 STOCK TRADER'S ALMANAC

## CONTENTS

# DIRECTORY OF TRADING PATTERNS AND DATABANK

# STRATEGY PLANNING AND RECORD SECTION

# INTRODUCTION TO THE FIFTY-SIXTH EDITION

Once again we have the honor of introducing the new edition of the *Stock Trader's Almanac*. The *Almanac* provides you with the necessary tools and data to invest and trade successfully in the twenty-first century.

J.P. Morgan's classic retort "Stocks will fluctuate" is often quoted with a wink-of-the-eye implication that the only prediction one can make about the stock market is that it will go up, down, or sideways. Many investors and traders agree that no one ever really knows which way the market will move. Nothing could be further from the truth.

We discovered that while stocks do indeed fluctuate, they do so in well-defined, often predictable patterns. These patterns recur too frequently to be the result of chance or coincidence. How else do we explain that since 1950 the Dow has gained 24884.34 points during November through April compared to just 7878.54 May through October? (See page 54.)

The *Almanac* is a practical investment tool. It alerts you to those little-known market patterns and tendencies on which shrewd professionals enhance profit potential. You will be able to forecast market trends with accuracy and confidence when you use the *Almanac* to help you understand:

- How our presidential elections affect the economy and the stock market—just as the moon affects the tides. Many investors have made fortunes following the political cycle. You can be sure that money managers who control billions of dollars are also political-cycle watchers. Astute people do not ignore a pattern that has been working effectively throughout most of our economic history.

- How the passage of the Twentieth Amendment to the Constitution fathered the January Barometer. This barometer has an outstanding record for predicting the general course of the stock market each year, with only 12 major errors since 1950, it has 83.3% accuracy ratio. (See page 18.)

- Why there is a significant market bias at certain times of the day, week, month and year.

Even if you are an investor who pays scant attention to cycles, indicators and patterns, your investment survival could hinge on your interpretation of one of the recurring patterns found within these pages. One of the most intriguing and important patterns is the symbiotic relationship between Washington and Wall Street. Aside from the potential profitability in seasonal patterns, there's the pure joy of seeing the market very often do just what you expected.

The *Stock Trader's Almanac* is also an organizer. Its wealth of information is presented on a calendar basis. The *Almanac* puts investing in a business framework and makes investing easier because it:

■ Updates investment knowledge and informs you of new techniques and tools.

■ Is a monthly reminder and refresher course.

■ Alerts you to both seasonal opportunities and dangers.

■ Furnishes a historical viewpoint by providing pertinent statistics on past market performance.

■ Supplies forms necessary for portfolio planning, record keeping and tax preparation.

 The WITCH Icon signifies THIRD FRIDAY OF THE MONTH on calendar pages and alerts you to extraordinary volatility due to expiration of monthly equity and index options and index futures contracts. "Triple-Witching" days (indicated by 3 WITCH Icons) appear during March, June, September and December. Some readers have questioned why we do not use the term "quadruple witching" as some in the business do. As we point out on page 108 the market for single-stock and ETF futures remains small and their impact on the market is virtually nonexistent. If and when single-stock futures trading volume expands and exerts influence on the market we will reconsider. Until such time, we do not believe the term "quadruple witching" is applicable.

 The BULL Icon on calendar pages signifies favorable trading days based on the S&P 500 rising 60% or more of the time on a particular trading day during the 21-year period January 2001 to December 2021.

 A BEAR Icon on calendar pages signifies unfavorable trading days based on the S&P falling 60% or more of the time for the same 21-year period.

Clusters of two or more BULLs or BEARs can be especially helpful in identifying periods of strength or weakness throughout the year. Clusters can also be three out of four days or three out of five days. An example of three BULLs in four days can be observed on page 43 during the first week of April.

On pages 123-130 you will find complete Market Probability Calendars for both long term and the recent 21-year period for the Dow, S&P and NASDAQ, as well as for the Russell 1000 and Russell 2000 indices. To give you even greater perspective we have listed next to the date every day that the market is open the Market Probability numbers for the same 21-year period for the Dow (D), S&P 500 (S) and NASDAQ (N). You will see a "D," "S" and "N" followed by a number signifying the actual Market Probability number for that trading day based on the recent 21-year period.

Other seasonalities near the ends, beginnings, and middles of months; options expirations; around holidays; and other times are noted for *Almanac* investors' convenience on the weekly planner pages. All other important economic releases are provided in the Strategy Calendar every month in our e-newsletter, *Almanac Investor*, available at our website *www.stocktradersalmanac.com*. Please see the insert for a special offer for new subscribers.

One-year seasonal pattern charts for Dow, S&P 500, NASDAQ, Russell 1000, and Russell 2000 appear on pages 42, 44 and 46. There are three charts each for Dow and S&P 500 spanning our entire database starting in 1901 and one each for the younger indices. As 2023 is a pre-election year, each chart contains typical pre-election year performance compared to all years.

The Russell 2000 is an excellent proxy for small- and mid-caps and the Russell 1000 provides a broader view of large caps. Annual highs and lows for all five indices covered in the *Almanac* appear on pages 151-155. Top 10 Best & Worst days, weeks, months, quarters and years for all five indices are listed on pages 174-183.

We have converted many of the paper forms in our Record Keeping section into spreadsheets for our own internal use. As a service to our faithful readers, we are making these forms available at our website *www.stocktradersalmanac.com*. Look for a link titled "Forms" located at the bottom of the homepage.

Pre-election years have historically been the best year of the four-year cycle over multiple time frames. You can find all the market charts of pre-election years since the Depression on page 26, "Pre-Presidential Election Years: Only One Loser In 84 Years" on page 28, "Why A 50% Gain in the Dow Is Possible From Its 2022 Low to Its 2023 High" on page 30, and "Welcome to the Sweet Spot Of The 4-Year Cycle: Q4 Midterm Year to Q2 Pre-Election Year" on page 34.

On page 80 we present "Bob Farrell's Market Rules to Remember & Justin Mamis' Sentiment Cycle." The return of the bear and increased market volatility in 2022 makes the lessons that can be learned from these two legends as relevant as ever. Our "2010 Super Boom Forecast Dow 38820 Ahead of Schedule" update can be found on page 104.

Our 2023 Outlook on pages 10-11 projects a more upbeat outlook following 2022's bear market. "How To Trade Best Months Switching Strategies" appears on page 38. How "Summer Market Volume Doldrums Drives Worst Six Months" is updated on page 48. Sector seasonalities including several consistent shorting opportunities, appear on pages 94-98.

We are constantly searching for new insights and nuances about the stock market and welcome any suggestions from our readers.

Have a healthy and prosperous 2023!

# 2023 OUTLOOK

Well, we got our midterm bear market in 2022. While that may not have felt so great in your portfolio at the time, it was in line with the cycles and seasonal patterns we track and rely on. As we suggested in last year's edition, gains have been harder to come by in 2022 and it does look like we will get a midterm bear market bottom. And we are still on pace with our annual 2022 newsletter forecast for early-year highs, a Worst Six Months correction and a Q4 rally.

For the first time since the 1980s the Federal Reserve is being forced to raise interest rates to fight runaway inflation. The Fed is finally aggressively moving away from the ZIRP (zero interest rate policy) and massive QE (quantitative easing) it has had in place for the better part of 15 years. In June 2022 they commenced an accelerated QT (quantitative tightening) process, culling assets from its $9 trillion balance sheet at the same time it increased interest rates at the fastest pace since 1994.

High inflation and a no-holds-barred Fed tightening policy are not the market's only concerns. There are the lingering impacts of the Covid-19 pandemic, especially China's zero-Covid policy and the likelihood of renewed lockdowns that will continue to exacerbate already strained and depleted supply chains and inventories. The Russia-Ukraine War appears likely to drag on into a Cold War 2.0 scenario. Energy prices are jumping faster than we have seen in decades. The current scenario is quite directly comparable to the 1970s.

But all these major risks and negative action may help reset imbalances and signal a return to normalcy for interest rates, valuations, and stock market returns. Price-earnings ratios have already fallen dramatically and are nearing historic averages, though they will likely fall further still.

Market weakness in 2022 during the Worst Six Months of the year (May-October) and the second and third quarter of the midterm election year also suggests historic seasonal and cyclical patterns and forces are at work. Adding in the drop in consumer confidence, recession fears and the incumbent's already low and dwindling approval ratings implies that we are poised for the usual loss of Congressional seats by the incumbent president's party, likely resulting in control of the U.S. House of Representatives changing hands, with the potential for control of both houses of Congress to flip.

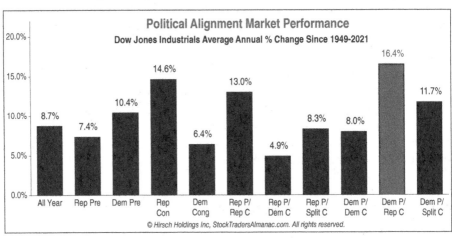

Political Alignment Market Performance
Dow Jones Industrials Average Annual % Change Since 1949-2021

© Hirsch Holdings Inc, StockTradersAlmanac.com. All rights reserved.

However, this would create the best political alignment for the stock market: a Democratic president with a Republican Congress. In the chart on page 10, you can see in the green bar this combination has produced the best market performance for an average gain on the Dow of 16.4% since 1949. It remains to be seen if President Biden can tack to the center and facilitate some bipartisan legislation as Bill Clinton did after the 1994 midterms.

In any event, we believe the Fed's recent 75-basis-point increase and their telegraphing of another one in July suggests they are likely to be done ahead of the midterm elections, which dovetails with the seasonal and 4-year cycle patterns. It sure has taken them long enough to get here, but we welcome it and the sooner they get to the end of the tightening cycle the better in our view. When we do get a clear indication of a pause or end to rate hikes that will likely be a signal the bear market is over.

This sets up well for Pre-Election Year 2023 as well as our 2010 Super Boom Forecast for Dow 38820 by 2025 (page 104). The 2022 bear market will likely bounce along sideways testing the June 2022 lows, reaching a bear market low in late Q3 or early Q4 in the August-October timeframe in typical midterm bottom fashion. Then we expect a new bull market to commence in the Sweet Spot of the 4-Year Cycle (page 34) that takes the market to new highs in Pre-Election Year 2023.

From the midterm low to the pre-election year high the Dow gains 46.8% on average since 1914 and NASDAQ gains a whopping 68.2% on average since 1974! If the Dow declines the average bear market drop of about 30% (page 133) to 25760 and rallies around 50% from the midterm low to the pre-election high (page 30) it would be at 38640.

The chart here of the S&P 500 Seasonal Pattern depicts four rather bullish scenarios for 2023. All pre-election years since 1949 have an average gain of 16.8%. Pre-election years after a midterm bear market like 2022 average 20.3% and first-term presidents' pre-election years average 20.1%. Our new Aggregate Cycle of the One-Year Seasonal Pattern, the 4-Year Presidential Election Cycle and the Decennial Cycle averages 12.3%. Despite current worrisome conditions, we believe a midterm bear market bottom and new bull market are on the horizon. Remember Warrant Buffet's wise words: "Be greedy when others are fearful."

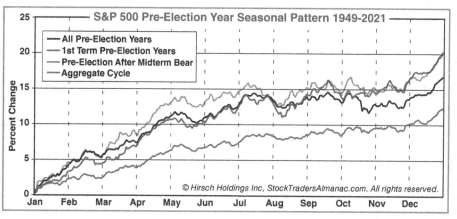

— *Jeffrey A. Hirsch, June 15, 2022*

# 2023 STRATEGY CALENDAR

### (Option expiration dates circled)

| | MONDAY | TUESDAY | WEDNESDAY | THURSDAY | FRIDAY | SATURDAY | SUNDAY |
|---|---|---|---|---|---|---|---|
| **JANUARY** | 26 | 27 | 28 | 29 | 30 | 31 | 1 JANUARY New Year's Day |
| | 2 | 3 | 4 | 5 | 6 | 7 | 8 |
| | 9 | 10 | 11 | 12 | 13 | 14 | 15 |
| | 16 Martin Luther King Day | 17 | 18 | 19 | (20) | 21 | 22 |
| | 23 | 24 | 25 | 26 | 27 | 28 | 29 |
| **FEBRUARY** | 30 | 31 | 1 FEBRUARY | 2 | 3 | 4 | 5 |
| | 6 | 7 | 8 | 9 | 10 | 11 | 12 |
| | 13 | 14 ♥ | 15 | 16 | (17) | 18 | 19 |
| | 20 Presidents' Day | 21 | 22 Ash Wednesday | 23 | 24 | 25 | 26 |
| **MARCH** | 27 | 28 | 1 MARCH | 2 | 3 | 4 | 5 |
| | 6 | 7 | 8 | 9 | 10 | 11 | 12 Daylight Saving Time Begins |
| | 13 | 14 | 15 | 16 | (17) ♣ St. Patrick's Day | 18 | 19 |
| | 20 | 21 | 22 | 23 | 24 | 25 | 26 |
| **APRIL** | 27 | 28 | 29 | 30 | 31 | 1 APRIL | 2 |
| | 3 | 4 | 5 | 6 Passover | 7 Good Friday | 8 | 9 Easter |
| | 10 | 11 | 12 | 13 | 14 | 15 | 16 |
| | 17 | 18 Tax Deadline | 19 | 20 | (21) | 22 | 23 |
| **MAY** | 24 | 25 | 26 | 27 | 28 | 29 | 30 |
| | 1 MAY | 2 | 3 | 4 | 5 | 6 | 7 |
| | 8 | 9 | 10 | 11 | 12 | 13 | 14 Mother's Day |
| | 15 | 16 | 17 | 18 | (19) | 20 | 21 |
| | 22 | 23 | 24 | 25 | 26 | 27 | 28 |
| **JUNE** | 29 Memorial Day | 30 | 31 | 1 JUNE | 2 | 3 | 4 |
| | 5 | 6 | 7 | 8 | 9 | 10 | 11 |
| | 12 | 13 | 14 | 15 | (16) | 17 | 18 Father's Day |
| | 19 Juneteenth | 20 | 21 | 22 | 23 | 24 | 25 |
| | 26 | 27 | 28 | 29 | 30 | 1 JULY | 2 |

12 *Market closed on shaded weekdays; closes early when half-shaded.*

# 2023 STRATEGY CALENDAR

(Option expiration dates circled)

| MONDAY | TUESDAY | WEDNESDAY | THURSDAY | FRIDAY | SATURDAY | SUNDAY | |
|--------|---------|-----------|----------|--------|----------|--------|---|
| 3 | 4 *Independence Day* | 5 | 6 | 7 | 8 | 9 | JULY |
| 10 | 11 | 12 | 13 | 14 | 15 | 16 | |
| 17 | 18 | 19 | 20 | (21) | 22 | 23 | |
| 24 | 25 | 26 | 27 | 28 | 29 | 30 | |
| 31 | 1 AUGUST | 2 | 3 | 4 | 5 | 6 | AUGUST |
| 7 | 8 | 9 | 10 | 11 | 12 | 13 | |
| 14 | 15 | 16 | 17 | (18) | 19 | 20 | |
| 21 | 22 | 23 | 24 | 25 | 26 | 27 | |
| 28 | 29 | 30 | 31 | 1 SEPTEMBER | 2 | 3 | SEPTEMBER |
| 4 *Labor Day* | 5 | 6 | 7 | 8 | 9 | 10 | |
| 11 | 12 | 13 | 14 | (15) | 16 *Rosh Hashanah* | 17 | |
| 18 | 19 | 20 | 21 | 22 | 23 | 24 | |
| 25 *Yom Kippur* | 26 | 27 | 28 | 29 | 30 | 1 OCTOBER | OCTOBER |
| 2 | 3 | 4 | 5 | 6 | 7 | 8 | |
| 9 *Columbus Day* | 10 | 11 | 12 | 13 | 14 | 15 | |
| 16 | 17 | 18 | 19 | (20) | 21 | 22 | |
| 23 | 24 | 25 | 26 | 27 | 28 | 29 | |
| 30 | 31 🎃 | 1 NOVEMBER | 2 | 3 | 4 | 5 *Daylight Saving Time Ends* | NOVEMBER |
| 6 | 7 *Election Day* | 8 | 9 | 10 | 11 *Veterans' Day* | 12 | |
| 13 | 14 | 15 | 16 | (17) | 18 | 19 | |
| 20 | 21 | 22 | 23 *Thanksgiving* | 24 | 25 | 26 | |
| 27 | 28 | 29 | 30 | 1 DECEMBER | 2 | 3 | DECEMBER |
| 4 | 5 | 6 | 7 | 8 *Chanukah* | 9 | 10 | |
| 11 | 12 | 13 | 14 | (15) | 16 | 17 | |
| 18 | 19 | 20 | 21 | 22 | 23 | 24 | |
| 25 *Christmas* | 26 | 27 | 28 | 29 | 30 | 31 | |

13

# JANUARY ALMANAC

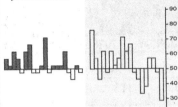

| JANUARY | | | | | | | FEBRUARY | | | | | | |
|---|---|---|---|---|---|---|---|---|---|---|---|---|---|
| S | M | T | W | T | F | S | S | M | T | W | T | F | S |
| 1 | 2 | 3 | 4 | 5 | 6 | 7 | | | | 1 | 2 | 3 | 4 |
| 8 | 9 | 10 | 11 | 12 | 13 | 14 | 5 | 6 | 7 | 8 | 9 | 10 | 11 |
| 15 | 16 | 17 | 18 | 19 | 20 | 21 | 12 | 13 | 14 | 15 | 16 | 17 | 18 |
| 22 | 23 | 24 | 25 | 26 | 27 | 28 | 19 | 20 | 21 | 22 | 23 | 24 | 25 |
| 29 | 30 | 31 | | | | | 26 | 27 | 28 | | | | |

*Market Probability Chart above is a graphic representation of the S&P 500 Recent Market Probability Calendar on page 126.*

◆ January Barometer predicts year's course with .722 batting average (page 18) ◆ 15 of last 18 pre-election years followed January's direction ◆ Every down January on the S&P since 1950, *without exception*, preceded a new or extended bear market, a flat market, or a 10% correction (page 22) ◆ S&P gains January's first five days preceded full-year gains 83.0% of the time, 13 of last 18 pre-election years followed first five day's direction (page 16) ◆ November, December and January constitute the year's best three-month span, a 4.2% S&P gain (pages 52 & 149) ◆ January NASDAQ powerful 2.5% since 1971 (pages 60 & 150) ◆ "January Effect" now starts in mid-December and favors small-cap stocks (pages 112 & 114) ◆ 2009 worst S&P 500 January ◆ Dow gained more than 1000 points in 2018 & 2019.

## January Vital Statistics

| | DJIA | S&P 500 | NASDAQ | Russell 1K | Russell 2K |
|---|---|---|---|---|---|
| Rank | 6 | 6 | 1 | 4 | 4 |
| Up | 45 | 43 | 34 | 26 | 24 |
| Down | 28 | 43 | 18 | 18 | 20 |
| Avg % Change | 0.9% | 1.0% | 2.5% | 0.9% | 1.4% |
| Pre-Election Year | 3.9% | 4.1% | 6.8% | 3.4% | 3.9% |
| **Best and Worst** | | | | | |
| | % Change | % Change | % Change | % Change | % Change |
| Best | 1976 14.4 | 1987 13.2 | 1975 16.6 | 1987 12.7 | 1985 13.1 |
| Worst | 2009 −8.8 | 2009 −8.6 | 2008 −9.9 | 2009 −8.3 | 2009 −11.2 |
| **Best and Worst Weeks** | | | | | |
| Best | 1/9/76 6.1 | 1/2/09 6.8 | 1/12/01 9.1 | 1/2/09 6.8 | 1/9/87 7.0 |
| Worst | 1/8/16 −6.2 | 1/8/16 −6.0 | 1/28/00 −8.2 | 1/8/16 −6.0 | 1/21/22 −8.1 |
| **Best and Worst Days** | | | | | |
| Best | 1/17/91 4.6 | 1/3/01 5.0 | 1/3/01 14.2 | 1/3/01 5.3 | 1/2/09 5.3 |
| Worst | 1/8/88 −6.9 | 1/8/88 −6.8 | 1/2/01 −7.2 | 1/8/88 −6.1 | 1/20/09 −7.0 |
| **First Trading Day of Expiration Week: 1980–2022** | | | | | |
| Record (#Up–#Down) | 27-16 | 24-19 | 22-21 | 22-21 | 22-21 |
| Current Streak | D1 | D1 | D1 | D1 | D1 |
| Avg % Change | 0.05 | 0.03 | 0.03 | 0.005 | −0.03 |
| **Options Expiration Day: 1980–2022** | | | | | |
| Record (#Up–#Down) | 24-19 | 24-19 | 25-18 | 24-19 | 25-18 |
| Current Streak | D2 | D2 | D1 | D2 | D1 |
| Avg % Change | −0.01 | 0.01 | −0.05 | −0.01 | 0.04 |
| **Options Expiration Week: 1980–2022** | | | | | |
| Record (#Up–#Down) | 24-19 | 20-23 | 28-18 | 20-23 | 24-19 |
| Current Streak | D1 | D1 | D1 | D1 | D1 |
| Avg % Change | −0.10 | −0.01 | 0.28 | −0.02 | 0.17 |
| **Week After Options Expiration: 1980–2022** | | | | | |
| Record (#Up–#Down) | 24-19 | 26-17 | 25-18 | 26-17 | 28-15 |
| Current Streak | U1 | U1 | U1 | U1 | D3 |
| Avg % Change | 0.03 | 0.18 | 0.11 | 0.15 | 0.05 |
| **First Trading Day Performance** | | | | | |
| % of Time Up | 60.3 | 50.7 | 57.7 | 47.7 | 47.7 |
| Avg % Change | 0.24 | 0.16 | 0.22 | 0.15 | 0.06 |
| **Last Trading Day Performance** | | | | | |
| % of Time Up | 54.8 | 60.3 | 63.5 | 56.8 | 70.5 |
| Avg % Change | 0.16 | 0.22 | 0.29 | 0.27 | 0.25 |

*Dow & S&P 1950-May 13, 2022, NASDAQ 1971-May 13, 2022, Russell 1K & 2K 1979-May 13, 2022.*

*20th Amendment made "lame ducks" disappear.*
*Now, "As January goes, so goes the year."*

(Market Closed - Christmas Day Observed)

**MONDAY**
**26**

*s for it being different this time, it is different every time. The question is in what way, and to what extent.*
- Tom McClellan (*The McClellan Market Report*)

**TUESDAY**
D 71.4
S 71.4
N 66.7
**27**

*e are nowhere near a capitulation point because it's at that point where it's despair, not hope,*
*at reigns supreme, and there was scant evidence of any despair at any of the meetings I gave.*
- David Rosenberg (Economist, Merrill Lynch, *Barron's* 4/21/2008)

**WEDNESDAY**
D 47.6
S 52.4
N 42.9
**28**

*u try to be greedy when others are fearful, and fearful when others are greedy.*
- Warren Buffett (CEO Berkshire Hathaway, investor and philanthropist, b. 1930)

**THURSDAY**
D 42.9
S 47.6
N 42.9
**29**

*e yourself!" is about the worst advice you can give to some people.*
- Thomas Lansing Masson (American anthropologist, editor and author, 1866–1934)

*st Trading Day of the Year, NASDAQ Down 16 of Last 22*
*ASDAQ Was Up 29 Years in a Row 1971-1999*

**FRIDAY**
D 42.9
S 38.1
N 28.6
**30**

*ry great advance in natural knowledge has involved the absolute rejection of authority.*
- Thomas H. Huxley (British scientist and humanist, defender of Darwinism, 1825-1895)

**SATURDAY**
**31**

**w Year's Day**
*nuary Almanac Investor Sector Seasonalities: See Pages 94, 96 and 98*

**SUNDAY**
**1**

# JANUARY'S FIRST FIVE DAYS: AN EARLY WARNING SYSTEM

The last 47 up First Five Days were followed by full-year gains 39 times for an 83.0% accuracy ratio and a 14.0% average gain in all 47 years. The eight exceptions include flat years 1994, 2011, 2015, four related to war and 2018. Vietnam military spending delayed start of 1966 bear market. Ceasefire imminence early in 1973 raised stocks temporarily. Saddam Hussein turned 1990 into a bear. The war on terrorism, instability in the Mideast and corporate malfeasance shaped 2002 into one of the worst years on record. In 2018 a partially inverted yield curve and trade tensions triggered a fourth-quarter selloff. The 25 down First Five Days were followed by 14 up years and 11 down (44.0% accurate) and an average gain of 1.0%.

In pre-election years this indicator has a respectable record. In the last 18 pre-election years 13 full years followed the direction of the First Five Days.

## THE FIRST-FIVE-DAYS-IN-JANUARY INDICATOR

| Chronological Data | | | | | Ranked by Performance | | | |
|---|---|---|---|---|---|---|---|---|
| | Previous Year's Close | January 5th Day | 5-Day Change | Year Change | Rank | Year | 5-Day Change | Year Change |
| 1950 | 16.76 | 17.09 | 2.0% | 21.8% | 1 | 1987 | 6.2% | 2.0% |
| 1951 | 20.41 | 20.88 | 2.3 | 16.5 | 2 | 1976 | 4.9 | 19.1 |
| 1952 | 23.77 | 23.91 | 0.6 | 11.8 | 3 | 1999 | 3.7 | 19.5 |
| 1953 | 26.57 | 26.33 | −0.9 | −6.6 | 4 | 2003 | 3.4 | 26.4 |
| 1954 | 24.81 | 24.93 | 0.5 | 45.0 | 5 | 2006 | 3.4 | 13.6 |
| 1955 | 35.98 | 35.33 | −1.8 | 26.4 | 6 | 1983 | 3.3 | 17.3 |
| 1956 | 45.48 | 44.51 | −2.1 | 2.6 | 7 | 1967 | 3.1 | 20.1 |
| 1957 | 46.67 | 46.25 | −0.9 | −14.3 | 8 | 1979 | 2.8 | 12.3 |
| 1958 | 39.99 | 40.99 | 2.5 | 38.1 | 9 | 2018 | 2.8 | −6.2 |
| 1959 | 55.21 | 55.40 | 0.3 | 8.5 | 10 | 2019 | 2.7 | 28.9 |
| 1960 | 59.89 | 59.50 | −0.7 | −3.0 | 11 | 2010 | 2.7 | 12.8 |
| 1961 | 58.11 | 58.81 | 1.2 | 23.1 | 12 | 1963 | 2.6 | 18.9 |
| 1962 | 71.55 | 69.12 | −3.4 | −11.8 | 13 | 1958 | 2.5 | 38.1 |
| 1963 | 63.10 | 64.74 | 2.6 | 18.9 | 14 | 1984 | 2.4 | 1.4 |
| 1964 | 75.02 | 76.00 | 1.3 | 13.0 | 15 | 1951 | 2.3 | 16.5 |
| 1965 | 84.75 | 85.37 | 0.7 | 9.1 | 16 | 2013 | 2.2 | 29.6 |
| 1966 | 92.43 | 93.14 | 0.8 | −13.1 | 17 | 1975 | 2.2 | 31.5 |
| 1967 | 80.33 | 82.81 | 3.1 | 20.1 | 18 | 1950 | 2.0 | 21.8 |
| 1968 | 96.47 | 96.62 | 0.2 | 7.7 | 19 | 2012 | 1.8 | 13.4 |
| 1969 | 103.86 | 100.80 | −2.9 | −11.4 | 20 | 2021 | 1.8 | 26.9 |
| 1970 | 92.06 | 92.68 | 0.7 | 0.1 | 21 | 2004 | 1.8 | 9.0 |
| 1971 | 92.15 | 92.19 | 0.04 | 10.8 | 22 | 1973 | 1.5 | −17.4 |
| 1972 | 102.09 | 103.47 | 1.4 | 15.6 | 23 | 1972 | 1.4 | 15.6 |
| 1973 | 118.05 | 119.85 | 1.5 | −17.4 | 24 | 1964 | 1.3 | 13.0 |
| 1974 | 97.55 | 96.12 | −1.5 | −29.7 | 25 | 2017 | 1.3 | 19.4 |
| 1975 | 68.56 | 70.04 | 2.2 | 31.5 | 26 | 1961 | 1.2 | 23.1 |
| 1976 | 90.19 | 94.58 | 4.9 | 19.1 | 27 | 1989 | 1.2 | 27.3 |
| 1977 | 107.46 | 105.01 | −2.3 | −11.5 | 28 | 2011 | 1.1 | −0.003 |
| 1978 | 95.10 | 90.64 | −4.7 | 1.1 | 29 | 2002 | 1.1 | −23.4 |
| 1979 | 96.11 | 98.80 | 2.8 | 12.3 | 30 | 1997 | 1.0 | 31.0 |
| 1980 | 107.94 | 108.95 | 0.9 | 25.8 | 31 | 1980 | 0.9 | 25.8 |
| 1981 | 135.76 | 133.06 | −2.0 | −9.7 | 32 | 1966 | 0.8 | −13.1 |
| 1982 | 122.55 | 119.55 | −2.4 | 14.8 | 33 | 1994 | 0.7 | −1.5 |
| 1983 | 140.64 | 145.23 | 3.3 | 17.3 | 34 | 1965 | 0.7 | 9.1 |
| 1984 | 164.93 | 168.90 | 2.4 | 1.4 | 35 | 2009 | 0.7 | 23.5 |
| 1985 | 167.24 | 163.99 | −1.9 | 26.3 | 36 | 2020 | 0.7 | 16.3 |
| 1986 | 211.28 | 207.97 | −1.6 | 14.6 | 37 | 1970 | 0.7 | 0.1 |
| 1987 | 242.17 | 257.28 | 6.2 | 2.0 | 38 | 1952 | 0.6 | 11.8 |
| 1988 | 247.08 | 243.40 | −1.5 | 12.4 | 39 | 1954 | 0.5 | 45.0 |
| 1989 | 277.72 | 280.98 | 1.2 | 27.3 | 40 | 1996 | 0.4 | 20.3 |
| 1990 | 353.40 | 353.79 | 0.1 | −6.6 | 41 | 1959 | 0.3 | 8.5 |
| 1991 | 330.22 | 314.90 | −4.6 | 26.3 | 42 | 1995 | 0.3 | 34.1 |
| 1992 | 417.09 | 418.10 | 0.2 | 4.5 | 43 | 1992 | 0.2 | 4.5 |
| 1993 | 435.71 | 429.05 | −1.5 | 7.1 | 44 | 1968 | 0.2 | 7.7 |
| 1994 | 466.45 | 469.90 | 0.7 | −1.5 | 45 | 2015 | 0.2 | −0.7 |
| 1995 | 459.27 | 460.83 | 0.3 | 34.1 | 46 | 1990 | 0.1 | −6.6 |
| 1996 | 615.93 | 618.46 | 0.4 | 20.3 | 47 | 1971 | 0.04 | 10.8 |
| 1997 | 740.74 | 748.41 | 1.0 | 31.0 | 48 | 2007 | −0.4 | 3.5 |
| 1998 | 970.43 | 956.04 | −1.5 | 26.7 | 49 | 2014 | −0.6 | 11.4 |
| 1999 | 1229.23 | 1275.09 | 3.7 | 19.5 | 50 | 1960 | −0.7 | −3.0 |
| 2000 | 1469.25 | 1441.46 | −1.9 | −10.1 | 51 | 1957 | −0.9 | −14.3 |
| 2001 | 1320.28 | 1295.86 | −1.8 | −13.0 | 52 | 1953 | −0.9 | −6.6 |
| 2002 | 1148.08 | 1160.71 | 1.1 | −23.4 | 53 | 1974 | −1.5 | −29.7 |
| 2003 | 879.82 | 909.93 | 3.4 | 26.4 | 54 | 1998 | −1.5 | 26.7 |
| 2004 | 1111.92 | 1131.91 | 1.8 | 9.0 | 55 | 1988 | −1.5 | 12.4 |
| 2005 | 1211.92 | 1186.19 | −2.1 | 3.0 | 56 | 1993 | −1.5 | 7.1 |
| 2006 | 1248.29 | 1290.15 | 3.4 | 13.6 | 57 | 1986 | −1.6 | 14.6 |
| 2007 | 1418.30 | 1412.11 | −0.4 | 3.5 | 58 | 2001 | −1.8 | −13.0 |
| 2008 | 1468.36 | 1390.19 | −5.3 | −38.5 | 59 | 1955 | −1.8 | 26.4 |
| 2009 | 903.25 | 909.73 | 0.7 | 23.5 | 60 | 2022 | −1.9 | ?? |
| 2010 | 1115.10 | 1144.98 | 2.7 | 12.8 | 61 | 2000 | −1.9 | −10.1 |
| 2011 | 1257.64 | 1271.50 | 1.1 | −0.003 | 62 | 1985 | −1.9 | 26.3 |
| 2012 | 1257.60 | 1280.70 | 1.8 | 13.4 | 63 | 1981 | −2.0 | −9.7 |
| 2013 | 1426.19 | 1457.15 | 2.2 | 29.6 | 64 | 1956 | −2.1 | 2.6 |
| 2014 | 1848.36 | 1837.49 | −0.6 | 11.4 | 65 | 2005 | −2.1 | 3.0 |
| 2015 | 2058.90 | 2062.14 | 0.2 | −0.7 | 66 | 1977 | −2.3 | −11.5 |
| 2016 | 2043.94 | 1922.03 | −6.0 | 9.5 | 67 | 1982 | −2.4 | 14.8 |
| 2017 | 2238.83 | 2268.90 | 1.3 | 19.4 | 68 | 1969 | −2.9 | −11.4 |
| 2018 | 2673.61 | 2747.71 | 2.8 | −6.2 | 69 | 1962 | −3.4 | −11.8 |
| 2019 | 2506.85 | 2574.41 | 2.7 | 28.9 | 70 | 1991 | −4.6 | 26.3 |
| 2020 | 3230.78 | 3253.05 | 0.7 | 16.3 | 71 | 1978 | −4.7 | 1.1 |
| 2021 | 3756.07 | 3824.68 | 1.8 | 26.9 | 72 | 2008 | −5.3 | −38.5 |
| 2022 | 4766.18 | 4677.03 | −1.9 | ?? | 73 | 2016 | −6.0 | 9.5 |

*Based on S&P 50*

# JANUARY

Market Closed – New Year's Day Observed)

**MONDAY**

**2**

---

*ll a parent can give a child is roots and wings.*
— Chinese proverb

First Trading Day of Year NASDAQ Up 18 of Last 25

**TUESDAY**

D 66.7
S 57.1
N 66.7

**3**

---

*hings may come to those who wait, but only the things left by those who hustle.*
— Abraham Lincoln (16th U.S. President, 1809-1865)

*econd Trading Day of the Year, Dow Up 20 of Last 29*
*anta Claus Rally Ends (Page 118)*

**WEDNESDAY**

D 61.9
S 52.4
N 47.6

**4**

---

*ie most important lesson in investing is humility.*
— Sir John Templeton (Founder Templeton Funds, philanthropist, 1912-2008)

**THURSDAY**

D 52.4
S 61.9
N 57.1

**5**

---

*ly those who will risk going too far can possibly find out how far one can go.*
— T.S. Eliot (English poet, essayist and critic, *The Wasteland*, 1888-1965)

**FRIDAY**

D 52.4
S 57.1
N 57.1

**6**

---

*thing has a stronger influence psychologically on their environment*
*d especially on their children than the unlived life of the parent.*
— C.G. Jung (Swiss psychiatrist)

**SATURDAY**

**7**

---

**SUNDAY**

**8**

# THE INCREDIBLE JANUARY BAROMETER (DEVISED 1972): ONLY 12 SIGNIFICANT ERRORS IN 72 YEARS

Devised by Yale Hirsch in 1972, our January Barometer states that as the S&P 500 goes in January, so goes the year. The indicator has registered **12 major errors since 1950 for an 83.3% accuracy ratio**. Vietnam affected 1966 and 1968; secular bull start in August boosted 1982; two January rate cuts and 9/11 affected 2001; the anticipation of military action in Iraq held down the market in January 2003; 2009 was the beginning of a new bull market; the Fed saved 2010 with QE2; QE3 likely staved off declines in 2014; global growth fears sparked selling in January 2016; inverted yield curve and trade tensions fueled Q4 selling in 2018; and Covid-19 disrupted 2020 and 2021. (*Almanac Investor* newsletter subscribers receive analysis with implications for the year.)

Including the eight flat-year errors (less than +/- 5%) yields a 72.2% accuracy ratio. A full comparison of all monthly barometers for the Dow, S&P and NASDAQ can be seen at *www.stocktradersalmanac.com* in the January 6, 2022 Alert. Full years followed January's direction in 15 of the last 18 pre-election years. See page 20 for more.

## Market Performance in January

| Year | Previous Year's Close | January Close | January Change | Year Change |
|---|---|---|---|---|
| 1950 | 16.76 | 17.05 | 1.7% | 21.8% |
| 1951 | 20.41 | 21.66 | 6.1 | 16.5 |
| 1952 | 23.77 | 24.14 | 1.6 | 11.8 |
| 1953 | 26.57 | 26.38 | -0.7 | -6.6 |
| 1954 | 24.81 | 26.08 | 5.1 | 45.0 |
| 1955 | 35.98 | 36.63 | 1.8 | 26.4 |
| 1956 | 45.48 | 43.82 | -3.6 | 2.6 flat |
| 1957 | 46.67 | 44.72 | -4.2 | -14.3 |
| 1958 | 39.99 | 41.70 | 4.3 | 38.1 |
| 1959 | 55.21 | 55.42 | 0.4 | 8.5 |
| 1960 | 59.89 | 55.61 | -7.1 | -3.0 flat |
| 1961 | 58.11 | 61.78 | 6.3 | 23.1 |
| 1962 | 71.55 | 68.84 | -3.8 | -11.8 |
| 1963 | 63.10 | 66.20 | 4.9 | 18.9 |
| 1964 | 75.02 | 77.04 | 2.7 | 13.0 |
| 1965 | 84.75 | 87.56 | 3.3 | 9.1 |
| 1966 | 92.43 | 92.88 | 0.5 | -13.1 X |
| 1967 | 80.33 | 86.61 | 7.8 | 20.1 |
| 1968 | 96.47 | 92.24 | -4.4 | 7.7 X |
| 1969 | 103.86 | 103.01 | -0.8 | -11.4 |
| 1970 | 92.06 | 85.02 | -7.6 | 0.1 flat |
| 1971 | 92.15 | 95.88 | 4.0 | 10.8 |
| 1972 | 102.09 | 103.94 | 1.8 | 15.6 |
| 1973 | 118.05 | 116.03 | -1.7 | -17.4 |
| 1974 | 97.55 | 96.57 | -1.0 | -29.7 |
| 1975 | 68.56 | 76.98 | 12.3 | 31.5 |
| 1976 | 90.19 | 100.86 | 11.8 | 19.1 |
| 1977 | 107.46 | 102.03 | -5.1 | -11.5 |
| 1978 | 95.10 | 89.25 | -6.2 | 1.1 flat |
| 1979 | 96.11 | 99.93 | 4.0 | 12.3 |
| 1980 | 107.94 | 114.16 | 5.8 | 25.8 |
| 1981 | 135.76 | 129.55 | -4.6 | -9.7 |
| 1982 | 122.55 | 120.40 | -1.8 | 14.8 X |
| 1983 | 140.64 | 145.30 | 3.3 | 17.3 |
| 1984 | 164.93 | 163.41 | -0.9 | 1.4 flat |
| 1985 | 167.24 | 179.63 | 7.4 | 26.3 |
| 1986 | 211.28 | 211.78 | 0.2 | 14.6 |
| 1987 | 242.17 | 274.08 | 13.2 | 2.0 flat |
| 1988 | 247.08 | 257.07 | 4.0 | 12.4 |
| 1989 | 277.72 | 297.47 | 7.1 | 27.3 |
| 1990 | 353.40 | 329.08 | -6.9 | -6.6 |
| 1991 | 330.22 | 343.93 | 4.2 | 26.3 |
| 1992 | 417.09 | 408.79 | -2.0 | 4.5 flat |
| 1993 | 435.71 | 438.78 | 0.7 | 7.1 |
| 1994 | 466.45 | 481.61 | 3.3 | -1.5 flat |
| 1995 | 459.27 | 470.42 | 2.4 | 34.1 |
| 1996 | 615.93 | 636.02 | 3.3 | 20.3 |
| 1997 | 740.74 | 786.16 | 6.1 | 31.0 |
| 1998 | 970.43 | 980.28 | 1.0 | 26.7 |
| 1999 | 1229.23 | 1279.64 | 4.1 | 19.5 |
| 2000 | 1469.25 | 1394.46 | -5.1 | -10.1 |
| 2001 | 1320.28 | 1366.01 | 3.5 | -13.0 X |
| 2002 | 1148.08 | 1130.20 | -1.6 | -23.4 |
| 2003 | 879.82 | 855.70 | -2.7 | 26.4 X |
| 2004 | 1111.92 | 1131.13 | 1.7 | 9.0 |
| 2005 | 1211.92 | 1181.27 | -2.5 | 3.0 flat |
| 2006 | 1248.29 | 1280.08 | 2.5 | 13.6 |
| 2007 | 1418.30 | 1438.24 | 1.4 | 3.5 flat |
| 2008 | 1468.36 | 1378.55 | -6.1 | -38.5 |
| 2009 | 903.25 | 825.88 | -8.6 | 23.5 X |
| 2010 | 1115.10 | 1073.87 | -3.7 | 12.8 X |
| 2011 | 1257.64 | 1286.12 | 2.3 | -0.003 flat |
| 2012 | 1257.60 | 1312.41 | 4.4 | 13.4 |
| 2013 | 1426.19 | 1498.11 | 5.0 | 29.6 |
| 2014 | 1848.36 | 1782.59 | -3.6 | 11.4 X |
| 2015 | 2058.90 | 1994.99 | -3.1 | -0.7 flat |
| 2016 | 2043.94 | 1940.24 | -5.1 | 9.5 X |
| 2017 | 2238.83 | 2278.87 | 1.8 | 19.4 |
| 2018 | 2673.61 | 2823.81 | 5.6 | -6.2 X |
| 2019 | 2506.85 | 2704.10 | 7.9 | 28.9 |
| 2020 | 3230.78 | 3225.52 | -0.2 | 16.3 X |
| 2021 | 3756.07 | 3714.24 | -1.1 | 26.9 X |
| 2022 | 4766.18 | 4515.55 | -5.3 | ?? |

## Ranked by Performance

| Rank | Year | January Change | Year Change |
|---|---|---|---|
| 1 | 1987 | 13.2% | 2.0% flat |
| 2 | 1975 | 12.3 | 31.5 |
| 3 | 1976 | 11.8 | 19.1 |
| 4 | 2019 | 7.9 | 28.9 |
| 5 | 1967 | 7.8 | 20.1 |
| 6 | 1985 | 7.4 | 26.3 |
| 7 | 1989 | 7.1 | 27.3 |
| 8 | 1961 | 6.3 | 23.1 |
| 9 | 1997 | 6.1 | 31.0 |
| 10 | 1951 | 6.1 | 16.5 |
| 11 | 1980 | 5.8 | 25.8 |
| 12 | 2018 | 5.6 | -6.2 X |
| 13 | 1954 | 5.1 | 45.0 |
| 14 | 2013 | 5.0 | 29.6 |
| 15 | 1963 | 4.9 | 18.9 |
| 16 | 2012 | 4.4 | 13.4 |
| 17 | 1958 | 4.3 | 38.1 |
| 18 | 1991 | 4.2 | 26.3 |
| 19 | 1999 | 4.1 | 19.5 |
| 20 | 1971 | 4.0 | 10.8 |
| 21 | 1988 | 4.0 | 12.4 |
| 22 | 1979 | 4.0 | 12.3 |
| 23 | 2001 | 3.5 | -13.0 X |
| 24 | 1965 | 3.3 | 9.1 |
| 25 | 1983 | 3.3 | 17.3 |
| 26 | 1996 | 3.3 | 20.3 |
| 27 | 1994 | 3.3 | -1.5 flat |
| 28 | 1964 | 2.7 | 13.0 |
| 29 | 2006 | 2.5 | 13.6 |
| 30 | 1995 | 2.4 | 34.1 |
| 31 | 2011 | 2.3 | -0.003 flat |
| 32 | 1972 | 1.8 | 15.6 |
| 33 | 1955 | 1.8 | 26.4 |
| 34 | 2017 | 1.8 | 19.4 |
| 35 | 1950 | 1.7 | 21.8 |
| 36 | 2004 | 1.7 | 9.0 |
| 37 | 1952 | 1.6 | 11.8 |
| 38 | 2007 | 1.4 | 3.5 flat |
| 39 | 1998 | 1.0 | 26.7 |
| 40 | 1993 | 0.7 | 7.1 |
| 41 | 1966 | 0.5 | -13.1 X |
| 42 | 1959 | 0.4 | 8.5 |
| 43 | 1986 | 0.2 | 14.6 |
| 44 | 2020 | -0.2 | 16.3 X |
| 45 | 1953 | -0.7 | -6.6 |
| 46 | 1969 | -0.8 | -11.4 |
| 47 | 1984 | -0.9 | 1.4 flat |
| 48 | 1974 | -1.0 | -29.7 |
| 49 | 2021 | -1.1 | 26.9 flat |
| 50 | 2002 | -1.6 | -23.4 |
| 51 | 1973 | -1.7 | -17.4 |
| 52 | 1982 | -1.8 | 14.8 X |
| 53 | 1992 | -2.0 | 4.5 flat |
| 54 | 2005 | -2.5 | 3.0 flat |
| 55 | 2003 | -2.7 | 26.4 X |
| 56 | 2015 | -3.1 | -0.7 flat |
| 57 | 2014 | -3.6 | 11.4 X |
| 58 | 1956 | -3.6 | 2.6 flat |
| 59 | 2010 | -3.7 | 12.8 X |
| 60 | 1962 | -3.8 | -11.8 |
| 61 | 1957 | -4.2 | -14.3 |
| 62 | 1968 | -4.4 | 7.7 X |
| 63 | 1981 | -4.6 | -9.7 |
| 64 | 1977 | -5.1 | -11.5 |
| 65 | 2000 | -5.1 | -10.1 |
| 66 | 2016 | -5.1 | 9.5 X |
| 67 | 2022 | -5.3 | ?? |
| 68 | 2008 | -6.1 | -38.5 |
| 69 | 1978 | -6.2 | 1.1 flat |
| 70 | 1990 | -6.9 | -6.6 |
| 71 | 1960 | -7.1 | -3.0 flat |
| 72 | 1970 | -7.6 | 0.1 flat |
| 73 | 2009 | -8.6 | 23.5 X |

*X – major errors   Based on S&P 500*

# JANUARY

uary's First Five Days Act as an "Early Warning" (Page 16)

**MONDAY**

D 38.1
S 47.6
N 66.7

**9**

*lways preached to my clients that how you do in bad markets is more important than how you good markets. Managing your risk is more important than finding avenues to make money.*
iomas Buck (*Barron's* Top 100 Advisor)

**TUESDAY**

D 52.4
S 61.9
N 61.9

**10**

*e is no great mystery to satisfying your customers.*
* *them a quality product and treat them with respect. It's that simple.*
ee Iacocca (American industrialist, Former Chrysler CEO, 1924-2019)

uary Ends "Best Three-Month Span" (Pages 52, 60, 149 and 150)

**WEDNESDAY**

D 57.1
S 66.7
N 71.4

**11**

*d general [or trader] plans in two ways: for an absolute victory and for absolute defeat. The one enables* *squeeze the last ounce of success out of a triumph; the other keeps a failure from turning into a catastrophe.* ederick Schiller Faust (AKA Max Brand, American author, *Way of the Lawless*, 1892-1944)

**THURSDAY**

D 47.6
S 47.6
N 52.4

**12**

*e end of the day, the most important thing is how good are you at risk control.* *y-percent of any great trader is going to be the risk control.* ul Tudor Jones II (Founder Tudor Investment Corporation, b. 1954)

**FRIDAY**

D 47.6
S 47.6
N 42.9

**13**

*e features and achievements of modern civilization are, directly or indirectly, the products of the capitalist process.* eph A. Schumpeter (Austrian-American economist, *Theory of Economic Development*, 1883-1950)

**SATURDAY**

**14**

**SUNDAY**

**15**

# JANUARY BAROMETER IN GRAPHIC FORM SINCE 1950

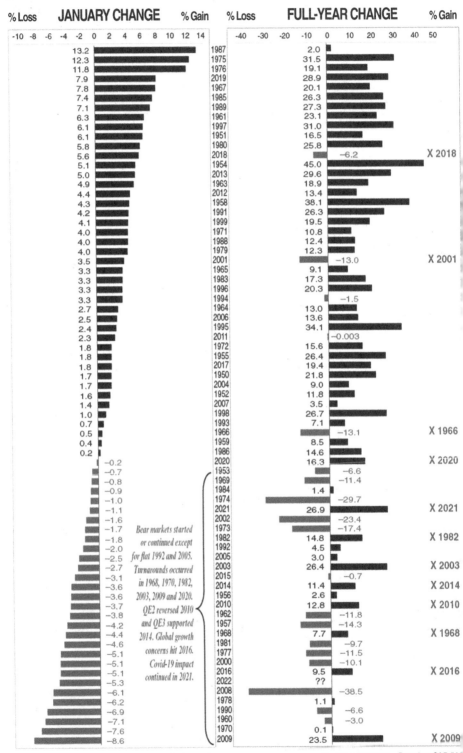

| % Loss | JANUARY CHANGE | % Gain | % Loss | FULL-YEAR CHANGE | % Gain |
|--------|----------------|--------|--------|------------------|--------|

| January | Year | Full-Year |
|---------|------|-----------|
| 13.2 | 1987 | 2.0 |
| 12.3 | 1975 | 31.5 |
| 11.8 | 1976 | 19.1 |
| 7.9 | 2019 | 28.9 |
| 7.8 | 1967 | 20.1 |
| 7.4 | 1985 | 26.3 |
| 7.1 | 1989 | 27.3 |
| 6.3 | 1961 | 23.1 |
| 6.1 | 1997 | 31.0 |
| 6.1 | 1951 | 16.5 |
| 5.8 | 1980 | 25.8 |
| 5.6 | 2018 | −6.2  X 2018 |
| 5.1 | 1954 | 45.0 |
| 5.0 | 2013 | 29.6 |
| 4.9 | 1963 | 18.9 |
| 4.4 | 2012 | 13.4 |
| 4.3 | 1958 | 38.1 |
| 4.2 | 1991 | 26.3 |
| 4.1 | 1999 | 19.5 |
| 4.0 | 1971 | 10.8 |
| 4.0 | 1988 | 12.4 |
| 4.0 | 1979 | 12.3 |
| 3.5 | 2001 | −13.0  X 2001 |
| 3.3 | 1965 | 9.1 |
| 3.3 | 1983 | 17.3 |
| 3.3 | 1996 | 20.3 |
| 3.3 | 1994 | −1.5 |
| 2.7 | 1964 | 13.0 |
| 2.5 | 2006 | 13.6 |
| 2.4 | 1995 | 34.1 |
| 2.3 | 2011 | −0.003 |
| 1.8 | 1972 | 15.6 |
| 1.8 | 1955 | 26.4 |
| 1.8 | 2017 | 19.4 |
| 1.7 | 1950 | 21.8 |
| 1.7 | 2004 | 9.0 |
| 1.6 | 1952 | 11.8 |
| 1.4 | 2007 | 3.5 |
| 1.0 | 1998 | 26.7 |
| 0.7 | 1993 | 7.1 |
| 0.5 | 1966 | −13.1  X 1966 |
| 0.4 | 1959 | 8.5 |
| 0.2 | 1986 | 14.6 |
| −0.2 | 2020 | 16.3  X 2020 |
| −0.7 | 1953 | −6.6 |
| −0.8 | 1969 | −11.4 |
| −0.9 | 1984 | 1.4 |
| −1.0 | 1974 | −29.7 |
| −1.1 | 2021 | 26.9  X 2021 |
| −1.6 | 2002 | −23.4 |
| −1.7 | 1973 | −17.4 |
| −1.8 | 1982 | 14.8  X 1982 |
| −2.0 | 1992 | 4.5 |
| −2.5 | 2005 | 3.0 |
| −2.7 | 2003 | 26.4  X 2003 |
| −3.1 | 2015 | −0.7 |
| −3.6 | 2014 | 11.4  X 2014 |
| −3.6 | 1956 | 2.6 |
| −3.7 | 2010 | 12.8  X 2010 |
| −3.8 | 1962 | −11.8 |
| −4.2 | 1957 | −14.3 |
| −4.4 | 1968 | 7.7  X 1968 |
| −4.6 | 1981 | −9.7 |
| −5.1 | 1977 | −11.5 |
| −5.1 | 2000 | −10.1 |
| −5.1 | 2016 | 9.5  X 2016 |
| −5.3 | 2022 | ?? |
| −6.1 | 2008 | −38.5 |
| −6.2 | 1978 | 1.1 |
| −6.9 | 1990 | −6.6 |
| −7.1 | 1960 | −3.0 |
| −7.6 | 1970 | 0.1 |
| −8.6 | 2009 | 23.5  X 2009 |

*Bear markets started or continued except for flat 1992 and 2005. Turnarounds occured in 1968, 1970, 1982, 2003, 2009 and 2020. QE2 reversed 2010 and QE3 supported 2014. Global growth concerns hit 2016. Covid-19 impact continued in 2021.*

X = 12 major errors   Based on S&P 500

# JANUARY

**tin Luther King Jr. Day** *(Market Closed)*

MONDAY
## 16

*eights by great men reached and kept, were not attained by sudden flight, but they,*
*their companions slept, were toiling upward in the night.*
enry Wadsworth Longfellow (American poet, 1807-1882)

*t Trading Day of January Expiration Week, Dow Up 19 of Last 30,*
*Down 6 of Last 9*

TUESDAY
D 52.4
S 52.4
N 38.1
## 17

*narket can stay irrational longer than you can stay solvent.*
hn Maynard Keynes (British economist, 1883-1946)

WEDNESDAY
D 57.1
S 71.4
N 71.4
## 18

*experience, selling a put is much safer than buying a stock.*
*le Rosen (Boston Capital Mgmt., Barron's 8/23/04)*

*lary Expiration Week, Dow Down 12 of Last 24, But Up 9 of Last 12*

THURSDAY
D 47.6
S 47.6
N 52.4
## 19

*new high ever seen in the indexes has been retraced, at least twice, save for those since August 2020 until now.*
lph Vince (Trader, programmer, author, 12/7/2021, b. 1958)

*lary Expiration Day Improving Since 2011, Dow Up 10 of Last 12*

FRIDAY
D 42.9
S 52.4
N 42.9
## 20

*rader that uses whatever he can find to get a leg up in a short-legged game. Sure, I use technical analysis, but much of it is mumbo*
*redundant, lacks a logical premise or does not hold up in testing. Fundamentals and technicals are both important and merge.*
rry Williams (Legendary trader, author, politician, b. 1942)

SATURDAY
## 21

SUNDAY
## 22

# DOWN JANUARYS: A REMARKABLE RECORD

In the first third of the 20th century there was no correlation between January markets and the year as a whole. Then in 1972 Yale Hirsch discovered that the 1933 "Lame Duck" Amendment to the Constitution changed the political calendar and the January Barometer was born—its record has been quite accurate (page 18).

Down Januarys are harbingers of trouble ahead, in the economic, political, or military arenas. Eisenhower's heart attack in 1955 cast doubt on whether he could run in 1956—a flat year. Two other election years with down Januarys were also flat (1984 & 1992). Fourteen bear markets began and 10 continued into second years with poor Januarys. 1968 started down as we were mired in Vietnam, but Johnson's "bombing halt" changed the climate. Imminent military action in Iraq held January 2003 down before the market triple-bottomed in March, but after Baghdad fell pre-election and recovery forces fueled 2003 into a banner year. 2005 was flat, registering the narrowest Dow trading range on record. 2008 was the worst January on record and preceded the worst bear market since the Great Depression. A negative reading in 2015 and 2016 preceded an official Dow bear market declaration in February 2016. In 2020 the shortest bear market in history began after the close on February 19. ZIRP and QE fueled a banner 2021 however, NASDAQ did correct 10.5% during February and March.

Unfortunately, bull and bear markets do not start conveniently at the beginnings and ends of months or years. Though some years ended higher, **every down January since 1950 was followed by a new or continuing bear market, a 10% correction or a flat year. Down Januarys were followed by substantial declines averaging *minus* 13.0%,** providing excellent buying opportunities later in most years.

## FROM DOWN JANUARY S&P CLOSES TO LOW NEXT 11 MONTHS

| Year | January Close | % Change | 11-Month Low | Date of Low | Jan Close to Low % | % Feb to Dec | Year % Change | |
|---|---|---|---|---|---|---|---|---|
| 1953 | 26.38 | −0.7% | 22.71 | 14-Sep | −13.9% | −6.0% | −6.6% | bear |
| 1956 | 43.82 | −3.6 | 43.42 | 14-Feb | −0.9 | 6.5 | 2.6 | FLAT/bear |
| 1957 | 44.72 | −4.2 | 38.98 | 22-Oct | −12.8 | −10.6 | −14.3 | Cont. bear |
| 1960 | 55.61 | −7.1 | 52.30 | 25-Oct | −6.0 | 4.5 | −3.0 | bear |
| 1962 | 68.84 | −3.8 | 52.32 | 26-Jun | −24.0 | −8.3 | −11.8 | bear |
| 1968 | 92.24 | −4.4 | 87.72 | 5-Mar | −4.9 | 12.6 | 7.7 | −10%/bear |
| 1969 | 103.01 | −0.8 | 89.20 | 17-Dec | −13.4 | −10.6 | −11.4 | Cont. bear |
| 1970 | 85.02 | −7.6 | 69.20 | 26-May | −18.6 | 8.4 | 0.1 | Cont. bear |
| 1973 | 116.03 | −1.7 | 92.16 | 5-Dec | −20.6 | −15.9 | −17.4 | bear |
| 1974 | 96.57 | −1.0 | 62.28 | 3-Oct | −35.5 | −29.0 | −29.7 | Cont. bear |
| 1977 | 102.03 | −5.1 | 90.71 | 2-Nov | −11.1 | −6.8 | −11.5 | bear |
| 1978 | 89.25 | −6.2 | 86.90 | 6-Mar | −2.6 | 7.7 | 1.1 | Cont. bear/bear |
| 1981 | 129.55 | −4.6 | 112.77 | 25-Sep | −13.0 | −5.4 | −9.7 | bear |
| 1982 | 120.40 | −1.8 | 102.42 | 12-Aug | −14.9 | 16.8 | 14.8 | Cont. bear |
| 1984 | 163.42 | −0.9 | 147.82 | 24-Jul | −9.5 | 2.3 | 1.4 | Cont. bear/FLAT |
| 1990 | 329.07 | −6.9 | 295.46 | 11-Oct | −10.2 | 0.4 | −6.6 | bear |
| 1992 | 408.79 | −2.0 | 394.50 | 8-Apr | −3.5 | 6.6 | 4.5 | FLAT |
| 2000 | 1394.46 | −5.1 | 1264.74 | 20-Dec | −9.3 | −5.3 | −10.1 | bear |
| 2002 | 1130.20 | −1.6 | 776.76 | 9-Oct | −31.3 | −22.2 | −23.4 | bear |
| 2003 | 855.70 | −2.7 | 800.73 | 11-Mar | −6.4 | 29.9 | 26.4 | Cont. bear |
| 2005 | 1181.27 | −2.5 | 1137.50 | 20-Apr | −3.7 | 5.7 | 3.0 | FLAT |
| 2008 | 1378.55 | −6.1 | 752.44 | 20-Nov | −45.4 | −34.5 | −38.5 | bear |
| 2009 | 825.88 | −8.6 | 676.53 | 9-Mar | −18.1 | 35.0 | 23.5 | Cont. bear |
| 2010 | 1073.87 | −3.7 | 1022.58 | 2-Jul | −4.8 | 17.1 | 12.8 | −10%/no bear |
| 2014 | 1782.59 | −3.6 | 1741.89 | 3-Feb | −2.3 | 15.5 | 11.4 | −10% intraday |
| 2015 | 1994.99 | −3.1 | 1867.61 | 25-Aug | −6.4 | 2.5 | −0.7 | bear |
| 2016 | 1940.24 | −5.1 | 1829.08 | 11-Feb | −5.7 | 15.4 | 9.5 | Cont. bear |
| 2020 | 3225.52 | −0.2 | 2237.40 | 23-Mar | −30.6 | 16.4 | 16.3 | bear |
| 2021 | 3714.24 | −1.1 | 3768.47 | 4-Mar | 1.5 | 28.3 | 26.9 | −10% NAS |
| 2022* | 4515.55 | −5.3 | 3900.79 | 16-Jun | −18.8 | | | |
| | | | | **Totals** | −378.0% | 77.0% | −32.8% | |
| | | | | **Average** | −13.0% | 2.7% | −1.1% | |

*As of 6/30/2022. Not included in averages.

**MONDAY**

D 33.3
S 52.4
N 42.9

**23**

*n this age of instant information, investors can experience both fear and greed at the exact same moment.*
— Sam Stovall (Chief Investment Strategist CFRA Research, October 2003)

**TUESDAY**

D 42.9
S 52.4
N 66.7

**24**

*People do not change when you tell them they should; they change when they tell themselves they must.*
— Michael Mandelbaum (Johns Hopkins foreign policy specialist, *NY Times*, 6/24/2009, b. 1946)

**WEDNESDAY**

D 57.1
S 61.9
N 52.4

**25**

*People have difficulty cutting losses, admitting an error, and moving on. I am rather frequently—and on occasion, quite spectacularly—wrong. However, if we expect to be wrong, then there should be no ego tied up in admitting the error, honoring the stop loss, selling the loser—and preserving your capital.*
— Barry L. Ritholtz (Founder/CIO Ritholtz Wealth Management, *Bailout Nation*, The Big Picture blog, 8/12/2010, b. 1961)

**THURSDAY**

D 57.1
S 47.6
N 66.7

**26**

*ood luck is what happens when preparation meets opportunity, bad luck is what happens when lack of preparation meets a challenge.*
— Paul Krugman (Economist, *NY Times*, 3/3/2006)

**FRIDAY**

D 52.4
S 42.9
N 57.1

**27**

*e who knows how will always work for he who knows why.*
— David Lee Roth (Lead singer of Van Halen, b. 1954)

**SATURDAY**

**28**

*ebruary Almanac Investor Sector Seasonalities: See Pages 94, 96 and 98*

**SUNDAY**

**29**

# FEBRUARY ALMANAC

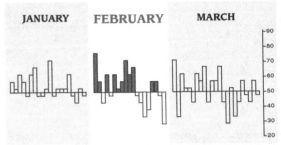

| FEBRUARY | | | | | | |
|---|---|---|---|---|---|---|
| S | M | T | W | T | F | S |
| | | | 1 | 2 | 3 | 4 |
| 5 | 6 | 7 | 8 | 9 | 10 | 11 |
| 12 | 13 | 14 | 15 | 16 | 17 | 18 |
| 19 | 20 | 21 | 22 | 23 | 24 | 25 |
| 26 | 27 | 28 | | | | |

| MARCH | | | | | | |
|---|---|---|---|---|---|---|
| S | M | T | W | T | F | S |
| | | | 1 | 2 | 3 | 4 |
| 5 | 6 | 7 | 8 | 9 | 10 | 11 |
| 12 | 13 | 14 | 15 | 16 | 17 | 18 |
| 19 | 20 | 21 | 22 | 23 | 24 | 25 |
| 26 | 27 | 28 | 29 | 30 | 31 | |

*Market Probability Chart above is a graphic representation of the S&P 500 Recent Market Probability Calendar on page 126.*

◆ February is the weak link in "Best Six Months" (pages 52, 54 & 149)
◆ RECENT RECORD: S&P up 9, down 6, average change +0.01% last 15 years
◆ #5 NASDAQ month in pre-election years average gain 2.8% up 10 down 3 (page 166), #5 Dow up 12 down 6 and #6 S&P up 12 down 6 (pages 156 & 162) ◆ Day before Presidents' Day weekend S&P down 18 of 31, 11 straight 1992-2002, day after up 8 of last 13 (see page 100 & 135) ◆ Many technicians modify market predictions based on January's market in February.

## February Vital Statistics

| | DJIA | S&P 500 | NASDAQ | Russell 1K | Russell 2K |
|---|---|---|---|---|---|
| Rank | 8 | 11 | 10 | 11 | 6 |
| Up | 43 | 40 | 28 | 26 | 26 |
| Down | 30 | 33 | 24 | 18 | 18 |
| Avg % Change | 0.1% | −0.04% | 0.5% | 0.2% | 1.1% |
| Pre-Election Year | 1.4% | 1.2% | 2.8% | 1.7% | 2.7% |
| **Best and Worst** | | | | | |
| | % Change | % Change | % Change | % Change | % Change |
| Best | 1986 8.8 | 1986 7.1 | 2000 19.2 | 1986 7.2 | 2000 16.4 |
| Worst | 2009 −11.7 | 2009 −11.0 | 2001 −22.4 | 2009 −10.7 | 2009 −12.3 |
| **Best and Worst Weeks** | | | | | |
| Best | 2/1/08 4.4 | 2/6/09 5.2 | 2/4/00 9.2 | 2/6/09 5.3 | 2/5/21 7.7 |
| Worst | 2/28/20 −12.4 | 2/28/20 −11.5 | 2/28/20 −10.5 | 2/28/20 −11.6 | 2/28/20 −12.0 |
| **Best and Worst Days** | | | | | |
| Best | 2/24/09 3.3 | 2/24/09 4.0 | 2/11/99 4.2 | 2/24/09 4.1 | 2/24/09 4.5 |
| Worst | 2/10/09 −4.6 | 2/10/09 −4.9 | 2/16/01 −5.0 | 2/10/09 −4.8 | 2/10/09 −4.7 |
| **First Trading Day of Expiration Week: 1980–2022** | | | | | |
| Record (#Up–#Down) | 25-18 | 29-14 | 28-18 | 29-14 | 25-18 |
| Current Streak | D1 | D3 | D2 | D3 | D3 |
| Avg % Change | 0.29 | 0.26 | 0.12 | 0.23 | 0.13 |
| **Options Expiration Day: 1980–2022** | | | | | |
| Record (#Up–#Down) | 22-21 | 18-25 | 18-25 | 19-24 | 21-22 |
| Current Streak | D1 | D3 | D1 | D3 | D1 |
| Avg % Change | −0.03 | −0.12 | −0.26 | −0.12 | −0.01 |
| **Options Expiration Week: 1980–2022** | | | | | |
| Record (#Up–#Down) | 26-17 | 23-20 | 23-20 | 23-20 | 27-16 |
| Current Streak | D1 | D3 | D3 | D3 | D3 |
| Avg % Change | 0.47 | 0.28 | 0.20 | 0.28 | 0.42 |
| **Week After Options Expiration: 1980–2022** | | | | | |
| Record (#Up–#Down) | 20-23 | 21-22 | 25-18 | 21-22 | 23-20 |
| Current Streak | D3 | U1 | U1 | U1 | U1 |
| Avg % Change | −0.51 | −0.42 | −0.41 | −0.39 | −0.32 |
| **First Trading Day Performance** | | | | | |
| % of Time Up | 64.4 | 63.0 | 71.2 | 68.2 | 68.2 |
| Avg % Change | 0.16 | 0.18 | 0.38 | 0.24 | 0.40 |
| **Last Trading Day Performance** | | | | | |
| % of Time Up | 45.2 | 50.7 | 50.0 | 47.7 | 52.3 |
| Avg % Change | −0.08 | −0.06 | −0.08 | −0.13 | −0.03 |

*Dow & S&P 1950-May 13, 2022, NASDAQ 1971-May 13, 2022, Russell 1K & 2K 1979-May 13, 2022.*

*Either go short, or stay away the day before Presidents' Day.*

# JANUARY/FEBRUARY

**MONDAY**

D 47.6
S 52.4
N 47.6
**30**

*The first panacea for a mismanaged nation is inflation of the currency; the second is war. Both bring a temporary prosperity; both bring a permanent ruin. But both are the refuge of political and economic opportunists.*
— Ernest Hemingway (American writer, 1954 Nobel Prize, 1899-1961)

*January Barometer" 83.3% Accurate (Page 18)*
*Almanac Investor Subscribers Emailed Official Results (See Insert)*

**TUESDAY**

D 42.9
S 47.6
N 47.6
**31**

*There's no trick to being a humorist when you have the whole government working for you.*
— Will Rogers (American humorist and showman, 1879-1935)

*First Day Trading in February, Dow Up 17 of Last 20*
*FOMC Meeting (2 Days)*

**WEDNESDAY**

D 81.0
S 76.2
N 76.2
**1**

*It is impossible to please all the world and one's father.*
— Jean de La Fontaine (French poet, 1621-1695)

**THURSDAY**

D 47.6
S 57.1
N 52.4
**2**

*If you can't deal with emotion, get out of trading.*
— J. Welles Wilder Jr. (Creator of several technical indicators including Relative Strength Index (RSI) 1935- 2021)

**FRIDAY**

D 52.4
S 42.9
N 33.3
**3**

*A fundamental analyst goes into each store and studies the products to decide whether to buy or not. A technical analyst sits on a bench watching people go into stores. Disregarding the intrinsic value, the technical analyst's decision is based on the patterns or activity of people.*
— Investopedia.com on Technical Analysis (Hat tip to JC Parets of All Star Charts via Ari Wald of Oppenheimer)

**SATURDAY**

**4**

**SUNDAY**

**5**

# MARKET CHARTS OF PRE-PRESIDENTIAL ELECTION YEARS

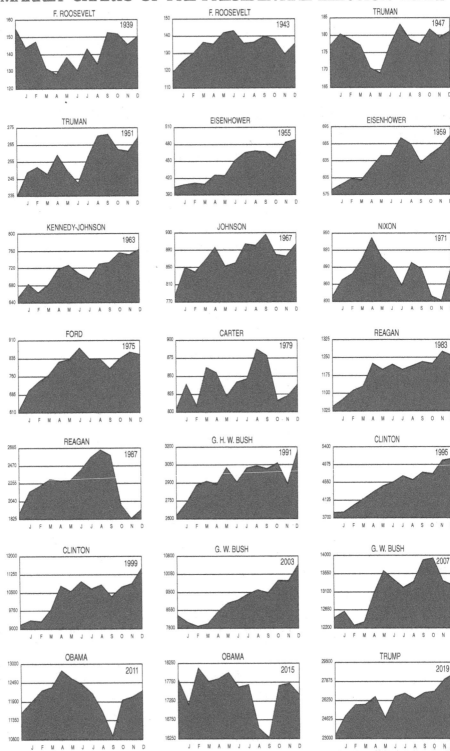

Based on Dow Jones Industrial Average monthly closing prices

# FEBRUARY

D 61.9
S 61.9
N 61.9

**6**

*The only thing I do know is that from chaos comes opportunity.*
– Daniel S. Loeb (American investor, hedge fund manager & philanthropist, founder CEO CIO Third Point, b. 1961)

TUESDAY

D 47.6
S 47.6
N 47.6

**7**

*People won't have time for you if you're always angry or complaining.*
– Professsor Stephen Hawking (English theoretical physicist, cosmologist, and author, 1942-2018)

*Week Before February Expiration Week, NASDAQ Down 12 of Last 22,*
*But Up 9 of Last 13*

🐾 WEDNESDAY

D 47.6
S 61.9
N 61.9

**8**

*Regret for the things we did can be tempered by time; it is regret for the things we did not do that is inconsolable.*
– Sydney J. Harris (American journalist and author, 1917-1986)

THURSDAY

D 52.4
S 52.4
N 57.1

**9**

*There's a lot of talk about self-esteem these days. It seems pretty basic to me.*
*If you want to feel good about yourself, you've got to do things that you can be proud of.*
– Oseola McCarty (American author, *Simple Wisdom for Rich Living*, 1908-1999)

FRIDAY

D 57.1
S 57.1
N 61.9

**10**

*A leader has the ability to create infectious enthusiasm.*
– Ted Turner (Billionaire, *New Yorker Magazine*, April 23, 2001)

SATURDAY

**11**

SUNDAY

**12**

# PRE-PRESIDENTIAL ELECTION YEARS: ONLY ONE LOSER IN 84 YEARS

Investors should feel somewhat secure going into 2023. There has only been one down year in the third year of a presidential term since war-torn 1939, Dow off 2.9%. That one loss occurred in 2015, Dow off 2.2%. The only severe loss in a pre-presidential election year going back 100 years occurred in 1931 during the Depression.

Electing a president every four years has set in motion a 4-year political stock market cycle. Most bear markets take place in the first or second years after elections (see pages 133-134). Then, the market improves. Typically each administration usually does everything in its power to juice up the economy so that voters are in a positive mood at election time.

Quite an impressive record. Chances are the winning streak will continue and that the market, in pre-presidential election year 2023 will gain ground.

## THE RECORD SINCE 1915

| | | |
|---|---|---|
| 1915 | Wilson (D) | World War I in Europe, but Dow up 81.7%. |
| 1919 | Wilson (D) | Post-Armistice 45.5% gain through Nov. 3rd top. Dow +30.5%. |
| 1923 | Harding/Coolidge (R) | Teapot Dome scandal a depressant. Dow loses 3.3%. |
| 1927 | Coolidge (R) | Bull market rolls on, up 28.8%. |
| 1931 | Hoover (R) | Depression, stocks slashed in half. Dow −52.7%, S&P −47.1%. |
| 1935 | Roosevelt (D) | Almost straight up year, S&P 500 up 41.2%, Dow 38.5%. |
| 1939 | Roosevelt (D) | War clouds, Dow −2.9% but 23.7% Apr.–Dec. gain. S&P −5.5%. |
| 1943 | Roosevelt (D) | U.S. at war, prospects brighter, S&P +19.4%, Dow +13.8%. |
| 1947 | Truman (D) | S&P unchanged, Dow up 2.2%. |
| 1951 | Truman (D) | Dow +14.4%, S&P +16.5%. |
| 1955 | Eisenhower (R) | Dow +20.8%, S&P +26.4%. |
| 1959 | Eisenhower (R) | Dow +16.4%, S&P +8.5%. |
| 1963 | Kennedy/Johnson (D) | Dow +17.0%, S&P +18.9%. |
| 1967 | Johnson (D) | Dow +15.2%, S&P +20.1%. |
| 1971 | Nixon (R) | Dow +6.1%, S&P +10.8%, NASDAQ +27.4%. |
| 1975 | Ford (R) | Dow +38.3%, S&P +31.5%, NASDAQ +29.8%. |
| 1979 | Carter (D) | Dow +4.2%, S&P +12.3%, NASDAQ +28.1%. |
| 1983 | Reagan (R) | Dow +20.3%, S&P +17.3%, NASDAQ +19.9%. |
| 1987 | Reagan (R) | Dow +2.3%, S&P +2.0% despite Oct. meltdown. NAS −5.4%. |
| 1991 | G.H.W. Bush (R) | Dow +20.3%, S&P +26.3%, NASDAQ +56.8%. |
| 1995 | Clinton (D) | Dow +33.5%, S&P +34.1%, NASDAQ +39.9%. |
| 1999 | Clinton (D) | Millennial fever crescendo: Dow +25.2%, S&P +19.5%, NASDAQ +85.6%. |
| 2003 | G.W. Bush (R) | Straight up after fall of Saddam: Dow +25.3% S&P +26.4%, NASDAQ +50.0% |
| 2007 | G.W. Bush (R) | Credit bubble fuels all-time market highs before bear starts & Great Recession: Dow: +6.4% S&P: +3.5% NASDAQ: 9.8%. |
| 2011 | Obama (D) | Debt Ceiling Debacle and U.S. credit rating downgrade: Dow +5.5%, S&P −0.003%, NASDAQ: −1.8% |
| 2015 | Obama (D) | Tepid growth: mild bear market ending February 2016: Dow −2.2%, S&P −0.7%, NASDAQ +5.7% |
| 2019 | Trump (R) | Dow +22.3%, S&P +26.9%, NASDAQ +35.2% |

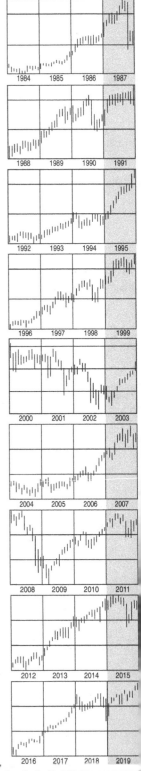

*Graph shows Pre-Presidential Election years screened*
*Based on Dow Jones Industrial Average monthly ranges*

# FEBRUARY

*First Trading Day of February Expiration Week Dow Down 10 of Last 18*    🐃 **MONDAY**

D 57.1
S 71.4
N 71.4

**13**

*weak currency is the sign of a weak economy, and a weak economy leads to a weak nation.*
*— H. Ross Perot (American businessman, The Dollar Crisis, 2-time 3rd-party presidential candidate 1992 & 1996, 1930-2019)*

**Valentine's Day** 🖤    🐃 **TUESDAY**

D 52.4
S 61.9
N 81.0

**14**

*nowing others is intelligence; knowing yourself is true wisdom. Mastering others is strength; mastering yourself is true power.*
*— Lao Tzu (Chinese philosopher, Shaolin monk, founder of Taoism, 6th century BCE)*

🐃 **WEDNESDAY**

D 66.7
S 66.7
N 66.7

**15**

*he whole problem with the world is that fools and fanatics are always so certain of themselves, but wiser people so full of doubts.*
*— Bertrand Russell (British mathematician and philosopher, 1872-1970)*

**THURSDAY**

D 61.9
S 47.6
N 42.9

**16**

*eryone times the market. Some people buy when they have money, and sell when they need money,*
*ile others use methods that are more sophisticated.*
Marian McClellan (Co-creator of the McClellan Oscillator and Summation Index, 1934-2003)

*bruary Expiration Day, NASDAQ Up 7 of Last 13*    🐃 **FRIDAY**
*ay Before Presidents' Day Weekend, S&P Up 10 of Last 12*

D 42.9
S 42.9
N 42.9

**17**

*sed on my own personal experience—both as an investor in recent years and an expert witness in years past—*
*ely do more than three or four variables really count. Everything else is noise.*
Martin J. Whitman (Founder Third Avenue Funds, 1924-2018)

**SATURDAY**

**18**

**SUNDAY**

**19**

# WHY A 50% GAIN IN THE DOW IS POSSIBLE FROM ITS 2022 LOW TO ITS 2023 HIGH

Normally, major corrections occur sometime in the first or second years following presidential elections. In the last 14 midterm election years, bear markets began or were in progress nine times—we experienced bull years in 1986, 2006, 2010 and 2014, while 1994 was flat. A correction in 2018 ended on Christmas Eve day.

The puniest midterm advance, 14.5% from the 1946 low, was during the industrial contraction after World War II. The next five smallest advances were: 2014 (tepid global growth) 19.1%, 1978 (OPEC–Iran) 21.0%, 1930 (economic collapse) 23.4%, 1966 (Vietnam) 26.7%, and 2018 (Fed interest rate tightening) 31.4%.

Since 1914 the Dow has gained 46.8% on average from its midterm election year low to its subsequent high in the following pre-election year. A swing of such magnitude is equivalent to a move from 20000 to 30000 or from 30000 to 45000.

## POST-ELECTION HIGH TO MIDTERM LOW: –20.1%

Conversely, since 1913 the Dow has dropped –20.1 on average from its post-election-year high to its subsequent low in the following midterm year. Dow's 2021 post-election year high was 36488.63. A 20.1% decline would put the Dow back at 29154 at the 2022 midterm bottom. Surging inflation has spurred the Fed to raise rates more quickly than expected, which makes a decline to this level possible. Whatever the level, the rally off the 2022 midterm low could be another great buying opportunity.

Pretty impressive seasonality! There is no reason to think the quadrennial Presidential Election/Stock Market Cycle will not continue. Page 132 shows how effectively most presidents "managed" to have much stronger economies in the third and fourth years of their terms than in their first two.

## % CHANGE IN DOW JONES INDUSTRIALS BETWEEN THE MIDTERM YEAR LOW AND THE HIGH IN THE FOLLOWING YEAR

| | Midterm Year Low | | | Pre-Election Year High | | | |
|---|---|---|---|---|---|---|---|
| | Date of Low | | Dow | Date of High | | Dow | % Gain |
| 1 | Jul | 30 1914* | 52.32 | Dec | 27 1915 | 99.21 | 89.6% |
| 2 | Jan | 15 1918** | 73.38 | Nov | 3 1919 | 119.62 | 63.0 |
| 3 | Jan | 10 1922** | 78.59 | Mar | 20 1923 | 105.38 | 34.1 |
| 4 | Mar | 30 1926* | 135.20 | Dec | 31 1927 | 202.40 | 49.7 |
| 5 | Dec | 16 1930* | 157.51 | Feb | 24 1931 | 194.36 | 23.4 |
| 6 | Jul | 26 1934* | 85.51 | Nov | 19 1935 | 148.44 | 73.6 |
| 7 | Mar | 31 1938* | 98.95 | Sep | 12 1939 | 155.92 | 57.6 |
| 8 | Apr | 28 1942* | 92.92 | Jul | 14 1943 | 145.82 | 56.9 |
| 9 | Oct | 9 1946 | 163.12 | Jul | 24 1947 | 186.85 | 14.5 |
| 10 | Jan | 13 1950** | 196.81 | Sep | 13 1951 | 276.37 | 40.4 |
| 11 | Jan | 11 1954** | 279.87 | Dec | 30 1955 | 488.40 | 74.5 |
| 12 | Feb | 25 1958** | 436.89 | Dec | 31 1959 | 679.36 | 55.5 |
| 13 | Jun | 26 1962* | 535.74 | Dec | 18 1963 | 767.21 | 43.2 |
| 14 | Oct | 7 1966* | 744.32 | Sep | 25 1967 | 943.08 | 26.7 |
| 15 | May | 26 1970* | 631.16 | Apr | 28 1971 | 950.82 | 50.6 |
| 16 | Dec | 6 1974* | 577.60 | Jul | 16 1975 | 881.81 | 52.7 |
| 17 | Feb | 28 1978* | 742.12 | Oct | 5 1979 | 897.61 | 21.0 |
| 18 | Aug | 12 1982* | 776.92 | Nov | 29 1983 | 1287.20 | 65.7 |
| 19 | Jan | 22 1986 | 1502.29 | Aug | 25 1987 | 2722.42 | 81.2 |
| 20 | Oct | 11 1990* | 2365.10 | Dec | 31 1991 | 3168.84 | 34.0 |
| 21 | Apr | 4 1994 | 3593.35 | Dec | 13 1995 | 5216.47 | 45.2 |
| 22 | Aug | 31 1998* | 7539.07 | Dec | 31 1999 | 11497.12 | 52.5 |
| 23 | Oct | 9 2002* | 7286.27 | Dec | 31 2003 | 10453.92 | 43.5 |
| 24 | Jan | 20 2006 | 10667.39 | Oct | 9 2007 | 14164.53 | 32.8 |
| 25 | Jul | 2 2010** | 9686.48 | Apr | 29 2011 | 12810.54 | 32.3 |
| 26 | Feb | 3 2014 | 15372.80 | May | 19 2015 | 18312.39 | 19.1 |
| 27 | Dec | 24 2018 | 21792.20 | Dec | 27 2019 | 28645.26 | 31.4 |
| | *Bear Market ended | **Bear previous year | | | | Average | 46.8% |

# FEBRUARY

residents' Day *(Market Closed)*

**MONDAY**
**20**

*ange is the law of life. And those who look only to the past or present are certain to miss the future.*
John F. Kennedy (35th U.S. President, 1917-1963)

ay After Presidents Day, NASDAQ Down 17 of Last 28, But Up 7 of Last 10  **TUESDAY**

D 38.1
S 33.3
N 38.1

**21**

*iting a book is an adventure. To begin with it is a toy, an amusement; then it is a mistress, and then a master, and then a tyrant.*
Winston Churchill (British statesman, 1874-1965)

sh Wednesday

**WEDNESDAY**

D 52.4
S 38.1
N 42.9

**22**

*olish consistency is the hobgoblin of little minds.*
Ralph Waldo Emerson (American author, poet and philosopher, *Self-Reliance*, 1803-1882)

eek After February Expiration Week, Dow Down 14 of Last 24,
t Up 7 of Last 11, 2020 Down 12.4% 5th Worst Week Since 1950

**THURSDAY**

D 52.4
S 57.1
N 52.4

**23**

*es are what we pay for civilized society.*
Oliver Wendell Holmes Jr. (U.S. Supreme Court Justice 1902-1932, "The Great Dissenter," inscribed above IRS HQ entrance, 1841-1935)

d of February Miserable in Recent Years, (Page 24 and 135)

**FRIDAY**

D 57.1
S 57.1
N 71.4

**24**

*facts are unimportant! It's what they are perceived to be that determines the course of events.*
R. Earl Hadady (*Bullish Consensus, Contrary Opinion*)

**SATURDAY**
**25**

rch Almanac Investor Sector Seasonalities: See Pages 94, 96 and 98

**SUNDAY**
**26**

# MARCH ALMANAC

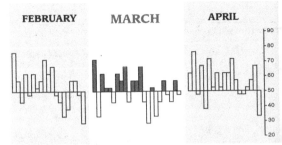

| MARCH | | | | | | |
|---|---|---|---|---|---|---|
| S | M | T | W | T | F | S |
| | | 1 | 2 | 3 | 4 | |
| 5 | 6 | 7 | 8 | 9 | 10 | 11 |
| 12 | 13 | 14 | 15 | 16 | 17 | 18 |
| 19 | 20 | 21 | 22 | 23 | 24 | 25 |
| 26 | 27 | 28 | 29 | 30 | 31 | |

| APRIL | | | | | | |
|---|---|---|---|---|---|---|
| S | M | T | W | T | F | S |
| | | | | | | 1 |
| 2 | 3 | 4 | 5 | 6 | 7 | 8 |
| 9 | 10 | 11 | 12 | 13 | 14 | 15 |
| 16 | 17 | 18 | 19 | 20 | 21 | 22 |
| 23 | 24 | 25 | 26 | 27 | 28 | 29 |
| 30 | | | | | | |

*Market Probability Chart above is a graphic representation of the S&P 500 Recent Market Probability Calendar on page 126.*

◆ Mid-month strength and late-month weakness are most evident above ◆ RECENT RECORD: S&P 13 up, 8 down, average gain 1.1%, fifth best ◆Rather turbulent in recent years with wild fluctuations and large gains and losses ◆ March 2020 Dow declined 13.7%, worst March loss since 1938 ◆ March has been taking some mean end-of-quarter hits (page 136), down 1469 Dow points March 9-22, 2001 ◆ Last three or four days Dow a net loser 22 out of last 33 years ◆NASDAQ hard hit in 2001, down 14.5% after 22.4% drop in February ◆ Fourth best NASDAQ month during pre-election years average gain 3.1%, up 11, down 2 ◆ Third Dow month to gain more than 1000 points in 2016.

## March Vital Statistics

| | DJIA | | S&P 500 | | NASDAQ | | Russell 1K | | Russell 2K | |
|---|---|---|---|---|---|---|---|---|---|---|
| Rank | 5 | | 5 | | 8 | | 6 | | 8 | |
| Up | 47 | | 47 | | 33 | | 29 | | 31 | |
| Down | 26 | | 26 | | 19 | | 15 | | 13 | |
| Avg % Change | 0.9% | | 1.1% | | 0.7% | | 0.9% | | 0.8% | |
| Pre-Election Year | 1.8% | | 1.9% | | 3.1% | | 2.0% | | 2.6% | |
| | **Best and Worst** | | | | | | | | | |
| | % Change | | % Change | | % Change | | % Change | | % Change | |
| Best | 2000 | 7.8 | 2000 | 9.7 | 2009 | 10.9 | 2000 | 8.9 | 1979 | 9.7 |
| Worst | 2020 | −13.7 | 2020 | −12.5 | 1980 | −17.1 | 2020 | −13.4 | 2020 | −21.9 |
| | **Best and Worst Weeks** | | | | | | | | | |
| Best | 3/27/20 | 12.8 | 3/13/09 | 10.7 | 3/13/09 | 10.6 | 3/13/09 | 10.7 | 3/13/09 | 12.0 |
| Worst | 3/20/20 | −17.3 | 3/20/20 | −15.0 | 3/20/20 | −12.6 | 3/20/20 | −15.3 | 3/13/20 | −16.5 |
| | **Best and Worst Days** | | | | | | | | | |
| Best | 3/24/20 | 11.4 | 3/24/20 | 9.4 | 3/13/20 | 9.4 | 3/24/20 | 9.5 | 3/24/20 | 9.4 |
| Worst | 3/16/20 | −12.9 | 3/16/20 | −12.0 | 3/16/20 | −12.3 | 3/16/20 | −12.2 | 3/16/20 | −14.3 |
| | **First Trading Day of Expiration Week: 1980–2022** | | | | | | | | | |
| Record (#Up–#Down) | 28-15 | | 27-16 | | 22-21 | | 25-18 | | 23-20 | |
| Current Streak | U2 | | D1 | | D1 | | D1 | | D1 | |
| Avg % Change | −0.12 | | −0.19 | | −0.48 | | −0.24 | | −0.59 | |
| | **Options Expiration Day: 1980–2022** | | | | | | | | | |
| Record (#Up–#Down) | 23-20 | | 25-18 | | 23-20 | | 24-19 | | 22-20 | |
| Current Streak | U1 | | U1 | | U2 | | U2 | | U2 | |
| Avg % Change | −0.01 | | −0.03 | | −0.03 | | −0.03 | | −0.04 | |
| | **Options Expiration Week: 1980–2022** | | | | | | | | | |
| Record (#Up–#Down) | 29-13 | | 28-15 | | 26-17 | | 27-16 | | 24-19 | |
| Current Streak | U1 | | U1 | | U1 | | U1 | | U1 | |
| Avg % Change | 0.53 | | 0.50 | | 0.04 | | 0.44 | | −0.02 | |
| | **Week After Options Expiration: 1980–2022** | | | | | | | | | |
| Record (#Up–#Down) | 19-24 | | 15-28 | | 20-23 | | 15-28 | | 18-25 | |
| Current Streak | U3 | | U3 | | U1 | | U3 | | D2 | |
| Avg % Change | −0.08 | | −0.02 | | 0.04 | | −0.03 | | −0.13 | |
| | **First Trading Day Performance** | | | | | | | | | |
| % of Time Up | 67.1 | | 64.4 | | 63.5 | | 61.4 | | 65.9 | |
| Avg % Change | 0.23 | | 0.25 | | 0.37 | | 0.28 | | 0.35 | |
| | **Last Trading Day Performance** | | | | | | | | | |
| % of Time Up | 41.1 | | 41.1 | | 63.5 | | 47.7 | | 79.5 | |
| Avg % Change | −0.12 | | −0.02 | | 0.18 | | 0.05 | | 0.37 | |

*Dow & S&P 1950-May 13, 2022, NASDAQ 1971-May 13, 2022, Russell 1K & 2K 1979-May 13, 2022.*

*March has Ides and St. Patrick's Day*
*Begins bullishly, then fades awa[y]*

# FEBRUARY/MARCH

MONDAY

D 42.9
S 47.6
N 57.1
**27**

*is totally unproductive to think the world has been unfair to you. Every tough stretch is an opportunity.*
— Charlie Munger (Vice-Chairman Berkshire Hathaway, 2007 Wesco Annual Meeting, b. 1924)

TUESDAY

D 28.6
S 28.6
N 28.6
**28**

*he mind is like the stomach. It is not how much you put into it that counts, but how much it digests—*
*you try to feed it with a shovel you get bad results.*
— Albert Jay Nock (Libertarian writer and social theorist, 1873-1945)

*irst Trading Day in March, S&P Up 16 of Last 23*          WEDNESDAY

D 61.9
S 71.4
N 66.7
**1**

*he inherent vice of capitalism is the unequal sharing of blessings; the inherent virtue of socialism is the equal sharing of miseries.*
— Winston Churchill (British statesman, 1874-1965)

THURSDAY

D 33.3
S 33.3
N 38.1
**2**

*ccessful innovation is not a feat of intellect, but of will.*
— Joseph A. Schumpeter (Austrian-American economist, *Theory of Economic Development*, 1883-1950)

*arch Historically Strong Early in the Month (Pages 32 and 136)*          FRIDAY

D 57.1
S 61.9
N 57.1
**3**

*market is the combined behavior of thousands of people responding to information, misinformation and whim.*
— Kenneth Chang (*NY Times* journalist)

SATURDAY

**4**

SUNDAY

**5**

# WELCOME TO THE SWEET SPOT OF THE 4-YEAR CYCLE: Q4 MIDTERM YEAR TO Q2 PRE-ELECTION YEAR

"Fourth Quarter Market Magic" is detailed on page 82 and the "50% Gain in the Dow" from the midterm year low to the pre-election year high is highlighted on page 30. The intersection of the annual seasonal pattern and the 4-Year Cycle produces the quadrennial "Sweet Spot." We created the charts here to highlight this critical juncture of 4-Year Cycle.

The second and third quarter of the midterm year has been the weakest period of the entire four-year pattern averaging losses over the two-quarter period of -1.2% for the Dow, -1.5% for the S&P 500 and -5.0% for the NASDAQ Composite Index. But thankfully, this sets up the even more important Sweet Spot of the cycle where on average the Dow gains 19.3%, S&P 500 increases 20.0% and NASDAQ jumps 29.3% over the three-quarter span from midterm year Q4 to pre-election year Q2.

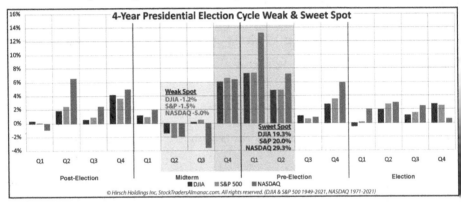

It is for this reason that we call midterm election years "A Bottom Pickers Paradise." From the midterm low to the pre-election year high DJIA gains 46.8% on average since 1914 (page 30) and NASDAQ gains a whopping 68.2% on average since 1974! As the 2022 bear market runs its course, the market will likely bounce along sideways, testing the lows, hitting its low point in late Q3 or early Q4 in the August-October period in prototypical midterm bottom fashion. Then be prepared for the rally off that low into the Sweet Spot and beyond to new highs.

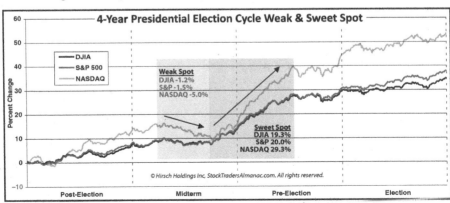

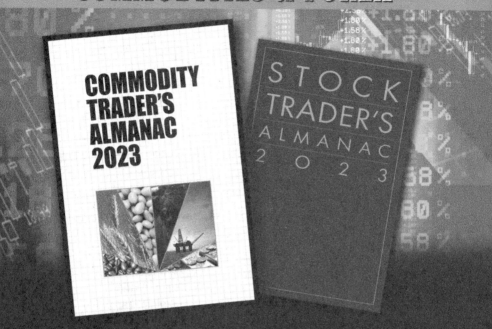

Returning after a 10-year hiatu[s]
*Commodity Trader's Almanac* for 2023 w[ill]
provide you the information needed [to]
effectively trade commodities and fore[x]
using futures, ETFs or highly correlate[d]
stocks. Futures traders will benefit fro[m]
the years of historical data available alo[ng]
with contract specific trade ideas. Sto[ck]
and ETF traders will be able to ta[ke]
advantage of seasonal moves [in]
commodities and forex by usi[ng]
highly-correlated individual stoc[ks]
and exchange-traded fund[s]

## Commodities & Forex Covered in the *Commodity Trader's Almanac* includ[es]

| | | | |
|---|---|---|---|
| ◆ S&P 500 | ◆ 30-year Treasury Bond | ◆ Crude Oil | ◆ Natural Gas |
| ◆ Heating Oil | ◆ Copper | ◆ Gold | ◆ Silver |
| ◆ Corn | ◆ Soybeans | ◆ Wheat | ◆ Cocoa |
| ◆ Coffee | ◆ Sugar | ◆ Live Cattle | ◆ Lean Hogs |
| ◆ British Pound | ◆ Euro | ◆ Swiss Franc | ◆ Japanese Y[en] |

As an existing *Stock Trader's Almanac* user, you can expect a similar calendar-st[yle]
layout in the *Commodity Trader's Almanac*. Each month will alert you to upcomi[ng]
trade setups with a full break down of their historical track record and chart of t[he]
commodity or currency overlaid with a correlating stock or ETF and seasonal tren[d.]
Armed with the data you will be better informed of potential risks and rewards befo[re]
placing any trade.

Weekly dairy pages are a place to put notes, quickly view when trade ideas beg[in]
and end plus key reminders for important dates. Carefully curated daily quotes le[nd]
support and spur creative thought.

It is impossible to predict the future. That is why we rely on seasonal and histori[cal]
analysis to help understand, or better yet, to remind us of what price trends ha[ve]
occurred in the past and how often these trends perform. These patterns typica[lly]
occur as a direct result of perennial supply and demand changes year after ye[ar.]
Every year has differences, from changes in monetary and fiscal policies to glo[bal]
macroeconomic situations to presidential election year cycles to extreme weath[er]
events and other exogenous events. With the *Commodity Trader's Almanac* a[s a]
reference guide you can compare current events against history and potentia[lly]
improve your trades.

**Get 20% off your 2023 *Commodity Trader's Almanac*!**

## ORDER YOURS TODAY!

Visit www.stocktradersalmanac.com and use promo code CTA2023

# MARCH

MONDAY

D 47.6
S 52.4
N 42.9

**6**

*o profession requires more hard work, intelligence, patience, and mental discipline than successful speculation.*
— Robert Rhea (Economist, trader, *The Dow Theory*, 1887-1952)

TUESDAY

D 52.4
S 52.4
N 38.1

**7**

*is not how right or how wrong you are that matters, but how much money you make when right and how much you do not lose when wrong.*
— George Soros (Financier, philanthropist, political activist, author and philosopher, b. 1930)

WEDNESDAY

D 47.6
S 42.9
N 42.9

**8**

*tock prices tend to discount what has been unanimously reported by the mass media.*
— Louis Ehrenkrantz (Wall Street broker, money manager, executive 1934-1999)

*ow Down 1469 Points March 9-22 in 2001*

🐃 THURSDAY

D 61.9
S 61.9
N 52.4

**9**

*hile markets often make double bottoms, three pushes to a high is the most common topping pattern.*
— John Bollinger (Bollinger Capital Management, *Capital Growth Letter, Bollinger on Bollinger Bands*)

FRIDAY

D 52.4
S 57.1
N 42.9

**10**

*ne determined person can make a significant difference; a small group of determined people can change the course of history.*
 Sonia Johnson (author, lecturer)

SATURDAY

**11**

aylight Saving Time Begins

SUNDAY

**12**

# THE DECEMBER LOW INDICATOR: A USEFUL PROGNOSTICATING TOOL

When the Dow closes below its December closing low in the first quarter, it is frequently an excellent warning sign. Jeffrey Saut brought this to our attention years ago. The December Low Indicator was originated by Lucien Hooper, a *Forbes* columnist and Wall Street analyst back in the 1970s. Hooper dismissed the importance of January and January's first week as reliable indicators. He noted that the trend could be random or even manipulated during a holiday-shortened week. Instead, said Hooper, "Pay much more attention to the December low. If that low is violated during the first quarter of the New Year, watch out!"

Twenty-one of the 36 occurrences were followed by gains for the rest of the year—and 19 full-year gains—after the low for the year was reached. For perspective we've included the January Barometer readings for the selected years. Hooper's "Watch Out" warning was absolutely correct, though. All but two of the instances since 1952 experienced further declines, as the Dow fell an additional 10.9% on average when December's low was breached in Q1. At press time, the Dow's subsequent 2022 decline is on par with the average drop.

Only three significant drops occurred (not shown) when December's low was not breached in Q1 (1974, 1981 [both down JBs] and 1987). Both indicators were wrong eight times and nine years ended flat. If the December low is not crossed, turn to our January Barometer for guidance (page 18).

## YEARS DOW FELL BELOW DECEMBER LOW IN FIRST QUARTER

| Year | Previous Dec Low | Date Crossed | Crossing Price | Subseq. Low | % Change Cross-Low | Rest of Year % Change | Full Year % Change | Jan Bar |
|------|-----------------|--------------|----------------|-------------|--------------------|-----------------------|--------------------|---------|
| 1952 | 262.29 | 2/19/52 | 261.37 | 256.35 | −1.9% | 11.7% | 8.4% | 1.6%[2] |
| 1953 | 281.63 | 2/11/53 | 281.57 | 255.49 | −9.3 | −0.2 | −3.8 | −0.7[3] |
| 1956 | 480.72 | 1/9/56 | 479.74 | 462.35 | −3.6 | 4.1 | 2.3 | −3.6[1, 2, 3] |
| 1957 | 480.61 | 1/18/57 | 477.46 | 419.79 | −12.1 | −8.7 | −12.8 | −4.2 |
| 1960 | 661.29 | 1/12/60 | 660.43 | 566.05 | −14.3 | −6.7 | −9.3 | −7.1 |
| 1962 | 720.10 | 1/5/62 | 714.84 | 535.76 | −25.1 | −8.8 | −10.8 | −3.8 |
| 1966 | 939.53 | 3/1/66 | 938.19 | 744.32 | −20.7 | −16.3 | −18.9 | 0.5[1] |
| 1968 | 879.16 | 1/22/68 | 871.71 | 825.13 | −5.3 | 8.3 | 4.3 | −4.4[1, 2, 3] |
| 1969 | 943.75 | 1/6/69 | 936.66 | 769.93 | −17.8 | −14.6 | −15.2 | −0.8 |
| 1970 | 769.93 | 1/26/70 | 768.88 | 631.16 | −17.9 | 9.1 | 4.8 | −7.6[2, 3] |
| 1973 | 1000.00 | 1/29/73 | 996.46 | 788.31 | −20.9 | −14.6 | −16.6 | −1.7 |
| 1977 | 946.64 | 2/7/77 | 946.31 | 800.85 | −15.4 | −12.2 | −17.3 | −5.1 |
| 1978 | 806.22 | 1/5/78 | 804.92 | 742.12 | −7.8 | 0.01 | −3.1 | −6.2[3] |
| 1980 | 819.62 | 3/10/80 | 818.94 | 759.13 | −7.3 | 17.7 | 14.9 | 5.8[2] |
| 1982 | 868.25 | 1/5/82 | 865.30 | 776.92 | −10.2 | 20.9 | 19.6 | −1.8[1, 2] |
| 1984 | 1236.79 | 1/25/84 | 1231.89 | 1086.57 | −11.8 | −1.6 | −3.7 | −0.9[3] |
| 1990 | 2687.93 | 1/15/90 | 2669.37 | 2365.10 | −11.4 | −1.3 | −4.3 | −6.9[3] |
| 1991 | 2565.59 | 1/7/91 | 2522.77 | 2470.30 | −2.1 | 25.6 | 20.3 | 4.2[2] |
| 1993 | 3255.18 | 1/8/93 | 3251.67 | 3241.95 | −0.3 | 15.5 | 13.7 | 0.7[2] |
| 1994 | 3697.08 | 3/30/94 | 3626.75 | 3593.35 | −0.9 | 5.7 | 2.1 | 3.3[2, 3] |
| 1996 | 5059.32 | 1/10/96 | 5032.94 | 5032.94 | NC | 28.1 | 26.0 | 3.3[2] |
| 1998 | 7660.13 | 1/9/98 | 7580.42 | 7539.07 | −0.5 | 21.1 | 16.1 | 1.0[2] |
| 2000 | 10998.39 | 1/4/00 | 10997.93 | 9796.03 | −10.9 | −1.9 | −6.2 | −5.1 |
| 2001 | 10318.93 | 3/12/01 | 10208.25 | 8235.81 | −19.3 | −1.8 | −7.1 | 3.5[1] |
| 2002 | 9763.96 | 1/16/02 | 9712.27 | 7286.27 | −25.0 | −14.1 | −16.8 | −1.6 |
| 2003 | 8303.78 | 1/24/03 | 8131.01 | 7524.06 | −7.5 | 28.6 | 25.3 | −2.7[1, 2] |
| 2005 | 10440.58 | 1/21/05 | 10392.99 | 10012.36 | −3.7 | 3.1 | −0.6 | −2.5[3] |
| 2006 | 10717.50 | 1/20/06 | 10667.39 | 10667.39 | NC | 16.8 | 16.3 | 2.5 |
| 2007 | 12194.13 | 3/2/07 | 12114.10 | 12050.41 | −0.5 | 9.5 | 6.4 | 1.4[2] |
| 2008 | 13167.20 | 1/2/08 | 13043.96 | 7552.29 | −42.1 | −32.7 | −33.8 | −6.1 |
| 2009 | 8149.09 | 1/20/09 | 7949.09 | 6547.05 | −17.6 | 31.2 | 18.8 | −8.6[1, 2] |
| 2010 | 10285.97 | 1/22/10 | 10172.98 | 9686.48 | −4.8 | 13.8 | 11.0 | −3.7[1, 2] |
| 2014 | 15739.43 | 1/31/14 | 15698.85 | 15372.80 | −2.1 | 13.5 | 7.5 | −3.6[1, 2] |
| 2016 | 17128.55 | 1/6/16 | 16906.51 | 15660.18 | −7.4 | 16.9 | 13.4 | −5.1[1, 2] |
| 2018 | 24140.91 | 2/8/18 | 23860.46 | 21792.20 | −8.7 | −2.2 | −5.6 | 5.6[1] |
| 2020 | 27502.81 | 2/25/20 | 27081.36 | 18591.93 | −31.3 | 13.0 | 7.2 | −0.2[1, 2] |
| 2022 | 34022.04 | 2/22/22 | 33596.61 | 29888.78 | −11.0 | *As of June 30, 2022 | | −5.3 |
| | | | | **Average Drop** | **−11.0%** | | | |

[1] January Barometer wrong    [2] December Low Indicator wrong    [3] Year Flat

# MARCH

Monday Before March Triple Witching, Dow Up 25 of Last 35
2020 Down 12.9% 2nd Worst Dow Day Since 1901

**MONDAY**
D 57.1
S 66.7
N 66.7
**13**

---

*The job of central banks: To take away the punch bowl just as the party is getting going.*
— William McChesney Martin (Federal Reserve Chairman 1951-1970, 1906-1998)

**TUESDAY**
D 66.7
S 42.9
N 42.9
**14**

---

*Every truth passes through three stages before it is recognized. In the first it is ridiculed; in the second it is opposed; in the third it is regarded as self evident.*
— Arthur Schopenhauer (German philosopher, 1788-1860)

**WEDNESDAY**
D 71.4
S 57.1
N 47.6
**15**

---

*So much hangs on the decisions of a small number of poorly educated people. That's democracy. A terrible way to run a country, but every other system is worse.*
— Kenneth Martin Follett (Welsh author, *Fall of Giants*, b. 1949)

**THURSDAY**
D 52.4
S 57.1
N 66.7
**16**

---

*Almost any insider purchase is worth investigating for a possible lead to a superior speculation. But very few insider sales justify concern.*
— William Chidester (*Scientific Investing*)

**St. Patrick's Day** ☘

March Triple Witching Day Mixed Last 30 Years, But NASDAQ Up 7 of Last 8

**FRIDAY**
D 66.7
S 66.7
N 71.4
**17**

---

*Some men see things as they are and say "why?" I dream things that never were and say "why not?"*
— George Bernard Shaw (Irish dramatist, 1856-1950)

**SATURDAY**
**18**

**SUNDAY**
**19**

# HOW TO TRADE BEST MONTHS SWITCHING STRATEGIES

Our Best Months Switching Strategies found on pages 54, 56, 62 and 64 are simple and reliable with a proven 72-year track record. Thus far we have failed to find a similar trading strategy that even comes close over the past six decades. And to top it off, the strategy has only been improving since we first discovered it in 1986.

Exogenous factors and cultural shifts must be considered. "Backward" tests that go back to 1925 or even 1896 and conclude that the pattern does not work are best ignored. They do not take into account these factors. Farming made August the best month from 1900-1951. Since 1987 it is the worst month of the year for Dow and S&P. Panic caused by financial crisis in 2007-08 caused every asset class aside from U.S. Treasuries to decline substantially. But the bulk of the major decline in equities in the worst months of 2008 was sidestepped using these strategies.

Our Best Months Switching Strategy will not make you an instant millionaire as other strategies claim they can do. What it will do is steadily build wealth over time with possibly less risk of a "buy-and-hold" approach.

A sampling of tradable funds for the Best and Worst Months appears in the table below. These are just a starting point and only skim the surface of possible trading vehicles currently available to take advantage of these strategies. Your specific situation and risk tolerance will dictate a suitable choice. If you are trading in a tax-advantaged account such as a company-sponsored 401(k) or Individual Retirement Account (IRA), your investment options may be limited to what has been selected by your employer or IRA administrator. But if you are a self-directed trader with a brokerage account, then you likely have unlimited choices (perhaps too many).

## TRADABLE BEST AND WORST MONTHS SWITCHING STRATEGY FUNDS

| Best Months | | Worst Months | |
|---|---|---|---|
| **Exchange Traded Funds (ETF)** | | **Exchange Traded Funds (ETF)** | |
| **Symbol** | **Name** | **Symbol** | **Name** |
| DIA | SPDR Dow Jones Industrial Average | SHY | iShares 1–3 Year Treasury Bond |
| SPY | SPDR S&P 500 | IEI | iShares 3–7 Year Treasury Bond |
| QQQ | Invesco QQQ | IEF | iShares 7–10 Year Treasury Bond |
| IWM | iShares Russell 2000 | TLT | iShares 20+ Year Treasury Bond |
| **Mutual Funds** | | **Mutual Funds** | |
| **Symbol** | **Name** | **Symbol** | **Name** |
| VWNDX | Vanguard Windsor Fund | VFSTX | Vanguard Short-Term Investment-Grade Bond Fund |
| FMAGX | Fidelity Magellan Fund | FBNDX | Fidelity Investment Grade Bond Fund |
| AMCPX | American Funds AMCAP Fund | ABNDX | American Funds Bond Fund of America |
| FCGAX | Franklin Growth Fund | FKUSX | Franklin U.S. Government Securities Fund |
| SECEX | Guggenheim Large Cap Core Fund | SIUSX | Guggenheim Intermediate Grade Bond Fund |

Generally speaking, during the Best Months you want to be invested in equities that offer similar exposure to the companies that constitute the Dow, S&P 500, and NASDAQ indices. These would typically be large-cap growth and value stocks as well as technology concerns. Reviewing the holdings of a particular ETF or mutual fund and comparing them to the index members is an excellent way to correlate.

During the Worst Months switch into Treasury bonds, money market funds or a bear/short fund. **Grizzly Short** (GRZZX) and **AdvisorShares Ranger Equity Bear** (HDGE) are two possible choices. Money market funds will be the safest, but are likely to offer the smallest return, while bear/short funds offer potentially greater returns, but more risk. If the market moves sideways or higher during the Worst Months, a bear/short fund is likely to lose money. Treasuries can offer a combination of fair returns with limited risk.

Additional Worst Month possibilities include precious metals and the companies that mine them. **SPDR Gold Shares** (GLD), **VanEck Vectors Gold Miners** (GDX) and **Aberdeen Standard Gold** (SGOL) are a few well recognized names available from the ETF universe.

## Become an *Almanac Investor*

*Almanac Investor* subscribers receive specific buy and sell trade ideas based upon the Best Months Switching Strategies online and via email. Sector Index Seasonalities, found on page 94, are also put into action throughout the year with corresponding ETF trades. Buy limits, stop losses, and auto-sell price points for the majority of seasonal trades are delivered directly to your inbox. Visit *www.stocktradersalmanac.com* or see the insert for details and a special offer for new subscribers.

# MARCH

Dow Lost 4012 Points (17.3%) on the Week Ending 3/20/2020
Worst Dow Weekly Point Loss and 2nd Worst Percent Loss Overall

**MONDAY**
D 52.4
S 42.9
N 66.7
**20**

*If there is something you really want to do, make your plan and do it. Otherwise, you'll just regret it forever.*
— Richard Rocco (PostNet franchisee, *Entrepreneur Magazine* 12/2006, b. 1946)

**TUESDAY**
D 33.3
S 28.6
N 42.9
**21**

*I hate to be wrong. That has aborted many a tempting error, but not all of them. But I hate much more to stay wrong.*
— Paul A. Samuelson (American economist, 12/23/03 University of Kansas interview, 1915-2009)

(FOMC Meeting 2 Days)

**WEDNESDAY**
D 52.4
S 52.4
N 61.9
**22**

*We can guarantee cash benefits as far out and at whatever size you like, but we cannot guarantee their purchasing power.*
— Alan Greenspan (Fed Chairman 1987-2006, on funding Social Security to Senate Banking Committee 2/15/05)

Week After Triple Witching, Dow Down 22 of Last 35, 2000 Up 4.9%,
2007 Up 3.1%, 2009 Up 6.8%, 2011 Up 3.1%,
2020 Up 12.8% Best Week Since 1931

**THURSDAY**
D 38.1
S 33.3
N 42.9
**23**

*A president is elected and tries to get rid of the dirty stuff in the economy as quickly as possible, so that by the time the next election comes around, he looks like a hero. The stock market is reacting to what the politicians are doing.*
— Yale Hirsch (Creator of *Stock Trader's Almanac*, N Y Times 10/10/2010, 1923-2021)

March Historically Weak Later in the Month (Pages 32 and 136)

**FRIDAY**
D 33.3
S 42.9
N 47.6
**24**

*Markets are constantly in a state of uncertainty and flux and money is made by discounting the obvious and betting on the unexpected.*
— George Soros (Financier, philanthropist, political activist, author and philosopher, b. 1930)

**SATURDAY**
**25**

April Almanac Investor Sector Seasonalities: See Pages 94, 96 and 98

**SUNDAY**
**26**

# APRIL ALMANAC

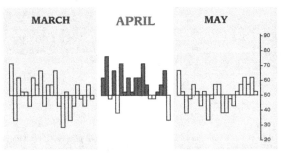

| APRIL | | | | | | | MAY | | | | | | |
|---|---|---|---|---|---|---|---|---|---|---|---|---|---|
| S | M | T | W | T | F | S | S | M | T | W | T | F | S |
|  |  |  |  |  |  | 1 |  | 1 | 2 | 3 | 4 | 5 | 6 |
| 2 | 3 | 4 | 5 | 6 | 7 | 8 | 7 | 8 | 9 | 10 | 11 | 12 | 13 |
| 9 | 10 | 11 | 12 | 13 | 14 | 15 | 14 | 15 | 16 | 17 | 18 | 19 | 20 |
| 16 | 17 | 18 | 19 | 20 | 21 | 22 | 21 | 22 | 23 | 24 | 25 | 26 | 27 |
| 23 | 24 | 25 | 26 | 27 | 28 | 29 | 28 | 29 | 30 | 31 |  |  |  |
| 30 |  |  |  |  |  |  |  |  |  |  |  |  |  |

*Market Probability Chart above is a graphic representation of the S&P 500 Recent Market Probability Calendar on page 126.*

◆ April is still the best Dow month (average 1.9%) since 1950 (page 52) ◆ April 1999 first month ever to gain 1000 Dow points, 856 in 2001, knocked off its high horse in 2002 down 458, 2003 up 488 ◆ Up 16 straight, 2006 to 2021 ◆ April 2020 Dow +11.1%, best April since 1938 ◆ Exhibits strength after tax deadline recent years ◆ Stocks anticipate great first quarter earnings by rising sharply before earnings are reported, rather than after ◆ Rarely a dangerous month, recent exceptions are 2002, 2004, 2005, and 2022 ◆ "Best Six Months" of the year end with April (page 54) ◆ Pre-election year Aprils since 1950, (Dow 3.9%, S&P 3.5%, NASDAQ 3.6%) ◆ End of April NASDAQ strength fading (pages 127 & 128).

## April Vital Statistics

| | DJIA | S&P 500 | NASDAQ | Russell 1K | Russell 2K |
|---|---|---|---|---|---|
| Rank | 1 | 2 | 4 | 2 | 3 |
| Up | 50 | 52 | 34 | 31 | 28 |
| Down | 23 | 21 | 18 | 13 | 16 |
| Avg % Change | 1.9% | 1.5% | 1.5% | 1.7% | 1.5% |
| Pre-Election Year | 3.9% | 3.5% | 3.6% | 2.9% | 2.9% |
| **Best and Worst** | | | | | |
| | % Change | % Change | % Change | % Change | % Change |
| Best | 2020 11.1 | 2020 12.7 | 2020 15.4 | 2020 13.1 | 2009 15.3 |
| Worst | 1970 −6.3 | 1970 −9.0 | 2000 −15.6 | 2022 −9.0 | 2022 −9.95 |
| **Best and Worst Weeks** | | | | | |
| Best | 4/9/20 12.7 | 4/9/20 12.1 | 4/12/01 14.0 | 4/9/20 12.6 | 4/9/20 18.5 |
| Worst | 4/14/00 −7.3 | 4/14/00 −10.5 | 4/14/00 −25.3 | 4/14/00 −11.2 | 4/14/00 −16.4 |
| **Best and Worst Days** | | | | | |
| Best | 4/6/20 7.7 | 4/6/20 7.0 | 4/5/01 8.9 | 4/6/20 7.1 | 4/6/20 8.2 |
| Worst | 4/14/00 −5.7 | 4/14/00 −5.8 | 4/14/00 −9.7 | 4/14/00 −6.0 | 4/14/00 −7.3 |
| **First Trading Day of Expiration Week: 1980–2022** | | | | | |
| Record (#Up–#Down) | 24-19 | 22-21 | 22-21 | 22-21 | 18-25 |
| Current Streak | D4 | D4 | D2 | D1 | D4 |
| Avg % Change | 0.13 | 0.06 | 0.07 | 0.05 | −0.08 |
| **Options Expiration Day: 1980–2022** | | | | | |
| Record (#Up–#Down) | 27-16 | 27-16 | 24-19 | 27-16 | 26-17 |
| Current Streak | D1 | D1 | D2 | D1 | D1 |
| Avg % Change | 0.21 | 0.17 | −0.08 | 0.16 | 0.23 |
| **Options Expiration Week: 1980–2022** | | | | | |
| Record (#Up–#Down) | 34-9 | 30-13 | 29-14 | 28-15 | 31-12 |
| Current Streak | D1 | D1 | D2 | D1 | U2 |
| Avg % Change | 1.02 | 0.83 | 0.94 | 0.82 | 0.74 |
| **Week After Options Expiration: 1980–2022** | | | | | |
| Record (#Up–#Down) | 26-17 | 27-16 | 28-15 | 27-1 | 29-14 |
| Current Streak | D5 | D3 | D3 | D3 | D1 |
| Avg % Change | 0.31 | 0.34 | 0.58 | 0.34 | 0.74 |
| **First Trading Day Performance** | | | | | |
| % of Time Up | 58.9 | 61.6 | 48.1 | 59.1 | 50.0 |
| Avg % Change | 0.10 | 0.08 | −0.15 | 0.06 | −0.20 |
| **Last Trading Day Performance** | | | | | |
| % of Time Up | 47.9 | 52.1 | 57.7 | 50.0 | 56.8 |
| Avg % Change | 0.001 | 0.02 | −0.02 | −0.10 | −0.18 |

*Dow & S&P 1950-May 13, 2022, NASDAQ 1971-May 13, 2022, Russell 1K & 2K 1979-May 13, 2022.*

*April "Best Month" for Dow since 1950;*
*Day-before-Good Friday gains are nifty.*

# MARCH/APRIL

Start Looking for Dow and S&P MACD SELL Signal on April 1 (Pages 56 & 64)
Almanac Investor Subscribers Emailed When It Triggers (See Insert)

**MONDAY**
D 61.9
S 57.1
N 66.7
**27**

---

*Trading is not a science. It's an art. But it helps to know a lot of science.*
— Senior Member of Central Bank of Spain. To Daniel Lacalle *The Energy World Is Flat: Opportunities from the End of Peak Oil*

**TUESDAY**
D 47.6
S 47.6
N 38.1
**28**

---

*To succeed in the markets, it is essential to make your own decisions. Numerous traders cited listening to others as their worst blunder.*
— Jack D. Schwager (Investment manager, author, *Stock Market Wizards: Interviews with America's Top Stock Traders*, b. 1948)

**WEDNESDAY**
D 42.9
S 42.9
N 42.9
**29**

---

*We may face more inflation pressure than currently shows up in formal data.*
— William Poole (Economist, president Federal Reserve Bank St. Louis 1998-2008, June 2006 speech, b. 1937)

**THURSDAY**
D 66.7
S 57.1
N 66.7
**30**

---

*There is a perfect inverse correlation between inflation rates and price/earnings ratios...*
*When inflation has been very high...P/E has been [low].*
— Liz Ann Sonders (Chief Investment Strategist Charles Schwab, June 2006)

Last Day of March, Dow Down 21 of Last 33, Russell 2000 Up 24 of Last 33

**FRIDAY**
D 42.9
S 47.6
N 57.1
**31**

---

*But how do we know when irrational exuberance has unduly escalated asset values, which then become subject to unexpected and prolonged contractions as they have in Japan over the past decade?*
— Alan Greenspan (Fed Chairman 1987-2006, 12/5/96 speech to American Enterprise Institute, b. 1926)

**SATURDAY**
**1**

---

**SUNDAY**
**2**

# DOW JONES INDUSTRIALS ONE-YEAR
# SEASONAL PATTERN CHARTS SINCE 1901

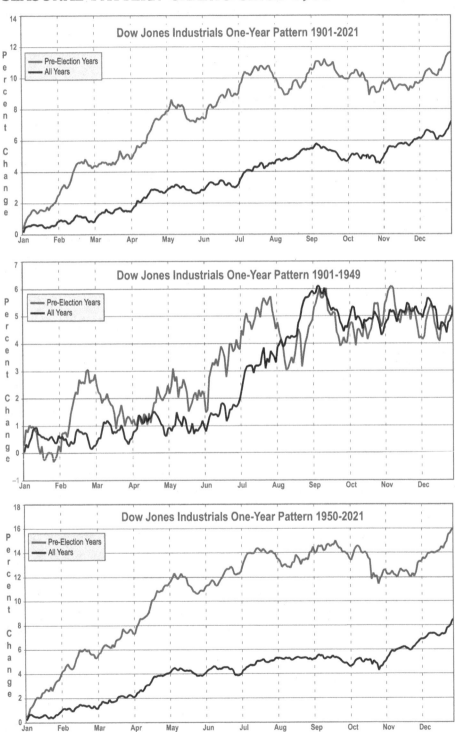

# APRIL

First Trading Day in April, Dow and S&P Up 20 of Last 28

🐃 **MONDAY**

D 61.9
S 61.9
N 61.9

**3**

*I look at the future from the standpoint of probabilities. It's like a branching stream of probabilities, and there are actions that we can take that affect those probabilities or that accelerate one thing or slow down another thing.*
— Elon Musk (South African engineer & industrialist, CEO Tesla, Founder SpaceX, b. 1971)

April is the Best Month for the Dow, Average 1.9% Gain Since 1950

💀 **TUESDAY**

D 71.4
S 76.2
N 71.4

**4**

*It was never my thinking that made the big money for me. It was always my sitting. Got that? My sitting tight!*
— Jesse Livermore (Early 20th century stock trader & speculator, *How to Trade in Stocks*, 1877-1940)

April is 2nd Best Month for S&P, 4th Best for NASDAQ (Since 1971)

**WEDNESDAY**

D 47.6
S 47.6
N 52.4

**5**

*History must repeat itself because we pay such little attention to it the first time.*
— Blackie Sherrod (Sportswriter, 1919-2016)

**Passover**

NASDAQ Up 20 of Last 22 Days Before Good Friday

💀 **THURSDAY**

D 66.7
S 66.7
N 57.1

**6**

*Leadership is the ability to hide your panic from others*
— Lao Tzu (Chinese philosopher, Shaolin monk, founder of Taoism, 6th century BCE)

**Good Friday** *(Market Closed)*

**FRIDAY**

**7**

*Experience is helpful, but it is judgment that matters.*
— General Colin Powell (Chairman Joint Chiefs 1989-93, Secretary of State 2001-05, *NY Times* 10/22/2008, b. 1937)

**SATURDAY**

**8**

**Easter**

**SUNDAY**

**9**

# S&P 500 ONE-YEAR
# SEASONAL PATTERN CHARTS SINCE 1930

# APRIL

*After Easter, Second Worst Post-Holiday (Page 100)*

🐻 **MONDAY**

D 42.9
S 38.1
N 28.6

**10**

*...utives owe it to the organization and to their fellow workers not to tolerate nonperforming individuals in important jobs.*
...ter Drucker (Austria-born pioneer management theorist, 1909-2005)

🐂 **TUESDAY**

D 61.9
S 71.4
N 71.4

**11**

*...ll Street, the man who does not change his mind will soon have no change to mind.*
...lliam D. Gann (Trader, technical analyst, author, publisher, 1878-1955)

**WEDNESDAY**

D 52.4
S 52.4
N 47.6

**12**

*...destroy a free market you create a black market. If you have ten thousand regulations you destroy all respect for the law.*
...nston Churchill (British statesman, 1874-1965)

🐂 **THURSDAY**

D 52.4
S 61.9
N 71.4

**13**

*...ieve satisfactory investment results is easier than most people realize.*
*...pical individual investor has a great advantage over the large institutions.*
...jamin Graham (Economist, investor, *Securities Analysis* 1934, *The Intelligent Investor* 1949, 1894-1976)

**FRIDAY**

D 52.4
S 52.4
N 42.9

**14**

*...ne of war, we need you to work for peace. At a time of inequality, we need you to work for opportunity.*
*...ne of so much cynicism and so much doubt, we need you to make us believe again.*
...ack H. Obama (44th U.S. President, Commencement Wesleyan University 5/28/2008, b. 1961)

**SATURDAY**

**15**

**SUNDAY**

**16**

# NASDAQ, RUSSELL 1000 & 2000 ONE-YEAR SEASONAL PATTERN CHARTS SINCE 1971

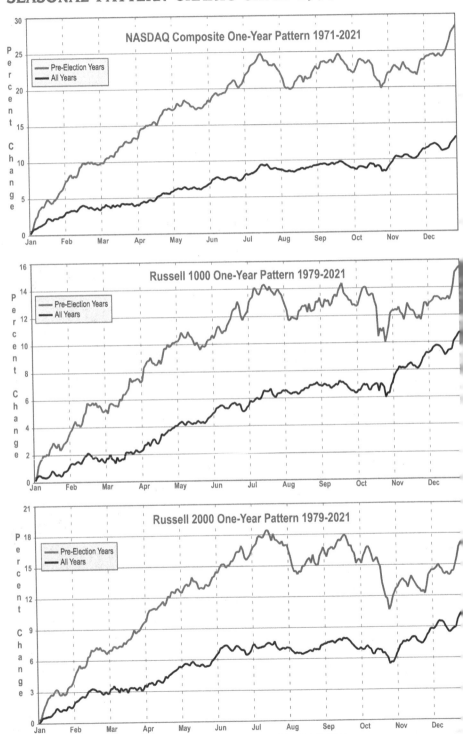

*Monday Before April Expiration, Dow Up 20 of Last 34, Down 11 of Last 18*   🦬 **MONDAY**

D 71.4
S 61.9
N 47.6

**17**

*measure what's going on, and I adapt to it. I try to get my ego out of the way. The market is smarter than I am so I bend.*
*— Martin Zweig (Fund manager, Winning on Wall Street, 1943-2013)*

**Income Tax Deadline**   🦬 **TUESDAY**

D 61.9
S 61.9
N 52.4

**18**

*always keep these seasonal patterns in the back of my mind. My antennae start to purr at certain times of the year.*
*— Kenneth Ward (VP Hayden Stone, General Technical Survey, 1899-1976)*

*April Exhibits Strength After Tax Deadline Recent Years (Pages 40 and 136)*   🦬 **WEDNESDAY**

D 61.9
S 71.4
N 71.4

**19**

*ever mind telling me what stocks to buy; tell me when to buy them.*
*— Humphrey B. Neill (Investor, analyst, author, Neill Letters of Contrary Opinion, 1895-1977)*

*April 1999 First Month Ever to Gain 1000 Dow Points*   **THURSDAY**

D 52.4
S 57.1
N 42.9

**20**

*anking establishments are more dangerous than standing armies; and that the principle of spending money*
*be paid by posterity, under the name of funding, is but swindling futurity on a large scale.*
*Thomas Jefferson (3rd U.S. President, 1743-7/4/1826, 1816 letter to John Taylor of Caroline)*

*April Expiration Day Dow Up 17 of Last 26, But Down 6 of Last 9*   🦬 **FRIDAY**

D 57.1
S 47.6
N 52.4

**21**

*e more feted by the media, the worse a pundit's accuracy.*
*Sharon Begley (Senior editor Newsweek, 2/23/2009, referencing Philip E. Tetlock's 2005 Expert Political Judgment)*

**SATURDAY**

**22**

**SUNDAY**

**23**

# SUMMER MARKET VOLUME DOLDRUMS
# DRIVE WORST SIX MONTHS

In recent years, Memorial Day weekend has become the unofficial start of summer. Not long afterwards trading activity typically begins to slowly decline (barring any external event triggers) towards a later summer low. We refer to this summertime slowdown in trading as the doldrums due to the anemic volume and uninspired trading on Wall Street. The individual trader, if they are looking to sell a stock, is generally met with disinterest from The Street. It becomes difficult to sell a stock at a good price. That is also why many summer rallies tend to be short lived and are quickly followed by a pullback or correction.

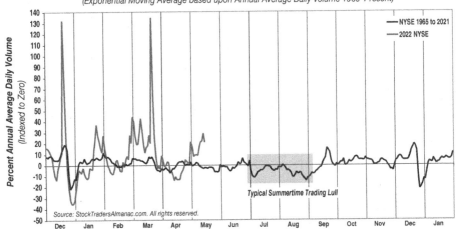

**NYSE Volume One-Year Seasonal Pattern**
*(Exponential Moving Average based upon Annual Average Daily Volume 1965–Present)*

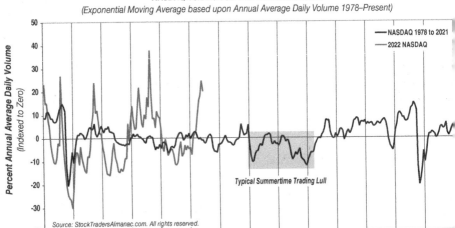

**NASDAQ Volume One-Year Seasonal Pattern**
*(Exponential Moving Average based upon Annual Average Daily Volume 1978–Present)*

Above are plotted the one-year seasonal volume patterns since 1965 for the NYSE and since 1978 for NASDAQ against the annual average daily volume moving average for 2022 as of the close on May 20, 2022. The typical summer lull is highlighted in green. A prolonged surge in volume during the typically quiet summer months, especially when accompanied by gains, can be an encouraging sign that the bull market will continue. However, should traders lose their conviction and participate in the annual summer exodus from The Street, a market pullback or correction could quickly unfold

# APRIL

**MONDAY**

D 42.9
S 47.6
N 52.4

**24**

*retending to know everything closes the door to finding out what's really there.*
- Neil deGrasse Tyson (American astrophysicist, cosmologist, Director Hayden Planetarium, *Cosmos: A Spacetime Odyssey*, b. 1958)

**TUESDAY**

D 61.9
S 52.4
N 42.9

**25**

*you torture the data long enough, it will confess to anything.*
- Ronald Coase (British economist, 1991 Nobel Prize in Economics, 1910-2013)

*nd of "Best Six Months" of the Year (Pages 54, 56, 64 and 149)*

**WEDNESDAY**

D 66.7
S 57.1
N 47.6

**26**

*vas absolutely unemotional about numbers. Losses did not have an effect on me because I viewed them as purely probability-driven, which eant sometimes you came up with a loss. Bad days, bad weeks, bad months never impacted the way I approached markets the next day.*
- James Leitner (Trader, hedge fund manager, Falcon Management Corp, b. 1953)

**THURSDAY**

D 66.7
S 66.7
N 76.2

**27**

*y best shorts come from research reports where there are recommendations to buy stocks on weakness; o, where a brokerage firm changes its recommendation from a buy to a hold.*
Marc Howard (Hedge fund manager, *New York Magazine* 1976, b. 1941)

**FRIDAY**

D 28.6
S 33.3
N 33.3

**28**

*he market does not rally, as it should during bullish seasonal periods, it is a sign that other forces stronger and that when the seasonal period ends those forces will really have their say.*
Edson Gould (Stock market analyst, *Findings & Forecasts*, 1902-1987)

**SATURDAY**

**29**

*ay Almanac Investor Sector Seasonalities: See Pages 94, 96 and 98*

**SUNDAY**

**30**

# MAY ALMANAC

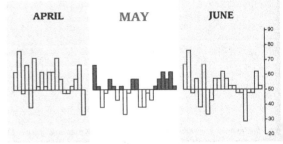

| MAY | JUNE |
|---|---|
| S M T W T F S | S M T W T F S |
| 1 2 3 4 5 6 | 1 2 3 |
| 7 8 9 10 11 12 13 | 4 5 6 7 8 9 10 |
| 14 15 16 17 18 19 20 | 11 12 13 14 15 16 17 |
| 21 22 23 24 25 26 27 | 18 19 20 21 22 23 24 |
| 28 29 30 31 | 25 26 27 28 29 30 |

*Market Probability Chart above is a graphic representation of the S&P 500 Recent Market Probability Calendar on page 126.*

◆ "May/June disaster area" between 1965 and 1984 with S&P down 15 out of 20 Mays ◆ Between 1985 and 1997 May was the best month with 13 straight gains, gaining 3.3% per year on average, up 15, down 9 since ◆ Worst six months of the year begin with May (page 54) ◆ A $10,000 investment compounded to gain $1,132,837 for November-April in 72 years compared to a $3,422 gain for May-October ◆ Dow Memorial Day week record: up 12 years in a row (1984-1995), down 15 of the last 26 years ◆ Since 1950 pre-election year Mays rank, #10 Dow, #11 S&P and #8 NASDAQ.

## May Vital Statistics

| | DJIA | S&P 500 | NASDAQ | Russell 1K | Russell 2K |
|---|---|---|---|---|---|
| Rank | 9 | 8 | 6 | 7 | 5 |
| Up | 39 | 43 | 31 | 30 | 28 |
| Down | 33 | 29 | 20 | 13 | 15 |
| Avg % Change | −0.01% | 0.2% | 1.0% | 0.9% | 1.3% |
| Pre-Election Year | −0.3% | −0.2% | 1.1% | 0.5% | 1.7% |
| **Best and Worst** | | | | | |
| | % Change | % Change | % Change | % Change | % Change |
| Best | 1990   8.3 | 1990   9.2 | 1997   11.1 | 1990   8.9 | 1997   11.0 |
| Worst | 2010  −7.9 | 1962  −8.6 | 2000 −11.9 | 2010  −8.1 | 2019  −7.9 |
| **Best and Worst Weeks** | | | | | |
| Best | 5/29/70   5.8 | 5/2/97   6.2 | 5/17/02   8.8 | 5/2/97   6.4 | 5/22/20   7.8 |
| Worst | 5/25/62  −6.0 | 5/25/62  −6.8 | 5/7/10  −8.0 | 5/7/10  −6.6 | 5/7/10  −8.9 |
| **Best and Worst Days** | | | | | |
| Best | 5/27/70   5.1 | 5/27/70   5.0 | 5/30/00   7.9 | 5/10/10   4.4 | 5/18/20   6.1 |
| Worst | 5/28/62  −5.7 | 5/28/62  −6.7 | 5/23/00  −5.9 | 5/20/10  −3.9 | 5/20/10  −5.1 |
| **First Trading Day of Expiration Week: 1980–2022** | | | | | |
| Record (#Up–#Down) | 25-17 | 27-15 | 23-19 | 25-16 | 21-21 |
| Current Streak | D3 | D1 | D1 | D1 | U1 |
| Avg % Change | 0.11 | 0.11 | 0.09 | 0.08 | −0.06 |
| **Options Expiration Day: 1980–2022** | | | | | |
| Record (#Up–#Down) | 22-20 | 23-19 | 20-22 | 23-19 | 22-20 |
| Current Streak | U2 | D1 | D1 | D1 | U2 |
| Avg % Change | −0.06 | −0.07 | −0.09 | −0.06 | 0.05 |
| **Options Expiration Week: 1980–2022** | | | | | |
| Record (#Up–#Down) | 19-23 | 19-23 | 21-21 | 18-24 | 21-21 |
| Current Streak | D6 | D5 | U1 | D5 | D3 |
| Avg % Change | −0.06 | −0.07 | 0.10 | −0.07 | −0.29 |
| **Week After Options Expiration: 1980–2022** | | | | | |
| Record (#Up–#Down) | 24-18 | 27-15 | 29-13 | 27-15 | 31-11 |
| Current Streak | U2 | U2 | U2 | U2 | U2 |
| Avg % Change | 0.13 | 0.26 | 0.37 | 0.29 | 0.57 |
| **First Trading Day Performance** | | | | | |
| % of Time Up | 55.6 | 58.3 | 60.8 | 58.1 | 60.5 |
| Avg % Change | 0.16 | 0.19 | 0.25 | 0.18 | 0.16 |
| **Last Trading Day Performance** | | | | | |
| % of Time Up | 56.9 | 59.7 | 64.7 | 53.5 | 58.1 |
| Avg % Change | 0.13 | 0.22 | 0.17 | 0.15 | 0.21 |

*Dow & S&P 1950-May 13, 2022, NASDAQ 1971-May 13, 2022, Russell 1K & 2K 1979-May 13, 2022.*

*Better to reposition in Ma*
*Than to sell in May and go away*

# MAY

*irst Trading Day in May, S&P Up 18 of Last 25*

**MONDAY**

D 57.1
S 66.7
N 66.7

**1**

*A contrarian's opportunity] If everybody is thinking alike, then somebody isn't thinking.*
— General George S. Patton, Jr. (U.S. Army field commander WWII, 1885-1945)

**TUESDAY**

D 66.7
S 52.4
N 57.1

**2**

*he game [or market] can be reduced to a social science; that it is simply a matter of figuring out the odds,*
*d exploiting the laws of probability; that baseball players [or investors] follow strikingly predictable patterns.*
— Michael Lewis (American author & journalist, what Oakland A's GM Billy Beane claims to believe,
*oneyball: The Art of Winning an Unfair Game*, b. 1960)

*OMC Meeting (2 Days)*

**WEDNESDAY**

D 42.9
S 38.1
N 38.1

**3**

*ere is a habitual nature to society and human activity.*
*ople's behavior and what they do with their money and time bears upon economics and the stock market.*
— Jeffrey A. Hirsch (Editor, *Stock Trader's Almanac*, b. 1966)

**THURSDAY**

D 42.9
S 47.6
N 52.4

**4**

*curities pricing is, in every sense a psychological phenomenon that arises from the interaction of human beings with fear.*
*hy not greed and fear as the equation is usually stated? Because greed is simply fear of not having enough.*
— John Bollinger (Bollinger Capital Management, *Capital Growth Letter, Bollinger on Bollinger Bands*)

**FRIDAY**

D 61.9
S 57.1
N 52.4

**5**

*ise men are instructed by reason, men of less understanding by experience, the most ignorant by necessity, the beasts by nature.*
— Marcus Tullius Cicero (Great Roman Orator, Politician, 106-43 B.C.)

**SATURDAY**

**6**

**SUNDAY**

**7**

# TOP PERFORMING MONTHS:
# STANDARD & POOR'S 500 AND DOW JONES INDUSTRIALS

Monthly performance of the S&P and the Dow are ranked over the past 72 1/3 years. NASDAQ monthly performance is shown on page 58.

April, November and December still hold the top three positions in both the Dow and S&P. Disastrous Januarys in 2008, 2009, 2016 and 2022 knocked January into sixth. This, in part, led to our discovery in 1986 of the market's most consistent seasonal pattern. You can divide the year into two sections and have practically all the gains in one six-month section and very little in the other. September is the worst month on both lists. (See "Best Six Months" on page 54.)

## MONTHLY % CHANGES (JANUARY 1950–APRIL 2022)

### Standard & Poor's 500

| Month | Total % Change | Avg. % Change | # Up | # Down |
|---|---|---|---|---|
| Jan | 71.5% | 1.0% | 43 | 30 |
| Feb | – 3.0 | – 0.04 | 40 | 33 |
| Mar | 77.8 | 1.1 | 47 | 26 |
| Apr | 113.0 | 1.5 | 52 | 21 |
| May | 16.3 | 0.2 | 43 | 29 |
| Jun | 9.8 | 0.1 | 40 | 32 |
| Jul | 82.7 | 1.1 | 42 | 30 |
| Aug | 5.1 | 0.07 | 40 | 32 |
| Sep* | – 39.0 | – 0.5 | 32 | 39 |
| Oct | 61.8 | 0.9 | 43 | 29 |
| Nov | 120.4 | 1.7 | 49 | 23 |
| Dec | 111.3 | 1.5 | 54 | 18 |

| % Rank | | | | |
|---|---|---|---|---|
| Nov | 120.4% | 1.7% | 49 | 23 |
| Apr | 113.0 | 1.5 | 52 | 21 |
| Dec | 111.3 | 1.5 | 54 | 18 |
| Jul | 82.7 | 1.1 | 42 | 30 |
| Mar | 77.8 | 1.1 | 47 | 26 |
| Jan | 71.5 | 1.0 | 43 | 30 |
| Oct | 61.8 | 0.9 | 43 | 29 |
| May | 16.3 | 0.2 | 43 | 29 |
| Jun | 9.8 | 0.1 | 40 | 32 |
| Aug | 5.1 | 0.07 | 40 | 32 |
| Feb | – 3.0 | – 0.04 | 40 | 33 |
| Sep* | – 39.0 | – 0.5 | 32 | 39 |
| **Totals** | **627.7%** | **8.6%** | | |
| **Average** | | **0.72%** | | |

*No change 1979.

### Dow Jones Industrials

| Month | Total % Change | Avg. % Change | # Up | # Down |
|---|---|---|---|---|
| Jan | 64.9% | 0.9% | 45 | 28 |
| Feb | 7.9 | 0.1 | 43 | 30 |
| Mar | 68.5 | 0.9 | 47 | 26 |
| Apr | 140.6 | 1.9 | 50 | 23 |
| May | – 0.6 | – 0.01 | 39 | 33 |
| Jun | – 11.3 | – 0.2 | 34 | 38 |
| Jul | 90.6 | 1.3 | 47 | 25 |
| Aug | – 2.6 | – 0.04 | 41 | 31 |
| Sep | – 51.3 | – 0.7 | 29 | 43 |
| Oct | 43.3 | 0.6 | 43 | 29 |
| Nov | 121.8 | 1.7 | 49 | 23 |
| Dec | 114.6 | 1.6 | 51 | 21 |

| % Rank | | | | |
|---|---|---|---|---|
| Apr | 140.6% | 1.9% | 50 | 23 |
| Nov | 121.8 | 1.7 | 49 | 23 |
| Dec | 114.6 | 1.6 | 51 | 21 |
| Jul | 90.6 | 1.3 | 47 | 25 |
| Mar | 68.5 | 0.9 | 47 | 26 |
| Jan | 64.9 | 0.9 | 45 | 28 |
| Oct | 43.3 | 0.6 | 43 | 29 |
| Feb | 7.9 | 0.1 | 43 | 30 |
| May | – 0.6 | – 0.01 | 39 | 33 |
| Aug | – 2.6 | – 0.04 | 41 | 31 |
| Jun | – 11.3 | – 0.2 | 34 | 38 |
| Sep | – 51.3 | – 0.7 | 29 | 43 |
| **Totals** | **586.4%** | **8.1%** | | |
| **Average** | | **0.67%** | | |

Anticipators, shifts in cultural behavior and faster information flow have altered seasonality in recent years. Here is how the months ranked over the past 15 1/3 years (184 months) using total percentage gains on the S&P 500: April 39.9, July 32.9, March 21.4, November 20.2, December 14.6, October 9.7, August 3.0, May 2.3, February –2.1, June –3.3, September –3.9 and January –8.4.

January has declined in 13 of the last 23 years. Sizeable turnarounds in "bear killing" October were a common occurrence from 1999 to 2007. Recent big Dow losses in the 21st Century were: September 2001 (9/11 attack), off 11.1%; September 2002 (Iraq war drums), off 12.4%; June 2008, off 10.2%, October 2008, off 14.1%, February 2009, off 11.7% (financial crisis) and March 2020, off 13.7% (pandemic shutdown).

# MAY

## MONDAY 8

D 66.7
S 52.4
N 71.4

*Anyone who believes that exponential growth can go on forever in a finite world is either a madman or an economist.*
– Kenneth Ewart Boulding (Economist, activist, poet, scientist, philosopher, cofounder General Systems Theory, 1910-1993)

## TUESDAY 9

D 38.1
S 42.9
N 47.6

*Civility is not a sign of weakness, and sincerity is always subject to proof.*
*Let us never negotiate out of fear. But let us never fear to negotiate.*
– John F. Kennedy (35th U.S. President, Inaugural Address 1/20/1961, 1917-1963)

## WEDNESDAY 10

D 61.9
S 52.4
N 42.9

*Today's Ponzi-style acute fragility and speculative dynamics dictate that he who panics first panics best.*
– Doug Noland (Prudent Bear Funds, *Credit Bubble Bulletin*, 10/26/07)

## THURSDAY 11

D 33.3
S 33.3
N 42.9

*Trending markets require different strategies than non-trending markets.*
– Larry Williams (Legendary trader, author, politician, b. 1942)

*Friday Before Mother's Day, Dow Up 19 of Last 28*

## FRIDAY 12

D 57.1
S 47.6
N 52.4

*We were fairly arrogant, until we realized the Japanese were selling quality products for what it cost us to make them.*
– Paul A. Allaire (former Chairman of Xerox)

## SATURDAY 13

Mother's Day

## SUNDAY 14

# "BEST SIX MONTHS": STILL AN EYE-POPPING STRATEGY

Our Best Six Months Switching Strategy consistently delivers. Investing in the Dow Jones Industrial Average between November 1st and April 30th each year and then switching into fixed income for the other six months has produced reliable returns with reduced risk since 1950.

The chart on page 149 shows November, December, January, March and April to be the top months since 1950. Add February, and an excellent strategy is born! These six consecutive months gained 24884.34 Dow points in 72 years, while the remaining May through October months gained 7878.54 points. The S&P gained 2721.33 points in the same best six months versus 1392.53 points in the worst six.

Percentage changes are shown along with a compounding $10,000 investment. The November-April $1,132,837 gain overshadows May-October's $3,422 gain. (S&P results were $906,861 to $14,918.) Just four November-April losses were double-digit: April 1970 (Cambodian invasion), 1973 (OPEC oil embargo), 2008 (financial crisis) and 2019 (coronavirus economic shutdown). Similarly, Iraq muted the Best Six and inflated the Worst Six in 2003. When we discovered this strategy in 1986, November-April outperformed May-October by $88,163 to minus $1,522. Results improved substantially these past 35 years, $1,044,674 to $1,900. A simple timing indicator nearly triples results (page 56).

## SIX-MONTH SWITCHING STRATEGY

| | DJIA % Change May 1–Oct 31 | Investing $10,000 | DJIA % Change Nov 1–Apr 30 | Investing $10,000 |
|---|---|---|---|---|
| 1950 | 5.0% | $10,500 | 15.2% | $11,520 |
| 1951 | 1.2 | 10,626 | −1.8 | 11,313 |
| 1952 | 4.5 | 11,104 | 2.1 | 11,551 |
| 1953 | 0.4 | 11,148 | 15.8 | 13,376 |
| 1954 | 10.3 | 12,296 | 20.9 | 16,172 |
| 1955 | 6.9 | 13,144 | 13.5 | 18,355 |
| 1956 | −7.0 | 12,224 | 3.0 | 18,906 |
| 1957 | −10.8 | 10,904 | 3.4 | 19,549 |
| 1958 | 19.2 | 12,998 | 14.8 | 22,442 |
| 1959 | 3.7 | 13,479 | −6.9 | 20,894 |
| 1960 | −3.5 | 13,007 | 16.9 | 24,425 |
| 1961 | 3.7 | 13,488 | −5.5 | 23,082 |
| 1962 | −11.4 | 11,950 | 21.7 | 28,091 |
| 1963 | 5.2 | 12,571 | 7.4 | 30,170 |
| 1964 | 7.7 | 13,539 | 5.6 | 31,860 |
| 1965 | 4.2 | 14,108 | −2.8 | 30,968 |
| 1966 | −13.6 | 12,189 | 11.1 | 34,405 |
| 1967 | −1.9 | 11,957 | 3.7 | 35,678 |
| 1968 | 4.4 | 12,483 | −0.2 | 35,607 |
| 1969 | −9.9 | 11,247 | −14.0 | 30,622 |
| 1970 | 2.7 | 11,551 | 24.6 | 38,155 |
| 1971 | −10.9 | 10,292 | 13.7 | 43,382 |
| 1972 | 0.1 | 10,302 | −3.6 | 41,820 |
| 1973 | 3.8 | 10,693 | −12.5 | 36,593 |
| 1974 | −20.5 | 8,501 | 23.4 | 45,156 |
| 1975 | 1.8 | 8,654 | 19.2 | 53,826 |
| 1976 | −3.2 | 8,377 | −3.9 | 51,727 |
| 1977 | −11.7 | 7,397 | 2.3 | 52,917 |
| 1978 | −5.4 | 6,998 | 7.9 | 57,097 |
| 1979 | −4.6 | 6,676 | 0.2 | 57,211 |
| 1980 | 13.1 | 7,551 | 7.9 | 61,731 |
| 1981 | −14.6 | 6,449 | −0.5 | 61,422 |
| 1982 | 16.9 | 7,539 | 23.6 | 75,918 |
| 1983 | −0.1 | 7,531 | −4.4 | 72,578 |
| 1984 | 3.1 | 7,764 | 4.2 | 75,626 |
| 1985 | 9.2 | 8,478 | 29.8 | 98,163 |
| 1986 | 5.3 | 8,927 | 21.8 | 119,563 |
| 1987 | −12.8 | 7,784 | 1.9 | 121,835 |
| 1988 | 5.7 | 8,228 | 12.6 | 137,186 |
| 1989 | 9.4 | 9,001 | 0.4 | 137,735 |
| 1990 | −8.1 | 8,272 | 18.2 | 162,803 |
| 1991 | 6.3 | 8,793 | 9.4 | 178,106 |
| 1992 | −4.0 | 8,441 | 6.2 | 189,149 |
| 1993 | 7.4 | 9,066 | 0.03 | 189,206 |
| 1994 | 6.2 | 9,628 | 10.6 | 209,262 |
| 1995 | 10.0 | 10,591 | 17.1 | 245,046 |
| 1996 | 8.3 | 11,470 | 16.2 | 284,743 |
| 1997 | 6.2 | 12,181 | 21.8 | 346,817 |
| 1998 | −5.2 | 11,548 | 25.6 | 435,602 |
| 1999 | −0.5 | 11,490 | 0.04 | 435,776 |
| 2000 | 2.2 | 11,743 | −2.2 | 426,189 |
| 2001 | −15.5 | 9,923 | 9.6 | 467,103 |
| 2002 | −15.6 | 8,375 | 1.0 | 471,774 |
| 2003 | 15.6 | 9,682 | 4.3 | 492,060 |
| 2004 | −1.9 | 9,498 | 1.6 | 499,933 |
| 2005 | 2.4 | 9,726 | 8.9 | 544,427 |
| 2006 | 6.3 | 10,339 | 8.1 | 588,526 |
| 2007 | 6.6 | 11,021 | −8.0 | 541,444 |
| 2008 | −27.3 | 8,012 | −12.4 | 474,305 |
| 2009 | 18.9 | 9,526 | 13.3 | 537,388 |
| 2010 | 1.0 | 9,621 | 15.2 | 619,071 |
| 2011 | −6.7 | 8,976 | 10.5 | 684,073 |
| 2012 | −0.9 | 8,895 | 13.3 | 775,055 |
| 2013 | 4.8 | 9,322 | 6.7 | 826,984 |
| 2014 | 4.9 | 9,779 | 2.6 | 848,486 |
| 2015 | −1.0 | 9,68 | 10.6 | 853,577 |
| 2016 | 2.1 | 9,884 | 15.4 | 985,223 |
| 2017 | 11.6 | 11,031 | 3.4 | 1,018,721 |
| 2018 | 3.9 | 11,461 | 5.9 | 1,078,826 |
| 2019 | 1.7 | 11,656 | −10.0 | 970,943 |
| 2020 | 8.9 | 12,693 | 27.8 | 1,240,865 |
| 2021 | 5.7 | 13,422 | −7.9 | 1,142,837 |
| **Average/Gain** | **0.8%** | **$3,422** | **7.3%** | **$1,132,837** |
| **# Up/Down** | **45/27** | | **56/16** | |

*Monday After Mother's Day, Dow Up 17 of Last 28, But Down 8 of Last 11*
*Monday Before May Expiration, Dow Up 25 of Last 35, But Down 7 of Last 12*

**MONDAY**

D 57.1
S 57.1
N 52.4

**15**

*Everything possible today was at one time impossible. Everything impossible today may at some time in the future be possible.*
— Edward Lindaman (Apollo space project, president Whitworth College, 1920-1982)

**TUESDAY**

D 52.4
S 57.1
N 61.9

**16**

*Financial markets will find and exploit hidden flaws, particularly in untested new innovations—*
*and do so at a time that will inflict the most damage to the most people.*
— Raymond F. DeVoe, Jr. (Market strategist Jesup & Lamont, *The DeVoe Report*, 3/30/07, 1929-2014)

**WEDNESDAY**

D 38.1
S 38.1
N 42.9

**17**

*The authority of a thousand is not worth the humble reasoning of a single individual.*
— Galileo Galilei (Italian physicist and astronomer, 1564-1642)

**THURSDAY**

D 38.1
S 38.1
N 38.1

**18**

*It isn't the incompetent who destroy an organization.*
*It is those who have achieved something and want to rest upon their achievements who are forever clogging things up.*
— Charles E. Sorenson (Danish-American engineer, officer, director of Ford Motor Co. 1907-1950,
helped develop first auto assembly line, 1881-1968)

*May Expiration Day, Dow Up 15 of Last 22*

**FRIDAY**

D 47.6
S 47.6
N 57.1

**19**

*My dad always said that you don't live in the world you were born into, and that's not going to change.*
*The rate of change is only going to accelerate.*
— Mark Cuban (American billionaire entrepreneur, b. 1958)

**SATURDAY**

**20**

**SUNDAY**

**21**

# MACD-TIMING TRIPLES "BEST SIX MONTHS" RESULTS

Using the simple MACD (Moving Average Convergence Divergence) indicator developed by our friend Gerald Appel to better time entries and exits into and out of the Best Six Months (page 54) period nearly triples the results. Several years ago Sy Harding enhanced our Best Six Months Switching Strategy with MACD triggers, dubbing it the "best mechanical system ever." In 2006 we improved it even more, achieving similar results with just four trades every four years (page 64).

*Almanac Investor eNewsletter* implements this system with quite a degree of success. Starting on the first trading day of October we look to catch the market's first hint of an uptrend after the summer doldrums, and beginning on the first trading day of April we prepare to exit these seasonal positions as soon as the market falters.

In up-trending markets MACD signals get you in earlier and keep you in longer. But if the market is trending down, entries are delayed until the market turns up and exit points can come a month earlier.

The results are astounding applying the simple MACD signals. Instead of $10,000 gaining $1,132,837 over the 72 recent years when invested only during the Best Six Months (page 54), the gain nearly tripled to $3,066,507. The $3,422 gain during the worst six months became a loss of $4,728.

Impressive results for being invested during only 6.3 months of the year on average! For the rest of the year consider money markets, bonds, puts, bear funds, covered calls or credit call spreads.

Updated signals are emailed to our *Almanac Investor eNewsletter* subscribers as soon as they are triggered. Visit *www.stocktradersalmanac.com* or see the insert for details and a special offer for new subscribers.

## SIX-MONTH SWITCHING STRATEGY+TIMING

| | DJIA % Change May 1–Oct 31* | Investing $10,000 | DJIA % Change Nov 1–Apr 30* | Investing $10,000 |
|---|---|---|---|---|
| 1950 | 7.3% | 10,730 | 13.3% | 11,330 |
| 1951 | 0.1 | 10,741 | 1.9 | 11,545 |
| 1952 | 1.4 | 10,891 | 2.1 | 11,787 |
| 1953 | 0.2 | 10,913 | 17.1 | 13,803 |
| 1954 | 13.5 | 12,386 | 16.3 | 16,053 |
| 1955 | 7.7 | 13,340 | 13.1 | 18,156 |
| 1956 | −6.8 | 12,433 | 2.8 | 18,664 |
| 1957 | −12.3 | 10,904 | 4.9 | 19,579 |
| 1958 | 17.3 | 12,790 | 16.7 | 22,849 |
| 1959 | 1.6 | 12,995 | −3.1 | 22,141 |
| 1960 | −4.9 | 12,358 | 16.9 | 25,883 |
| 1961 | 2.9 | 12,716 | −1.5 | 25,495 |
| 1962 | −15.3 | 10,770 | 22.4 | 31,206 |
| 1963 | 4.3 | 11,233 | 9.6 | 34,202 |
| 1964 | 6.7 | 11,986 | 6.2 | 36,323 |
| 1965 | 2.6 | 12,298 | −2.5 | 35,415 |
| 1966 | −16.4 | 10,281 | 14.3 | 40,479 |
| 1967 | −2.1 | 10,065 | 5.5 | 42,705 |
| 1968 | 3.4 | 10,407 | 0.2 | 42,790 |
| 1969 | −11.9 | 9,169 | −6.7 | 39,923 |
| 1970 | −1.4 | 9,041 | 20.8 | 48,227 |
| 1971 | −11.0 | 8,046 | 15.4 | 55,654 |
| 1972 | −0.6 | 7,998 | −1.4 | 54,875 |
| 1973 | −11.0 | 7,118 | 0.1 | 54,930 |
| 1974 | −22.4 | 5,524 | 28.2 | 70,420 |
| 1975 | 0.1 | 5,530 | 18.5 | 83,448 |
| 1976 | −3.4 | 5,342 | −3.0 | 80,945 |
| 1977 | −11.4 | 4,733 | 0.5 | 81,350 |
| 1978 | −4.5 | 4,520 | 9.3 | 88,916 |
| 1979 | −5.3 | 4,280 | 7.0 | 95,140 |
| 1980 | 9.3 | 4,678 | 4.7 | 99,612 |
| 1981 | −14.6 | 3,995 | 0.4 | 100,010 |
| 1982 | 15.5 | 4,614 | 23.5 | 123,512 |
| 1983 | 2.5 | 4,729 | −7.3 | 114,496 |
| 1984 | 3.3 | 4,885 | 3.9 | 118,961 |
| 1985 | 7.0 | 5,227 | 38.1 | 164,285 |
| 1986 | −2.8 | 5,081 | 28.2 | 210,613 |
| 1987 | −14.9 | 4,324 | 3.0 | 216,931 |
| 1988 | 6.1 | 4,588 | 11.8 | 242,529 |
| 1989 | 9.8 | 5,038 | 3.3 | 250,532 |
| 1990 | −6.7 | 4,700 | 15.8 | 290,116 |
| 1991 | 4.8 | 4,926 | 11.3 | 322,899 |
| 1992 | −6.2 | 4,621 | 6.6 | 344,210 |
| 1993 | 5.5 | 4,875 | 5.6 | 363,486 |
| 1994 | 3.7 | 5,055 | 13.1 | 411,103 |
| 1995 | 7.2 | 5,419 | 16.7 | 479,757 |
| 1996 | 9.2 | 5,918 | 21.9 | 584,824 |
| 1997 | 3.6 | 6,131 | 18.5 | 693,016 |
| 1998 | −12.4 | 5,371 | 39.9 | 969,529 |
| 1999 | −6.4 | 5,027 | 5.1 | 1,018,975 |
| 2000 | −6.0 | 4,725 | 5.4 | 1,074,000 |
| 2001 | −17.3 | 3,908 | 15.8 | 1,243,692 |
| 2002 | −25.2 | 2,923 | 6.0 | 1,318,314 |
| 2003 | 16.4 | 3,402 | 7.8 | 1,421,142 |
| 2004 | −0.9 | 3,371 | 1.8 | 1,446,723 |
| 2005 | −0.5 | 3,354 | 7.7 | 1,558,121 |
| 2006 | 4.7 | 3,512 | 14.4 | 1,782,490 |
| 2007 | 5.6 | 3,709 | −12.7 | 1,556,114 |
| 2008 | −24.7 | 2,793 | −14.0 | 1,338,258 |
| 2009 | 23.8 | 3,458 | 10.8 | 1,482,790 |
| 2010 | 4.6 | 3,617 | 7.3 | 1,591,034 |
| 2011 | −9.4 | 3,277 | 18.7 | 1,888,557 |
| 2012 | 0.3 | 3,287 | 10.0 | 2,077,413 |
| 2013 | 4.1 | 3,422 | 7.1 | 2,224,909 |
| 2014 | 2.3 | 3,501 | 7.4 | 2,389,552 |
| 2015 | −6.0 | 3,291 | 4.9 | 2,506,640 |
| 2016 | 3.5 | 3,406 | 13.1 | 2,835,010 |
| 2017 | 15.7 | 3,941 | 0.4 | 2,846,350 |
| 2018 | 5.0 | 4,138 | 5.2 | 2,994,360 |
| 2019 | 1.5 | 4,200 | −13.3 | 2,596,110 |
| 2020 | 22.1 | 5,128 | 19.1 | 3,091,967 |
| 2021 | 2.8 | 5,272 | −0.5 | 3,076,507 |
| **Average** | **−0.4%** | | **8.8%** | |
| **# Up** | **41** | | **61** | |
| **# Down** | **31** | | **11** | |
| **72-Year Gain (Loss)** | | **($4,728)** | | **$3,066,507** |

*MACD generated entry and exit points (earlier or later) can lengthen or shorten six month periods.

# MAY

**MONDAY**

D 33.3
S 42.9
N 47.6

**22**

*If you spend more than 14 minutes a year worrying about the market, you've wasted 12 minutes.*
— Peter Lynch (Fidelity Investments, *One Up On Wall Street*, b. 1944)

**TUESDAY**

D 52.4
S 52.4
N 52.4

**23**

*Nothing is more uncertain than the favor of the crowd.*
— Marcus Tullius Cicero (Great Roman Orator, Politician, 106-43 B.C.)

Start Looking for NASDAQ MACD Sell Signal on June 1 (Page 62)
Almanac Investor Subscribers Emailed When It Triggers (See Insert)

**WEDNESDAY**

D 47.6
S 57.1
N 52.4

**24**

*When you lose, say little. When you win, say less. Everyone can see the score.*
— Al Shaver (Hockey sportscaster)

**THURSDAY**

D 57.1
S 61.9
N 61.9

**25**

*Averaging down in a bear market is tantamount to taking a seat on the down escalator at Macy's.*
— Richard Russell (*Dow Theory Letters*, 1984, 1924-2015)

Friday Before Memorial Day Tends to Be Lackluster with Light Trading,
Dow Down 12 of Last 23, Average -0.1%

**FRIDAY**

D 52.4
S 57.1
N 61.9

**26**

*Brevity is the soul of wit.*
— William Shakespeare (English playwright, 1564-1616)

**SATURDAY**

**27**

June Almanac Investor Sector Seasonalities: See Pages 94, 96 and 98

**SUNDAY**

**28**

# JUNE ALMANAC

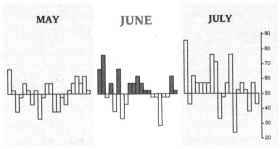

| JUNE | | | | | | | JULY | | | | | | |
|---|---|---|---|---|---|---|---|---|---|---|---|---|---|
| S | M | T | W | T | F | S | S | M | T | W | T | F | S |
| | | | | 1 | 2 | 3 | | | | | | | 1 |
| 4 | 5 | 6 | 7 | 8 | 9 | 10 | 2 | 3 | 4 | 5 | 6 | 7 | 8 |
| 11 | 12 | 13 | 14 | 15 | 16 | 17 | 9 | 10 | 11 | 12 | 13 | 14 | 15 |
| 18 | 19 | 20 | 21 | 22 | 23 | 24 | 16 | 17 | 18 | 19 | 20 | 21 | 22 |
| 25 | 26 | 27 | 28 | 29 | 30 | | 23 | 24 | 25 | 26 | 27 | 28 | 29 |
| | | | | | | | 30 | 31 | | | | | |

*Market Probability Chart above is a graphic representation of the S&P 500 Recent Market Probability Calendar on page 126.*

◆ The "summer rally" in most years is the weakest rally of all four seasons (page 74) ◆ Week after June Triple-Witching Day Dow down 27 of last 32 (page 108) ◆ RECENT RECORD: S&P up 12, down 9, average loss 0.5%, ranks eleventh ◆ Stronger for NASDAQ, average gain 0.2% last 21 years ◆ Watch out for end-of-quarter "portfolio pumping" on last day of June, Dow down 17 of last 31, NASDAQ up 9 of last 11 ◆ Pre-election year Junes: #5 S&P, #6 Dow, #6 NASDAQ ◆ June ends NASDAQ's Best Eight Months.

## June Vital Statistics

| | DJIA | | S&P 500 | | NASDAQ | | Russell 1K | | Russell 2K | |
|---|---|---|---|---|---|---|---|---|---|---|
| Rank | 11 | | 9 | | 5 | | 9 | | 7 | |
| Up | 34 | | 40 | | 29 | | 27 | | 28 | |
| Down | 38 | | 32 | | 22 | | 16 | | 15 | |
| Avg % Change | −0.2% | | 0.1% | | 0.9% | | 0.4% | | 0.9% | |
| Pre-Election Year | 1.1% | | 1.5% | | 2.4% | | 1.6% | | 1.9% | |
| **Best and Worst** | | | | | | | | | | |
| | % Change | | % Change | | % Change | | % Change | | % Change | |
| Best | 2019 | 7.2 | 1955 | 8.2 | 2000 | 16.6 | 2019 | 6.9 | 2000 | 8.6 |
| Worst | 2008 | −10.2 | 2008 | −8.6 | 2002 | −9.4 | 2008 | −8.5 | 2010 | −7.9 |
| **Best and Worst Weeks** | | | | | | | | | | |
| Best | 6/5/20 | 6.8 | 6/2/00 | 7.2 | 6/2/00 | 19.0 | 6/2/00 | 8.0 | 6/2/00 | 12.2 |
| Worst | 6/30/50 | −6.8 | 6/30/50 | −7.6 | 6/15/01 | −8.4 | 6/12/20 | −4.8 | 6/12/20 | −7.9 |
| **Best and Worst Days** | | | | | | | | | | |
| Best | 6/28/62 | 3.8 | 6/28/62 | 3.4 | 6/2/00 | 6.4 | 6/10/10 | 3.0 | 6/2/00 | 4.2 |
| Worst | 6/11/20 | −6.9 | 6/11/20 | −5.9 | 6/11/20 | −5.3 | 6/11/20 | −5.9 | 6/11/20 | −7.6 |
| **First Trading Day of Expiration Week: 1980–2022** | | | | | | | | | | |
| Record (#Up–#Down) | 22-20 | | 25-17 | | 20-22 | | 23-19 | | 17-24 | |
| Current Streak | D1 | | U4 | | U4 | | U4 | | D1 | |
| Avg % Change | −0.03 | | −0.07 | | −0.17 | | −0.08 | | −0.25 | |
| **Options Expiration Day: 1980–2022** | | | | | | | | | | |
| Record (#Up–#Down) | 23-19 | | 24-18 | | 21-20 | | 24-18 | | 21-21 | |
| Current Streak | D4 | | D4 | | D1 | | D4 | | D7 | |
| Avg % Change | −0.11 | | −0.030 | | −0.06 | | −0.05 | | −0.08 | |
| **Options Expiration Week: 1980–2022** | | | | | | | | | | |
| Record (#Up–#Down) | 24-18 | | 23-19 | | 19-23 | | 21-21 | | 20-22 | |
| Current Streak | D1 | | D1 | | D1 | | D1 | | D1 | |
| Avg % Change | −0.08 | | −0.04 | | −0.12 | | −0.09 | | −0.24 | |
| **Week After Options Expiration: 1980–2022** | | | | | | | | | | |
| Record (#Up–#Down) | 13-29 | | 19-23 | | 23-19 | | 19-23 | | 22-20 | |
| Current Streak | U1 | | U1 | | U1 | | U1 | | U1 | |
| Avg % Change | −0.47 | | −0.20 | | 0.12 | | −0.17 | | −0.12 | |
| **First Trading Day Performance** | | | | | | | | | | |
| % of Time Up | 58.3 | | 54.2 | | 58.8 | | 60.5 | | 67.4 | |
| Avg % Change | 0.16 | | 0.13 | | 0.12 | | 0.10 | | 0.23 | |
| **Last Trading Day Performance** | | | | | | | | | | |
| % of Time Up | 56.9 | | 54.2 | | 68.6 | | 58.1 | | 66.7 | |
| Avg % Change | 0.08 | | 0.13 | | 0.35 | | 0.10 | | 0.44 | |

*Dow & S&P 1950-May 13, 2022, NASDAQ 1971-May 13, 2022, Russell 1K & 2K 1979-May 13, 2022.*

*Last Day of June not hot for the Dow;*
*Down 17 of 31, WOW!*

# MAY/JUNE

Memorial Day *(Market Closed)*

**MONDAY**

## 29

*It's no coincidence that three of the top five stock option traders in a recent trading contest were all former Marines.*
— Robert Prechter, Jr. (American financial author & stock market analyst, *The Elliott Wave Theorist*, b. 1949)

*Day After Memorial Day, Dow Up 23 of Last 37, But Down 6 of Last 8*

🐂 **TUESDAY**

D 61.9
S 61.9
N 66.7

## 30

*The only function of economic forecasting is to make astrology look respectable.*
— John Kenneth Galbraith (Canadian/American economist and diplomat, 1908-2006)

*Memorial Day Week Dow Down 15 of Last 26, Up 12 Straight 1984-1995*

**WEDNESDAY**

D 38.1
S 52.4
N 52.4

## 31

*Never attribute to malevolence what is merely due to incompetence.*
— Arthur C. Clarke (British sci-fi writer, *3001: The Final Odyssey*, 1917-2008)

*First Trading Day in June, Dow Up 26 of Last 33, Down 4 of 5 2008-2012*

🐂 **THURSDAY**

D 76.2
S 66.7
N 57.1

## 1

*An economist is someone who sees something happen, and then wonders if it would work in theory.*
— Ronald Reagan (40th U.S. President, 1911-2004)

🐂 **FRIDAY**

D 61.9
S 76.2
N 71.4

## 2

*War is God's way of teaching Americans geography.*
— Ambrose Bierce (Writer, satirist, Civil War hero, *The Devil's Dictionary*, 1842-1914?)

**SATURDAY**

## 3

**SUNDAY**

## 4

# TOP PERFORMING NASDAQ MONTHS

NASDAQ stocks continue to run away during three consecutive months, November, December and January, with an average gain of 6.0% despite the slaughter of November 2000, down 22.9%, December 2000, –4.9%, December 2002, –9.7%, November 2007, –6.9%, January 2008, –9.9%, November 2008, –10.8%, January 2009, –6.4%, January 2010, –5.4% January 2016, –7.9%, December 2018, –9.5% and January 2022, –9.0%. Solid gains in November and December 2004 offset January 2005's 5.2% Iraq-turmoil-fueled drop.

You can see the months graphically on page 150. January by itself is impressive, up 2.5% on average. April, May and June also shine, creating our NASDAQ Best Eight Months strategy. What appears as a Death Valley abyss occurs during NASDAQ's leanest months: July, August and September. NASDAQ's Best Eight Months seasonal strategy using MACD timing is displayed on page 62.

## MONTHLY % CHANGES (JANUARY 1971 TO APRIL 2022)

### NASDAQ Composite*

| Month | Total % Change | Avg. % Change | # Up | # Down |
|---|---|---|---|---|
| Jan | 131.4% | 2.5% | 34 | 18 |
| Feb | 27.0 | 0.5 | 28 | 24 |
| Mar | 36.1 | 0.7 | 33 | 19 |
| Apr | 76.4 | 1.5 | 34 | 18 |
| May | 48.6 | 1.0 | 31 | 20 |
| Jun | 50.0 | 1.0 | 29 | 22 |
| Jul | 31.8 | 0.6 | 29 | 22 |
| Aug | 23.4 | 0.5 | 29 | 22 |
| Sep | – 34.1 | – 0.7 | 27 | 24 |
| Oct | 37.5 | 0.7 | 28 | 23 |
| Nov | 93.6 | 1.8 | 36 | 15 |
| Dec | 85.6 | 1.7 | 31 | 20 |

| % Rank | | | | |
|---|---|---|---|---|
| Jan | 131.4% | 2.5% | 34 | 18 |
| Nov | 93.6 | 1.8 | 36 | 15 |
| Dec | 85.6 | 1.7 | 31 | 20 |
| Apr | 76.4 | 1.5 | 34 | 18 |
| Jun | 50.0 | 1.0 | 29 | 22 |
| May | 48.6 | 1.0 | 31 | 20 |
| Oct | 37.5 | 0.7 | 28 | 23 |
| Mar | 36.1 | 0.7 | 33 | 19 |
| Jul | 31.8 | 0.6 | 29 | 22 |
| Feb | 27.0 | 0.5 | 28 | 24 |
| Aug | 23.4 | 0.5 | 29 | 22 |
| Sep | – 34.1 | – 0.7 | 27 | 24 |
| Totals | 607.3% | 11.8% | | |
| Average | | 0.98% | | |

### Dow Jones Industrials

| Month | Total % Change | Avg. % Change | # Up | # Down |
|---|---|---|---|---|
| Jan | 55.2% | 1.1% | 31 | 21 |
| Feb | 13.5 | 0.3 | 31 | 21 |
| Mar | 47.3 | 0.9 | 34 | 18 |
| Apr | 109.6 | 2.1 | 35 | 17 |
| May | 12.8 | 0.3 | 29 | 22 |
| Jun | 5.9 | 0.1 | 26 | 25 |
| Jul | 47.1 | 0.9 | 31 | 20 |
| Aug | – 5.3 | – 0.1 | 29 | 22 |
| Sep | – 47.4 | – 0.9 | 19 | 32 |
| Oct | 31.9 | 0.6 | 31 | 20 |
| Nov | 77.8 | 1.5 | 35 | 16 |
| Dec | 78.3 | 1.5 | 36 | 15 |

| % Rank | | | | |
|---|---|---|---|---|
| Apr | 109.6% | 2.1% | 35 | 17 |
| Dec | 78.3 | 1.5 | 36 | 15 |
| Nov | 77.8 | 1.5 | 35 | 16 |
| Jan | 55.2 | 1.1 | 31 | 21 |
| Mar | 47.3 | 0.9 | 34 | 18 |
| Jul | 47.1 | 0.9 | 31 | 20 |
| Oct | 31.9 | 0.6 | 31 | 20 |
| Feb | 13.5 | 0.3 | 31 | 21 |
| May | 12.8 | 0.3 | 29 | 22 |
| Jun | 5.9 | 0.1 | 26 | 25 |
| Aug | – 5.3 | – 0.1 | 29 | 22 |
| Sep | – 47.4 | – 0.9 | 19 | 32 |
| Totals | 426.7% | 8.3% | | |
| Average | | 0.69% | | |

*Based on NASDAQ composite, prior to Feb. 5, 1971 based on National Quotation Bureau indices.

For comparison, Dow figures are shown. During this period NASDAQ averaged a 0.98% gain per month, 42.0% more than the Dow's 0.69% per month. Between January 1971 and January 1982 NASDAQ's composite index doubled in twelve years, while the Dow stayed flat. But while NASDAQ plummeted 77.9% from its 2000 highs to the 2002 bottom, the Dow only lost 37.8%. The Great Recession and bear market of 2007 2009 spread its carnage equally across Dow and NASDAQ. Recent market moves are increasingly more correlated, but NASDAQ still has an advantage.

# JUNE

**MONDAY**

D 42.9
S 47.6
N 52.4

# 5

*ee will is your mind's freedom to think or not, the only will you have, your only freedom,*
*e choice that controls all the choices you make and determines your life and your character.*
— Ayn Rand (Russian-born American novelist and philosopher, from Galt's Speech, *Atlas Shrugged*, 1957, 1905-1982)

*une Ends NASDAQ's "Best Eight Months" (Pages 60, 62 and 150)*  **TUESDAY**

D 61.9
S 57.1
N 57.1

# 6

*ople with a sense of fulfillment think the world is good, while the frustrated blame the world for their failure.*
— Eric Hoffer (*The True Believer*, 1951)

**WEDNESDAY**

D 61.9
S 38.1
N 42.9

# 7

*erson's greatest virtue is his ability to correct his mistakes and continually make a new person of himself.*
— Yang-Ming Wang (Chinese philosopher, 1472-1529)

*08 Second Worst June Ever, Dow -10.2%, S&P -8.6%,*  **THURSDAY**
*ly 1930 Was Worse, NASDAQ June 2008 -9.1%, June 2002 -9.4%*

D 66.7
S 66.7
N 52.4

# 8

*ou are ready to give up everything else to study the whole history of the market as carefully as a medical student studies anatomy and*
*have the cool nerves of a great gambler, the sixth sense of a clairvoyant, and the courage of a lion, you have a ghost of a chance.*
— Bernard Baruch (Financier, speculator, statesman, presidential adviser, 1870-1965)

**FRIDAY**

D 38.1
S 33.3
N 33.3

# 9

*market is a voting machine, whereon countless individuals register choices*
*ch are the product partly of reason and partly of emotion.*
— Graham & Dodd

**SATURDAY**

# 10

**SUNDAY**

# 11

# GET MORE OUT OF NASDAQ'S "BEST EIGHT MONTHS" WITH MACD TIMING

NASDAQ's amazing eight-month run from November through June is hard to miss on pages 60 and 150. A $10,000 investment in these eight months since 1971 gained $897,988 versus 1,613 during the void that is the four-month period July-October (as of May 20, 2022).

Using the same MACD timing indicators on the NASDAQ as is done for the Dow (page 56) has enabled us to capture much of October's improved performance, pumping up NASDAQ's results considerably. Over the 51 years since NASDAQ began, the gain on the same $10,000 more than doubles to $2,333,643 and the gain during the four-month void becomes a loss of $5,581. Only five sizeable losses occurred during the favorable period and the bulk of NASDAQ's bear markets were avoided including the worst of the 2000-2002 bear.

Updated signals are emailed to our monthly newsletter subscribers as soon as they are triggered. Visit *www.stocktradersalmanac.com*, or see insert for details and a special offer for new subscribers.

## BEST EIGHT MONTHS STRATEGY + TIMING

| MACD Signal Date | Worst 4 Months July 1–Oct 31* NASDAQ | % Change | Investing $10,000 | MACD Signal Date | Best 8 Months Nov 1–June 30* NASDAQ | % Change | Investing $10,000 |
|---|---|---|---|---|---|---|---|
| 22-Jul-71 | 109.54 | −3.6 | $9,640 | 4-Nov-71 | 105.56 | 24.1 | $12,410 |
| 7-Jun-72 | 131.00 | −1.8 | 9,466 | 23-Oct-72 | 128.66 | −22.7 | 9,593 |
| 25-Jun-73 | 99.43 | −7.2 | 8,784 | 7-Dec-73 | 92.32 | −20.2 | 7,655 |
| 3-Jul-74 | 73.66 | −23.2 | 6,746 | 7-Oct-74 | 56.57 | 47.8 | 11,314 |
| 11-Jun-75 | 83.60 | −9.2 | 6,125 | 7-Oct-75 | 75.88 | 20.8 | 13,667 |
| 22-Jul-76 | 91.66 | −2.4 | 5,978 | 19-Oct-76 | 89.45 | 13.2 | 15,471 |
| 27-Jul-77 | 101.25 | −4.0 | 5,739 | 4-Nov-77 | 97.21 | 26.6 | 19,586 |
| 7-Jun-78 | 123.10 | −6.5 | 5,366 | 6-Nov-78 | 115.08 | 19.1 | 23,327 |
| 3-Jul-79 | 137.03 | −1.1 | 5,307 | 30-Oct-79 | 135.48 | 15.5 | 26,943 |
| 20-Jun-80 | 156.51 | 26.2 | 6,697 | 9-Oct-80 | 197.53 | 11.2 | 29,961 |
| 4-Jun-81 | 219.68 | −17.6 | 5,518 | 1-Oct-81 | 181.09 | −4.0 | 28,763 |
| 7-Jun-82 | 173.84 | 12.5 | 6,208 | 7-Oct-82 | 195.59 | 57.4 | 45,273 |
| 1-Jun-83 | 307.95 | −10.7 | 5,544 | 3-Nov-83 | 274.86 | −14.2 | 38,844 |
| 1-Jun-84 | 235.90 | 5.0 | 5,821 | 15-Oct-84 | 247.67 | 17.3 | 45,564 |
| 3-Jun-85 | 290.59 | −3.0 | 5,646 | 1-Oct-85 | 281.77 | 39.4 | 63,516 |
| 10-Jun-86 | 392.83 | −10.3 | 5,064 | 1-Oct-86 | 352.34 | 20.5 | 76,537 |
| 30-Jun-87 | 424.67 | −22.7 | 3,914 | 2-Nov-87 | 328.33 | 20.1 | 91,921 |
| 8-Jul-88 | 394.33 | −6.6 | 3,656 | 29-Nov-88 | 368.15 | 22.4 | 112,511 |
| 13-Jun-89 | 450.73 | 0.7 | 3,682 | 9-Nov-89 | 454.07 | 1.9 | 114,649 |
| 11-Jun-90 | 462.79 | −23.0 | 2,835 | 2-Oct-90 | 356.39 | 39.3 | 159,706 |
| 11-Jun-91 | 496.62 | 6.4 | 3,016 | 1-Oct-91 | 528.51 | 7.4 | 171,524 |
| 11-Jun-92 | 567.68 | 1.5 | 3,061 | 14-Oct-92 | 576.22 | 20.5 | 206,686 |
| 7-Jun-93 | 694.61 | 9.9 | 3,364 | 1-Oct-93 | 763.23 | −4.4 | 197,592 |
| 17-Jun-94 | 729.35 | 5.0 | 3,532 | 11-Oct-94 | 765.57 | 13.5 | 224,267 |
| 1-Jun-95 | 868.82 | 17.2 | 4,140 | 13-Oct-95 | 1018.38 | 21.6 | 272,709 |
| 3-Jun-96 | 1238.73 | 1.0 | 4,181 | 7-Oct-96 | 1250.87 | 10.3 | 300,798 |
| 4-Jun-97 | 1379.67 | 24.4 | 5,201 | 3-Oct-97 | 1715.87 | 1.8 | 306,212 |
| 1-Jun-98 | 1746.82 | −7.8 | 4,795 | 15-Oct-98 | 1611.01 | 49.7 | 458,399 |
| 1-Jun-99 | 2412.03 | 18.5 | 5,682 | 6-Oct-99 | 2857.21 | 35.7 | 622,047 |
| 29-Jun-00 | 3877.23 | −18.2 | 4,648 | 18-Oct-00 | 3171.56 | −32.2 | 421,748 |
| 1-Jun-01 | 2149.44 | −31.1 | 3,202 | 1-Oct-01 | 1480.46 | 5.5 | 444,944 |
| 3-Jun-02 | 1562.56 | −24.0 | 2,434 | 2-Oct-02 | 1187.30 | 38.5 | 616,247 |
| 20-Jun-03 | 1644.72 | 15.1 | 2,802 | 6-Oct-03 | 1893.46 | 4.3 | 642,746 |
| 21-Jun-04 | 1974.38 | −1.6 | 2,757 | 1-Oct-04 | 1942.20 | 6.1 | 681,954 |
| 8-Jun-05 | 2060.18 | 1.5 | 2,798 | 19-Oct-05 | 2091.76 | 6.1 | 723,553 |
| 1-Jun-06 | 2219.86 | 3.9 | 2,907 | 5-Oct-06 | 2306.34 | 9.5 | 792,291 |
| 7-Jun-07 | 2541.38 | 7.9 | 3,137 | 1-Oct-07 | 2740.99 | −9.1 | 724,796 |
| 2-Jun-08 | 2491.53 | −31.3 | 2,155 | 17-Oct-08 | 1711.29 | 6.1 | 769,009 |
| 15-Jun-09 | 1816.38 | 17.8 | 2,539 | 9-Oct-09 | 2139.28 | 1.6 | 781,313 |
| 7-Jun-10 | 2173.90 | 18.6 | 3,011 | 4-Nov-10 | 2577.34 | 7.4 | 839,130 |
| 1-Jun-11 | 2769.19 | −10.5 | 2,695 | 7-Oct-11 | 2479.35 | 10.8 | 929,756 |
| 1-Jun-12 | 2747.48 | 9.6 | 2,954 | 6-Nov-12 | 3011.93 | 16.2 | 1,080,376 |
| 4-Jun-13 | 3445.26 | 10.1 | 3,252 | 15-Oct-13 | 3794.01 | 15.4 | 1,227,442 |
| 26-Jun-14 | 4379.05 | 0.9 | 3,281 | 21-Oct-14 | 4419.48 | 14.5 | 1,405,427 |
| 4-Jun-15 | 5059.12 | −5.5 | 3,101 | 5-Oct-15 | 4781.26 | 1.4 | 1,425,097 |
| 13-Jun-16 | 4848.44 | 9.5 | 3,396 | 24-Oct-16 | 5309.83 | 18.8 | 1,693,015 |
| 9-Jun-17 | 6207.92 | 11.3 | 3,780 | 28-Nov-17 | 6912.36 | 11.6 | 1,859,187 |
| 21-Jun-18 | 7712.95 | −5.3 | 3,580 | 31-Oct-18 | 7305.90 | 7.9 | 2,006,063 |
| 19-Jul-19 | 8146.49 | −1.1 | 3,541 | 11-Oct-19 | 8057.04 | 17.8 | 2,441,987 |
| 11-Jun-20 | 9492.73 | 25.3 | 4,437 | 5-Nov-20 | 11890.93 | 18.3 | 2,888,877 |
| 14-Jul-21 | 14644.95 | −0.4 | 4,419 | 8-Oct-21 | 14579.54 | −25.9 | 2,343,643 |
| 13-Jun-22 | 11354.62 | | | | | | |
| | **51-Year Loss** | ($5,581) | | | **51-Year Gain** | | $2,333,643 |

*MACD-generated entry and exit points (earlier or later) can lengthen or shorten eight-month periods.*

Monday of Triple Witching Week, Dow Down 14 of Last 26

**MONDAY**

D 42.9
S 42.9
N 42.9

**12**

*The difference between the almost right word [or trade] and the right word [trade] is really a large matter—is the difference between the lightning-bug and the lightning.*
— Mark Twain (American novelist and satirist, pen name of Samuel Longhorne Clemens, 1835-1910)

**TUESDAY**

D 57.1
S 57.1
N 52.4

**13**

*When you're one step ahead of the crowd, you're a genius. When you're two steps ahead, you're a crackpot.*
— Shlomo Riskin (Rabbi, author, b. 1940)

Triple Witching Week Often Up in Bull Markets and Down in Bears (Page 108)
FOMC Meeting (2 Days)

**WEDNESDAY**

D 52.4
S 57.1
N 61.9

**14**

*Successful investing is anticipating the anticipations of others.*
— John Maynard Keynes (British economist, 1883-1946)

**THURSDAY**

D 52.4
S 61.9
N 61.9

**15**

*A good manager is a man who isn't worried about his own career but rather the careers of those who work for him… Don't worry about yourself! Take care of those who work for you and you'll float to greatness on their achievements.*
— H.S.M. Burns (Scottish CEO Shell Oil 1947-1960, 1900-1971)

June Triple Witching Day, Dow Up 10 of Last 19, But Down 6 of Last 7

**FRIDAY**

D 61.9
S 57.1
N 52.4

**16**

*When the public buys toilet paper, I buy stocks.*
— Larry Williams (Legendary trader, author, politician, 3/16/2020, b. 1942)

**SATURDAY**

**17**

Father's Day

**SUNDAY**

**18**

# TRIPLE RETURNS, FEWER TRADES: BEST 6 + 4-YEAR CYCLE

We first introduced this strategy to *Almanac Investor* newsletter subscribers in October 2006. Recurring seasonal stock market patterns and the Four-Year Presidential Election/Stock Market Cycle (page 132) have been integral to our research since the first *Almanac* over 50 years ago. Yale Hirsch discovered the Best Six Months in 1986 (page 54) and it has been a cornerstone of our seasonal investment analysis and strategies ever since.

Most of the market's gains have occurred during the Best Six Months and the market generally hits a low point every four years in the first (post-election) or second (midterm) year and exhibits the greatest gains in the third (pre-election) year. This strategy combines the best of these two market phenomena, the Best Six Months and the 4-Year Cycle, timing entries and exits with MACD (page 56 & 62).

We've gone back to 1949 to include the full four-year cycle that began with post-election year 1949. Only four trades every four years are needed to nearly triple the results of the Best Six Months. Buy and sell during the post-election and midterm years and then hold from the midterm MACD seasonal buy signal sometime after October 1 until the post-election MACD seasonal sell signal sometime after April 1, approximately 2.5 years. Solid returns, less effort, lower transaction fees and fewer taxable events.

| FOUR TRADES EVERY FOUR YEARS | | |
|---|---|---|
| | Worst | Best |
| | Six Months | Six Months |
| Year | May-Oct | Nov-April |
| Post-election | Sell | Buy |
| Midterm | Sell | Buy |
| Pre-election | Hold | Hold |
| Election | Hold | Hold |

| | DJIA % Change May 1–Oct 31* | Investing $10,000 | DJIA % Change Nov 1–Apr 30* | Investing $10,000 |
|---|---|---|---|---|
| BEST SIX MONTHS+TIMING+4-YEAR CYCLE STRATEGY | | | | |
| 1949 | 3.0% | $10,300 | 17.5% | $11,750 |
| 1950 | 7.3 | 14,065 | 19.7 | 14,065 |
| 1951 | | 11,052 | | 14,065 |
| 1952 | | 11,052 | | 14,065 |
| 1953 | 0.2 | 11,074 | 17.1 | 16,470 |
| 1954 | 13.5 | 12,569 | 35.7 | 22,350 |
| 1955 | | 12,569 | | 22,350 |
| 1956 | | 12,569 | | 22,350 |
| 1957 | −12.3 | 11,023 | 4.9 | 23,445 |
| 1958 | 17.3 | 12,930 | 27.8 | 29,963 |
| 1959 | | 12,930 | | 29,963 |
| 1960 | | 12,930 | | 29,963 |
| 1961 | 2.9 | 13,305 | −1.5 | 29,514 |
| 1962 | −15.3 | 11,269 | 58.5 | 46,780 |
| 1963 | | 11,269 | | 46,780 |
| 1964 | | 11,269 | | 46,780 |
| 1965 | 2.6 | 11,562 | −2.5 | 45,611 |
| 1966 | −16.4 | 9,666 | 22.2 | 55,737 |
| 1967 | | 9,666 | | 55,737 |
| 1968 | | 9,666 | | 55,737 |
| 1969 | −11.9 | 8,516 | −6.7 | 52,003 |
| 1970 | −1.4 | 8,397 | 21.5 | 63,184 |
| 1971 | | 8,397 | | 63,184 |
| 1972 | | 8,397 | | 63,184 |
| 1973 | −11.0 | 7,473 | 0.1 | 63,247 |
| 1974 | −22.4 | 5,799 | 42.5 | 90,127 |
| 1975 | | 5,799 | | 90,127 |
| 1976 | | 5,799 | | 90,127 |
| 1977 | −11.4 | 5,138 | 0.5 | 90,578 |
| 1978 | −4.5 | 4,907 | 26.8 | 114,853 |
| 1979 | | 4,907 | | 114,853 |
| 1980 | | 4,907 | | 114,853 |
| 1981 | −14.6 | 4,191 | 0.4 | 115,312 |
| 1982 | 15.5 | 4,841 | 25.9 | 145,178 |
| 1983 | | 4,841 | | 145,178 |
| 1984 | | 4,841 | | 145,178 |
| 1985 | 7.0 | 5,180 | 38.1 | 200,491 |
| 1986 | −2.8 | 5,035 | 33.2 | 267,054 |
| 1987 | | 5,035 | | 267,054 |
| 1988 | | 5,035 | | 267,054 |
| 1989 | 9.8 | 5,528 | 3.3 | 275,867 |
| 1990 | −6.7 | 5,158 | 35.1 | 372,696 |
| 1991 | | 5,158 | | 372,696 |
| 1992 | | 5,158 | | 372,696 |
| 1993 | 5.5 | 5,442 | 5.6 | 393,455 |
| 1994 | 3.7 | 5,643 | 88.2 | 740,482 |
| 1995 | | 5,643 | | 740,482 |
| 1996 | | 5,643 | | 740,482 |
| 1997 | 3.6 | 5,846 | 18.5 | 877,471 |
| 1998 | −12.4 | 5,121 | 36.3 | 1,195,993 |
| 1999 | | 5,121 | | 1,195,993 |
| 2000 | | 5,121 | | 1,195,993 |
| 2001 | −17.3 | 4,235 | 15.8 | 1,384,960 |
| 2002 | −25.2 | 3,168 | 34.2 | 1,858,616 |
| 2003 | | 3,168 | | 1,858,616 |
| 2004 | | 3,168 | | 1,858,616 |
| 2005 | −0.5 | 3,152 | 7.7 | 2,001,729 |
| 2006 | 4.7 | 3,300 | −31.7 | 1,367,181 |
| 2007 | | 3,300 | | 1,367,181 |
| 2008 | | 3,300 | | 1,367,181 |
| 2009 | 23.8 | 4,085 | 10.8 | 1,514,738 |
| 2010 | 4.6 | 4,273 | 27.4 | 1,929,777 |
| 2011 | | 4,273 | | 1,929,777 |
| 2012 | | 4,273 | | 1,929,777 |
| 2013 | 4.1 | 4,448 | 7.1 | 2,066,791 |
| 2014 | 2.3 | 4,550 | 24.0 | 2,562,820 |
| 2015 | | 4,550 | | 2,562,820 |
| 2016 | | 4,550 | | 2,562,820 |
| 2017 | 15.7 | 5,265 | 0.4 | 2,573,072 |
| 2018 | 5.0 | 5,528 | 34.6 | 3,463,354 |
| 2019 | | 5,528 | | 3,463,354 |
| 2020 | | 5,528 | | 3,463,354 |
| 2021** | 2.8 | 5,683 | −0.5 | 3,446,038 |
| Average | −0.4% | | 9.6% | |
| # Up | 21 | | 32 | |
| # Down | 16 | | 5 | |
| 73-Year Gain (Loss) | ($4,317) | | | $3,436,038 |

*MACD and 2.5-year hold lengthen and shorten six-month periods.
** As of April 7, 2022 Seasonal Sell signal.

# JUNE

eteenth National Independence Day *(Market Closed)*

MONDAY
**19**

---

*ss you've interpreted changes before they've occurred, you'll be decimated trying to follow them.*
*bert J. Nurock (Stock market analyst, Wall Street Week panelist, 1938-2017)*

TUESDAY
D 47.6
S 52.4
N 66.7 **20**

---

*olitical party does not have its foundation in the determination to advance a cause that is right*
*hat is moral, then it is not a political party; it is merely a conspiracy to seize power.*
*wight D. Eisenhower (34th U.S. President, 1890-1969)*

*ek After June Triple Witching, Dow Down 27 of Last 32*
*rage Loss Since 1990, 1.0%*

WEDNESDAY
D 47.6
S 52.4
N 47.6 **21**

---

*never you see a successful business, someone once made a courageous decision.*
*ter Drucker (Austrian-born pioneer management theorist, 1909-2005)*

THURSDAY
D 42.9
S 47.6
N 47.6 **22**

---

*n new money is created on a grand scale, it must go somewhere and have some major consequences.*
*of these will be greatly increased volatility and instability in the economy and financial system.*
Anthony Boeckh, Ph.D (Chairman Bank Credit Analyst 1968-2002, *The Great Reflation, Boeckh Investment Letter*)

FRIDAY
D 38.1
S 47.6
N 42.9 **23**

---

*it has been well said, think in herds; it will be seen that they go mad in herds, while they only recover their senses slowly, and one by one.*
*harles Mackay (Scottish poet, journalist, author, anthologist, novelist, and songwriter,*
*iordinary Popular Delusions and the Madness of Crowds, 1814-1889)*

SATURDAY
**24**

---

*Almanac Investor Sector Seasonalities: See Pages 94, 96 and 98*

SUNDAY
**25**

# JULY ALMANAC

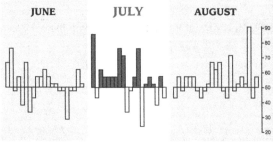

| JULY | | | | | | |
|---|---|---|---|---|---|---|
| S | M | T | W | T | F | S |
| | | | | | | 1 |
| 2 | 3 | 4 | 5 | 6 | 7 | 8 |
| 9 | 10 | 11 | 12 | 13 | 14 | 15 |
| 16 | 17 | 18 | 19 | 20 | 21 | 22 |
| 23 | 24 | 25 | 26 | 27 | 28 | 29 |
| 30 | 31 | | | | | |

| AUGUST | | | | | | |
|---|---|---|---|---|---|---|
| S | M | T | W | T | F | S |
| | | 1 | 2 | 3 | 4 | 5 |
| 6 | 7 | 8 | 9 | 10 | 11 | 12 |
| 13 | 14 | 15 | 16 | 17 | 18 | 19 |
| 20 | 21 | 22 | 23 | 24 | 25 | 26 |
| 27 | 28 | 29 | 30 | 31 | | |

*Market Probability Chart above is a graphic representation of the S&P 500 Recent Market Probability Calendar on page 126.*

◆ July is the best month of the third quarter (page 68) ◆ Start of second half brings an inflow of retirement funds ◆ First trading day Dow up 27 of last 33 ◆ Graph above shows strength in the first half of July ◆ Huge gain in July usually provides better buying opportunity over next four months ◆ Start of NASDAQ's worst four months of the year (page 60) ◆ Pre-election Julys are ranked #7 Dow (up 11, down 7), #7 S&P (up 11, down 7), and #9 NASDAQ (up 7, down 6).

## July Vital Statistics

| | DJIA | S&P 500 | NASDAQ | Russell 1K | Russell 2K |
|---|---|---|---|---|---|
| Rank | 4 | 4 | 9 | 5 | 10 |
| Up | 47 | 42 | 29 | 23 | 22 |
| Down | 25 | 30 | 22 | 20 | 21 |
| Avg % Change | 1.3% | 1.1% | 0.6% | 0.9% | −0.2% |
| Pre-Election Year | 1.0% | 0.9% | 1.0% | 0.6% | 0.3% |
| **Best and Worst** | | | | | |
| | % Change | % Change | % Change | % Change | % Change |
| Best | 1989 9.0 | 1989 8.8 | 1997 10.5 | 1989 8.2 | 1980 11.0 |
| Worst | 1969 −6.6 | 2002 −7.9 | 2002 −9.2 | 2002 −7.5 | 2002 −15.2 |
| **Best and Worst Weeks** | | | | | |
| Best | 7/17/09 7.3 | 7/17/09 7.0 | 7/17/09 7.4 | 7/17/09 7.0 | 7/17/09 8.0 |
| Worst | 7/19/02 −7.7 | 7/19/02 −8.0 | 7/28/00 −10.5 | 7/19/02 −7.4 | 7/2/10 −7.2 |
| **Best and Worst Days** | | | | | |
| Best | 7/24/02 6.4 | 7/24/02 5.7 | 7/29/02 5.8 | 7/24/02 5.6 | 7/29/02 4.9 |
| Worst | 7/19/02 −4.6 | 7/19/02 −3.8 | 7/28/00 −4.7 | 7/19/02 −3.6 | 7/23/02 −4.1 |
| **First Trading Day of Expiration Week: 1980–2022** | | | | | |
| Record (#Up–#Down) | 27-15 | 26-16 | 28-14 | 26-16 | 23-19 |
| Current Streak | U4 | U1 | U1 | U1 | U1 |
| Avg % Change | 0.13 | 0.03 | 0.02 | 0.01 | −0.07 |
| **Options Expiration Day: 1980–2022** | | | | | |
| Record (#Up–#Down) | 17-23 | 20-22 | 17-25 | 20-22 | 16-26 |
| Current Streak | D5 | D1 | D1 | D1 | D1 |
| Avg % Change | −0.25 | −0.27 | −0.39 | −0.28 | −0.44 |
| **Options Expiration Week: 1980–2022** | | | | | |
| Record (#Up–#Down) | 26-16 | 24-18 | 21-21 | 24-18 | 23-19 |
| Current Streak | D1 | D1 | D4 | D1 | D1 |
| Avg % Change | 0.46 | 0.16 | 0.04 | 0.10 | −0.09 |
| **Week After Options Expiration: 1980–2022** | | | | | |
| Record (#Up–#Down) | 23-19 | 21-21 | 19-23 | 22-20 | 16-26 |
| Current Streak | U1 | U1 | U1 | U1 | U1 |
| Avg % Change | 0.03 | −0.06 | −0.30 | −0.07 | −0.30 |
| **First Trading Day Performance** | | | | | |
| % of Time Up | 66.7 | 73.6 | 64.7 | 76.7 | 67.4 |
| Avg % Change | 0.26 | 0.27 | 0.17 | 0.33 | 0.13 |
| **Last Trading Day Performance** | | | | | |
| % of Time Up | 50.0 | 59.7 | 49.0 | 55.8 | 60.5 |
| Avg % Change | 0.01 | 0.05 | −0.04 | −0.04 | −0.05 |

*Dow & S&P 1950-May 13, 2022, NASDAQ 1971-May 13, 2022, Russell 1K & 2K 1979-May 13, 2022.*

*When Dow and S&P in July are inferior, NASDAQ days tend to be even drearier.*

# Those who study market history are bound to profit from it!

*"I'm a mechanical engineer, and an investment advisor, and been in this business for over 30 years. Throughout [?] years I subscribed to the most expensive newsletters in the country, and never made a profit because of [?] momentum stocks they all recommend, and most of their recommendations made a round trip no exception [?] 8 weeks I followed your recommendations regarding the seasonality trends and I made over $135,000.0[?]* – Sam C. from Mississippi*

Now you can find out which seasonal trends are on schedule and which are not, and how to take advantage of them. You will be kept abreast of upcoming market-moving events and what our indicators are saying about the next major market move. Every week you will receive timely dispatches about bullish and bearish seasonal patterns.

Our digital subscription service, *Almanac Investor*, provides all this plus unusual investing opportunities – exciting small-, mid- and large-cap stocks; seasoned, undervalued equities; timely sector ETF trades and more. Our **Data-Rich and Data-Driven Market Cycle Analysis** is the only investment tool of its kind that helps traders and investors forecast market trends with accuracy and confidence.

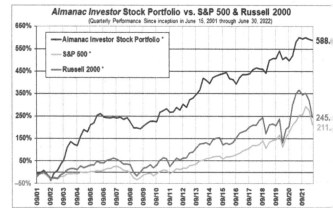

Almanac Investor Stock Portfolio vs. S&P 500 & Russell 2000
(Quarterly Performance Since inception in June 15, 2001 through June 30, 2022)
- Almanac Investor Stock Portfolio *
- S&P 500 *
- Russell 2000 *

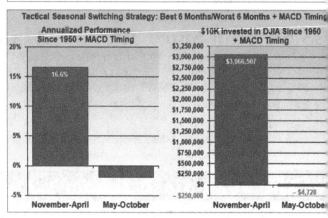

Tactical Seasonal Switching Strategy: Best 6 Months/Worst 6 Months + MACD Timing

Annualized Performance Since 1950 + MACD Timing

$10K invested in DJIA Since 1950 + MACD Timing

| | YOU RECEIVE WEEKLY EMAIL ALERTS CONTAINING: |
|---|---|
| | ◆ Opportune ETF and Stock Trading Ideas with Specific Buy and Sell Price Limits |
| | ◆ Timely Data-Rich and Data-Driven Market Analysis |
| | ◆ Access to Webinars, Videos, Tools and Resources |
| | ◆ Market-Tested and Time-Proven Short- and Long-term Trading Strategies |
| | ◆ Best Six-Months Switching Strategy MACD Timing Signals. |

# JUNE/JULY

*_aws are like sausages. It's better not to see them being made.*
— Otto von Bismarck (German-Prussian politician, first Chancellor of Germany, 1815-1898)

**TUESDAY**
D 42.9
S 47.6
N 52.4 **27**

*The thing you do obsessively between age 13 and 18, that's the thing you have the most chance of being world-class at.*
— William H. Gates (Microsoft founder, "Charlie Rose" interview 2/22/2016, b. 1955)

**WEDNESDAY**
D 47.6
S 47.6
N 66.7 **28**

*_believe in the exceptional man—the entrepreneur who is always out of money, _ot the bureaucrat who generates cash flow and pays dividends.*
— Armand Erpf (Investment banker, partner Loeb Rhoades, 1897-1971)

🐃 **THURSDAY**
D 57.1
S 61.9
N 66.7 **29**

*)on't be the last bear or last bull standing, let history guide you, be contrary to the crowd, and let the tape tell you when to act.*
— Jeffrey A. Hirsch (Editor, *Stock Trader's Almanac*, b. 1966)

*_ast Day of Q2 Bearish for Dow, Down 17 of Last 31, But Up 9 of Last 11,*
*ʒullish for NASDAQ, Up 21 of 30*

**FRIDAY**
D 52.4
S 52.4
N 57.1 **30**

*_he only person who never makes a mistake is someone who does nothing.*
— Albert Einstein (German/American physicist, 1921 Nobel Prize, 1879-1955)

**SATURDAY**
**1**

**SUNDAY**
**2**

# FIRST MONTH OF QUARTERS IS THE MOST BULLISH

We have observed over the years that the investment calendar reflects the annual, semi-annual and quarterly operations of institutions during January, April and July. The opening month of the first three quarters produces the greatest gains in the Dow Jones Industrials, S&P 500 and NASDAQ.

The fourth quarter had behaved quite differently since it is affected by year-end portfolio adjustments and Presidential and Congressional elections in even-numbered years. Since 1991 major turnarounds have helped October join the ranks of bullish first months of quarters. October transformed into a bear-killing, turnaround month, posting Dow gains in 17 of the last 24 years, 2008 was a significant exception (See pages 156-173.)

After experiencing the most powerful bull market of all time during the 1990s, followed by two ferocious bear markets early in the millennium, we divided the monthly average percent changes into two groups: before 1991 and after. Comparing the month-by-month quarterly behavior of the three major U.S. averages in the table, you'll see that first months of the first three quarters perform best overall. Nasty sell-offs in April 2000, 2002, 2004, 2005 and 2022, and in July 2000-2002 and 2004 hit the NASDAQ hardest. The bear market of October 2007-March 2009, which more than cut the markets in half, took a toll on every first month except April. October 2008 was the worst month in a decade. January was also a difficult month in 9 of the last 15 years, pulling its performance lower. (See pages 156-173.)

Between 1950 and 1990, the S&P 500 gained 1.3% (Dow, 1.4%) on average in first months of the first three quarters. Second months barely eked out any gain, while third months, thanks to March, moved up 0.23% (Dow, 0.07%) on average. NASDAQ's first month of the first three quarters averages 1.67% from 1971-1990 with July being a negative drag.

## DOW JONES INDUSTRIALS, S&P 500 AND NASDAQ
## AVERAGE MONTHLY % CHANGES BY QUARTER

| | DJIA 1950–1990 | | | S&P 500 1950–1990 | | | NASDAQ 1971–1990 | | |
|---|---|---|---|---|---|---|---|---|---|
| | 1st Mo | 2nd Mo | 3rd Mo | 1st Mo | 2nd Mo | 3rd Mo | 1st Mo | 2nd Mo | 3rd Mo |
| 1Q | 1.5% | −0.01% | 1.0% | 1.5% | −0.1% | 1.1% | 3.8% | 1.2% | 0.9% |
| 2Q | 1.6 | −0.4 | 0.1 | 1.3 | −0.1 | 0.3 | 1.7 | 0.8 | 1.1 |
| 3Q | 1.1 | 0.3 | −0.9 | 1.1 | 0.3 | −0.7 | −0.5 | 0.1 | −1.6 |
| Tot | 4.2% | −0.1% | 0.2% | 3.9% | 0.1% | 0.7% | 5.0% | 2.1% | 0.4% |
| Avg | 1.40% | −0.04% | 0.07% | 1.30% | 0.03% | 0.23% | 1.67% | 0.70% | 0.13% |
| 4Q | −0.1% | 1.4% | 1.7% | 0.4% | 1.7% | 1.6% | −1.4% | 1.6% | 1.4% |
| | DJIA 1991–April 2022 | | | S&P 500 1991–April 2022 | | | NASDAQ 1991–April 2022 | | |
| 1Q | 0.1% | 0.3% | 0.8% | 0.3% | 0.01% | 1.0% | 1.7% | 0.1% | 0.6% |
| 2Q | 2.3 | 0.5 | −0.4 | 1.9 | 0.7 | −0.03 | 1.3 | 1.0 | 0.9 |
| 3Q | 1.5 | −0.5 | −0.5 | 1.2 | −0.2 | −0.4 | 1.4 | 0.7 | −0.1 |
| Tot | 3.9% | 0.3% | −0.1% | 3.4% | 0.5% | 0.6% | 4.4% | 1.8% | 1.4% |
| Avg | 1.30% | 0.09% | −0.03% | 1.13% | 0.17% | 0.19% | 1.47% | 0.59% | 0.47% |
| 4Q | 1.5% | 2.0% | 1.5% | 1.5% | 1.7% | 1.5% | 2.1% | 2.0% | 1.8% |
| | DJIA 1950–April 2022 | | | S&P 500 1950–April 2022 | | | NASDAQ 1971–April 2022 | | |
| 1Q | 0.9% | 0.1% | 0.9% | 1.0% | −0.04% | 1.1% | 2.5% | 0.5% | 0.7% |
| 2Q | 1.9 | −0.01 | −0.2 | 1.5 | 0.2 | 0.1 | 1.5 | 1.0 | 1.0 |
| 3Q | 1.3 | −0.0 | −0.7 | 1.1 | 0.07 | −0.5 | 0.6 | 0.5 | −0.7 |
| Tot | 4.1% | 0.1% | 0.1% | 3.6% | 0.2% | 0.7% | 4.6% | 2.0% | 1.0% |
| Avg | 1.37% | 0.02% | 0.02% | 1.20% | 0.08% | 0.25% | 1.54% | 0.65% | 0.33% |
| 4Q | 0.6% | 1.7% | 1.6% | 0.9% | 1.7% | 1.5% | 0.7% | 1.8% | 1.7% |

# JULY

**(Shortened Trading Day)**
*First Trading Day in July, S&P Up 29 of Last 33, Average Gain 0.5%*

 **MONDAY**

D 76.2
S 85.7
N 76.2

**3**

*Entrepreneurs who believe they're in business to vanquish the competition are less successful than those who believe their goal is to maximize profits or increase their company's value.*
— Kaihan Krippendorff (Business consultant, strategist, author, *The Art of the Advantage*, The Strategic Learning Center, b. 1971)

**Independence Day**
**(Market Closed)**

**TUESDAY**

**4**

*Politics ought to be the part-time profession of every citizen who would protect the rights and privileges of free people and who would preserve what is good and fruitful in our national heritage.*
— Dwight D. Eisenhower (34th U.S. President, 1890-1969)

*Market Subject to Elevated Volatility After July 4th*

**WEDNESDAY**

D 38.1
S 42.9
N 42.9

**5**

*Your chances for success in any undertaking can be measured by your belief in yourself.*
— Robert Collier (Direct marketing copywriter & author, 1885-1950)

*July Begins NASDAQ's "Worst Four Months" (Pages 60, 62 and 150)*

 **THURSDAY**

D 57.1
S 61.9
N 61.9

**6**

*Wall Street's graveyards are filled with men who were right too soon.*
— William Peter Hamilton (Editor, *Wall Street Journal, The Stock Market Barometer*, 1922, 1867-1929)

*July is the Best Performing Dow and S&P Month of the Third Quarter (Page 68)*

**FRIDAY**

D 57.1
S 57.1
N 61.9

**7**

*I'm not better than the next trader, just quicker at admitting my mistakes and moving on to the next opportunity.*
— George Soros (Financier, philanthropist, political activist, author and philosopher, b. 1930)

**SATURDAY**

**8**

**SUNDAY**

**9**

# 2021 DAILY DOW POINT CHANGES (DOW JONES INDUSTRIAL AVERAGE)

| Week # | | Monday** | Tuesday | Wednesday | Thursday | Friday** 2020 Close | Weekly Dow Close 30606.48 | Net Point Change |
|---|---|---|---|---|---|---|---|---|
| 1 | | | | | | | | |
| 2 | J | − 382.59 | 167.71 | 437.80 | 211.73 | 56.84 | 31097.97 | 491.49 |
| 3 | A | − 89.28 | 60.00 | − 8.22 | − 68.95 | − 177.26 | 30814.26 | − 283.71 |
| 4 | N | Holiday | 116.26 | 257.86 | − 12.37 | − 179.03 | 30996.98 | 182.72 |
| 5 | | − 36.98 | − 22.96 | − 633.87 | 300.19 | − 620.74 | 29982.62 | − 1014.36 |
| 6 | F | 229.29 | 475.57 | 36.12 | 332.26 | 92.38 | 31148.24 | 1165.62 |
| 7 | E | 237.52 | − 9.93 | 61.97 | − 7.10 | 27.70 | 31458.40 | 310.16 |
| 8 | B | Holiday | 64.35 | 90.27 | − 119.68 | 0.98 | 31494.32 | 35.92 |
| 9 | | 27.37 | 15.66 | 424.51 | − 559.85 | − 469.64 | 30932.37 | − 561.95 |
| 10 | M | 603.14 | − 143.99 | − 121.43 | − 345.95 | 572.16 | 31496.30 | 563.93 |
| 11 | A | 306.14 | 30.30 | 464.28 | 188.57 | 293.05 | 32778.64 | 1282.34 |
| 12 | R | 174.82 | − 127.51 | 189.42 | − 153.07 | − 234.33 | 32627.97 | − 150.67 |
| 13 | | 103.23 | − 308.05 | − 3.09 | 199.42 | 453.40 | 33072.88 | 444.91 |
| 14 | | 98.49 | − 104.41 | − 85.41 | 171.66 | Holiday | 33153.21 | 80.33 |
| 15 | A | 373.98 | − 96.95 | 16.02 | 57.31 | 297.03 | 33800.60 | 647.39 |
| 16 | P | − 55.20 | − 68.13 | 53.62 | 305.10 | 164.68 | 34200.67 | 400.07 |
| 17 | R | − 123.04 | − 256.33 | 316.01 | − 321.41 | 227.59 | 34043.49 | − 157.18 |
| 18 | | − 61.92 | 3.36 | − 164.55 | 239.98 | − 185.51 | 33874.85 | − 168.64 |
| 19 | M | 238.38 | 19.80 | 97.31 | 318.19 | 229.23 | 34777.76 | 902.91 |
| 20 | A | − 34.94 | − 473.66 | − 681.50 | 433.79 | 360.68 | 34382.13 | − 395.63 |
| 21 | Y | − 54.34 | − 267.13 | − 164.62 | 188.11 | 123.69 | 34207.84 | − 174.29 |
| 22 | | 186.14 | − 81.52 | 10.59 | 141.59 | 64.81 | 34529.45 | 321.61 |
| 23 | | Holiday | 45.86 | 25.07 | − 23.34 | 179.35 | 34756.39 | 226.94 |
| 24 | J | − 126.15 | − 30.42 | − 152.68 | 19.10 | 13.36 | 34479.60 | − 276.79 |
| 25 | U | − 85.85 | − 94.42 | − 265.66 | − 210.22 | − 533.37 | 33290.08 | − 1189.52 |
| 26 | N | 586.89 | 68.61 | − 71.34 | 322.58 | 237.02 | 34433.84 | 1143.76 |
| 27 | | − 150.57 | 9.02 | 210.22 | 131.02 | 152.82 | 34786.35 | 352.51 |
| 28 | J | Holiday | − 208.98 | 104.42 | − 259.86 | 448.23 | 34870.16 | 83.81 |
| 29 | U | 126.02 | − 107.39 | 44.44 | 53.79 | − 299.17 | 34687.85 | − 182.31 |
| 30 | L | − 725.81 | 549.95 | 286.01 | 25.35 | 238.20 | 35061.55 | 373.70 |
| 31 | | 82.76 | − 85.79 | − 127.59 | 153.60 | − 149.06 | 34935.47 | − 126.08 |
| 32 | | − 97.31 | 278.24 | − 323.73 | 271.58 | 144.26 | 35208.51 | 273.04 |
| 33 | A | − 106.66 | 162.82 | 220.30 | 14.88 | 15.53 | 35515.38 | 306.87 |
| 34 | U | 110.02 | − 282.12 | − 382.59 | − 66.57 | 225.96 | 35120.08 | − 395.30 |
| 35 | G | 215.63 | 30.55 | 39.24 | − 192.38 | 242.68 | 35455.80 | 335.72 |
| 36 | | − 55.96 | − 39.11 | − 48.20 | 131.29 | − 74.73 | 35369.09 | − 86.71 |
| 37 | S | Holiday | − 269.09 | − 68.93 | − 151.69 | − 271.66 | 34607.72 | − 761.37 |
| 38 | E | 261.91 | − 312.06 | 256.82 | − 63.07 | − 166.44 | 34584.88 | − 22.84 |
| 39 | P | − 614.41 | − 50.63 | 338.48 | 506.50 | 33.18 | 34798.00 | 213.12 |
| 40 | | 71.37 | − 569.38 | 90.73 | − 546.80 | 482.54 | 34326.46 | − 471.54 |
| 41 | O | − 323.54 | 311.75 | 102.32 | 337.95 | − 8.69 | 34746.25 | 419.79 |
| 42 | C | − 250.19 | − 117.72 | − 0.53 | 534.75 | 382.20 | 35294.76 | 548.51 |
| 43 | T | − 36.15 | 198.70 | 152.03 | − 6.26 | 73.94 | 35677.02 | 382.26 |
| 44 | | 64.13 | 15.73 | − 266.19 | 239.79 | 89.08 | 35819.56 | 142.54 |
| 45 | | 94.28 | 138.79 | 104.95 | − 33.35 | 203.72 | 36327.95 | 508.39 |
| 46 | N | 104.27 | − 112.24 | − 240.04 | − 158.71 | 179.08 | 36100.31 | − 227.64 |
| 47 | O | − 12.86 | 54.77 | − 211.17 | − 60.10 | − 268.97 | 35601.98 | − 498.33 |
| 48 | V | 17.27 | 194.55 | − 9.42 | Holiday | − 905.04* | 34899.34 | − 702.64 |
| 49 | | 236.60 | − 652.22 | − 461.68 | 617.75 | − 59.71 | 34580.08 | − 319.26 |
| 50 | | 646.95 | 492.40 | 35.32 | − 0.06 | 216.30 | 35970.99 | 1390.91 |
| 51 | D | − 320.04 | − 106.77 | 383.25 | − 29.79 | − 532.20 | 35365.44 | − 605.55 |
| 52 | E | − 433.28 | 560.54 | 261.19 | 196.67 | Holiday | 35950.56 | 585.12 |
| 53 | C | 351.82 | 95.83 | 90.42 | − 90.55 | − 59.78 | 36338.30 | 387.74 |
| TOTALS | | 1119.75 | − 586.19 | 708.55 | 2795.04 | 1694.67 | | 5731.82 |

Outline Bold Color: Down Friday, Down Monday          * Shortened trading day: Nov 26

** Monday denotes first trading day of week, Friday denotes last trading day of week.

# JULY

**MONDAY**
D 57.1
S 57.1
N 57.1
**10**

*Pullbacks near the 30-week moving average are often good times to take action.*
— Michael L. Burke (*Investors Intelligence*)

**TUESDAY**
D 57.1
S 57.1
N 71.4
**11**

*The only thing that saves us from the bureaucracy is its inefficiency.*
— Eugene McCarthy (U.S. Congressman and Senator Minnesota 1949-1971, 3-time presidential candidate, 1916-2005)

*Beware the "Summer Rally" Hype*
*Historically the Weakest Rally of All Seasons (Page 74)*

**WEDNESDAY**
D 52.4
S 57.1
N 61.9
**12**

*You are your own Promised Land, your own new frontier.*
— Julia Margaret Cameron (19th century English photographer)

**THURSDAY**
D 76.2
S 76.2
N 61.9
**13**

*Investors operate with limited funds and limited intelligence; they don't need to know everything.*
*As long as they understand something better than others, they have an edge.*
— George Soros (Financier, philanthropist, political activist, author and philosopher, b. 1930)

**FRIDAY**
D 76.2
S 71.4
N 71.4
**14**

*Letting your emotions override your plan or system is the biggest cause of failure.*
— J. Welles Wilder Jr. (Creator of several technical indicators including Relative Strength Index (RSI) 1935-2021)

**SATURDAY**
**15**

**SUNDAY**
**16**

# DON'T SELL STOCKS ON MONDAY OR FRIDAY

Since 1989, Monday*, Tuesday and Wednesday have been the most consistently bullish days of the week for the Dow, Thursday and Friday* the least bullish, as traders have become reluctant to stay long going into the weekend. Since 1989 Mondays and Tuesdays gained 18985.05 Dow points, while Thursdays and Fridays have gained 2232.86 points. Note Monday's and Friday's poor performance in bear market years 2001-2002 and 2008-2009. See pages 70, 78, and 143-146 for more.

## ANNUAL DOW POINT CHANGES FOR DAYS OF THE WEEK SINCE 1953

| Year | Monday* | Tuesday | Wednesday | Thursday | Friday* | Year's DJIA Closing | Year's Point Change |
|---|---|---|---|---|---|---|---|
| 1953 | −36.16 | −7.93 | 19.63 | 5.76 | 7.70 | 280.90 | −11.00 |
| 1954 | 15.68 | 3.27 | 24.31 | 33.96 | 46.27 | 404.39 | 123.49 |
| 1955 | −48.36 | 26.38 | 46.03 | −0.66 | 60.62 | 488.40 | 84.01 |
| 1956 | −27.15 | −9.36 | −15.41 | 8.43 | 64.56 | 499.47 | 11.07 |
| 1957 | −109.50 | −7.71 | 64.12 | 3.32 | −14.01 | 435.69 | −63.78 |
| 1958 | 17.50 | 23.59 | 29.10 | 22.67 | 55.10 | 583.65 | 147.96 |
| 1959 | −44.48 | 29.04 | 4.11 | 13.60 | 93.44 | 679.36 | 95.71 |
| 1960 | −111.04 | −3.75 | −5.62 | 6.74 | 50.20 | 615.89 | −63.47 |
| 1961 | −23.65 | 10.18 | 87.51 | −5.96 | 47.17 | 731.14 | 115.25 |
| 1962 | −101.60 | 26.19 | 9.97 | −7.70 | −5.90 | 652.10 | −79.04 |
| 1963 | −8.88 | 47.12 | 16.23 | 22.39 | 33.99 | 762.95 | 110.85 |
| 1964 | −0.29 | −17.94 | 39.84 | 5.52 | 84.05 | 874.13 | 111.18 |
| 1965 | −73.23 | 39.65 | 57.03 | 3.20 | 68.48 | 969.26 | 95.13 |
| 1966 | −153.24 | −27.73 | 56.13 | −46.19 | −12.54 | 785.69 | −183.57 |
| 1967 | −68.65 | 31.50 | 25.42 | 92.25 | 38.90 | 905.11 | 119.42 |
| 1968† | −6.41 | 34.94 | 25.16 | −72.06 | 44.19 | 943.75 | 38.64 |
| 1969 | −164.17 | −36.70 | 18.33 | 23.79 | 15.36 | 800.36 | −143.39 |
| 1970 | −100.05 | −46.09 | 116.07 | −3.48 | 72.11 | 838.92 | 38.56 |
| 1971 | −2.99 | 9.56 | 13.66 | 8.04 | 23.01 | 890.20 | 51.28 |
| 1972 | −87.40 | −1.23 | 65.24 | 8.46 | 144.75 | 1020.02 | 129.82 |
| 1973 | −174.11 | 10.52 | −5.94 | 36.67 | −36.30 | 850.86 | −169.16 |
| 1974 | −149.37 | 47.51 | −20.31 | −13.70 | −98.75 | 616.24 | −234.62 |
| 1975 | 39.46 | −109.62 | 56.93 | 124.00 | 125.40 | 852.41 | 236.17 |
| 1976 | 70.72 | 71.76 | 50.88 | −33.70 | −7.42 | 1004.65 | 152.24 |
| 1977 | −65.15 | −44.89 | −79.61 | −5.62 | 21.79 | 831.17 | −173.48 |
| 1978 | −31.29 | −70.84 | 71.33 | −64.67 | 69.31 | 805.01 | −26.16 |
| 1979 | −32.52 | 9.52 | −18.84 | 75.18 | 0.39 | 838.74 | 33.73 |
| 1980 | −86.51 | 135.13 | 137.67 | −122.00 | 60.96 | 963.99 | 125.25 |
| 1981 | −45.68 | −49.51 | −13.95 | −14.67 | 34.82 | 875.00 | −88.99 |
| 1982 | 5.71 | 86.20 | 28.37 | −1.47 | 52.73 | 1046.54 | 171.54 |
| 1983 | 30.51 | −30.92 | 149.68 | 61.16 | 1.67 | 1258.64 | 212.10 |
| 1984 | −73.80 | 78.02 | −139.24 | 92.79 | −4.84 | 1211.57 | −47.07 |
| 1985 | 80.36 | 52.70 | 51.26 | 46.32 | 104.46 | 1546.67 | 335.10 |
| 1986 | −39.94 | 97.63 | 178.65 | 29.31 | 83.63 | 1895.95 | 349.28 |
| 1987 | −559.15 | 235.83 | 392.03 | 139.73 | −165.56 | 1938.83 | 42.88 |
| 1988 | 268.12 | 166.44 | −60.48 | −230.84 | 86.50 | 2168.57 | 229.74 |
| 1989 | −53.31 | 143.33 | 233.25 | 90.25 | 171.11 | 2753.20 | 584.63 |
| **SubTotal** | **−1937.20** | **941.79** | **1708.54** | **330.82** | **1417.35** | | **2461.30** |
| 1990 | 219.90 | −25.22 | 47.96 | −352.55 | −9.63 | 2633.66 | −119.54 |
| 1991 | 191.13 | 47.97 | 174.53 | 254.79 | −133.25 | 3168.83 | 535.17 |
| 1992 | 237.80 | −49.67 | 3.12 | 108.74 | −167.71 | 3301.11 | 132.28 |
| 1993 | 322.82 | −37.03 | 243.87 | 4.97 | −81.65 | 3754.09 | 452.98 |
| 1994 | 206.41 | −95.33 | 29.98 | −168.87 | 108.16 | 3834.44 | 80.35 |
| 1995 | 262.97 | 210.06 | 357.02 | 140.07 | 312.56 | 5117.12 | 1282.68 |
| 1996 | 626.41 | 155.55 | −34.24 | 268.52 | 314.91 | 6448.27 | 1331.15 |
| 1997 | 1136.04 | 1989.17 | −590.17 | −949.80 | −125.26 | 7908.25 | 1459.98 |
| 1998 | 649.10 | 679.95 | 591.63 | −1579.43 | 931.93 | 9181.43 | 1273.18 |
| 1999 | 980.49 | −1587.23 | 826.68 | 735.94 | 1359.81 | 11497.12 | 2315.69 |
| 2000 | 2265.45 | 306.47 | −1978.34 | 238.21 | −1542.06 | 10786.85 | −710.27 |
| **SubTotal** | **7098.52** | **1594.69** | **−327.96** | **−1299.41** | **967.81** | | **8033.65** |
| 2001 | −389.33 | 336.86 | −396.53 | 976.41 | −1292.76 | 10021.50 | −765.35 |
| 2002 | −1404.94 | −823.76 | 1443.69 | −428.12 | −466.74 | 8341.63 | −1679.87 |
| 2003 | 978.87 | 482.11 | −425.46 | 566.22 | 510.55 | 10453.92 | 2112.29 |
| 2004 | 201.12 | 523.28 | 358.76 | −409.72 | −344.35 | 10783.01 | 329.09 |
| 2005 | 316.23 | −305.62 | 27.67 | −128.75 | 24.96 | 10717.50 | −65.51 |
| 2006 | 95.74 | 573.98 | 1283.87 | 193.34 | −401.28 | 12463.15 | 1745.65 |
| 2007 | 278.23 | −157.93 | 1316.74 | −766.63 | 131.26 | 13264.82 | 801.67 |
| 2008 | −1387.20 | 1704.51 | −3073.72 | −940.88 | −791.14 | 8776.39 | −4488.43 |
| 2009 | −45.22 | 161.76 | 617.56 | 932.68 | −15.12 | 10428.05 | 1651.66 |
| 2010 | 1236.88 | −421.80 | 1019.66 | −76.73 | −608.55 | 11577.51 | 1149.46 |
| 2011 | −571.02 | 1423.66 | −776.05 | 246.27 | 317.19 | 12217.56 | 640.05 |
| 2012 | 254.59 | −49.28 | −456.37 | 847.34 | 299.30 | 13104.14 | 886.58 |
| 2013 | −79.63 | 1091.75 | 170.93 | 653.64 | 1635.83 | 16576.66 | 3472.52 |
| 2014 | −171.63 | 817.56 | 265.07 | −337.48 | 672.89 | 17823.07 | 1246.41 |
| 2015 | 308.28 | −879.14 | 926.70 | 982.16 | −1736.04 | 17425.03 | −398.04 |
| 2016 | 602.00 | 594.09 | 636.92 | 678.40 | −173.84 | 19762.60 | 2337.57 |
| 2017 | 1341.29 | 1184.32 | 882.40 | 445.43 | 1103.18 | 24719.22 | 4956.62 |
| 2018 | −1694.23 | 252.29 | 754.24 | −47.39 | −656.67 | 23327.46 | −1391.76 |
| 2019 | −1723.31 | 1364.93 | 656.12 | 1156.52 | 3756.72 | 28538.44 | 5210.98 |
| 2020 | 1126.98 | 3852.74 | 1067.54 | −4418.94 | 439.72 | 30606.48 | 2068.04 |
| 2021 | 1119.75 | −586.19 | 708.55 | 2795.04 | 1694.67 | 36338.30 | 5731.82 |
| 2022‡ | −2357.02 | 1115.29 | 1557.22 | −3068.36 | −1385.77 | | |
| **Subtotal** | **−1963.57** | **12255.41** | **8565.51** | **−149.55** | **2714.01** | | **25551.45** |
| **Totals** | **3197.75** | **14791.89** | **9946.09** | **−1118.14** | **5099.17** | | **36046.40** |

\* Monday denotes first trading day of week, Friday denotes last trading day of week.
†Most Wednesdays closed last 7 months of 1968. ‡Partial year through May 13, 2022.

# JULY

Monday Before July Expiration, Dow Up 15 of Last 19

🐻 **MONDAY**

D 57.1
S 33.3
N 47.6

**17**

*He who wants to persuade should put his trust not in the right argument, but in the right word.*
*The power of sound has always been greater than the power of sense.*
— Joseph Conrad (Polish/British novelist, 1857-1924)

**TUESDAY**

D 47.6
S 47.6
N 52.4

**18**

*If banking institutions are protected by the taxpayer and they are given free reign to speculate,*
*I may not live long enough to see the crisis, but my soul is going to come back and haunt you.*
— Paul A. Volcker (Fed Chairman 1979-1987, Chair Economic Recovery Advisory Board, 2/2/2010, b. 1927)

**WEDNESDAY**

D 57.1
S 57.1
N 61.9

**19**

*In the business world, everyone is paid in two coins: cash and experience. Take the experience first; the cash will come later.*
— Harold S. Geneen (British-American businessman, CEO ITT Corp, 1910-1977)

🐃 **THURSDAY**

D 76.2
S 76.2
N 76.2

**20**

*Washington is run by people who think there is a 1% difference between 2% growth and 3% growth.*
— George Will (American political commentator & journalist, b. 1941)

July Expiration Day, Dow Down 15 of Last 22, -4.6% 2002, -2.5% 2010

🐻 🐃 **FRIDAY**

D 19.0
S 23.8
N 14.3

**21**

*We will have to pay more and more attention to what the funds are doing.*
*They are the ones who have been contributing to the activity, especially in the high-fliers.*
— Humphrey B. Neill (Investor, analyst, author, *NY Times* 6/11/1966, 1895-1977)

**SATURDAY**

**22**

**SUNDAY**

**23**

# A RALLY FOR ALL SEASONS

Most years, especially when the market sells off during the first half, prospects for the perennial summer rally become the buzz on the street. Parameters for this "rally" were defined by the late Ralph Rotnem as the lowest close in the Dow Jones Industrials in May or June to the highest close in July, August, or September. Such a big deal is made of the "summer rally" that one might get the impression the market puts on its best performance in the summertime. Nothing could be further from the truth! Not only does the market "rally" in every season of the year, but it does so with more gusto in the winter, spring, and fall than in the summer.

Winters in 59 years averaged a 13.0% gain as measured from the low in November or December to the first quarter closing high. Spring rose 11.8% followed by fall with 11.0%. Last and least was the average 9.4% "summer rally." Even 2020's impressive 25.2% "summer rally" was outmatched by spring. Nevertheless, no matter how thick the gloom or grim the outlook, don't despair! There's always a rally for all seasons, statistically.

## SEASONAL GAINS IN DOW JONES INDUSTRIALS

| | WINTER RALLY Nov/Dec Low to Q1 High | SPRING RALLY Feb/Mar Low to Q2 High | SUMMER RALLY May/Jun Low to Q3 High | FALL RALLY Aug/Sep Low to Q4 High |
|---|---|---|---|---|
| 1964 | 15.3% | 6.2% | 9.4% | 8.3% |
| 1965 | 5.7 | 6.6 | 11.6 | 10.3 |
| 1966 | 5.9 | 4.8 | 3.5 | 7.0 |
| 1967 | 11.6 | 8.7 | 11.2 | 4.4 |
| 1968 | 7.0 | 11.5 | 5.2 | 13.3 |
| 1969 | 0.9 | 7.7 | 1.9 | 6.7 |
| 1970 | 5.4 | 6.2 | 22.5 | 19.0 |
| 1971 | 21.6 | 9.4 | 5.5 | 7.4 |
| 1972 | 19.1 | 7.7 | 5.2 | 11.4 |
| 1973 | 8.6 | 4.8 | 9.7 | 15.9 |
| 1974 | 13.1 | 8.2 | 1.4 | 11.0 |
| 1975 | 36.2 | 24.2 | 8.2 | 8.7 |
| 1976 | 23.3 | 6.4 | 5.9 | 4.6 |
| 1977 | 8.2 | 3.1 | 2.8 | 2.1 |
| 1978 | 2.1 | 16.8 | 11.8 | 5.2 |
| 1979 | 11.0 | 8.9 | 8.9 | 6.1 |
| 1980 | 13.5 | 16.8 | 21.0 | 8.5 |
| 1981 | 11.8 | 9.9 | 0.4 | 8.3 |
| 1982 | 4.6 | 9.3 | 18.5 | 37.8 |
| 1983 | 15.7 | 17.8 | 6.3 | 10.7 |
| 1984 | 5.9 | 4.6 | 14.1 | 9.7 |
| 1985 | 11.7 | 7.1 | 9.5 | 19.7 |
| 1986 | 31.1 | 18.8 | 9.2 | 11.4 |
| 1987 | 30.6 | 13.6 | 22.9 | 5.9 |
| 1988 | 18.1 | 13.5 | 11.2 | 9.8 |
| 1989 | 15.1 | 12.9 | 16.1 | 5.7 |
| 1990 | 8.8 | 14.5 | 12.4 | 8.6 |
| 1991 | 21.8 | 11.2 | 6.6 | 9.3 |
| 1992 | 14.9 | 6.4 | 3.7 | 3.3 |
| 1993 | 8.9 | 7.7 | 6.3 | 7.3 |
| 1994 | 9.7 | 5.2 | 9.1 | 5.0 |
| 1995 | 13.6 | 19.3 | 11.3 | 13.9 |
| 1996 | 19.2 | 7.5 | 8.7 | 17.3 |
| 1997 | 17.7 | 18.4 | 18.4 | 7.3 |
| 1998 | 20.3 | 13.6 | 8.2 | 24.3 |
| 1999 | 15.1 | 21.6 | 8.2 | 12.6 |
| 2000 | 10.8 | 15.2 | 9.8 | 3.5 |
| 2001 | 6.4 | 20.8 | 1.7 | 23.1 |
| 2002 | 14.8 | 7.9 | 2.8 | 17.6 |
| 2003 | 6.5 | 23.9 | 14.3 | 15.7 |
| 2004 | 11.6 | 5.2 | 4.4 | 10.6 |
| 2005 | 9.0 | 2.1 | 5.6 | 5.3 |
| 2006 | 8.8 | 8.3 | 9.5 | 13.0 |
| 2007 | 6.7 | 13.5 | 6.6 | 10.3 |
| 2008 | 2.5 | 11.2 | 3.8 | 4.5 |
| 2009 | 19.6 | 34.4 | 19.7 | 15.5 |
| 2010 | 11.6 | 13.1 | 11.1 | 16.0 |
| 2011 | 12.6 | 10.3 | 7.0 | 14.7 |
| 2012 | 18.0 | 4.5 | 12.4 | 5.7 |
| 2013 | 16.2 | 11.8 | 6.9 | 12.2 |
| 2014 | 6.0 | 10.2 | 5.5 | 10.3 |
| 2015 | 7.1 | 5.5 | 3.0 | 14.4 |
| 2016 | 3.4 | 15.6 | 8.7 | 10.8 |
| 2017 | 18.0 | 8.3 | 8.8 | 14.6 |
| 2018 | 14.4 | 7.6 | 11.8 | 6.6 |
| 2019 | 19.7 | 6.8 | 10.3 | 12.4 |
| 2020 | 8.1 | 48.3 | 25.2 | 14.8 |
| 2021 | 23.2 | 15.1 | 7.0 | 7.8 |
| 2022 | 8.2 | 7.7* | | |
| **Totals** | **766.3%** | **698.2%** | **542.7%** | **637.2%** |
| **Average** | **13.0%** | **11.8%** | **9.4%** | **11.0%** |

* As of 5/20/2022.

# JULY

**MONDAY**

D 38.1
S 52.4
N 47.6 **24**

*ll there is to investing is picking good stocks at good times and staying with them as long as they remain good companies.*
— Warren Buffett (CEO Berkshire Hathaway, investor & philanthropist, b. 1930)

**TUESDAY**

D 61.9
S 57.1
N 57.1 **25**

*elf-discipline is a form of freedom. Freedom from laziness and lethargy, freedom from expectations*
*d demands of others, freedom from weakness and fear—and doubt.*
— Harvey A. Dorfman (Sports psychologist, *The Mental ABC's of Pitching*, b. 1935)

*OMC Meeting (2 Days)*

**WEDNESDAY**

D 52.4
S 52.4
N 57.1 **26**

*o other wisdom is better than the financial markets themselves.*
*ey incorporate the total wisdom of everyone that has money that is willing to vote their wisdom every second of every day.*
— Don R. Hays (Hays Advisory, 3/14/07)

*'eek After July Expiration Prone to Wild Swings, Dow Up 14 of Last 24*
*998 -4.3%, 2002 +3.1%, 2006 +3.2%, 2007 -4.2%, 2009 +4.0%, 2010 +3.2*

**THURSDAY**

D 42.9
S 38.1
N 42.9 **27**

*plosive growth of shadow banking was about the invisible hand having a party,*
*on-regulated drinking party, with rating agencies handing out fake IDs.*
Paul McCulley (Economist, bond investor, PIMCO, coined "shadow banking" in 2007, *NY Times* 4/26/2010, b. 1957)

**FRIDAY**

D 38.1
S 57.1
N 66.7 **28**

*nnot people realize how large an income is thrift?*
Marcus Tullius Cicero (Great Roman Orator, Politician, 106-43 B.C.)

**SATURDAY**

**29**

*gust Almanac Investor Sector Seasonalities: See Pages 94, 96 and 98*

**SUNDAY**

**30**

# AUGUST ALMANAC

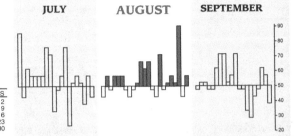

| AUGUST | | | | | | | | SEPTEMBER | | | | | | |
|---|---|---|---|---|---|---|---|---|---|---|---|---|---|---|
| S | M | T | W | T | F | S | | S | M | T | W | T | F | S |
| | | 1 | 2 | 3 | 4 | 5 | | | | | | | 1 | 2 |
| 6 | 7 | 8 | 9 | 10 | 11 | 12 | | 3 | 4 | 5 | 6 | 7 | 8 | 9 |
| 13 | 14 | 15 | 16 | 17 | 18 | 19 | | 10 | 11 | 12 | 13 | 14 | 15 | 16 |
| 20 | 21 | 22 | 23 | 24 | 25 | 26 | | 17 | 18 | 19 | 20 | 21 | 22 | 23 |
| 27 | 28 | 29 | 30 | 31 | | | | 24 | 25 | 26 | 27 | 28 | 29 | 30 |

*Market Probability Chart above is a graphic representation of the S&P 500 Recent Market Probability Calendar on page 126.*

◆Harvesting made August the best stock market month 1901-1951 ◆ Now that about 2% farm, August is the worst Dow and second worst S&P (2000 up 11.7%, 2001 down 10.9%) month since 1987 ◆ Second shortest bear in history (45 days) caused by turmoil in Russia, currency crisis and hedge fund debacle ended here in 1998, 1344.22-point drop in the Dow, ninth worst point loss, off 15.1% ◆ Saddam Hussein triggered a 10.0% slide in 1990 ◆ Best Dow gains: 1982 (11.5%) and 1984 (9.8%) as bear markets ended ◆ Next to last day S&P up only nine times last 26 years ◆ Pre-election year Augusts' rankings #9 S&P, #8 Dow, and #10 NASDAQ.

## August Vital Statistics

| | DJIA | S&P 500 | NASDAQ | Russell 1K | Russell 2K |
|---|---|---|---|---|---|
| Rank | 10 | 10 | 11 | 10 | 9 |
| Up | 41 | 40 | 29 | 27 | 25 |
| Down | 31 | 32 | 22 | 16 | 18 |
| Avg % Change | −0.04% | 0.10% | 0.5% | 0.4% | 0.3% |
| Pre-Election Year | 0.8% | 0.4% | 0.5% | 0.05% | −0.5% |
| **Best and Worst** | | | | | |
| | % Change | % Change | % Change | % Change | % Change |
| Best | 1982  11.5 | 1982  11.6 | 2000  11.7 | 1982  11.3 | 1984  11.5 |
| Worst | 1998 −15.1 | 1998 −14.6 | 1998 −19.9 | 1998 −15.1 | 1998 −19.5 |
| **Best and Worst Weeks** | | | | | |
| Best | 8/20/82  10.3 | 8/20/82  8.8 | 8/3/84  7.4 | 8/20/82  8.5 | 8/3/84  7.0 |
| Worst | 8/23/74  −6.1 | 8/5/11  −7.2 | 8/28/98  −8.8 | 8/5/11  −7.7 | 8/5/11  −10.3 |
| **Best and Worst Days** | | | | | |
| Best | 8/17/82  4.9 | 8/17/82  4.8 | 8/9/11  5.3 | 8/9/11  5.0 | 8/9/11  6.9 |
| Worst | 8/31/98  −6.4 | 8/31/98  −6.8 | 8/31/98  −8.6 | 8/8/11  −6.9 | 8/8/11  −8.9 |
| **First Trading Day of Expiration Week: 1980–2022** | | | | | |
| Record (#Up–#Down) | 26-16 | 30-12 | 30-12 | 30-12 | 26-16 |
| Current Streak | U1 | U2 | D1 | U2 | D1 |
| Avg % Change | 0.21 | 0.25 | 0.31 | 0.23 | 0.24 |
| **Options Expiration Day: 1980–2022** | | | | | |
| Record (#Up–#Down) | 22-20 | 23-19 | 24-18 | 24-18 | 24-18 |
| Current Streak | U4 | U4 | U4 | U4 | U1 |
| Avg % Change | −0.07 | −0.01 | −0.06 | −0.01 | 0.14 |
| **Options Expiration Week: 1980–2022** | | | | | |
| Record (#Up–#Down) | 19-23 | 23-19 | 22-20 | 23-19 | 24-18 |
| Current Streak | D3 | D1 | D1 | D1 | D3 |
| Avg % Change | −0.03 | 0.16 | 0.33 | 0.17 | 0.26 |
| **Week After Options Expiration: 1980–2022** | | | | | |
| Record (#Up–#Down) | 26-16 | 28-14 | 27-15 | 28-14 | 28-14 |
| Current Streak | U2 | U2 | U2 | U2 | U2 |
| Avg % Change | 0.34 | 0.40 | 0.63 | 0.41 | 0.28 |
| **First Trading Day Performance** | | | | | |
| % of Time Up | 45.8 | 48.6 | 54.9 | 44.2 | 46.5 |
| Avg % Change | 0.01 | 0.04 | −0.02 | 0.08 | −0.01 |
| **Last Trading Day Performance** | | | | | |
| % of Time Up | 58.3 | 62.5 | 64.7 | 58.1 | 67.4 |
| Avg % Change | 0.10 | 0.11 | 0.06 | −0.04 | 0.05 |

*Dow & S&P 1950-May 13, 2022, NASDAQ 1971-May 13, 2022, Russell 1K & 2K 1979-May 13, 2022.*

*August's a good month to go on vacation;*
*Trading stocks will likely lead to frustration.*

# JULY/AUGUST

*Trading Day in July, NASDAQ and S&P Down 12 of Last 17,*
*Down 13 of Last 17*

**MONDAY**

D 38.1
S 42.9
N 38.1

**31**

*...are many people who think they want to be matadors [or money managers or traders] only to find themselves in the ring with two ...nd pounds of bull bearing down on them, and then discover that what they really wanted was to wear tight pants and hear the crowd roar.*
...rry Pearce (Founder and President of Leadership Communication, b. 1941)

*Trading Day in August, Dow Down 17 of Last 25*

**TUESDAY**

D 33.3
S 42.9
N 57.1

**1**

*...ry big on having clarified principles. I don't believe in being reactive. You can't do that in the markets effectively.*
*. I need perspective. I need a game plan.*
...y Dalio (Money manager, founder Bridgewater Associates, *Fortune* 3/16/2009, b. 1949)

**WEDNESDAY**

D 52.4
S 57.1
N 47.6

**2**

*...nin Graham was correct in suggesting that while the stock market in the short run may be a voting mechanism,*
*...long run it is a weighing mechanism. True value will win out in the end.*
...ton G. Malkiel (Economist, April 2003 Princeton Paper, *A Random Walk Down Wall Street*, b. 1932)

*Nine Trading Days of August Are Historically Weak (Pages 76 and 126)*

**THURSDAY**

D 52.4
S 47.6
N 52.4

**3**

*...could kick the person in the pants responsible for most of your trouble, you wouldn't sit for a month.*
...:odore Roosevelt (26th U.S. President, 1858-1919)

**FRIDAY**

D 52.4
S 57.1
N 52.4

**4**

*...nics is a very difficult subject. I've compared it to trying to learn how to repair a car when the engine is running.*
... Bernanke (Fed Chairman 2006-2014, June 2004 *Region* interview as Fed Govenor, b. 1953)

**SATURDAY**

**5**

**SUNDAY**

**6**

# TAKE ADVANTAGE OF
# DOWN FRIDAY/DOWN MONDAY WARNING

Fridays and Mondays* are the most important days of the week. Friday* is the day for squaring positions—trimming longs or covering shorts before taking off for the weekend. Traders want to limit their exposure (particularly to stocks that are not acting well) since there could be unfavorable developments before trading resumes two or more days later.

Monday* is important because the market then has the chance to reflect any weekend news, plus what traders think after digesting the previous week's action and the many Monday morning research and strategy comments.

For over 30 years a down Friday* followed by down Monday* has frequently corresponded with important market inflection points that exhibit a clearly negative bias, often coinciding with market tops and on a few climactic occasions, such as in October 2002, March 2009 and in March 2020 near major market bottoms.

One simple way to get a quick reading on which way the market may be heading is to keep track of the performance of the Dow Jones Industrial Average on Fridays* and the following Mondays*. Since 1995 there have been 274 occurrences of Down Friday/Down Monday* (DF/DM) with 77 falling in the bear market years of 2001, 2002, 2008, 2011, 2015 and 2020 producing an average decline of 13.3%.

To illustrate how Down Friday/Down Monday* can telegraph market infection points we created the chart below of the Dow Jones Industrials from November 2020 to May 20, 2022 with arrows pointing to occurrences of DF/DM. Use DF/DM as a warning to examine market conditions carefully.

## DOWN FRIDAY/DOWN MONDAYS

| Year | Total Number Down Friday/ Down Monday | Subsequent Average % Dow Loss* | Average Number of Days it took |
|---|---|---|---|
| 1995 | 8 | −1.2% | 18 |
| 1996 | 9 | −3.0% | 28 |
| 1997 | 6 | −5.1% | 45 |
| 1998 | 9 | −6.4% | 47 |
| 1999 | 9 | −6.4% | 39 |
| 2000 | 11 | −6.6% | 32 |
| 2001 | 13 | −13.5% | 53 |
| 2002 | 18 | −11.9% | 54 |
| 2003 | 9 | −3.0% | 17 |
| 2004 | 9 | −3.7% | 51 |
| 2005 | 10 | −3.0% | 37 |
| 2006 | 11 | −2.0% | 14 |
| 2007 | 8 | −6.0% | 33 |
| 2008 | 15 | −17.0% | 53 |
| 2009 | 10 | −8.7% | 15 |
| 2010 | 7 | −3.1% | 10 |
| 2011 | 11 | −9.0% | 53 |
| 2012 | 11 | −4.0% | 38 |
| 2013 | 7 | −2.4% | 15 |
| 2014 | 7 | −2.5% | 8 |
| 2015 | 12 | −9.2% | 44 |
| 2016 | 10 | −2.7% | 25 |
| 2017 | 11 | −1.2% | 18 |
| 2018 | 14 | −5.8% | 45 |
| 2019 | 7 | −4.3% | 32 |
| 2020 | 8 | −19.0% | 27 |
| 2021 | 7 | −4.4% | 38 |
| 2022** | 7 | −8.0% | 55 |
| **Average** | **10** | **−6.2%** | **34** |

*Over next 3 months; **Ending May 20, 2022.

## DOW JONES INDUSTRIALS (November 2020 to May 20, 2022)

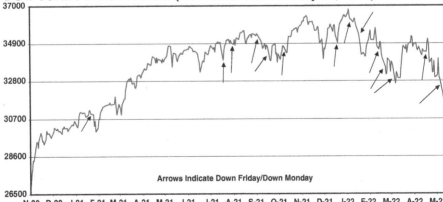

Arrows Indicate Down Friday/Down Monday

N-20  D-20  J-21  F-21  M-21  A-21  M-21  J-21  J-21  A-21  S-21  O-21  N-21  D-21  J-22  F-22  M-22  A-22  M-22

*Monday denotes first trading day of week, Friday denotes last trading day of week.*

# AUGUST

**MONDAY**

D 57.1
S 57.1
N 38.1

**7**

---

*...be a bum on the street with a tin cup, if the markets were always efficient.*
Warren Buffett (CEO Berkshire Hathaway, investor & philanthropist, b. 1930)

**TUESDAY**

D 52.4
S 57.1
N 47.6

**8**

---

*...earned that courage was not the absence of fear, but the triumph over it.*
*...e brave man is not he who does not feel afraid, but he who conquers that fear.*
Nelson Mandela (1st President of South Africa, 1918-2013)

*...ugust Worst Dow and S&P Month 1988-2022*
*...arvesting Made August Best Dow Month 1901-1951*

**WEDNESDAY**

D 47.6
S 47.6
N 42.9

**9**

---

*...mplexity is the enemy of execution.*
Tony Robbins (American author, coach, speaker, and philanthropist, b. 1960)

**THURSDAY**

D 33.3
S 42.9
N 38.1

**10**

---

*...ere are two kinds of people who lose money: those who know nothing and those who know everything.*
Henry Kaufman (German-American economist, b. 1927, to Robert Lenzner in *Forbes* 10/19/98 who added,
*...ith two Nobel Prize winners in the house, Long-Term Capital clearly fits the second case.*")

**FRIDAY**

D 47.6
S 47.6
N 57.1

**11**

---

*...nvesting is entertaining, if you're having fun, you're probably not making any money. Good investing is boring.*
George Soros (Financier, philanthropist, political activist, author and philosopher, b. 1930)

**SATURDAY**

**12**

---

**SUNDAY**

**13**

# BOB FARRELL'S MARKET RULES TO REMEMBER & JUSTIN MAMIS' SENTIMENT CYCLE

Lessons learned from these two legends of Wall Street have been paramount and more relevant than ever with market volatility on the rise in 2022 and the return of the bear. Justin Mamis passed away in 2019, but his books and wisdom are still relied upon regularly to this day. 90-year-old Bob Farrell has retired to Florida, but he still imparts his forecasts and outlook to investors and traders from time to time.

Justin Mamis was a renowned market analyst and technician who authored three of the most highly regarded books on the stock market: *When to Sell* (1977), *How to Buy* (1982), and *The Nature of Risk* (1991). Just before we presented at the CMT Association's 2022 Annual Symposium veteran technical analyst Helene Meisler shared Mamis' Sentiment Cycle (pictured below) along with her analysis of where in the cycle the market was at the time at the end of April 2022—in that brief pause between disbelief and panic (green circle). At this writing in mid-June, we are likely nearing that panic point in our view.

Back in the day when Jeff started working for Yale full-time in 1990 Bob Farrell was chief stock market analyst at Merrill Lynch. Farrell's weekly market comments were required reading. It was in one of these reports circa 1998 when he was a senior investment adviser at Merrill that he first revealed his 10 Market Rules to Remember. In an

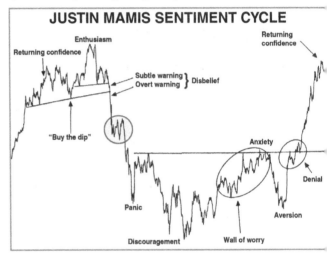

April 27 interview with David Rosenberg, a veteran market strategist who was chief economist at Merrill from 2002-2009, Mr. Farrell relayed his current bearish analysis with respect to his original 10 rules.

### Bob Farrell's 10 Market Rules to Remember

1. Markets tend to return to the mean over time.
2. Excesses in one direction will lead to an opposite excess in the other direction.
3. There are no new eras—excesses are never permanent.
4. Exponential rapidly rising or falling markets usually go further than you think but they do not correct by going sideways.
5. The public buys the most at the top and the least at the bottom.
6. Fear and greed are stronger than long-term resolve.
7. Markets are strongest when they are broad and weakest when they narrow to a handful of blue-chip names.
8. Bear markets have three stages—sharp down, reflexive rebound and a drawn-out fundamental downtrend.
9. When all the experts and forecasts agree—something else is going to happen.
10. Bull markets are more fun than bear markets.

# AUGUST

Monday Before August Expiration, Dow Up 17 of Last 27, Average Gain 0.2%    **MONDAY**

D 61.9
S 52.4
N 57.1

# 14

*your highest moment be careful, that's when the devil comes for you.*
Denzel Washington (American actor, director, and producer, b. 1954)

**TUESDAY**

D 57.1
S 66.7
N 57.1

# 15

*man should always hold something in reserve, a surprise to spring when things get tight.*
Christy Mathewson (MLB Hall of Fame Pitcher, one of the first 5 members, 3rd most wins, 1880-1925)

*d-August Stronger Than Beginning and End*    **WEDNESDAY**

D 52.4
S 61.9
N 61.9

# 16

*me and Money are two sides of a single coin. No person gives you his money until he has first given you his time.*
*in the time of the people, their money will follow.*
Roy H. Williams (*The Wizard of Ads*)

**THURSDAY**

D 66.7
S 66.7
N 61.9

# 17

*nong the simplest truths is that market risk tends to be unusually rewarding*
*en market valuations are low and interest rates are falling.*
John P. Hussman, Ph.D. (Hussman Funds, 5/22/06)

*gust Expiration Day Less Bullish Lately, Dow Down 7 of Last 12*    **FRIDAY**
*wn 531 Points (3.1%) in 2015*

D 47.6
S 47.6
N 47.6

# 18

*all want progress, but if you're on the wrong road, progress means doing an about-turn*
*l walking back to the right road; in that case, the man who turns back soonest is the most progressive.*
C. S. Lewis (Irish novelist, poet, academic, 1898-1963)

**SATURDAY**

# 19

**SUNDAY**

# 20

# FOURTH QUARTER MARKET MAGIC

Examining market performance on a quarterly basis reveals several intriguing and helpful patterns. Fourth quarter market gains have been magical, providing the greatest and most consistent gains over the years. First quarter performance runs a respectable second. This should not be surprising as cash inflows, trading volume and buying bias are generally elevated during these two quarters.

Positive market psychology hits a fever pitch as the holiday season approaches and does not begin to wane until spring. Professionals drive the market higher as they make portfolio adjustments to maximize yearend numbers. Bonuses are paid and invested around the turn of the year.

The market's sweet spot of the Four-Year Cycle begins in the fourth quarter of the midterm year (page 34). The best two-quarter span runs from the fourth quarter of the midterm year through the first quarter of the pre-election year, averaging 13.7% for the Dow, 14.4% for the S&P 500 and an amazing 19.9% for NASDAQ. Pre-election Q2 is smoking too, the third best quarter of the cycle, creating a three-quarter sweet spot from midterm Q4 to pre-election Q2 (page 34).

Quarterly strength fades in the latter half of the pre-election year, but stays impressively positive through the election year. Losses dominate the first quarter of post-election years and the second and third quarters of midterm years.

## QUARTERLY % CHANGES

| | Q1 | Q2 | Q3 | Q4 | Year | Q2–Q3 | Q4–Q1 |
|---|---|---|---|---|---|---|---|
| **Dow Jones Industrials (1949 to March 2022)** | | | | | | | |
| Average | 2.0% | 1.8% | 0.7% | 4.0% | 8.7% | 2.5% | 6.2% |
| *Post-Election* | 0.3% | 1.9% | 0.4% | 4.3% | 7.4% | 2.3% | 5.4% |
| *Midterm* | 0.9% | −1.4% | 0.1% | 6.1% | 6.0% | −1.2% | 13.7% |
| *Pre-Election* | 7.3% | 4.8% | 1.0% | 2.7% | 16.2% | 5.8% | 2.3% |
| *Election* | −0.5% | 1.9% | 1.1% | 2.8% | 5.4% | 3.2% | 3.3% |
| | | | | | | | |
| **S&P 500 (1949 to March 2022)** | | | | | | | |
| Average | 2.0% | 2.0% | 0.9% | 4.2% | 9.5% | 3.0% | 6.4% |
| *Post-Election* | 0.1% | 2.5% | 0.8% | 4.0% | 8.0% | 3.5% | 4.8% |
| *Midterm* | 0.6% | −2.1% | 0.5% | 6.6% | 6.0% | −1.5% | 14.4% |
| *Pre-Election* | 7.4% | 4.9% | 0.6% | 3.5% | 16.8% | 5.5% | 3.7% |
| *Election* | 0.2% | 2.8% | 1.5% | 2.5% | 7.3% | 4.4% | 2.9% |
| | | | | | | | |
| **NASDAQ Composite (1971 to March 2022)** | | | | | | | |
| Average | 3.9% | 3.8% | 0.6% | 4.5% | 13.6% | 4.7% | 8.5% |
| *Post-Election* | −0.9% | 6.6% | 2.2% | 5.2% | 13.2% | 8.8% | 6.3% |
| *Midterm* | 1.1% | −1.9% | −3.5% | 6.4% | 2.2% | −5.0% | 19.9% |
| *Pre-Election* | 13.2% | 7.2% | 0.9% | 5.9% | 29.3% | 8.1% | 8.3% |
| *Election* | 2.0% | 3.0% | 2.5% | 0.6% | 8.9% | 6.0% | 0.3% |

# AUGUST

*he number one thing that has made us successful, by far, is obsessive, ompulsive focus on the customer, as opposed to obsession over the competitor.*
— Jeff Bezos (Founder & CEO Amazon, technology entrepreneur, investor & philanthropist, b. 1964)

**TUESDAY**
D 61.9
S 71.4
N 81.0
**22**

*eing uneducated is sometimes beneficial. Then you don't know what can't be done.*
— Michael Ott (Venture capitalist)

*Veek After August Expiration Mixed, Dow Up 9 of Last 17*

**WEDNESDAY**
D 52.4
S 47.6
N 47.6
**23**

*e always live in an uncertain world. What is certain is that the United States will go forward over time.*
— Warren Buffett (CEO Berkshire Hathaway, investor & philanthropist, CNBC 9/22/2010, b. 1930)

**THURSDAY**
D 57.1
S 52.4
N 52.4
**24**

*government which robs Peter to pay Paul can always depend on the support of Paul.*
George Bernard Shaw (Irish dramatist, 1856-1950)

**FRIDAY**
D 47.6
S 57.1
N 57.1
**25**

*ar markets don't act like a medicine ball rolling down a smooth hill. Instead, they behave like a basketball bouncing wn a rock-strewn mountainside; there's lots of movement up and sideways before the bottom is reached.*
Daniel Turov (*Turov on Timing, Barron's* May 21, 2001, b. 1947)

**SATURDAY**
**26**

*eptember Almanac Investor Sector Seasonalities: See Pages 94, 96 and 98*

**SUNDAY**
**27**

# SEPTEMBER ALMANAC

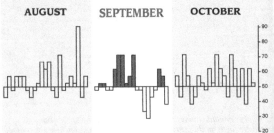

| SEPTEMBER | | | | | | | OCTOBER | | | | | | |
|---|---|---|---|---|---|---|---|---|---|---|---|---|---|
| S | M | T | W | T | F | S | S | M | T | W | T | F | S |
| | | | | | 1 | 2 | | | | | 1 | 2 | 3 |
| 3 | 4 | 5 | 6 | 7 | 8 | 9 | 8 | 9 | 10 | 11 | 12 | 13 | 14 |
| 10 | 11 | 12 | 13 | 14 | 15 | 16 | 15 | 16 | 17 | 18 | 19 | 20 | 21 |
| 17 | 18 | 19 | 20 | 21 | 22 | 23 | 22 | 23 | 24 | 25 | 26 | 27 | 28 |
| 24 | 25 | 26 | 27 | 28 | 29 | 30 | 29 | 30 | 31 | | | | |

*Market Probability Chart above is a graphic representation of the S&P 500 Recent Market Probability Calendar on page 126.*

◆Start of business year, end of vacations, and back to school made September a leading barometer month in first 60 years of 20th century. Now portfolio managers back after Labor Day tend to clean house ◆ Biggest % loser on the S&P, Dow and NASDAQ since 1950 (pages 52 & 60) ◆ Streak of four great Dow Septembers averaging 4.2% gains ended in 1999 with six losers in a row averaging –5.9% (see page 157), up three straight 2005-2007, down 6% in 2008 and 2011 ◆ Day after Labor Day Dow up 16 of last 28 ◆ S&P opened strong 16 of last 27 years but tends to close weak due to end-of-quarter mutual fund portfolio restructuring; last trading day: S&P down 18 of past 29 ◆ September Triple-Witching Week can be dangerous; week after is pitiful (see page 108).

## September Vital Statistics

| | DJIA | S&P 500 | NASDAQ | Russell 1K | Russell 2K |
|---|---|---|---|---|---|
| Rank | 12 | 12 | 12 | 12 | 12 |
| Up | 29 | 32 | 27 | 21 | 23 |
| Down | 43 | 39 | 24 | 22 | 20 |
| Avg % Change | –0.7% | –0.5% | –0.7% | –0.7% | –0.5% |
| Pre-Election Year | –0.8% | –0.8% | –0.8% | –0.7% | –1.3% |
| **Best and Worst** | | | | | |
| | % Change | % Change | % Change | % Change | % Change |
| Best | 2010  7.7 | 2010  8.8 | 1998  13.0 | 2010  9.0 | 2010  12.3 |
| Worst | 2002 –12.4 | 1974 –11.9 | 2001 –17.0 | 2002 –10.9 | 2001 –13.6 |
| **Best and Worst Weeks** | | | | | |
| Best | 9/28/01  7.4 | 9/28/01  7.8 | 9/16/11  6.3 | 9/28/01  7.6 | 9/28/01  6.9 |
| Worst | 9/21/01 –14.3 | 9/21/01 –11.6 | 9/21/01 –16.1 | 9/21/01 –11.7 | 9/21/01 –14.0 |
| **Best and Worst Days** | | | | | |
| Best | 9/8/98  5.0 | 9/30/08  5.4 | 9/8/98  6.0 | 9/30/08  5.3 | 9/18/08  7.0 |
| Worst | 9/17/01 –7.1 | 9/29/08 –8.8 | 9/29/08 –9.1 | 9/29/08 –8.7 | 9/29/08 –6.7 |
| **First Trading Day of Expiration Week: 1980–2022** | | | | | |
| Record (#Up–#Down) | 27-15 | 23-19 | 16-26 | 23-19 | 19-23 |
| Current Streak | U2 | U2 | D1 | U2 | U3 |
| Avg % Change | 0.01 | –0.04 | –0.22 | –0.05 | –0.09 |
| **Options Expiration Day: 1980–2022** | | | | | |
| Record (#Up–#Down) | 20-22 | 20-22 | 24-18 | 21-21 | 25-17 |
| Current Streak | D3 | D4 | D4 | D4 | U1 |
| Avg % Change | –0.08 | 0.01 | 0.02 | 0.004 | 0.09 |
| **Options Expiration Week: 1980–2022** | | | | | |
| Record (#Up–#Down) | 22-20 | 24-18 | 23-19 | 24-18 | 23-19 |
| Current Streak | D3 | D3 | D4 | D3 | U2 |
| Avg % Change | –0.10 | 0.05 | 0.08 | 0.06 | 0.20 |
| **Week After Options Expiration: 1980–2022** | | | | | |
| Record (#Up–#Down) | 15-27 | 13-29 | 19-23 | 13-28 | 15-27 |
| Current Streak | U1 | U1 | U2 | U1 | U1 |
| Avg % Change | –0.67 | –0.70 | –0.79 | –0.71 | –1.29 |
| **First Trading Day Performance** | | | | | |
| % of Time Up | 58.3 | 59.7 | 56.9 | 53.5 | 51.2 |
| Avg % Change | –0.01 | –0.02 | –0.03 | –0.07 | 0.001 |
| **Last Trading Day Performance** | | | | | |
| % of Time Up | 41.7 | 43.1 | 51.0 | 51.2 | 62.8 |
| Avg % Change | –0.10 | –0.04 | 0.04 | 0.06 | 0.24 |

*Dow & S&P 1950-May 13, 2022, NASDAQ 1971-May 13, 2022, Russell 1K & 2K 1979-May 13, 2022.*

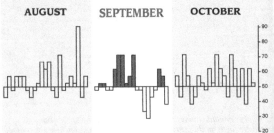

*September is when leaves and stocks tend to fall*
*On Wall Street it's the worst month of all*

# AUGUST/SEPTEMBER

**MONDAY**

D 42.9
S 52.4
N 52.4

**28**

*The two most abundant elements in the universe are Hydrogen and Stupidity.*
— Harlan Ellison (Science fiction writer, b. 1934)

*August's Third-to-Last Trading Day, S&P Up 19 Years In A Row 2003-2021*

**TUESDAY**

D 85.7
S 90.5
N 81.0

**29**

*Buy a stock the way you would buy a house. Understand and like it such that you'd be content to own it in the absence of any market.*
— Warren Buffett (CEO Berkshire Hathaway, investor and philanthropist, b. 1930)

*August's Next-to-Last Trading Day, S&P Down 17 of Last 26 Years*

**WEDNESDAY**

D 38.1
S 42.9
N 61.9

**30**

*Every time everyone's talking about something, that's the time to sell.*
— George Lindemann (Billionaire, *Forbes*)

*Last Trading Day in August, S&P Up 13 of Last 22 Years*

**THURSDAY**

D 52.4
S 57.1
N 52.4

**31**

*The future now belongs to societies that organize themselves for learning. What we know and can do holds the key to economic progress.*
— Ray Marshall (b. 1928) and Marc Tucker ( b. 1939) (*Thinking for a Living: Education and the Wealth of Nations*, 1992)

*First Trading Day in September, S&P Down 9 of Last 14*

**FRIDAY**

D 42.9
S 47.6
N 57.1

**1**

*During the first period of a man's life the greatest danger is not to take the risk.*
— Soren Kierkegaard (Danish philosopher, 1813-1855)

**SATURDAY**

**2**

**SUNDAY**

**3**

# MARKET GAINS MORE ON SUPER-8 DAYS EACH MONTH THAN ON ALL 13 REMAINING DAYS COMBINED

For many years the last day plus the first four days were the best days of the month. The market currently exhibits greater bullish bias from the last three trading days of the previous month through the first two days of the current month, and now shows significant bullishness during the middle three trading days, nine to eleven, due to 401(k) cash inflows (see pages 147 and 148). This pattern was not as pronounced during the boom years of the 1990s, with market strength all month long. Since the 2009 market bottom, the "Super Eight" advantage has been sporadic. So far in 2022 the "Super Eight" have a clear advantage. The "Super Eight" were destroyed in 2020 through the end of June. When compared to the last twenty-three and a third year record (at the bottom of the page), the "Super Eight" edge has dulled recently.

## SUPER-8 DAYS* DOW % CHANGES VS. REST OF MONTH

| | Super-8 Days | Rest of Month | | Super-8 Days | Rest of Month | | Super-8 Days | Rest of Month |
|---|---|---|---|---|---|---|---|---|
| | **2014** | | | **2015** | | | **2016** | |
| Jan | 0.92% | − 4.26% | | − 3.64% | − 0.07% | | − 2.95% | − 4.93% |
| Feb | − 1.99 | 3.66 | | 2.65 | 2.00 | | 1.69 | 0.30 |
| Mar | 0.77 | − 0.21 | | 1.91 | − 4.78 | | 4.02 | 2.21 |
| Apr | 2.44 | − 1.82 | | 1.20 | 0.83 | | 2.14 | 0.43 |
| May | − 0.56 | 2.50 | | 1.31 | − 1.28 | | − 1.33 | 0.57 |
| Jun | − 0.09 | 1.24 | | − 1.32 | 0.49 | | − 1.33 | − 2.68 |
| Jul | 1.79 | − 1.10 | | − 0.11 | − 1.31 | | 4.97 | 2.66 |
| Aug | − 1.81 | 2.61 | | 0.37 | − 8.02 | | − 0.11 | − 0.30 |
| Sep | 0.32 | − 1.26 | | 2.27 | − 2.04 | | 0.84 | − 1.72 |
| Oct | − 3.28 | 3.82 | | 1.03 | 6.57 | | − 0.65 | 0.49 |
| Nov | 2.42 | 2.28 | | 0.68 | 0.68 | | − 0.71 | 5.93 |
| Dec | − 1.66 | 3.14 | | − 0.74 | − 0.86 | | 0.38 | 3.73 |
| **Totals** | **− 0.73%** | **10.60%** | | **5.61%** | **− 7.79%** | | **6.96%** | **6.69%** |
| **Average** | **− 0.06%** | **0.88%** | | **0.47%** | **− 0.65%** | | **0.58%** | **0.56%** |
| | **2017** | | | **2018** | | | **2019** | |
| Jan | − 0.44% | 1.24% | | 2.83% | 4.54% | | 0.04% | 7.10% |
| Feb | 0.62 | 2.90 | | − 1.68 | − 3.17 | | 4.70 | 1.54 |
| Mar | 1.16 | − 1.66 | | − 4.26 | − 0.09 | | 0.11 | − 1.77 |
| Apr | − 0.39 | 1.83 | | 0.89 | − 1.34 | | 2.90 | 0.21 |
| May | − 0.03 | 0.45 | | − 0.79 | 3.59 | | − 1.71 | − 2.56 |
| Jun | 1.18 | − 0.09 | | − 0.67 | − 1.17 | | 0.35 | 4.32 |
| Jul | 0.89 | 0.98 | | 0.33 | 4.72 | | 1.81 | 0.60 |
| Aug | 2.12 | − 1.65 | | − 1.39 | 3.53 | | − 3.87 | − 1.41 |
| Sep | 0.53 | 1.65 | | 0.05 | 1.59 | | 1.98 | 2.62 |
| Oct | 1.97 | 2.96 | | − 0.30 | − 6.62 | | − 1.32 | 1.85 |
| Nov | − 0.15 | 0.93 | | 1.97 | − 1.68 | | 2.50 | 1.05 |
| Dec | 3.61 | 1.27 | | − 2.63 | − 5.08 | | − 0.85 | 2.85 |
| **Totals** | **11.07%** | **10.81%** | | **− 5.65%** | **− 1.18%** | | **6.64%** | **16.40%** |
| **Average** | **0.92%** | **0.90%** | | **− 0.47%** | **− 0.10%** | | **0.55%** | **1.37%** |
| | **2020** | | | **2021** | | | **2022** | |
| Jan | 1.40% | − 1.01% | | − 0.46% | 2.22% | | − 1.44% | − 4.78% |
| Feb | − 0.78 | − 4.78 | | − 0.54 | 2.49 | | 3.56 | − 6.40 |
| Mar | − 18.59 | 2.59 | | 1.57 | 3.25 | | 3.41 | 2.09 |
| Apr | − 4.42 | 11.77 | | 2.92 | − 0.18 | | 0.46 | − 5.41 |
| May | − 1.92 | 5.59 | | 2.64 | − 1.64 | | | |
| Jun | − 1.56 | 4.78 | | 0.36 | 0.00 | | | |
| Jul | 2.81 | − 0.33 | | 0.44 | 1.36 | | | |
| Aug | 1.23 | 6.03 | | 0.57 | − 0.11 | | | |
| Sep | 4.04 | − 7.99 | | 0.32 | − 1.28 | | | |
| Oct | 0.68 | 0.55 | | 0.19 | 2.41 | | | |
| Nov | 1.94 | 7.30 | | 0.85 | − 0.71 | | | |
| Dec | 0.13 | 1.06 | | − 3.37 | 5.15 | | | |
| **Totals** | **− 15.04%** | **25.56%** | | **5.49%** | **12.96%** | | **5.99%** | **− 14.50%** |
| **Average** | **− 1.25%** | **2.13%** | | **0.46%** | **1.08%** | | **1.50%** | **− 3.63%** |

| | Super-8 Days* | | | Rest of Month (13 Days) | |
|---|---|---|---|---|---|
| 280 | Net % Changes | 126.20% | | Net % Changes | 34.23% |
| Month | Average Period | 0.45% | | Average Period | 0.12% |
| Totals | Average Day | 0.06% | | Average Day | 0.01% |

* Super-8 Days = Last 3 + First 2 + Middle 3

# SEPTEMBER

abor Day *(Market Closed)*

**MONDAY**

**4**

*ake care of your employees and they'll take care of your customers.*
- John W. Marriott (Founder Marriott International, 1900-1985)

*Day After Labor Day, Dow Up 16 of Last 28, But Down 9 of Last 12*

**TUESDAY**

D 76.2
S 52.4
N 52.4

**5**

*"tired businessman" is one whose business is usually not a successful one.*
- Joseph R. Grundy (U.S. Senator Pennsylvania 1929-1930, businessman, 1863-1961)

**WEDNESDAY**

D 57.1
S 52.4
N 52.4

**6**

*n Wall Street, to know what everyone else knows is to know nothing.*
- Newton Zinder (Investment advisor and analyst, E.F. Hutton, b. 1927)

**THURSDAY**

D 42.9
S 47.6
N 52.4

**7**

*etnam, the original domino in the Cold War, now faces the prospect of becoming, in the words of political scientist*
*nai Phasuk of Chulalongkorn University in Bangkok, one of the new "dominos of democracy."*
Quoted by Seth Mydans *(NY Times, Jan. 6, 2001)*

**FRIDAY**

D 52.4
S 47.6
N 52.4

**8**

*n't delay! A good plan, violently executed now, is better than a perfect plan next week. War is a very simple thing,*
*ke stock trading] and the determining characteristics are self-confidence, speed, and audacity.*
General George S. Patton, Jr. (U.S. Army field commander WWII, 1885-1945)

**SATURDAY**

**9**

**SUNDAY**

**10**

# A CORRECTION FOR ALL SEASONS

While there's a rally for every season (page 74), almost always there's a decline or correction, too. Fortunately, corrections tend to be smaller than rallies, and that's what gives the stock market its long-term upward bias. In each season the average bounce outdoes the average setback. On average the net gain between the rally and the correction is smallest in summer and fall.

The summer setback tends to be slightly outdone by the average correction in the fall. Tax-loss selling and portfolio cleaning are the usual explanations. The October jinx also plays a major part. Since 1964, there have been 19 fall declines of over 10%, and in 11 of them (1966, 1974, 1978, 1979, 1987, 1990, 1997, 2000, 2002, 2008 and 2018) much damage was done in October, where so many bear markets end. Recent October lows were also seen in 1998, 1999, 2004, 2005 and 2011. Most often, it has paid to buy after fourth-quarter or late-third-quarter "waterfall declines" for a rally that may continue into January or even beyond. Covid-19 caused the worst Winter and Spring slumps in 2020 since 1932. Easy money and strong earnings spared Q1 2011 and 2012 a Winter slump. Tax cut expectations lifted the market in Q4 2017.

## SEASONAL CORRECTIONS IN DOW JONES INDUSTRIALS

| | WINTER SLUMP Nov/Dec High to Q1 Low | SPRING SLUMP Feb/Mar High to Q2 Low | SUMMER SLUMP May/Jun High to Q3 Low | FALL SLUMP Aug/Sep High to Q4 Low |
|---|---|---|---|---|
| 1964 | −0.1% | −2.4% | −1.0% | −2.1% |
| 1965 | −2.5 | −7.3 | −8.3 | −0.9 |
| 1966 | −6.0 | −13.2 | −17.7 | −12.7 |
| 1967 | −4.2 | −3.9 | −5.5 | −9.9 |
| 1968 | −8.8 | −0.3 | −5.5 | +0.4 |
| 1969 | −8.7 | −8.7 | −17.2 | −8.1 |
| 1970 | −13.8 | −20.2 | −8.8 | −2.5 |
| 1971 | −1.4 | −4.8 | −10.7 | −13.4 |
| 1972 | −0.5 | −2.6 | −6.3 | −5.3 |
| 1973 | −11.0 | −12.8 | −10.9 | −17.3 |
| 1974 | −15.3 | −10.8 | −29.8 | −27.6 |
| 1975 | −6.3 | −5.5 | −9.9 | −6.7 |
| 1976 | −0.2 | −5.1 | −4.7 | −8.9 |
| 1977 | −8.5 | −7.2 | −11.5 | −10.2 |
| 1978 | −12.3 | −4.0 | −7.0 | −13.5 |
| 1979 | −2.5 | −5.8 | −3.7 | −10.9 |
| 1980 | −10.0 | −16.0 | −1.7 | −6.8 |
| 1981 | −6.9 | −5.1 | −18.6 | −12.9 |
| 1982 | −10.9 | −7.5 | −10.6 | −3.3 |
| 1983 | −4.1 | −2.8 | −6.8 | −3.6 |
| 1984 | −11.9 | −10.5 | −8.4 | −6.2 |
| 1985 | −4.8 | −4.4 | −2.8 | −2.3 |
| 1986 | −3.3 | −4.7 | −7.3 | −7.6 |
| 1987 | −1.4 | −6.6 | −1.7 | −36.1 |
| 1988 | −6.7 | −7.0 | −7.6 | −4.5 |
| 1989 | −1.7 | −2.4 | −3.1 | −6.6 |
| 1990 | −7.9 | −4.0 | −17.3 | −18.4 |
| 1991 | −6.3 | −3.6 | −4.5 | −6.3 |
| 1992 | +0.1 | −3.3 | −5.4 | −7.6 |
| 1993 | −2.7 | −3.1 | −3.0 | −2.0 |
| 1994 | −4.4 | −9.6 | −4.4 | −7.1 |
| 1995 | −0.8 | −0.1 | −0.2 | −2.0 |
| 1996 | −3.5 | −4.6 | −7.5 | +0.2 |
| 1997 | −1.8 | −9.8 | −2.2 | −13.3 |
| 1998 | −7.0 | −3.1 | −18.2 | −13.1 |
| 1999 | −2.7 | −1.7 | −8.0 | −11.5 |
| 2000 | −14.8 | −7.4 | −4.1 | −11.8 |
| 2001 | −14.5 | −13.6 | −27.4 | −16.2 |
| 2002 | −5.1 | −14.2 | −26.7 | −19.5 |
| 2003 | −15.8 | −5.3 | −3.1 | −2.1 |
| 2004 | −3.9 | −7.7 | −6.3 | −5.7 |
| 2005 | −4.5 | −8.5 | −3.3 | −4.5 |
| 2006 | −2.4 | −5.4 | −7.8 | −0.4 |
| 2007 | −3.7 | −3.2 | −6.1 | −8.4 |
| 2008 | −14.5 | −11.0 | −20.6 | −35.9 |
| 2009 | −32.0 | −6.3 | −7.4 | −3.5 |
| 2010 | −6.1 | −10.4 | −13.1 | −1.0 |
| 2011 | +0.2 | −4.0 | −16.3 | −12.2 |
| 2012 | +0.5 | −8.7 | −5.3 | −7.8 |
| 2013 | −0.2 | −0.3 | −4.1 | −5.7 |
| 2014 | −7.3 | −2.6 | −3.4 | −6.7 |
| 2015 | −4.9 | −3.8 | −14.4 | −7.6 |
| 2016 | −12.6 | −3.3 | −0.9 | −4.0 |
| 2017 | −1.2 | −3.4 | −1.0 | +0.6 |
| 2018 | −5.3 | −9.7 | −4.5 | −18.5 |
| 2019 | −13.4 | −4.9 | −4.8 | −4.2 |
| 2020 | −35.1 | −29.1 | −6.8 | −8.9 |
| 2021 | −2.0 | −0.1 | −2.7 | −4.6 |
| 2022* | −10.6 | −12.6* | | |
| **Totals** | **−410.0%** | **−400.0%** | **−487.9%** | **−509.1%** |
| **Average** | **−6.9%** | **−6.8%** | **−8.4%** | **−8.8%** |

*As of 5/20/2022.*

# SEPTEMBER

*Monday Before September Triple Witching, NASDAQ Down 14 of Last 23*  🐂 **MONDAY**

D 57.1
S 61.9
N 57.1

**11**

🏴 *"In Memory"*

*Success isn't measured by the position you reach in life; it's measured by the obstacles you overcome.*
— Booker T. Washington (Founder of Tuskegee Institute, 1856-1915)

*2001 4-Day Closing, Longest Since 9-Day Banking Moratorium in March 1933*  🐻 **TUESDAY**

D 71.4
S 71.4
N 61.9

**12**

*Regulatory agencies within five years become controlled by industries they were set up to regulate.*
— Gabriel Kolko (American historian and author, 1932-2014)

*Expiration Week 2001, Dow Lost 1370 Points (14.3%)*
*2th Worst Weekly Point Loss Ever, 6th Worst Week Overall*  🐻 **WEDNESDAY**

D 66.7
S 71.4
N 61.9

**13**

*Even being right 3 or 4 times out of 10 should yield a person a fortune,*
*if he has the sense to cut his losses quickly on the ventures where he has been wrong.*
— Bernard Baruch (Financier, speculator, statesman, presidential adviser, 1870-1965)

**THURSDAY**

D 52.4
S 52.4
N 61.9

**14**

*There is nothing more powerful than a market that has changed its mind.*
— Arthur D. Cashin, Jr. (Legendary NYSE floor trader, director of floor operations UBS Financial Services, b. 1941)

*September Triple Witching, Dow Up 11 of Last 18, Down 7 of Last 10*  🐻🐻🐻 **FRIDAY**

D 61.9
S 57.1
N 42.9

**15**

*Make sure you have a jester because people in high places are seldom told the truth.*
— Radio caller to President Ronald Reagan

**Rosh Hashanah**

**SATURDAY**

**16**

**SUNDAY**

**17**

# FIRST-TRADING-DAY-OF-THE-MONTH PHENOMENON

Dow Jones Industrial Average has gained 23,639.48 points between September 2, 1997 (7622.42) and May 20, 2022 (31,261.90). It is incredible that 8,910.04 points were gained on the first trading days of these 297 months. The remaining 6222 trading days combined gained 14,729.44 points during the period. This averages out to gains of 30.00 points on first days, in contrast to just 2.49 points on all others.

Note September 1997 through October 2000 racked up a total gain of 2632.39 Dow points on the first trading days of these 38 months (winners except for seven occasions). But between November 2000 and September 2002, when the 2000-2002 bear markets did the bulk of their damage, frightened investors switched from pouring money into the market on that day to pulling it out, fourteen months out of twenty-three, netting a 404.80 Dow point loss. The 2007-2009 bear market lopped off 964.14 Dow points on first days in 17 months November 2007-March 2009. First days had their worst year in 2014, declining eight times for a total loss of 820.86 Dow points.

First days of August have performed worst, declining 16 times in the last 23 years. July's first trading day is third best by points but best based upon frequency of gains with only six declines in the last 32 years. In rising market trends first days tend to perform much better as institutions are likely anticipating strong performance at each month's outset. S&P 500 and NASDAQ first days differ slightly from Dow's pattern. December's first trading day is worst for S&P 500. April is worst for NASDAQ while October and December are also net decliners.

## DOW POINTS GAINED FIRST DAY OF MONTH
## SEPTEMBER 1997 TO MAY 20, 2022

| | Jan | Feb | Mar | Apr | May | Jun | Jul | Aug | Sep | Oct | Nov | Dec | Totals |
|---|---|---|---|---|---|---|---|---|---|---|---|---|---|
| 1997 | | | | | | | | | 257.36 | 70.24 | 232.31 | 189.98 | 749.89 |
| 1998 | 56.79 | 201.28 | 4.73 | 68.51 | 83.70 | 22.42 | 96.65 | −96.55 | 288.36 | −210.09 | 114.05 | 16.99 | 646.84 |
| 1999 | 2.84 | −13.13 | 18.20 | 46.35 | 225.65 | 36.52 | 95.62 | −9.19 | 108.60 | −63.95 | −81.35 | 120.58 | 486.74 |
| 2000 | −139.61 | 100.52 | 9.62 | 300.01 | 77.87 | 129.87 | 112.78 | 84.97 | 23.68 | 49.21 | −71.67 | −40.95 | 636.30 |
| 2001 | −140.70 | 96.27 | −45.14 | −100.85 | 163.37 | 78.47 | 91.32 | −12.80 | 47.74 | −10.73 | 188.76 | −87.60 | 268.11 |
| 2002 | 51.90 | −12.74 | 262.73 | −41.24 | 113.41 | −215.46 | −133.47 | −229.97 | −355.45 | 346.86 | 120.61 | −33.52 | −126.34 |
| 2003 | 265.89 | 56.01 | −53.22 | 77.73 | −25.84 | 47.55 | 55.51 | −79.83 | 107.45 | 194.14 | 57.34 | 116.59 | 819.32 |
| 2004 | −44.07 | 11.11 | 94.22 | 15.63 | 88.43 | 14.20 | −101.32 | 39.45 | −5.46 | 112.38 | 26.92 | 162.20 | 413.69 |
| 2005 | −53.58 | 62.00 | 63.77 | −99.46 | 59.19 | 82.39 | 28.47 | −17.76 | −21.97 | −33.22 | −33.30 | 106.70 | 143.23 |
| 2006 | 129.91 | 89.09 | 60.12 | 35.62 | −23.85 | 91.97 | 77.80 | −59.95 | 83.00 | −8.72 | −49.71 | −27.80 | 397.48 |
| 2007 | 11.37 | 51.99 | −34.29 | 27.95 | 73.23 | 40.47 | 126.81 | 150.38 | 91.12 | 191.92 | −362.14 | −57.15 | 311.66 |
| 2008 | −220.86 | 92.83 | −7.49 | 391.47 | 189.87 | −134.50 | 32.25 | −51.70 | −26.63 | −19.59 | −5.18 | −679.95 | −439.48 |
| 2009 | 258.30 | −64.03 | −299.64 | 152.68 | 44.29 | 221.11 | 57.06 | 114.95 | −185.68 | −203.00 | 76.71 | 126.74 | 299.49 |
| 2010 | 155.91 | 118.20 | 78.53 | 70.44 | 143.22 | −112.61 | −41.49 | 208.44 | 254.75 | 41.63 | 6.13 | 249.76 | 1172.91 |
| 2011 | 93.24 | 148.23 | −168.32 | 56.99 | −3.18 | −279.65 | 168.43 | −10.75 | −119.96 | −258.08 | −297.05 | −25.65 | −695.75 |
| 2012 | 179.82 | 83.55 | 28.23 | 52.45 | 65.69 | −274.88 | −8.70 | −37.62 | −54.90 | 77.98 | 136.16 | −59.98 | 187.80 |
| 2013 | 308.41 | 149.21 | 35.17 | −15.69 | −138.85 | 138.46 | 65.36 | 128.48 | 23.65 | 62.03 | 69.80 | −77.64 | 758.39 |
| 2014 | −135.31 | −326.05 | −153.68 | 74.95 | −21.97 | 26.46 | 129.47 | −69.93 | −30.89 | −238.19 | −24.28 | −51.44 | −820.86 |
| 2015 | 9.92 | 196.09 | 155.93 | −77.94 | 185.54 | 29.69 | 138.40 | −91.66 | −469.68 | −11.99 | 165.22 | 168.43 | 395.95 |
| 2016 | −276.09 | −17.12 | 348.58 | 107.66 | 117.52 | 2.47 | 19.38 | −27.73 | 18.42 | −54.30 | −105.32 | 68.35 | 201.82 |
| 2017 | 119.16 | 26.85 | 303.31 | −13.01 | −27.05 | 135.53 | 129.64 | 72.80 | 39.46 | 152.51 | 57.77 | −40.76 | 956.21 |
| 2018 | 104.79 | 37.32 | −420.22 | −458.92 | −64.10 | 219.37 | 35.77 | −81.37 | −12.34 | 192.90 | 264.98 | 287.97 | 106.15 |
| 2019 | 18.78 | 64.22 | 110.32 | 329.74 | −162.77 | 4.74 | 117.47 | −280.85 | −285.26 | −343.79 | 301.13 | −268.37 | −394.64 |
| 2020 | 330.36 | 143.78 | 1293.96 | −973.65 | −622.03 | 91.91 | −77.91 | 236.00 | 215.61 | 35.20 | 423.45 | 185.28 | 1282.04 |
| 2021 | −382.59 | 229.29 | 603.14 | 171.66 | 238.38 | 45.86 | 131.02 | −97.31 | −48.20 | 482.54 | 94.28 | −461.68 | 1006.39 |
| 2022 | 246.76 | 273.38 | −597.65 | 139.92 | 84.29 | | | | | | | | 146.79 |
| Totals | 951.34 | 1798.15 | 1690.91 | 349.00 | 862.01 | 442.36 | 1346.32 | −219.42 | −57.22 | 553.89 | 1305.62 | −112.92 | 8910.04 |

## SUMMARY FIRST DAYS VS. OTHER DAYS OF MONTH

| | # of Days | Total Points Gained | Average Daily Point Gain |
|---|---|---|---|
| First days | 297 | 8910.04 | 30.00 |
| Other days | 5925 | 14729.44 | 2.49 |

# SEPTEMBER

**🐂 MONDAY**

D 81.0
S 71.4
N 81.0

**18**

*imes of panic... these old fellows will be seen in Wall Street, hobbling down on their canes to their brokers' offices....
e panic usually rages until enough of these cash purchases of stock is made to afford a big rake in.*
— Henry Clews (British-American financier, author, *Fifty Years in Wall Street*, 1888, 1834-1923)

eek After September Triple Witching Dow Down 24 of Last 32,
erage Loss Since 1990, 1.0%

**TUESDAY**

D 47.6
S 47.6
N 42.9

**19**

*enever you find the key to the market, they change the locks.*
— Lucien Hooper

MC Meeting (2 Days)

**WEDNESDAY**

D 52.4
S 47.6
N 47.6

**20**

*atever method you use to pick stocks..., your ultimate success or failure will depend on your ability to ignore the worries of the
ld long enough to allow your investments to succeed. It isn't the head but the stomach that determines the fate of the stockpicker.*
— Peter Lynch (Fidelity Investments, *Beating the Street*, 1994)

**🐻 THURSDAY**

D 47.6
S 33.3
N 42.9

**21**

*fool can buy. It is the wise man who knows how to sell.*
— Albert W. Thomas (Trader, investor, *Over My Shoulder*, mutualfundmagic.com, *If It Doesn't Go Up, Don't Buy It!*, b. 1927)

**🐻 FRIDAY**

D 28.6
S 28.6
N 38.1

**22**

*words that spell business success: create concept, communicate concept, sustain momentum.*
— ale Hirsch (Creator of *Stock Trader's Almanac*, 1923-2021)

**SATURDAY**

**23**

ober Almanac Investor Sector Seasonalities: See Pages 94, 96 and 98

**SUNDAY**

**24**

# OCTOBER ALMANAC

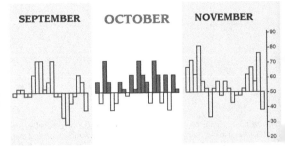

SEPTEMBER   OCTOBER   NOVEMBER

| OCTOBER | | | | | | | NOVEMBER | | | | | | |
|---|---|---|---|---|---|---|---|---|---|---|---|---|---|
| S | M | T | W | T | F | S | S | M | T | W | T | F | S |
| 1 | 2 | 3 | 4 | 5 | 6 | 7 | | | | 1 | 2 | 3 | 4 |
| 8 | 9 | 10 | 11 | 12 | 13 | 14 | 5 | 6 | 7 | 8 | 9 | 10 | 11 |
| 15 | 16 | 17 | 18 | 19 | 20 | 21 | 12 | 13 | 14 | 15 | 16 | 17 | 18 |
| 22 | 23 | 24 | 25 | 26 | 27 | 28 | 19 | 20 | 21 | 22 | 23 | 24 | 25 |
| 29 | 30 | 31 | | | | | 26 | 27 | 28 | 29 | 30 | | |

*Market Probability Chart above is a graphic representation of the S&P 500 Recent Market Probability Calendar on page 126.*

◆ Known as the jinx month because of crashes in 1929, 1987, the 554-point drop on October 27, 1997, back-to-back massacres in 1978 and 1979, Friday the 13th in 1989 and the meltdown in 2008 ◆ Yet October is a "bear killer" and turned the tide in 12 post-WWII bear markets: 1946, 1957, 1960, 1962, 1966, 1974, 1987, 1990, 1998, 2001, 2002 and 2011 ◆ First October Dow top in 2007, 20-year 1987 Crash anniversary –2.6% ◆ Worst six months of the year ends with October (page 54) ◆ No longer worst month (pages 52 & 60) ◆ Best Dow, S&P and NASDAQ month from 1993 to 2007 ◆ Pre-election year Octobers since 1950, #11 Dow (–0.4%), #10 S&P (0.2%) and #11 NASDAQ (0.3%) ◆ October is a great time to buy ◆ Big October gains five years 1999-2003 after atrocious Septembers ◆ Can get into Best Six Months earlier using MACD (page 56) ◆ October 2011, second month to gain 1000 Dow points and again in 2015.

## October Vital Statistics

| | DJIA | S&P 500 | NASDAQ | Russell 1K | Russell 2K |
|---|---|---|---|---|---|
| Rank | 7 | 7 | 7 | 8 | 11 |
| Up | 43 | 43 | 28 | 27 | 25 |
| Down | 29 | 29 | 23 | 16 | 18 |
| Avg % Change | 0.6% | 0.9% | 0.7% | 0.9% | –0.3% |
| Pre-Election Year | –0.4% | 0.2% | 0.3% | 0.4% | –1.5% |
| **Best and Worst** | | | | | |
| | % Change | % Change | % Change | % Change | % Change |
| Best | 1982  10.7 | 1974  16.3 | 1974  17.2 | 1982  11.3 | 2011  15.0 |
| Worst | 1987 –23.2 | 1987 –21.8 | 1987 –27.2 | 1987 –21.9 | 1987 –30.8 |
| **Best and Worst Weeks** | | | | | |
| Best | 10/11/74  12.6 | 10/11/74  14.1 | 10/31/08  10.9 | 10/31/08  10.8 | 10/31/08  14.1 |
| Worst | 10/10/08 –18.2 | 10/10/08 –18.2 | 10/23/87 –19.2 | 10/10/08 –18.2 | 10/23/87 –20.4 |
| **Best and Worst Days** | | | | | |
| Best | 10/13/08  11.1 | 10/13/08  11.6 | 10/13/08  11.8 | 10/13/08  11.7 | 10/13/08  9.3 |
| Worst | 10/19/87 –22.6 | 10/19/87 –20.5 | 10/19/87 –11.4 | 10/19/87 –19.0 | 10/19/87 –12.5 |
| **First Trading Day of Expiration Week: 1980–2022** | | | | | |
| Record (#Up–#Down) | 31-11 | 29-13 | 27-15 | 30-12 | 29-13 |
| Current Streak | D1 | D1 | D1 | D1 | D1 |
| Avg % Change | 0.63 | 0.60 | 0.50 | 0.58 | 0.34 |
| **Options Expiration Day: 1980–2022** | | | | | |
| Record (#Up–#Down) | 21-21 | 22-20 | 23-19 | 21-21 | 16-26 |
| Current Streak | U2 | U2 | U1 | U1 | D4 |
| Avg % Change | –0.10 | –0.17 | –0.11 | –0.16 | –0.21 |
| **Options Expiration Week: 1980–2022** | | | | | |
| Record (#Up–#Down) | 30-12 | 31-11 | 25-17 | 30-12 | 25-17 |
| Current Streak | U2 | U7 | U3 | U3 | U1 |
| Avg % Change | 0.62 | 0.66 | 0.70 | 0.65 | 0.43 |
| **Week After Options Expiration: 1980–2022** | | | | | |
| Record (#Up–#Down) | 21-21 | 19-23 | 22-20 | 19-23 | 20-22 |
| Current Streak | U1 | U1 | U1 | U1 | U3 |
| Avg % Change | –0.31 | –0.31 | –0.30 | –0.34 | –0.55 |
| **First Trading Day Performance** | | | | | |
| % of Time Up | 50.0 | 51.4 | 49.0 | 55.8 | 48.8 |
| Avg % Change | 0.07 | 0.06 | –0.11 | 0.21 | –0.20 |
| **Last Trading Day Performance** | | | | | |
| % of Time Up | 52.8 | 54.2 | 62.7 | 62.8 | 67.4 |
| Avg % Change | 0.06 | 0.13 | 0.44 | 0.29 | 0.50 |

*Dow & S&P 1950-May 13, 2022, NASDAQ 1971-May 13, 2022, Russell 1K & 2K 1979-May 13, 2022.*

*October has killed many a bea*
*Buy techs and small caps and soon wear a grin ear to ea*

# SEPTEMBER/OCTOBER

om Kippur

D 42.9
S 42.9
N 47.6
**25**

---

*eal knowledge is to know the extent of one's ignorance.*
*- Confucius (Chinese philosopher, 551-478 B.C.)*

D 57.1
S 47.6
N 52.4
**26**

---

*he riskiest moment is when you are right. That's when you're in the most trouble, because you tend to overstay the good decisions.*
*- Peter L. Bernstein (Economist, Money Magazine 10/15/2004, 1919-2009)*

*nd of September Prone to Weakness*
*rom End-of-Q3 Institutional Portfolio Restructuring*

🐻 WEDNESDAY

D 61.9
S 61.9
N 47.6
**27**

---

*he stock market is that creation of man which humbles him the most.*
*- Anonymous*

D 57.1
S 57.1
N 38.1
**28**

---

*committee is a cul-de-sac down which ideas are lured and then quietly strangled.*
*- Sir Barnett Cocks (Member of Parliament, 1907-1989)*

*ast Day of Q3, S&P Down 16 of Last 25, But Up 5 of Last 7,*
*assive 5.4% Rally in 2008*

🐂 FRIDAY

D 42.9
S 38.1
N 47.6
**29**

---

*e are all born originals; why is it so many die copies?*
*Edward Young (English poet, 1683-1765)*

**30**

---

**1**

# SECTOR SEASONALITY: SELECTED PERCENTAGE PLAYS

Sector seasonality was featured in the first 1968 *Almanac*. A Merrill Lynch study showed that buying seven sectors around September or October and selling in the first few months of 1954-1964 tripled the gains of holding them for 10 years. Over the years we have honed this strategy significantly and now devote a significant portion of our time and resources to investing and trading during positive and negative seasonal periods for the different sector indexes below with highly correlated exchange-traded funds (ETFs).

Updated seasonalities appear in the table below. We specify whether the seasonality starts or finishes in the beginning third (B), middle third (M) or last third (E) of the month. These Selected Percentage Plays are geared to take advantage of the bulk of seasonal sector strength or weakness.

By design, entry points are in advance of the major seasonal moves, providing traders ample opportunity to accumulate positions at favorable prices. Conversely, exit points have been selected to capture the majority of the move.

From the major seasonalities in the table below we created the Sector Index Seasonality Strategy Calendar on pages 96 and 98. Note the concentration of bullish sector seasonalities during the Best Six Months, November-April and bearish sector seasonalities during the Worst Six Months, May-October.

*Almanac Investor* e-newsletter subscribers receive specific entry and exit points for highly correlated ETFs and detailed analysis in our *ETF Trades Alerts*. Visit *www.stocktradersalmanac.com* or see the insert for additional details and a special offer for new subscribers.

## SECTOR INDEX SEASONALITY TABLE

| Ticker | Sector Index | Type | Start | | Finish | | 25-Year | 10-Year | 5-Year |
|--------|-------------|------|-------|---|--------|---|---------|---------|--------|
| | | | | | | | | Average % Return[†] | |
| XCI | Computer Tech | Short | January | B | March | B | −6.7 | −3.8 | −8.1 |
| XNG | Natural Gas | Long | February | E | June | B | 16.5 | 13.6 | 12.4 |
| S5INFT | InfoTech | Long | March | M | July | B | 10.8 | 11.3 | 18.5 |
| UTY | Utilities | Long | March | M | October | B | 9.8 | 7.9 | 12.9 |
| XCI | Computer Tech | Long | April | M | July | M | 11.6 | 10.3 | 14.1 |
| BKX | Banking | Short | May | B | July | B | −5.2 | −2.8 | −2.9 |
| XAU | Gold & Silver | Short | May | M | June | E | −6.9 | −5.0 | −3.1 |
| S5MATR | Materials | Short | May | M | October | M | −5.7 | −0.2 | 3.0 |
| XNG | Natural Gas | Short | June | M | July | E | −7.3 | −6.0 | −7.0 |
| XAU | Gold & Silver | Long | July | E | December | E | 7.0 | −2.7 | 3.5 |
| S5INDU | Industrials | Short | July | M | October | B | −4.6 | −1.3 | 0.7 |
| DJT | Transports | Short | July | M | October | M | −5.3 | −0.5 | 1.8 |
| BTK | Biotech | Long | August | B | March | B | 17.5 | 7.8 | 8.5 |
| S5INFT | InfoTech | Long | August | M | January | M | 11.9 | 9.6 | 13.6 |
| SOX | Semiconductor | Short | August | M | October | E | −7.7 | −0.8 | 0.1 |
| XOI | Oil | Short | September | B | November | E | −3.3 | −1.2 | 0.9 |
| BKX | Banking | Long | October | B | May | B | 15.7 | 18.0 | 19.3 |
| XBD | Broker/Dealer | Long | October | B | April | M | 26.7 | 17.4 | 15.7 |
| XCI | Computer Tech | Long | October | B | January | B | 14.1 | 8.6 | 11.1 |
| S5COND | Consumer Discretionary | Long | October | B | June | B | 16.5 | 16.0 | 14.4 |
| S5CONS | Consumer Staples | Long | October | B | June | B | 9.6 | 9.1 | 5.4 |
| S5HLTH | Healthcare | Long | October | B | May | B | 10.5 | 11.8 | 7.7 |
| S5INDU | Industrials | Long | October | E | May | M | 12.7 | 10.9 | 11.0 |
| S5MATR | Materials | Long | October | B | May | B | 15.7 | 13.6 | 10.7 |
| DRG | Pharmaceutical | Long | October | M | January | B | 7.1 | 6.5 | 7.1 |
| RMZ | Real Estate | Long | October | E | May | B | 10.9 | 8.0 | 3.9 |
| SOX | Semiconductor | Long | October | E | December | B | 14.5 | 11.3 | 13.7 |
| XTC | Telecom | Long | October | M | December | E | 7.6 | 2.0 | 0.3 |
| DJT | Transports | Long | October | B | May | B | 17.6 | 14.0 | 9.4 |
| XOI | Oil | Long | December | M | July | B | 11.2 | 8.0 | 6.6 |

[†]*Average % Return based on full seasonality completion through April 14, 2022.*

t Trading Day in October, Dow Down 9 of Last 17, Off 2.4% in 2011

**MONDAY**

D 52.4
S 57.1
N 52.4

**2**

tock market is a device for transferring money from the impatient to the patient.
arren Buffett (CEO Berkshire Hathaway, investor & philanthropist, b. 1930)

t Looking for MACD BUY Signals on October 1 (Pages 56, 62 and 64)
anac Investor Subscribers Emailed When It Triggers (See Insert)

**TUESDAY**

D 38.1
S 42.9
N 47.6

**3**

overnment would not look fondly on Caesar's Palace if it opened a table for wagering on corporate failure.
uld not give greater encouragement for Goldman Sachs [et al] to do so.
ger Lowenstein (Financial journalist and author, *End of Wall Street*, NY TimesOpEd 4/20/2010, b. 1954)

**WEDNESDAY**

D 71.4
S 71.4
N 76.2

**4**

ursuit of gain is the only way in which people can serve the needs of others whom they do not know.
iedrich von Hayek (*Counterrevolution of Science*)

ober Ends Dow and S&P "Worst Six Months" (Pages 52, 54, 56, 64 and 149)
NASDAQ "Worst Four Months" (Pages 60, 62 and 150)

**THURSDAY**

D 61.9
S 57.1
N 57.1

**5**

sts are supposed to be critics of corporations. They often end up being public relations spokesmen for them.
lph Wanger (Chief Investment Officer, Acorn Fund)

**FRIDAY**

D 38.1
S 38.1
N 47.6

**6**

sn't pay to anticipate the correction; there are already plenty who have been carried out on their shields trying to do that.
r, we will wait for some confirmed sell signals before altering our still-bullish view.
wrence G. McMillan (Professional trader, author, speaker, OptionStrategist.com, b. 1946)

**SATURDAY**

**7**

**SUNDAY**

**8**

# SECTOR INDEX SEASONALITY STRATEGY CALENDAR*

* Graphic representation of the Sector Index Seasonality Percentage Plays on page 94.
L = Long Trade, S = Short Trade, ➡ = Start of Trade

96

# OCTOBER

**Columbus Day** *(Bond Market Closed)*

MONDAY

D 47.6
S 42.9
N 52.4

# 9

*Doubt is the father of invention.*
— Galileo Galilei (Italian physicist and astronomer, 1564-1642)

*Dow Lost 1874 Points (18.2%) on the Week Ending 10/10/2008*
*Worst Dow Week in the History of Wall Street*

TUESDAY

D 57.1
S 57.1
N 57.1

# 10

*Your organization will never get better unless you are willing to admit that there is something wrong with it.*
— General Norman Schwartzkof (Ret. Commander of Allied Forces in 1990-1991 Gulf War)

WEDNESDAY

D 52.4
S 52.4
N 57.1

# 11

*First-rate people hire first-rate people; second-rate people hire third-rate people.*
— Leo Rosten (American author, 1908-1997)

*October 2011, Second Dow Month to Gain 1000 Points*

THURSDAY

D 38.1
S 47.6
N 57.1

# 12

*History is replete with episodes in which the real patriots were the ones who defied their governments.*
— Jim Rogers (Financier, *Adventure Capitalist*, b. 1942)

FRIDAY

D 61.9
S 61.9
N 66.7

# 13

*If you can buy more of your best idea, why put [the money] into your 10th-best idea or your 20th-best idea?*
*The more positions you have, the more average you are.*
— Bruce Berkowitz (Fairholme Fund, *Barron's* 3/17/08)

SATURDAY

# 14

SUNDAY

# 15

# SECTOR INDEX SEASONALITY STRATEGY CALENDAR*

* Graphic representation of the Sector Index Seasonality Percentage Plays on page 94.
L = Long Trade, S = Short Trade, → = Start of Trade

98

# OCTOBER

*Monday Before October Expiration, Dow Up 30 of 40*

**MONDAY**

D 52.4
S 52.4
N 52.4

**16**

*Inflation is the modern way that governments default on their debt.*
— Mike Epstein (CMT Association, MIT/Sloan Lab for Financial Engineering)

**TUESDAY**

D 57.1
S 71.4
N 61.9

**17**

*What investors really get paid for is holding dogs. Small stocks tend to have higher average returns than big stocks, and value stocks tend to have higher average returns than growth stocks.*
— Kenneth R. French (Economist, Dartmouth, NBER, b. 1954)

**WEDNESDAY**

D 52.4
S 61.9
N 57.1

**18**

*For a country, everything will be lost when the jobs of an economist and a banker become highly respected professions.*
— Montesquieu (French philosopher, 1689-1755)

*Crash of October 19, 1987, Dow down 22.6% in One Day*

**THURSDAY**

D 52.4
S 57.1
N 52.4

**19**

*That's the American way. If little kids don't aspire to make money like I did, what the hell good is this country?*
— Lee Iacocca (American industrialist, Former Chrysler CEO, b. 1924)

*October Expiration Day, Dow Down 6 Straight 2005-2010, But Up 7 of Last 9*

**FRIDAY**

D 33.3
S 42.9
N 38.1

**20**

*The critical ingredient is getting off your butt and doing something. It's as simple as that. A lot of people have ideas, but there are few who decide to do something about them now. Not tomorrow. Not next week. But today. The true entrepreneur is a doer, not a dreamer.*
— Nolan Bushnell (Founder Atari & Chuck E. Cheese's, b. 1943)

**SATURDAY**

**21**

**SUNDAY**

**22**

# MARKET BEHAVIOR THREE DAYS BEFORE AND THREE DAYS AFTER HOLIDAYS

The *Stock Trader's Almanac* has tracked holiday seasonality annually since the first edition in 1968. Stocks used to rise on the day before holidays and sell off the day after, but nowadays each holiday moves to its own rhythm. Eight holidays are separated into six groups. Average percent changes for the Dow, S&P 500, NASDAQ and Russell 2000 are shown.

The Dow and S&P consist of blue chips and the largest cap stocks, whereas NASDAQ and the Russell 2000 would be more representative of smaller cap stocks. This is evident on the last day of the year with NASDAQ and the Russell 2000 having a field day, while their larger brethren in the Dow and S&P are showing losses on average.

Thanks to the Santa Claus Rally the three days before and after New Year's Day and Christmas are best. NASDAQ and the Russell 2000 average gains of 1.0% to 1.6% over the six-day spans. However, trading around the first day of the year has been mixed recently. Traders have been selling more the first trading day of the year, pushing gains and losses into the New Year.

Bullishness before Labor Day and after Memorial Day is often affected by strength the first day of September and June. The second worst day after a holiday is the day after Easter. Surprisingly, the following day is the best second day after a holiday, eclipsing the second day after New Year's Day.

Presidents' Day is the least bullish of all the holidays, bearish the day before and three days after. NASDAQ has dropped 21 of the last 33 days before Presidents' Day (Dow, 18 of 33; S&P 19 of 33; Russell 2000, 16 of 33).

## HOLIDAYS: 3 DAYS BEFORE, 3 DAYS AFTER (Average % Change 1980 to April 2022)

| | −3 | −2 | −1 | | +1 | +2 | +3 |
|---|---|---|---|---|---|---|---|
| S&P 500 | 0.04 | 0.16 | − 0.09 | **Mixed** | 0.20 | 0.21 | 0.06 |
| DJIA | 0.03 | 0.11 | − 0.14 | **New Year's** | 0.29 | 0.20 | 0.19 |
| NASDAQ | 0.07 | 0.19 | 0.12 | **Day** | 0.23 | 0.41 | 0.13 |
| Russell 2K | 0.01 | 0.34 | 0.34 | *1/1/23* | 0.04 | 0.19 | 0.12 |
| S&P 500 | 0.35 | − 0.01 | − 0.10 | **Negative Before & After** | − 0.16 | − 0.08 | − 0.10 |
| DJIA | 0.33 | − 0.03 | − 0.03 | **Presidents'** | − 0.13 | − 0.08 | − 0.13 |
| NASDAQ | 0.53 | 0.22 | − 0.25 | **Day** | − 0.42 | − 0.08 | − 0.05 |
| Russell 2K | 0.41 | 0.13 | − 0.02 | *2/20/23* | − 0.32 | − 0.17 | − 0.04 |
| S&P 500 | 0.09 | 0.05 | 0.38 | **Positive Before &** | − 0.18 | 0.42 | 0.06 |
| DJIA | 0.08 | 0.02 | 0.31 | **Negative After** | − 0.14 | 0.39 | 0.08 |
| NASDAQ | 0.26 | 0.29 | 0.45 | **Good Friday** | − 0.26 | 0.51 | 0.15 |
| Russell 2K | 0.20 | 0.17 | 0.56 | *4/7/23* | − 0.37 | 0.38 | 0.02 |
| S&P 500 | 0.10 | 0.01 | 0.01 | **Positive After** | 0.25 | 0.15 | 0.21 |
| DJIA | 0.07 | − 0.02 | − 0.04 | **Memorial** | 0.30 | 0.16 | 0.11 |
| NASDAQ | 0.17 | 0.17 | 0.06 | **Day** | 0.21 | 0.01 | 0.40 |
| Russell 2K | 0.07 | 0.25 | 0.13 | *5/29/23* | 0.30 | 0.13 | 0.30 |
| S&P 500 | 0.20 | 0.16 | 0.10 | **Negative After** | − 0.09 | 0.02 | 0.06 |
| DJIA | 0.16 | 0.13 | 0.10 | **Independence** | − 0.04 | 0.03 | 0.05 |
| NASDAQ | 0.33 | 0.18 | 0.08 | **Day** | − 0.06 | − 0.11 | 0.23 |
| Russell 2K | 0.33 | 0.04 | 0.01 | *7/4/23* | − 0.22 | − 0.11 | 0.05 |
| S&P 500 | 0.25 | − 0.22 | 0.11 | **Positive Before** | − 0.01 | 0.12 | − 0.09 |
| DJIA | 0.22 | − 0.26 | 0.11 | **& Mixed After** | 0.001 | 0.16 | − 0.15 |
| NASDAQ | 0.45 | − 0.06 | 0.12 | **Labor Day** | − 0.09 | 0.01 | 0.04 |
| Russell 2K | 0.53 | 0.04 | 0.10 | *9/4/23* | − 0.03 | 0.13 | 0.02 |
| S&P 500 | 0.12 | 0.03 | 0.24 | **Positive Before** | 0.10 | − 0.35 | 0.27 |
| DJIA | 0.14 | 0.04 | 0.21 | **& After** | 0.06 | − 0.32 | 0.26 |
| NASDAQ | 0.03 | − 0.16 | 0.41 | **Thanksgiving** | 0.35 | − 0.33 | 0.11 |
| Russell 2K | 0.20 | − 0.02 | 0.38 | *11/23/23* | 0.18 | − 0.52 | 0.22 |
| S&P 500 | 0.18 | 0.17 | 0.14 | **Christmas** | 0.31 | 0.01 | 0.22 |
| DJIA | 0.22 | 0.20 | 0.17 | *12/25/23* | 0.32 | 0.04 | 0.19 |
| NASDAQ | − 0.003 | 0.32 | 0.32 | | 0.31 | 0.02 | 0.25 |
| Russell 2K | 0.28 | 0.31 | 0.29 | | 0.30 | − 0.03 | 0.41 |

# OCTOBER

*Let me end my talk by abusing slightly my status as an official representative of the Federal Reserve. I would like to say to Milton Friedman]: regarding the Great Depression, you're right; we did it. We're very sorry. But thanks to you, we won't do it again.*
— Ben Bernanke (Fed Chairman 2006-2014, 11/8/02 speech as Fed Govenor, b. 1953)

### Late October Is Time to Buy Depressed Stocks Especially Techs and Small Caps

🐃 TUESDAY
D 52.4
S 61.9
N 57.1
**24**

*Politicians use statistics in the same way that a drunk uses lamp-posts—for support rather than illumination.*
— Andrew Lang (Scottish writer, literary critic, anthropologist, 1844-1912)

WEDNESDAY
D 47.6
S 42.9
N 52.4
**25**

*Government is like fire—useful when used legitimately, but dangerous when not.*
— David Brooks (*NY Times* columnist, 10/5/07)

🐃 THURSDAY
D 66.7
S 61.9
N 52.4
**26**

*The price of a stock varies inversely with the thickness of its research file.*
— Martin Sosnoff (Atalanta Sosnoff Capital, *Silent Investor, Silent Loser*)

### 84th Anniversary of 1929 Crash, Dow Down 23.0% in Two Days, October 28 and 29

🐻 FRIDAY
D 42.9
S 38.1
N 52.4
**27**

*What technology does is make people more productive. It doesn't replace them.*
— Michael Bloomberg (Founder Bloomberg L.P., philanthropist, New York Mayor 2002-2013, b. 1942)

SATURDAY
**28**

*November Almanac Investor Sector Seasonalities: See Pages 94, 96 and 98*

SUNDAY
**29**

# NOVEMBER ALMANAC

OCTOBER  NOVEMBER  DECEMBER

*Market Probability Chart above is a graphic representation of the S&P 500 Recent Market Probability Calendar on page 126.*

◆ #1 S&P and #2 Dow month since 1950, #2 on NASDAQ since 1971 (pages 52 & 60) ◆ Start of the "Best Six Months" of the year (page 54), NASDAQ's Best Eight Months and Best Three (pages 149 & 150) ◆ Simple timing indicator almost triples "Best Six Months" strategy (page 56), doubles NASDAQ's Best Eight (page 62) ◆ Day before and after Thanksgiving Day combined, only 19 losses in 70 years (page 106) ◆ Week before Thanksgiving Dow up 19 of last 29 ◆ Pre-election year Novembers rank #9 Dow, #8 S&P, NASDAQ #7.

## November Vital Statistics

| | DJIA | S&P 500 | NASDAQ | Russell 1K | Russell 2K |
|---|---|---|---|---|---|
| Rank | 2 | 1 | 2 | 1 | 1 |
| Up | 49 | 49 | 36 | 32 | 29 |
| Down | 23 | 23 | 15 | 11 | 14 |
| Avg % Change | 1.7% | 1.7% | 1.8% | 1.9% | 2.3% |
| Pre-Election Year | 0.5% | 0.5% | 1.2% | 0.1% | 1.4% |
| **Best and Worst** | | | | | |
| | % Change | % Change | % Change | % Change | % Change |
| Best | 2020 11.8 | 2020 10.8 | 2001 14.2 | 2020 11.6 | 2020 18.3 |
| Worst | 1973 −14.0 | 1973 −11.4 | 2000 −22.9 | 2000 −9.3 | 2008 −12.0 |
| **Best and Worst Weeks** | | | | | |
| Best | 11/28/08 9.7 | 11/28/08 12.0 | 11/28/08 10.9 | 11/28/08 12.5 | 11/28/08 16.4 |
| Worst | 11/21/08 −5.3 | 11/21/08 −8.4 | 11/10/00 −12.2 | 11/21/08 −8.8 | 11/21/08 −11.0 |
| **Best and Worst Days** | | | | | |
| Best | 11/13/08 6.7 | 11/13/08 6.9 | 11/13/08 6.5 | 11/13/08 7.0 | 11/13/08 8.5 |
| Worst | 11/20/08 −5.6 | 11/20/08 −6.7 | 11/19/08 −6.5 | 11/20/08 −6.9 | 11/19/08 −7.9 |
| **First Trading Day of Expiration Week: 1980–2022** | | | | | |
| Record (#Up–#Down) | 23-19 | 19-23 | 16-26 | 21-21 | 18-24 |
| Current streak | D1 | D1 | D1 | D1 | D1 |
| Avg % Change | −0.02 | −0.05 | −0.16 | −0.06 | −0.06 |
| **Options Expiration Day: 1980–2022** | | | | | |
| Record (#Up–#Down) | 26-16 | 24-18 | 22-20 | 24-18 | 24-17 |
| Current Streak | D2 | D2 | U1 | D2 | D1 |
| Avg % Change | 0.20 | 0.15 | 0.04 | 0.14 | 0.14 |
| **Options Expiration Week: 1980–2022** | | | | | |
| Record (#Up–#Down) | 26-16 | 25-17 | 24-18 | 24-18 | 21-21 |
| Current Streak | D2 | U1 | U3 | U1 | D1 |
| Avg % Change | 0.23 | 0.09 | 0.10 | 0.08 | −0.16 |
| **Week After Options Expiration: 1980–2022** | | | | | |
| Record (#Up–#Down) | 24-18 | 26-16 | 27-15 | 26-16 | 25-17 |
| Current Streak | D1 | D1 | D1 | D1 | D1 |
| Avg % Change | 0.52 | 0.52 | 0.62 | 0.54 | 0.71 |
| **First Trading Day Performance** | | | | | |
| % of Time Up | 65.3 | 65.3 | 66.7 | 74.4 | 62.8 |
| Avg % Change | 0.31 | 0.32 | 0.33 | 0.42 | 0.35 |
| **Last Trading Day Performance** | | | | | |
| % of Time Up | 54.2 | 51.4 | 60.8 | 44.2 | 62.8 |
| Avg % Change | 0.08 | 0.10 | −0.10 | −0.03 | 0.03 |

*Dow & S&P 1950-May 13, 2022, NASDAQ 1971-May 13, 2022, Russell 1K & 2K 1979-May 13, 2022.*

*Astute investors always smile and remember,*
*When stocks seasonally start soaring, and salute November.*

**MONDAY**

D 61.9
S 61.9
N 61.9 **30**

---

*Statements by high officials are practically always misleading when they are designed to bolster a falling market.*
— Gerald M. Loeb (E.F. Hutton, *The Battle for Investment Survival*, predicted 1929 Crash, 1900-1974)

Halloween

**TUESDAY**

D 47.6
S 52.4
N 52.4 **31**

---

*Analyzing the chart is the easy part. Actually doing what the chart says? That's the tough part.*
— Ralph Acampora (Godfather of Technical Analysis, co-founder CMT Association, Altaira Wealth Management, b. 1941)

*First Trading Day in November, Dow Up 10 of Last 13*
*FOMC Meeting (2 Days)*

**WEDNESDAY**

D 66.7
S 66.7
N 66.7 **1**

---

*If the market prefers a system that looks inefficient that's a good sign that its more efficient than it looks.*
— Matt Levine (Bloomberg View columnist, former investment banker, lawyer & high school Latin teacher)

**THURSDAY**

D 66.7
S 71.4
N 61.9 **2**

---

*When everybody thinks alike, everyone is likely to be wrong.*
— Humphrey B. Neill (Investor, analyst, author, *Art of Contrary Thinking* 1954, 1895-1977)

*November Begins Dow and S&P "Best Six Months" (Pages 52, 54, 56, 64 and 149)*
*and NASDAQ "Best Eight Months" (Pages 60, 62 and 150)*

**FRIDAY**

D 66.7
S 61.9
N 61.9 **3**

---

*Those that forget the past are condemned to repeat its mistakes, and those that mis-state the past should be condemned.*
— Eugene D. Cohen (*Letter to the Editor Financial Times* 10/30/06)

**SATURDAY**

**4**

---

**Daylight Savings Time Ends**

**SUNDAY**

**5**

# 2010 SUPER BOOM FORECAST DOW 38820 AHEAD OF SCHEDULE

Our Super Boom Forecast for Dow 38820 by the year 2025 still appears to be ahead of schedule. In fact, we outlined a sharp decline for 2022 in our original 15-Year Projection (chart below) first drawn in 2011 when our book *Super Boom: Why the Dow Jones Will Hit 38,820 and How You Can Profit From It* (Wiley) hit the stores.

Few believed us when we first released this forecast in our newsletter in May 2010 and published it in the *Stock Trader's Almanac 2011* with the Dow around 10,000. At the all-time high of 36799.95 on January 4, 2022, the Dow was only 5.5% below 38820. This extraordinary forecast was and is based upon the seminal research and reports our late founder Yale Hirsch (1923-2021) undertook and published back in the mid-seventies when he discovered this iconic market cycle, which led him to the greatest market call in history for a 500% move in the market from the 1974 low to 1990.

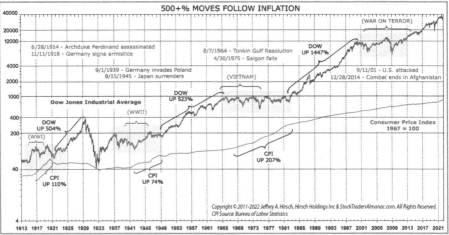

The pattern shows how the market failed to make any sustained advance while the world was at war and enduring other crises. Inflation caused by government spending kicked in and the stock market made 500+% moves.

The War on Terror began on 9/11 and ended when the U.S. and NATO formally declared their combat mission in Afghanistan over on December 28, 2014. This appears to be the Super Boom launching ramp noted in the chart below. Inflation as measured by CPI came a bit later this cycle, but it has come on strong now. Years of ZIRP, QE and fiscal stimulus to quell the 2007-2008 Financial Crisis and the Covid-19 pandemic have finally come home to roost.

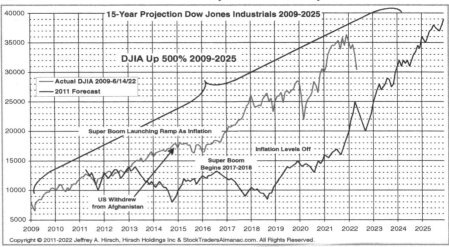

# NOVEMBER

**MONDAY**

D 71.4
S 81.0
N 71.4

**6**

*The four most expensive words in the English language, "This time it's different."*
— Sir John Templeton (Founder Templeton Funds, philanthropist, 1912-2008)

**Election Day**

**TUESDAY**

D 66.7
S 57.1
N 66.7

**7**

*I know nothing grander, better exercise...more positive proof of the past,
the triumphant result of faith in humankind, than a well-contested national election.*
— Walt Whitman (American poet, 1819-1892)

**WEDNESDAY**

D 61.9
S 52.4
N 52.4

**8**

*It is better to be out wishing you were in, than in wishing you were out.*
— Albert W. Thomas (Trader, investor, *Over My Shoulder*, mutualfundmagic.com, *If It Doesn't Go Up, Don't Buy It!*, b. 1927)

*Week Before November Options Expiration, S&P 500 Up 8 of Last 13*

**THURSDAY**

D 47.6
S 33.3
N 33.3

**9**

*There are ways for the individual investor to make money in the securities markets.
Buying value and holding long term while collecting dividends has been proven over and over again.*
— Robert M. Sharp (Author, *The Lore and Legends of Wall Street*)

**FRIDAY**

D 38.1
S 52.4
N 61.9

**10**

*Exercising the right of occasional suppression and slight modification, it is truly absurd to see
how plastic a limited number of observations become, in the hands of men with preconceived ideas.*
— Sir Francis Galton, FRS (English polymath, statistical pioneer, *Meteorographica* 1863, 1822-1911)

**Veterans' Day**

**SATURDAY**

**11**

**SUNDAY**

**12**

# TRADING THE THANKSGIVING MARKET

For 35 years the "holiday spirit" gave Wednesday before Thanksgiving and Friday after a great track record, except for two occasions. Publishing it in the 1987 *Almanac* was the "kiss of death." Since 1988 Wednesday-Friday gained 18 of 34 times with a total Dow point-loss of 519.28. The best strategy appears to be coming into the week long and exiting into strength before the holiday. Omicron Covid-19 variant cancelled Thanksgiving in 2021.

## DOW JONES INDUSTRIALS BEFORE AND AFTER THANKSGIVING

| | Tuesday Before | Wednesday Before | Friday After | Total Gain Dow Points | Dow Close | Next Monday |
|---|---|---|---|---|---|---|
| 1952 | − 0.18 | 1.54 | 1.22 | 2.76 | 283.66 | 0.04 |
| 1953 | 1.71 | 0.65 | 2.45 | 3.10 | 280.23 | 1.14 |
| 1954 | 3.27 | 1.89 | 3.16 | 5.05 | 387.79 | 0.72 |
| 1955 | 4.61 | 0.71 | 0.26 | 0.97 | 482.88 | − 1.92 |
| 1956 | − 4.49 | − 2.16 | 4.65 | 2.49 | 472.56 | − 2.27 |
| 1957 | − 9.04 | 10.69 | 3.84 | 14.53 | 449.87 | − 2.96 |
| 1958 | − 4.37 | 8.63 | 8.31 | 16.94 | 557.46 | 2.61 |
| 1959 | 2.94 | 1.41 | 1.42 | 2.83 | 652.52 | 6.66 |
| 1960 | − 3.44 | 1.37 | 4.00 | 5.37 | 606.47 | − 1.04 |
| 1961 | − 0.77 | 1.10 | 2.18 | 3.28 | 732.60 | − 0.61 |
| 1962 | 6.73 | 4.31 | 7.62 | 11.93 | 644.87 | − 2.81 |
| 1963 | 32.03 | − 2.52 | 9.52 | 7.00 | 750.52 | 1.39 |
| 1964 | − 1.68 | − 5.21 | − 0.28 | − 5.49 | 882.12 | − 6.69 |
| 1965 | 2.56 | N/C | − 0.78 | − 0.78 | 948.16 | − 1.23 |
| 1966 | − 3.18 | 1.84 | 6.52 | 8.36 | 803.34 | − 2.18 |
| 1967 | 13.17 | 3.07 | 3.58 | 6.65 | 877.60 | 4.51 |
| 1968 | 8.14 | − 3.17 | 8.76 | 5.59 | 985.08 | − 1.74 |
| 1969 | − 5.61 | 3.23 | 1.78 | 5.01 | 812.30 | − 7.26 |
| 1970 | 5.21 | 1.98 | 6.64 | 8.62 | 781.35 | 12.74 |
| 1971 | − 5.18 | 0.66 | 17.96 | 18.62 | 816.59 | 13.14 |
| 1972 | 8.21 | 7.29 | 4.67 | 11.96 | 1025.21 | − 7.45 |
| 1973 | − 17.76 | 10.08 | − 0.98 | 9.10 | 854.00 | − 29.05 |
| 1974 | 5.32 | 2.03 | − 0.63 | 1.40 | 618.66 | − 15.64 |
| 1975 | 9.76 | 3.15 | 2.12 | 5.27 | 860.67 | − 4.33 |
| 1976 | − 6.57 | 1.66 | 5.66 | 7.32 | 956.62 | − 6.57 |
| 1977 | 6.41 | 0.78 | 1.12 | 1.90 | 844.42 | − 4.85 |
| 1978 | − 1.56 | 2.95 | 3.12 | 6.07 | 810.12 | 3.72 |
| 1979 | − 6.05 | − 1.80 | 4.35 | 2.55 | 811.77 | 16.98 |
| 1980 | 3.93 | 7.00 | 3.66 | 10.66 | 993.34 | − 23.89 |
| 1981 | 18.45 | 7.90 | 7.80 | 15.70 | 885.94 | 3.04 |
| 1982 | − 9.01 | 9.01 | 7.36 | 16.37 | 1007.36 | − 4.51 |
| 1983 | 7.01 | − 0.20 | 1.83 | 1.63 | 1277.44 | − 7.62 |
| 1984 | 9.83 | 6.40 | 18.78 | 25.18 | 1220.30 | − 7.95 |
| 1985 | 0.12 | 18.92 | − 3.56 | 15.36 | 1472.13 | − 14.22 |
| 1986 | 6.05 | 4.64 | − 2.53 | 2.11 | 1914.23 | − 1.55 |
| 1987 | 40.45 | − 16.58 | − 36.47 | − 53.05 | 1910.48 | − 76.93 |
| 1988 | 11.73 | 14.58 | − 17.60 | − 3.02 | 2074.68 | 6.76 |
| 1989 | 7.25 | 17.49 | 18.77 | 36.26 | 2675.55 | 19.42 |
| 1990 | − 35.15 | 9.16 | − 12.13 | − 2.97 | 2527.23 | 5.94 |
| 1991 | 14.08 | − 16.10 | − 5.36 | − 21.46 | 2894.68 | 40.70 |
| 1992 | 25.66 | 17.56 | 15.94 | 33.50 | 3282.20 | 22.96 |
| 1993 | 3.92 | 13.41 | − 3.63 | 9.78 | 3683.95 | − 6.15 |
| 1994 | − 91.52 | − 3.36 | 33.64 | 30.28 | 3708.27 | 31.29 |
| 1995 | 40.46 | 18.06 | 7.23* | 25.29 | 5048.84 | 22.04 |
| 1996 | − 19.38 | − 29.07 | 22.36* | − 6.71 | 6521.70 | N/C |
| 1997 | 41.03 | − 14.17 | 28.35* | 14.18 | 7823.13 | 189.98 |
| 1998 | − 73.12 | 13.13 | 18.80* | 31.93 | 9333.08 | − 216.53 |
| 1999 | − 93.89 | 12.54 | − 19.26* | − 6.72 | 10988.91 | − 40.99 |
| 2000 | 31.85 | − 95.18 | 70.91* | − 24.27 | 10470.23 | 75.84 |
| 2001 | − 75.08 | − 66.70 | 125.03* | 58.33 | 9959.71 | 23.04 |
| 2002 | − 172.98 | 255.26 | − 35.59* | 219.67 | 8896.09 | − 33.52 |
| 2003 | 16.15 | 15.63 | 2.89* | 18.52 | 9782.46 | 116.59 |
| 2004 | 3.18 | 27.71 | 1.92* | 29.63 | 10522.23 | − 46.33 |
| 2005 | 51.15 | 44.66 | 15.53* | 60.19 | 10931.62 | − 40.90 |
| 2006 | 5.05 | 5.36 | − 46.78* | − 41.42 | 12280.17 | − 158.46 |
| 2007 | 51.70 | − 211.10 | 181.84* | − 29.26 | 12980.88 | − 237.44 |
| 2008 | 36.08 | 247.14 | 102.43* | 349.57 | 8829.04 | − 679.95 |
| 2009 | − 17.24 | 30.69 | − 154.48* | − 123.79 | 10309.92 | 34.92 |
| 2010 | − 142.21 | 150.91 | − 95.28* | 55.63 | 11092.00 | − 39.51 |
| 2011 | − 53.59 | − 236.17 | − 25.77* | − 261.94 | 11231.78 | 291.23 |
| 2012 | − 7.45 | 48.38 | 172.79* | 221.17 | 13009.68 | − 42.31 |
| 2013 | 0.26 | 24.53 | − 10.92* | 13.61 | 16086.41 | − 77.64 |
| 2014 | − 2.96 | − 2.69 | 15.99* | 13.30 | 17828.24 | − 51.44 |
| 2015 | 19.51 | 1.20 | − 14.90* | − 13.70 | 17798.49 | − 78.57 |
| 2016 | 67.18 | 59.31 | 68.96* | 128.27 | 19152.14 | − 54.24 |
| 2017 | 160.50 | − 64.65 | 31.81* | − 32.84 | 23557.99 | 22.79 |
| 2018 | − 551.80 | − 0.95 | − 178.74* | − 179.69 | 24285.95 | 354.29 |
| 2019 | 55.21 | 42.32 | − 112.59* | −70.27 | 28051.41 | − 268.37 |
| 2020 | 454.97 | − 173.77 | 37.90* | − 135.87 | 29910.02 | − 271.73 |
| 2021 | 194.55 | − 9.42 | − 905.04* | − 914.46 | 34899.34 | 236.60 |

*Shortened trading day

# NOVEMBER

*londay Before November Expiration, Dow Up 12 of Last 18,*
*)08 –2.6%, 2018 –2.3%*

**MONDAY**

D 61.9
S 57.1
N 66.7

# 13

*ne only gets to the top rung on the ladder by steadily climbing up one at a time, and suddenly all sorts of powers,*
*l sorts of abilities, which you thought never belonged to you-suddenly become within your own possibility….*
*— Margaret Thatcher (British, prime minister, 1979-1990, 1925-2013)*

**TUESDAY**

D 47.6
S 47.6
N 42.9

# 14

*ver tell people how to do things. Tell them what to do and they will surprise you with their ingenuity.*
*General George S. Patton, Jr. (U.S. Army field commander WWII, 1885-1945)*

*'eek Before Thanksgiving, Dow Up 19 of Last 29, Down Last 5*
*)03 –1.4%, 2004 –0.8%, 2008 –5.3%, 2011 –2.9%, 2012 –1.8%, 2018 –2.2%*

**WEDNESDAY**

D 66.7
S 57.1
N 47.6

# 15

*ople somehow think you must buy at the bottom and sell at the top. That's nonsense.*
*e idea is to buy when the probability is greatest that the market is going to advance.*
*Martin Zweig (Fund manager, Winning on Wall Street, 1943-2013)*

**THURSDAY**

D 57.1
S 52.4
N 57.1

# 16

*ien investment decisions need to consider the speed of light, something is seriously wrong.*
*Frank M. Bifulco (Senior Portfolio Manager Alcott Capital Management, Barron's Letters to the Editor, 5/24/2010)*

*)vember Expiration Day, Dow Up 14 of Last 20*
*)w Surged in 2008, Up 494 Points (6.5%)*

**FRIDAY**

D 38.1
S 42.9
N 42.9

# 17

*not nearly so concerned about the return on my capital as I am the return of my capital.*
*Will Rogers (American humorist and showman, 1879-1935)*

**SATURDAY**

# 18

**SUNDAY**

# 19

# AURA OF THE TRIPLE WITCH—4TH QUARTER MOST BULLISH: DOWN WEEKS TRIGGER MORE WEAKNESS WEEK AFTER

Options expire the third Friday of every month but in March, June, September and December a powerful coven gathers. Since the S&P index futures began trading on April 21, 1982, stock options, index options as well as index futures all expire at the same time four times each year—known as Triple Witching. Traders have long sought to understand and master the magic of this quarterly phenomenon.

The impact of single-stock and ETF futures on the market has thus far been subdued. Until their influence broadens, we do not believe the term "quadruple witching" is applicable just yet.

We have analyzed what the market does prior, during and following Triple Witching expirations in search of consistent trading patterns. Here are some of our findings of how the Dow Jones Industrials perform around Triple-Witching Week (TWW).

- TWWs have become more bullish since 1990, except in the second quarter.
- Following weeks became more bearish. Since Q1 2000 only 36 of 88 were up, and 17 occurred in December, 10 in March, 6 in September, 3 in June.
- TWWs have tended to be down in flat periods and dramatically so during bear markets.
- DOWN WEEKS TEND TO FOLLOW DOWN TWWs is a interesting pattern. Since 1991, of 44 down TWWs, 28 following weeks were also down. This is surprising inasmuch as the previous decade had an exactly opposite pattern: There were 13 down TWWs then, but 12 up weeks followed them.
- TWWs in the second and third quarter (Worst Six Months May through October) are much weaker and the weeks following, horrendous. But in the first and fourth quarter (Best Six Months period November through April) only the week after Q1 expiration is negative.

Throughout the *Almanac* you will also see notations on the performance of Mondays and Fridays of TWW as we place considerable significance on the beginnings and ends of weeks (pages 72, 78 and 143-146).

## TRIPLE WITCHING WEEK AND WEEK AFTER DOW POINT CHANGES

| | Expiration Week Q1 | Week After | Expiration Week Q2 | Week After | Expiration Week Q3 | Week After | Expiration Week Q4 | Week After |
|---|---|---|---|---|---|---|---|---|
| 1991 | −6.93 | −89.36 | −34.98 | −58.81 | 33.54 | −13.19 | 20.12 | 167.04 |
| 1992 | 40.48 | −44.95 | −69.01 | −2.94 | 21.35 | −76.73 | 9.19 | 12.97 |
| 1993 | 43.76 | −31.60 | −10.24 | −3.88 | −8.38 | −70.14 | 10.90 | 6.15 |
| 1994 | 32.95 | −120.92 | 3.33 | −139.84 | 58.54 | −101.60 | 116.08 | 26.24 |
| 1995 | 38.04 | 65.02 | 86.80 | 75.05 | 96.85 | −33.42 | 19.87 | −78.76 |
| 1996 | 114.52 | 51.67 | 55.78 | −50.60 | 49.94 | −15.54 | 179.53 | 76.51 |
| 1997 | −130.67 | −64.20 | 14.47 | −108.79 | 174.30 | 4.91 | −82.01 | −76.98 |
| 1998 | 303.91 | −110.35 | −122.07 | 231.67 | 100.16 | 133.11 | 81.87 | 314.36 |
| 1999 | 27.20 | −81.31 | 365.05 | −303.00 | −224.80 | −524.30 | 32.73 | 148.33 |
| 2000 | 666.41 | 517.49 | −164.76 | −44.55 | −293.65 | −79.63 | −277.95 | 200.60 |
| 2001 | −821.21 | −318.63 | −353.36 | −19.05 | −1369.70 | 611.75 | 224.19 | 101.65 |
| 2002 | 34.74 | −179.56 | −220.42 | −10.53 | −326.67 | −284.57 | 77.61 | −207.54 |
| 2003 | 662.26 | −376.20 | 83.63 | −211.70 | 173.27 | −331.74 | 236.06 | 46.45 |
| 2004 | −53.48 | 26.37 | 6.31 | −44.57 | −28.61 | −237.22 | 106.70 | 177.20 |
| 2005 | −144.69 | −186.80 | 110.44 | −325.23 | −36.62 | −222.35 | 97.01 | 7.68 |
| 2006 | 203.31 | 0.32 | 122.63 | −25.46 | 168.66 | −52.67 | 138.03 | −102.30 |
| 2007 | −165.91 | 370.60 | 215.09 | −279.22 | 377.67 | 75.44 | 110.80 | −84.78 |
| 2008 | 410.23 | −144.92 | −464.66 | −496.18 | −33.55 | −245.31 | −50.57 | −63.56 |
| 2009 | 54.40 | 497.80 | −259.53 | −101.34 | 214.79 | −155.01 | −142.61 | 191.21 |
| 2010 | 117.29 | 108.38 | 239.57 | −306.83 | 145.08 | 252.41 | 81.59 | 81.58 |
| 2011 | −185.88 | 362.07 | 52.45 | −69.78 | 516.96 | −737.61 | −317.87 | 427.61 |
| 2012 | 310.60 | −151.89 | 212.97 | −126.39 | −13.90 | −142.34 | 55.83 | −252.73 |
| 2013 | 117.04 | −2.08 | −270.78 | 110.20 | 75.03 | −192.85 | 465.78 | 257.27 |
| 2014 | 237.10 | 20.29 | 171.34 | −95.24 | 292.23 | −166.59 | 523.97 | 248.91 |
| 2015 | 378.34 | −414.99 | 117.11 | −69.27 | −48.51 | −69.91 | −136.66 | 423.62 |
| 2016 | 388.99 | −86.57 | −190.18 | −274.41 | 38.35 | 137.65 | 86.56 | 90.40 |
| 2017 | 11.64 | −317.90 | 112.31 | 10.48 | 470.55 | 81.25 | 322.58 | 102.32 |
| 2018 | −389.23 | −1413.31 | −226.05 | −509.59 | 588.83 | −285.19 | −1655.14 | 617.03 |
| 2019 | 398.63 | −346.55 | 629.52 | −119.17 | −284.45 | −114.82 | 319.71 | 190.17 |
| 2020 | −4011.64 | 2462.80 | 265.92 | −855.91 | −8.22 | −483.46 | 132.68 | 20.82 |
| 2021 | −150.67 | 444.91 | −1189.52 | 1143.76 | −22.84 | 213.12 | −605.55 | 585.12 |
| 2022 | 1810.74 | 106.31 | | | | | | |
| Up | 22 | 13 | 18 | 5 | 18 | 8 | 23 | 24 |
| Down | 10 | 19 | 13 | 26 | 13 | 23 | 8 | 7 |

108

# NOVEMBER

*ading Thanksgiving Market: Long into Weakness Prior,*
*xit into Strength (Page 106)*

**MONDAY**

D 42.9
S 47.6
N 52.4
**20**

*ll stocks whenever the market is 30% higher over a year ago.*
— Eugene D. Brody (Oppenheimer Capital)

**TUESDAY**

D 42.9
S 47.6
N 52.4
**21**

*'hat's money? A man is a success if he gets up in the morning and goes to bed at night and in between does what he wants to do.*
— Bob Dylan (American singer-songwriter, musician and artist, b. 1941)

**WEDNESDAY**

D 57.1
S 52.4
N 61.9
**22**

*ost people can bear adversity. But if you wish to know what a man really is, give him power.*
— Robert G. Ingersoll (American lawyer, politician and orator, "The Great Agnostic," 1833-1899)

**hanksgiving** *(Market Closed)*

**THURSDAY**

**23**

*wering genius disdains a beaten path. It scorns to tread in the footsteps of any predecessor, however illustrious. It thirsts for distinction.*
— Abraham Lincoln (16th U.S. President, 1809-1865)

*hortened Trading Day)*

🐂 **FRIDAY**

D 66.7
S 61.9
N 61.9
**24**

*l great truths begin as blasphemies.*
— George Bernard Shaw (Irish dramatist, 1856-1950)

**SATURDAY**

**25**

*ecember Almanac Investor Sector Seasonalities: See Pages 94, 96 and 98*

**SUNDAY**

**26**

# DECEMBER ALMANAC

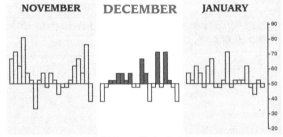

| NOVEMBER | DECEMBER | JANUARY |
|----------|----------|---------|

| DECEMBER | | | | | | | JANUARY | | | | | | |
|---|---|---|---|---|---|---|---|---|---|---|---|---|---|
| S | M | T | W | T | F | S | S | M | T | W | T | F | S |
|   |   |   |   |   | 1 | 2 |   | 1 | 2 | 3 | 4 | 5 | 6 |
| 3 | 4 | 5 | 6 | 7 | 8 | 9 | 7 | 8 | 9 | 10 | 11 | 12 | 13 |
| 10 | 11 | 12 | 13 | 14 | 15 | 16 | 14 | 15 | 16 | 17 | 18 | 19 | 20 |
| 17 | 18 | 19 | 20 | 21 | 22 | 23 | 21 | 22 | 23 | 24 | 25 | 26 | 27 |
| 24 | 25 | 26 | 27 | 28 | 29 | 30 | 28 | 29 | 30 | 31 |   |   |   |
| 31 |   |   |   |   |   |   |   |   |   |   |   |   |   |

*Market Probability Chart above is a graphic representation of the S&P 500 Recent Market Probability Calendar on page 126.*

◆ #3 S&P (+1.5%) and Dow (+1.6%) month since 1950 (page 52), #3 NASDAQ (+1.7%) since 1971 ◆ 2018 worst December since 1931, down over 8% Dow and S&P, –9.5% on NASDAQ (pages 156, 162 & 166) ◆ "Free lunch" served on Wall Street before Christmas (page 116) ◆ Small caps start to outperform larger caps near middle of month (pages 112 and 114) ◆ "Santa Claus Rally" visible in graph above and on page 118 ◆ In 1998 was part of best fourth quarter since 1928 (page 180) ◆ Fourth quarter expiration week most bullish triple witching week, Dow up 23 of last 31 (page 108) ◆ Pre-election years Decembers rankings: #3 Dow, #3 S&P and #1 NASDAQ.

## December Vital Statistics

| | DJIA | S&P 500 | NASDAQ | Russell 1K | Russell 2K |
|---|---|---|---|---|---|
| Rank | 3 | 3 | 3 | 3 | 2 |
| Up | 51 | 54 | 31 | 33 | 33 |
| Down | 21 | 18 | 20 | 10 | 10 |
| Avg % Change | 1.6% | 1.5% | 1.7% | 1.4% | 2.3% |
| Pre-Election Year | 2.7% | 2.9% | 4.2% | 2.9% | 3.0% |
| **Best and Worst** | | | | | |
| | % Change | % Change | % Change | % Change | % Change |
| Best | 1991 9.5 | 1991 11.2 | 1999 22.0 | 1991 11.2 | 1999 11.2 |
| Worst | 2018 –8.7 | 2018 –9.2 | 2002 –9.7 | 2018 –9.3 | 2018 –12.0 |
| **Best and Worst Weeks** | | | | | |
| Best | 12/2/11 7.0 | 12/2/11 7.4 | 12/8/00 10.3 | 12/2/11 7.4 | 12/2/11 10.3 |
| Worst | 12/4/87 –7.5 | 12/6/74 –7.1 | 12/15/00 –9.1 | 12/21/18 –7.1 | 12/21/18 –8.4 |
| **Best and Worst Days** | | | | | |
| Best | 12/26/18 5.0 | 12/16/08 5.1 | 12/5/00 10.5 | 12/16/08 5.2 | 12/16/08 6.7 |
| Worst | 12/1/08 –7.7 | 12/1/08 –8.9 | 12/1/08 –9.0 | 12/1/08 –9.1 | 12/1/08 –11.9 |
| **First Trading Day of Expiration Week: 1980–2022** | | | | | |
| Record (#Up–#Down) | 24-18 | 24-18 | 19-23 | 24-18 | 18-24 |
| Current Streak | D2 | D2 | D1 | D2 | D1 |
| Avg % Change | 0.09 | 0.06 | –0.10 | 0.03 | –0.24 |
| **Options Expiration Day: 1980–2022** | | | | | |
| Record (#Up–#Down) | 25-17 | 28-14 | 27-15 | 28-14 | 26-16 |
| Current Streak | D2 | D2 | D2 | D2 | U1 |
| Avg % Change | 0.15 | 0.23 | 0.22 | 0.23 | 0.34 |
| **Options Expiration Week: 1980–2022** | | | | | |
| Record (#Up–#Down) | 31-11 | 29-13 | 24-18 | 28-14 | 22-20 |
| Current Streak | D1 | D1 | D1 | D1 | D1 |
| Avg % Change | 0.51 | 0.54 | 0.13 | 0.50 | 0.43 |
| **Week After Options Expiration: 1980–2022** | | | | | |
| Record (#Up–#Down) | 31-10 | 27-15 | 29-13 | 27-15 | 30-12 |
| Current Streak | U9 | U1 | U9 | U1 | U2 |
| Avg % Change | 0.83 | 0.61 | 0.82 | 0.64 | 0.98 |
| **First Trading Day Performance** | | | | | |
| % of Time Up | 47.2 | 48.6 | 56.9 | 48.8 | 48.8 |
| Avg % Change | –0.05 | –0.03 | 0.08 | –0.05 | –0.18 |
| **Last Trading Day Performance** | | | | | |
| % of Time Up | 52.8 | 59.7 | 68.6 | 51.2 | 62.8 |
| Avg % Change | 0.07 | 0.09 | 0.26 | –0.05 | 0.34 |

*Dow & S&P 1950-May 13, 2022, NASDAQ 1971-May 13, 2022, Russell 1K & 2K 1979-May 13, 2022.*

*If Santa Claus should fail to call,*
*Bears may come to Broad and Wall.*

# NOVEMBER/DECEMBER

### 🐂 MONDAY
D 71.4
S 66.7
N 71.4
**27**

*he CROWD is always wrong at market turning points but often times right once a trend sets in. The reason many*
*arket fighters go broke is they believe the CROWD is always wrong. There is nothing further from the truth.*
*nless volatility is extremely low or very high one should think twice before betting against the CROWD.*
— Shawn Andrew (Trader, Ricercar Fund /SA, 12/21/01)

### TUESDAY
D 61.9
S 57.1
N 57.1
**28**

*ou have to keep digging, keep asking questions, because otherwise you'll be seduced or brainwashed*
*to the idea that it's somehow a great privilege, an honor, to report the lies they've been feeding you.*
— David Halberstam (American writer, war reporter, 1964 Pulitzer Prize, 1934-2007)

### 🐂 WEDNESDAY
D 66.7
S 76.2
N 71.4
**29**

*order to be a great writer (or "investor") a person must have a built-in, shockproof crap detector.*
— Ernest Hemingway (American writer, 1954 Nobel Prize, 1899-1961)

*ast Trading Day of November, S&P Down 16 of Last 24*

### 🐻 THURSDAY
D 52.4
S 38.1
N 42.9
**30**

*ducation is our passport to the future, for tomorrow belongs only to the people who prepare for it today.*
— Malcom X (Minister, human rights activist and civil rights leader, 1925-1965)

*rst Trading Day in December, NASDAQ Up 22 of 35, But Down 7 of Last 10*

### 🐻 FRIDAY
D 42.9
S 38.1
N 47.6
**1**

*e're not believers that the government is bigger than the business cycle.*
— David Rosenberg (Economist, Merrill Lynch, *Barron's* 4/21/2008)

### SATURDAY
**2**

### SUNDAY
**3**

# MOST OF THE SO-CALLED "JANUARY EFFECT" TAKES PLACE IN THE LAST HALF OF DECEMBER

Over the years we reported annually on the fascinating January Effect, showing that small-cap stocks handily outperformed large-cap stocks during January 40 out of 43 years between 1953 and 1995. Readers saw that "Cats and Dogs" on average quadrupled the returns of blue chips in this period. Then, the January Effect disappeared over the next four years.

Looking at the graph on page 114, comparing the Russell 1000 index of large capitalization stocks to the Russell 2000 smaller capitalization stocks, shows small cap stocks beginning to outperform the blue chips in mid-December. Narrowing the comparison down to half-month segments was an inspiration and proved to be quite revealing, as you can see in the table below.

### 35-YEAR AVERAGE RATES OF RETURN (DEC 1987 TO FEB 2022)

| | Russell 1000 | | Russell 2000 | |
|---|---|---|---|---|
| Mid-Dec* | Change | Annualized | Change | Annualized |
| 12/15-12/31 | 1.6% | 43.9% | 2.9% | 92.5% |
| 12/15-01/15 | 1.9 | 24.1 | 3.4 | 46.7 |
| 12/15-01/31 | 2.0 | 17.5 | 3.3 | 30.2 |
| 12/15-02/15 | 3.2 | 20.8 | 5.2 | 35.5 |
| 12/15-02/28 | 2.3 | 12.1 | 4.6 | 25.4 |
| | | | | |
| End-Dec* | | | | |
| 12/31-01/15 | 0.4 | 8.7 | 0.5 | 11.0 |
| 12/31-01/31 | 0.5 | 6.2 | 0.4 | 4.9 |
| 12/31-02/15 | 1.6 | 13.3 | 2.3 | 19.6 |
| 12/31-02/28 | 0.7 | 4.5 | 1.7 | 11.2 |

### 43-YEAR AVERAGE RATES OF RETURN (DEC 1979 TO FEB 2022)

| | Russell 1000 | | Russell 2000 | |
|---|---|---|---|---|
| Mid-Dec* | Change | Annualized | Change | Annualized |
| 12/15-12/31 | 1.5% | 40.6% | 2.6% | 80.0% |
| 12/15-01/15 | 2.1 | 26.9 | 3.8 | 53.3 |
| 12/15-01/31 | 2.3 | 20.3 | 3.8 | 35.4 |
| 12/15-02/15 | 3.4 | 22.2 | 5.6 | 38.7 |
| 12/15-02/28 | 2.6 | 13.5 | 5.2 | 28.5 |
| | | | | |
| End-Dec* | | | | |
| 12/31-01/15 | 0.7 | 15.8 | 1.1 | 25.8 |
| 12/31-01/31 | 0.9 | 11.4 | 1.2 | 15.4 |
| 12/31-02/15 | 1.9 | 16.0 | 2.9 | 25.2 |
| 12/31-02/28 | 1.2 | 7.8 | 2.5 | 16.8 |

*Mid-month dates are the 11th trading day of the month; month end dates are monthly closes.*

Small-cap strength in the last half of December became even more magnified after the 1987 market crash. Note the shift in gains in the last half of December during the 35-year period starting in 1987, versus the 43 years from 1979 to 2022. With all the beaten-down small stocks being dumped for tax loss purposes, it generally pays to get a head start on the January Effect in mid-December. You don't have to wait until December either; the small-cap sector often begins to turnaround near the beginning of November.

# DECEMBER

**MONDAY**

D 38.1
S 47.6
N 52.4

**4**

*he principles of successful stock speculation are based on the supposition that people*
*ll continue in the future to make the mistakes that they have made in the past.*
— Thomas F. Woodlock (*Wall Street Journal* editor & columnist, quoted in *Reminiscences of a Stock Operator*, 1866-1945)

**TUESDAY**

D 61.9
S 52.4
N 61.9

**5**

*l has fostered massive corruption in almost every country that has been "blessed" with it,*
*d the expectation that oil wealth will transform economies has lead to disastrous policy choices.*
— Ted Tyson (Chief Investment Officer, Mastholm Asset Management)

*mall Cap Strength Starts in Mid-December (Pages 112 and 114)*

**WEDNESDAY**

D 52.4
S 52.4
N 66.7

**6**

*he average man is always waiting for something to happen to him instead of setting to work to make things happen.*
*r one person who dreams of making 50,000 pounds, a hundred people dream of being left 50,000 pounds.*
— A. A. Milne (British author, *Winnie-the-Pooh*, 1882-1956)

**THURSDAY**

D 61.9
S 57.1
N 52.4

**7**

*me traders are born with an innate discipline. Most have to learn it the hard way.*
— J. Welles Wilder Jr. (Creator of several technical indicators including Relative Strength Index (RSI) 1935-2021)

**hanukah**

**FRIDAY**

D 57.1
S 57.1
N 61.9

**8**

*the stock market those who expect history to repeat itself exactly are doomed to failure.*
Yale Hirsch (Creator of *Stock Trader's Almanac*, 1923-2021)

**SATURDAY**

**9**

**SUNDAY**

**10**

# JANUARY EFFECT NOW STARTS IN MID-DECEMBER

Small-cap stocks tend to outperform big caps in January. Known as the "January Effect," the tendency is clearly revealed by the graph below. Daily data for the Russell 2000 index of smaller companies are divided by the Russell 1000 index of largest companies since July 1, 1979, and then compressed into a single year to show an idealized yearly pattern. When the graph is descending, big blue chips are outperforming smaller companies; when the graph is rising, smaller companies are moving up faster than their larger brethren.

In a typical year the smaller fry stay on the sidelines while the big boys are on the field. Then, around early November, small stocks begin to wake up and in mid-December, they take off. Anticipated year-end dividends, payouts and bonuses could be a factor. Other major moves are quite evident just before Labor Day—possibly because individual investors are back from vacations. Small caps tend to hold the lead through the beginning of May, though the bulk of the move is complete by early March.

## RUSSELL 2000/RUSSELL 1000 ONE-YEAR SEASONAL PATTERN

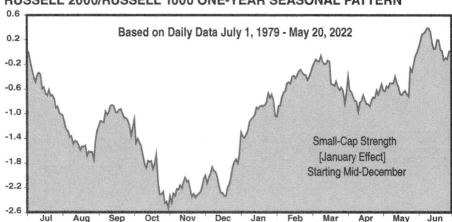

The bottom graph shows the actual ratio of the Russell 2000 divided by the Russell 1000 from 1979. Smaller companies had the upper hand for five years into 1983 as the major bear trend wound to a close and the nascent bull market logged its first year. After falling behind for about eight years, they came back after the Persian Gulf War bottom in 1990, moving up until 1994 when big caps ruled the latter stages of the millennial bull. For six years the picture was bleak for small fry as the blue chips and tech stocks moved to stratospheric PE ratios. Small caps spiked in late 2020 and early 2021 and have been in retreat since. Note how the small cap advantage has waned during major bull moves and intensified during periods of uncertainty as traders may begin bargain hunting early.

## RUSSELL 2000/RUSSELL 1000 (1979 TO APRIL 2022)

# DECEMBER

*Monday Before December Triple Witching S&P Up 13 of Last 22,*
*2018 Down 2.1%*

**MONDAY**

D 47.6
S 52.4
N 61.9

**11**

---

*I have a dream that my four little children will one day live in a nation*
*where they will not be judged by the color of their skin but by the content of their character.*
*— Martin Luther King Jr. (Civil rights leader, 1964 Nobel Peace Prize, 1929-1968)*

**TUESDAY**

D 57.1
S 57.1
N 52.4

**12**

---

*On [TV financial news programs], if the stock is near its high, 90% of the guests like it,*
*if it is near its lows, 90% of the guests hate it.*
*— Michael L. Burke (Investors Intelligence, May 2002, 1935-2014)*

*December Triple Witching Week, S&P Up 28 of Last 38, 2018 Down 7.1%*
*FOMC Meeting (2 Days)*

**WEDNESDAY**

D 57.1
S 47.6
N 42.9

**13**

---

*The finest thought runs the risk of being irrevocably forgotten if we do not write it down.*
*— Arthur Schopenhauer (German philosopher, 1788-1860)*

**THURSDAY**

D 52.4
S 47.6
N 52.4

**14**

---

*Charts not only tell what was, they tell what is; and a trend from was to is*
*projected linearly into the will be) contains better percentages than clumsy guessing.*
*— Robert A. Levy (Chairman, Cato Institute, founder, CDA Investment Technologies,*
*The Relative Strength Concept of Common Stock Forecasting, 1968, b. 1941)*

*December Triple Witching Day, S&P Up 26 of Last 40, 2018 -2.1%*

**FRIDAY**

D 66.7
S 66.7
N 66.7

**15**

---

*The average bottom-of-the-ladder person is potentially as creative as the top executive who sits in the big office. The problem*
*that the person on the bottom of the ladder doesn't trust his own brilliance and doesn't, therefore, believe in his own ideas.*
*— Robert Schuller (Minister)*

*The Only FREE LUNCH on Wall Street is Served (Page 116)*
*Almanac Investors Emailed Alert Before the Open, Monday (See Insert)*

**SATURDAY**

**16**

---

**SUNDAY**

**17**

# WALL STREET'S ONLY "FREE LUNCH" SERVED BEFORE CHRISTMAS

Investors tend to get rid of their losers near year-end for tax purposes, often hammering these stocks down to bargain levels. Over the years the *Almanac* has shown that NYSE stocks selling at their lows on December 15 will usually outperform the market by February 15 in the following year. Preferred stocks, closed-end funds, splits and new issues are eliminated.

## BARGAIN STOCKS VS. THE MARKET*

| Short Span* Late Dec–Jan/Feb | New Lows Late Dec | % Change Jan/Feb | % Change NYSE Composite | Bargain Stocks Advantage |
|---|---|---|---|---|
| 1974–75 | 112 | 48.9% | 22.1% | 26.8% |
| 1975–76 | 21 | 34.9 | 14.9 | 20.0 |
| 1976–77 | 2 | 1.3 | –3.3 | 4.6 |
| 1977–78 | 15 | 2.8 | –4.5 | 7.3 |
| 1978–79 | 43 | 11.8 | 3.9 | 7.9 |
| 1979–80 | 5 | 9.3 | 6.1 | 3.2 |
| 1980–81 | 14 | 7.1 | –2.0 | 9.1 |
| 1981–82 | 21 | –2.6 | –7.4 | 4.8 |
| 1982–83 | 4 | 33.0 | 9.7 | 23.3 |
| 1983–84 | 13 | –3.2 | –3.8 | 0.6 |
| 1984–85 | 32 | 19.0 | 12.1 | 6.9 |
| 1985–86 | 4 | –22.5 | 3.9 | –26.4 |
| 1986–87 | 22 | 9.3 | 12.5 | –3.2 |
| 1987–88 | 23 | 13.2 | 6.8 | 6.4 |
| 1988–89 | 14 | 30.0 | 6.4 | 23.6 |
| 1989–90 | 25 | –3.1 | –4.8 | 1.7 |
| 1990–91 | 18 | 18.8 | 12.6 | 6.2 |
| 1991–92 | 23 | 51.1 | 7.7 | 43.4 |
| 1992–93 | 9 | 8.7 | 0.6 | 8.1 |
| 1993–94 | 10 | –1.4 | 2.0 | –3.4 |
| 1994–95 | 25 | 14.6 | 5.7 | 8.9 |
| 1995–96 | 5 | –11.3 | 4.5 | –15.8 |
| 1996–97 | 16 | 13.9 | 11.2 | 2.7 |
| 1997–98 | 29 | 9.9 | 5.7 | 4.2 |
| 1998–99 | 40 | –2.8 | 4.3 | –7.1 |
| 1999–00 | 26 | 8.9 | –5.4 | 14.3 |
| 2000–01 | 51 | 44.4 | 0.1 | 44.3 |
| 2001–02 | 12 | 31.4 | –2.3 | 33.7 |
| 2002–03 | 33 | 28.7 | 3.9 | 24.8 |
| 2003–04 | 15 | 16.7 | 2.3 | 14.4 |
| 2004–05 | 36 | 6.8 | –2.8 | 9.6 |
| 2005–06 | 71 | 12.0 | 2.6 | 9.4 |
| 2006–07 | 43 | 5.1 | –0.5 | 5.6 |
| 2007–08 | 71 | –3.2 | –9.4 | 6.2 |
| 2008–09 | 88 | 11.4 | –2.4 | 13.8 |
| 2009–10 | 25 | 1.8 | –3.0 | 4.8 |
| 2010–11 | 20 | 8.3 | 3.4 | 4.9 |
| 2011–12 | 65 | 18.1 | 6.1 | 12.0 |
| 2012–13 | 17 | 20.9 | 3.4 | 17.5 |
| 2013–14 | 18 | 25.7 | 1.7 | 24.0 |
| 2014–15 | 17 | 0.2 | –0.4 | 0.6 |
| 2015–16 | 38 | –9.2 | 5.6 | –14.8 |
| 2016–17 | 19 | 2.8 | 0.6 | 2.2 |
| 2017–18 | 18 | 3.3 | 1.2 | 2.1 |
| 2018–19 | 23 | 24.9 | 15.1 | 9.8 |
| 2019–20 | 13 | –1.1 | –0.3 | –0.7 |
| 2020–21 | 3 | –4.9 | 3.6 | –8.5 |
| 2021–22 | 26 | –1.5 | –0.02 | –1.5 |
| **48-Year Totals** | | **542.3%** | **149.9%** | **392.3%** |
| **Average** | | **11.3%** | **3.1%** | **8.2%** |

*\* Dec 15 to Feb 15 (1974–1999), Dec 1999–2022 based on actual newsletter portfolio.*

In response to changing market conditions we tweaked the strategy the last 23 years adding selections from NASDAQ and AMEX, and selling in mid-January some years. We email the list of stocks to our *Almanac Investor* e-newsletter subscribers. Visit *www.stocktradersalmanac.com* or see the insert for additional details and a special offer for new subscribers.

We have come to the conclusion that the most prudent course of action is to compile our list from the stocks making new lows on Triple-Witching Friday before Christmas, capitalizing on the Santa Claus Rally (page 118). This also gives us the weekend to evaluate the issues in greater depth and weed out any glaringly problematic stocks. Subscribers will receive the list of stocks selected from the new lows made on December 16, 2022 and December 15, 2023 via email.

This "Free Lunch" strategy is an extremely short-term strategy reserved for the nimblest traders. It has performed better after market corrections and when there are more new lows to choose from. The object is to buy bargain stocks near their 52-week lows and sell any quick, generous gains, as these issues can be real dogs.

# DECEMBER

**MONDAY**

D 47.6
S 57.1
N 57.1

**18**

*Big money is made in the stock market by being on the right side of major moves. I don't believe in swimming against the tide.*
— Martin Zweig (Fund manager, *Winning on Wall Street*, 1943-2013)

🐻 **TUESDAY**

D 33.3
S 38.1
N 33.3

**19**

*Another factor contributing to productivity is technology, particularly the rapid introduction of new microcomputers based on single-chip circuits.... The results over the next decade will be a second industrial revolution.*
— Yale Hirsch (Creator of *Stock Trader's Almanac, Smart Money Newsletter* 9/22/1976, 1923-2021)

### Week After December Triple Witching Dow Up 24 of Last 31, Average Gain 0.9% Since 1991

**WEDNESDAY**

D 47.6
S 47.6
N 42.9

**20**

*If more of us valued food and cheer and song above hoarded gold, it would be a merrier world.*
— J. R. R. Tolkien (English writer, poet, philologist, and academic, *The Hobbit*, 1892-1973)

🦃 **THURSDAY**

D 71.4
S 71.4
N 61.9

**21**

*We like what's familiar, and we dislike change. So, we push the familiar until it starts working against us big-time—a crisis. Then, MAYBE we can accept change.*
— Kevin Cameron (Journalist, *Cycle World* April 2013)

### Santa Claus Rally Begins December 22 (Page 118)
### Last Trading Day Before Christmas, NASDAQ Up 11 of Last 15, 2018 Down 2.2%

**FRIDAY**

D 42.9
S 47.6
N 61.9

**22**

*Only buy stocks when the market declines 10% from that date a year ago, which happens once or twice a decade.*
— Eugene D. Brody (Oppenheimer Capital)

**SATURDAY**

**23**

**SUNDAY**

**24**

# IF SANTA CLAUS SHOULD FAIL TO CALL, BEARS MAY COME TO BROAD AND WALL

Santa Claus tends to come to Wall Street nearly every year, bringing a short, sweet, respectable rally within the last five days of the year and the first two in January. This has been good for an average 1.3% gain since 1969 (1.3% since 1950). Santa's failure to show tends to precede bear markets, or times stocks could be purchased later in the year at much lower prices. We discovered this phenomenon in 1972.

## DAILY % CHANGE IN S&P 500 AT YEAR END

| | Trading Days Before Year End | | | | | | First Days in January | | | Rally % Change |
|------|------|------|------|------|------|------|------|------|------|------|
| | 6 | 5 | 4 | 3 | 2 | 1 | 1 | 2 | 3 | |
| 1969 | −0.4 | 1.1 | 0.8 | −0.7 | 0.4 | 0.5 | 1.0 | 0.5 | −0.7 | 3.6 |
| 1970 | 0.1 | 0.6 | 0.5 | 1.1 | 0.2 | −0.1 | −1.1 | 0.7 | 0.6 | 1.9 |
| 1971 | −0.4 | 0.2 | 1.0 | 0.3 | −0.4 | 0.3 | −0.4 | 0.4 | 1.0 | 1.3 |
| 1972 | −0.3 | −0.7 | 0.6 | 0.4 | 0.5 | 1.0 | 0.9 | 0.4 | −0.1 | 3.1 |
| 1973 | −1.1 | −0.7 | 3.1 | 2.1 | −0.2 | 0.01 | 0.1 | 2.2 | −0.9 | 6.7 |
| 1974 | −1.4 | 1.4 | 0.8 | −0.4 | 0.03 | 2.1 | 2.4 | 0.7 | 0.5 | 7.2 |
| 1975 | 0.7 | 0.8 | 0.9 | −0.1 | −0.4 | 0.5 | 0.8 | 1.8 | 1.0 | 4.3 |
| 1976 | 0.1 | 1.2 | 0.7 | −0.4 | 0.5 | 0.5 | −0.4 | −1.2 | −0.9 | 0.8 |
| 1977 | 0.8 | 0.9 | N/C | 0.1 | 0.2 | 0.2 | −1.3 | −0.3 | −0.8 | −0.3 |
| 1978 | 0.03 | 1.7 | 1.3 | −0.9 | −0.4 | −0.2 | 0.6 | 1.1 | 0.8 | 3.3 |
| 1979 | −0.6 | 0.1 | 0.1 | 0.2 | −0.1 | 0.1 | −2.0 | −0.5 | 1.2 | −2.2 |
| 1980 | −0.4 | 0.4 | 0.5 | −1.1 | 0.2 | 0.3 | 0.4 | 1.2 | 0.1 | 2.0 |
| 1981 | −0.5 | 0.2 | −0.2 | −0.5 | 0.5 | 0.2 | 0.2 | −2.2 | −0.7 | −1.8 |
| 1982 | 0.6 | 1.8 | −1.0 | 0.3 | −0.7 | 0.2 | −1.6 | 2.2 | 0.4 | 1.2 |
| 1983 | −0.2 | −0.03 | 0.9 | 0.3 | −0.2 | 0.05 | −0.5 | 1.7 | 1.2 | 2.1 |
| 1984 | −0.5 | 0.8 | −0.2 | −0.4 | 0.3 | 0.6 | −1.1 | −0.5 | −0.5 | −0.6 |
| 1985 | −1.1 | −0.7 | 0.2 | 0.9 | 0.5 | 0.3 | −0.8 | 0.6 | −0.1 | 1.1 |
| 1986 | −1.0 | 0.2 | 0.1 | −0.9 | −0.5 | −0.5 | 1.8 | 2.3 | 0.2 | 2.4 |
| 1987 | 1.3 | −0.5 | −2.6 | −0.4 | 1.3 | −0.3 | 3.6 | 1.1 | 0.1 | 2.2 |
| 1988 | −0.2 | 0.3 | −0.4 | 0.1 | 0.8 | −0.6 | −0.9 | 1.5 | 0.2 | 0.9 |
| 1989 | 0.6 | 0.8 | −0.2 | 0.6 | 0.5 | 0.8 | 1.8 | −0.3 | −0.9 | 4.1 |
| 1990 | 0.5 | −0.6 | 0.3 | −0.8 | 0.1 | 0.5 | −1.1 | −1.4 | −0.3 | −3.0 |
| 1991 | 2.5 | 0.6 | 1.4 | 0.4 | 2.1 | 0.5 | 0.04 | 0.5 | −0.3 | 5.7 |
| 1992 | −0.3 | 0.2 | −0.1 | −0.3 | 0.2 | −0.7 | −0.1 | −0.2 | 0.04 | −1.1 |
| 1993 | 0.01 | 0.7 | 0.1 | −0.1 | −0.4 | −0.5 | −0.2 | 0.3 | 0.1 | −0.1 |
| 1994 | 0.01 | 0.2 | 0.4 | −0.3 | 0.1 | −0.4 | −0.03 | 0.3 | −0.1 | 0.2 |
| 1995 | 0.8 | 0.2 | 0.4 | 0.04 | −0.1 | 0.3 | 0.8 | 0.1 | −0.6 | 1.8 |
| 1996 | −0.3 | 0.5 | 0.6 | 0.1 | −0.4 | −1.7 | −0.5 | 1.5 | −0.1 | 0.1 |
| 1997 | −1.5 | −0.7 | 0.4 | 1.8 | 1.8 | −0.04 | 0.5 | 0.2 | −1.1 | 4.0 |
| 1998 | 2.1 | −0.2 | −0.1 | 1.3 | −0.8 | −0.2 | −0.1 | 1.4 | 2.2 | 1.3 |
| 1999 | 1.6 | −0.1 | 0.04 | 0.4 | 0.1 | 0.5 | −1.0 | −3.8 | 0.2 | −4.0 |
| 2000 | 0.8 | 2.4 | 0.7 | 1.0 | 0.4 | −1.0 | −2.8 | 5.0 | −1.1 | 5.7 |
| 2001 | 0.4 | −0.02 | 0.4 | 0.7 | 0.3 | −1.1 | 0.6 | 0.9 | 0.6 | 1.8 |
| 2002 | 0.2 | −0.5 | −0.3 | −1.6 | 0.5 | 0.05 | 3.3 | −0.05 | 2.2 | 1.2 |
| 2003 | 0.3 | −0.2 | 0.2 | 1.2 | 0.01 | 0.2 | −0.3 | 1.2 | 0.1 | 2.4 |
| 2004 | 0.1 | −0.4 | 0.7 | −0.01 | 0.01 | −0.1 | −0.8 | −1.2 | −0.4 | −1.8 |
| 2005 | 0.4 | 0.04 | −1.0 | 0.1 | −0.3 | −0.5 | 1.6 | 0.4 | 0.002 | 0.4 |
| 2006 | −0.4 | −0.5 | 0.4 | 0.7 | −0.1 | −0.5 | −0.1 | 0.1 | −0.6 | 0.003 |
| 2007 | 1.7 | 0.8 | 0.1 | −1.4 | 0.1 | −0.7 | −1.4 | N/C | −2.5 | −2.5 |
| 2008 | −1.0 | 0.6 | 0.5 | −0.4 | 2.4 | 1.4 | 3.2 | −0.5 | 0.8 | 7.4 |
| 2009 | 0.2 | 0.5 | 0.1 | −0.1 | 0.02 | −1.0 | 1.6 | 0.3 | 0.05 | 1.4 |
| 2010 | −0.2 | 0.1 | 0.1 | 0.1 | −0.2 | −0.02 | 1.1 | −0.1 | 0.5 | 1.1 |
| 2011 | 0.8 | 0.9 | 0.01 | −1.3 | 1.1 | −0.4 | 1.6 | 0.02 | 0.3 | 1.9 |
| 2012 | −0.9 | −0.2 | −0.5 | −0.1 | −1.1 | 1.7 | 2.5 | −0.2 | 0.5 | 2.0 |
| 2013 | 0.5 | 0.3 | 0.5 | −0.03 | −0.02 | 0.4 | −0.9 | −0.03 | −0.3 | 0.2 |
| 2014 | 0.2 | −0.01 | 0.3 | 0.1 | −0.5 | −1.0 | −0.03 | −1.8 | −0.9 | −3.0 |
| 2015 | 1.2 | −0.2 | −0.2 | 1.1 | −0.7 | −0.9 | −1.5 | 0.2 | −1.3 | −2.3 |
| 2016 | −0.2 | 0.1 | 0.2 | −0.8 | −0.03 | −0.5 | 0.9 | 0.6 | −0.1 | 0.4 |
| 2017 | 0.2 | −0.05 | −0.1 | 0.1 | 0.2 | −0.5 | 0.8 | 0.6 | 0.4 | 1.1 |
| 2018 | −2.1 | −2.7 | 5.0 | 0.9 | −0.1 | 0.9 | 0.1 | −2.5 | 3.4 | 1.3 |
| 2019 | 0.1 | −0.02 | 0.5 | 0.003 | −0.6 | 0.3 | 0.8 | −0.7 | 0.4 | 0.3 |
| 2020 | 0.1 | 0.4 | 0.9 | −0.2 | 0.1 | 0.6 | −1.5 | 0.7 | 0.6 | 1.0 |
| 2021 | 0.6 | 1.4 | −0.1 | 0.1 | −0.3 | −0.3 | 0.6 | −0.1 | −1.9 | 1.4 |
| Avg | 0.09 | 0.25 | 0.35 | 0.06 | 0.13 | 0.02 | 0.21 | 0.29 | 0.04 | 1.3 |

The couplet above was certainly on the mark in 1999, as the period suffered a horrendous 4.0% loss. On January 14, 2000, the Dow started its 33-month 37.8% slide to the October 2002 midterm election year bottom. NASDAQ cracked eight weeks later falling 37.3% in 10 weeks, eventually dropping 77.9% by October 2002. Energy prices and Middle East terror woes may have grounded Santa in 2004. In 2007 the third worst reading since 1950 was recorded as a full-blown financial crisis lead to the second worst bear market in history. In 2016, the period was hit again as global growth concerns escalated and the market digested the first interest rate hike in nearly a decade.

# DECEMBER

**Christmas Day** *(Market Closed)*

MONDAY
## 25

---

*Each day is a building block to the future. Who I am today is dependent on who I was yesterday.*
— Matthew McConaughey (Actor, *Parade Magazine*)

🐃 TUESDAY

D 71.4
S 71.4
N 66.7
## 26

---

*The death of contrarians has been greatly exaggerated. The reason is that the crowd is the market for most of any cycle. You cannot be contrarian all the time, otherwise you end up simply fighting the tape the whole way up (or down), therefore being wildly wrong.*
— Barry L. Ritholtz (Founder/CIO Ritholtz Wealth Management, Bloomberg View 12/20/2013, b. 1961)

WEDNESDAY

D 47.6
S 52.4
N 42.9
## 27

---

*Over time, you weed out luck.*
— Billy Beane (American baseball player and general manager, b. 1962)

THURSDAY

D 42.9
S 47.6
N 42.9
## 28

---

*Throughout the centuries there were men who took first steps down new roads armed with nothing but their own vision.*
— Ayn Rand (Russian-born American novelist and philosopher, *The Fountainhead*, 1943, 1905-1982)

Last Trading Day of the Year, NASDAQ Down 16 of last 22
NASDAQ Was Up 29 Years in a Row 1971-1999

🐻 FRIDAY

D 42.9
S 38.1
N 28.6
## 29

---

*Remember to look up at the stars and not down at your feet.*
— Professsor Stephen Hawking (English theoretical physicist, cosmologist, and author, 1942-2018)

SATURDAY
## 30

---

January Almanac Investor Sector Seasonalities: See Pages 94, 96 and 98

SUNDAY
## 31

# 2024 STRATEGY CALENDAR

### (Option expiration dates circled)

| | MONDAY | TUESDAY | WEDNESDAY | THURSDAY | FRIDAY | SATURDAY | SUNDAY |
|---|---|---|---|---|---|---|---|
| **JANUARY** | 1 JANUARY New Year's Day | 2 | 3 | 4 | 5 | 6 | 7 |
| | 8 | 9 | 10 | 11 | 12 | 13 | 14 |
| | 15 Martin Luther King Day | 16 | 17 | 18 | ⑲ | 20 | 21 |
| | 22 | 23 | 24 | 25 | 26 | 27 | 28 |
| | 29 | 30 | 31 | 1 FEBRUARY | 2 | 3 | 4 |
| **FEBRUARY** | 5 | 6 | 7 | 8 | 9 | 10 | 11 |
| | 12 | 13 | 14 ♥ Ash Wednesday | 15 | ⑯ | 17 | 18 |
| | 19 Presidents' Day | 20 | 21 | 22 | 23 | 24 | 25 |
| | 26 | 27 | 28 | 29 | 1 MARCH | 2 | 3 |
| **MARCH** | 4 | 5 | 6 | 7 | 8 | 9 | 10 Daylight Saving Time Begins |
| | 11 | 12 | 13 | 14 | ⑮ | 16 | 17 ♣ St. Patrick's Day |
| | 18 | 19 | 20 | 21 | 22 Passover | 23 | 24 |
| | 25 | 26 | 27 | 28 | 29 Good Friday | 30 | 31 Easter |
| **APRIL** | 1 APRIL | 2 | 3 | 4 | 5 | 6 | 7 |
| | 8 | 9 | 10 | 11 | 12 | 13 | 14 |
| | 15 Tax Deadline | 16 | 17 | 18 | ⑲ | 20 | 21 |
| | 22 | 23 | 24 | 25 | 26 | 27 | 28 |
| | 29 | 30 | 1 MAY | 2 | 3 | 4 | 5 |
| **MAY** | 6 | 7 | 8 | 9 | 10 | 11 | 12 Mother's Day |
| | 13 | 14 | 15 | 16 | ⑰ | 18 | 19 |
| | 20 | 21 | 22 | 23 | 24 | 25 | 26 |
| | 27 Memorial Day | 28 | 29 | 30 | 31 | 1 JUNE | 2 |
| **JUNE** | 3 | 4 | 5 | 6 | 7 | 8 | 9 |
| | 10 | 11 | 12 | 13 | 14 | 15 | 16 Father's Day |
| | 17 | 18 | 19 Juneteenth | 20 | ㉑ | 22 | 23 |
| | 24 | 25 | 26 | 27 | 28 | 29 | 30 |

*Market closed on shaded weekdays; closes early when half-shaded.*

# 2024 STRATEGY CALENDAR

## (Option expiration dates circled)

| MONDAY | TUESDAY | WEDNESDAY | THURSDAY | FRIDAY | SATURDAY | SUNDAY | |
|---|---|---|---|---|---|---|---|
| 1 JULY | 2 | 3 | 4 Independence Day | 5 | 6 | 7 | JULY |
| 8 | 9 | 10 | 11 | 12 | 13 | 14 | |
| 15 | 16 | 17 | 18 | (19) | 20 | 21 | |
| 22 | 23 | 24 | 25 | 26 | 27 | 28 | |
| 29 | 30 | 31 | 1 AUGUST | 2 | 3 | 4 | |
| 5 | 6 | 7 | 8 | 9 | 10 | 11 | AUGUST |
| 12 | 13 | 14 | 15 | (16) | 17 | 18 | |
| 19 | 20 | 21 | 22 | 23 | 24 | 25 | |
| 26 | 27 | 28 | 29 | 30 | 31 | 1 SEPTEMBER | |
| 2 Labor Day | 3 | 4 | 5 | 6 | 7 | 8 | SEPTEMBER |
| 9 | 10 | 11 | 12 | 13 | 14 | 15 | |
| 16 | 17 | 18 | 19 | (20) | 21 | 22 | |
| 23 | 24 | 25 | 26 | 27 | 28 | 29 | |
| 30 | 1 OCTOBER | 2 | 3 Rosh Hashanah | 4 | 5 | 6 | OCTOBER |
| 7 | 8 | 9 | 10 | 11 Yom Kippur | 12 | 13 | |
| 14 Columbus Day | 15 | 16 | 17 | (18) | 19 | 20 | |
| 21 | 22 | 23 | 24 | 25 | 26 | 27 | |
| 28 | 29 | 30 | 31 | 1 NOVEMBER | 2 | 3 Daylight Saving Time Ends | NOVEMBER |
| 4 | 5 Election Day | 6 | 7 | 8 | 9 | 10 | |
| 11 Veterans' Day | 12 | 13 | 14 | (15) | 16 | 17 | |
| 18 | 19 | 20 | 21 | 22 | 23 | 24 | |
| 25 | 26 | 27 | 28 Thanksgiving | 29 | 30 | 1 DECEMBER | DECEMBER |
| 2 | 3 | 4 | 5 | 6 | 7 | 8 | |
| 9 | 10 | 11 | 12 | 13 | 14 | 15 | |
| 16 | 17 | 18 | 19 | (20) | 21 | 22 | |
| 23 | 24 | 25 Chanukah Christmas | 26 | 27 | 28 | 29 | |
| 30 | 31 | 1 JANUARY New Year's Day | 2 | 3 | 4 | 5 | |

# DIRECTORY OF TRADING PATTERNS AND DATABANK

## CONTENTS

# DOW JONES INDUSTRIALS MARKET PROBABILITY CALENDAR 2023

## THE % CHANCE OF THE MARKET RISING ON ANY TRADING DAY OF THE YEAR*

(Based on the number of times the DJIA rose on a particular trading day during January 1953 to December 2021.)

| Date | Jan | Feb | Mar | Apr | May | Jun | Jul | Aug | Sep | Oct | Nov | Dec |
|------|-----|-----|-----|-----|-----|-----|-----|-----|-----|-----|-----|-----|
| 1 | S | 62.3 | 66.7 | S | 55.1 | 60.9 | S | 43.5 | 56.5 | S | 63.8 | 44.9 |
| 2 | H | 55.1 | 59.4 | S | 63.8 | 55.1 | S | 46.4 | S | 49.3 | 55.1 | S |
| 3 | 59.4 | 43.5 | 58.0 | 59.4 | 52.2 | S | 66.7 | 49.3 | S | 55.1 | 68.1 | S |
| 4 | 71.0 | S | S | 60.9 | 46.4 | S | H | 53.6 | H | 56.5 | S | 52.2 |
| 5 | 49.3 | S | S | 50.7 | 49.3 | 50.7 | 58.0 | S | 62.3 | 60.9 | S | 62.3 |
| 6 | 56.5 | 56.5 | 49.3 | 60.9 | S | 59.4 | 60.9 | S | 59.4 | 44.9 | 58.0 | 58.0 |
| 7 | S | 46.4 | 46.4 | H | S | 55.1 | 56.5 | 55.1 | 43.5 | S | 50.7 | 50.7 |
| 8 | S | 42.0 | 53.6 | S | 55.1 | 47.8 | S | 46.4 | 47.8 | S | 62.3 | 46.4 |
| 9 | 46.4 | 46.4 | 62.3 | S | 47.8 | 36.2 | S | 44.9 | S | 52.2 | 53.6 | S |
| 10 | 49.3 | 60.9 | 52.2 | 50.7 | 50.7 | S | 60.9 | 46.4 | S | 44.9 | 53.6 | S |
| 11 | 47.8 | S | S | 60.9 | 44.9 | S | 58.0 | 49.3 | 46.4 | 42.0 | S | 52.2 |
| 12 | 47.8 | S | S | 60.9 | 55.1 | 52.2 | 52.2 | S | 59.4 | 49.3 | S | 58.0 |
| 13 | 56.5 | 47.8 | 55.1 | 59.4 | S | 59.4 | 46.4 | S | 60.9 | 59.4 | 47.8 | 46.4 |
| 14 | S | 50.7 | 53.6 | 56.5 | S | 56.5 | 68.1 | 63.8 | 47.8 | S | 47.8 | 49.3 |
| 15 | S | 56.5 | 62.3 | S | 55.1 | 49.3 | S | 56.5 | 56.5 | S | 59.4 | 52.2 |
| 16 | H | 44.9 | 60.9 | S | 44.9 | 50.7 | S | 50.7 | S | 52.2 | 53.6 | S |
| 17 | 55.1 | 47.8 | 56.5 | 71.0 | 49.3 | S | 52.2 | 47.8 | S | 53.6 | 46.4 | S |
| 18 | 60.9 | S | S | 62.3 | 44.9 | S | 46.4 | 53.6 | 58.0 | 46.4 | S | 55.1 |
| 19 | 42.0 | S | S | 56.5 | 50.7 | H | 50.7 | S | 42.0 | 59.4 | S | 46.4 |
| 20 | 40.6 | H | 52.2 | 53.6 | S | 50.7 | 55.1 | S | 49.3 | 44.9 | 47.8 | 53.6 |
| 21 | S | 49.3 | 42.0 | 53.6 | S | 44.9 | 39.1 | 40.6 | 44.9 | S | 56.5 | 53.6 |
| 22 | S | 40.6 | 42.0 | S | 43.5 | 47.8 | S | 59.4 | 39.1 | S | 63.8 | 59.4 |
| 23 | 40.6 | 47.8 | 46.4 | S | 36.2 | 43.5 | S | 50.7 | S | 43.5 | H | S |
| 24 | 46.4 | 60.9 | 36.2 | 50.7 | 52.2 | S | 44.9 | 52.2 | S | 50.7 | 60.9 | S |
| 25 | 56.5 | S | S | 59.4 | 44.9 | S | 59.4 | 49.3 | 49.3 | 30.4 | S | H |
| 26 | 58.0 | S | S | 56.5 | 44.9 | 36.2 | 53.6 | S | 55.1 | 53.6 | S | 71.0 |
| 27 | 49.3 | 44.9 | 50.7 | 52.2 | S | 49.3 | 46.4 | S | 52.2 | 52.2 | 66.7 | 49.3 |
| 28 | S | 46.4 | 47.8 | 47.8 | S | 46.4 | 56.5 | 44.9 | 49.3 | S | 59.4 | 53.6 |
| 29 | S | | 53.6 | S | H | 55.1 | S | 63.8 | 42.0 | S | 55.1 | 53.6 |
| 30 | 59.4 | | 46.4 | S | 56.5 | 56.5 | S | 42.0 | S | 60.9 | 52.2 | S |
| 31 | 55.1 | | 42.0 | | 55.1 | | 49.3 | 58.0 | | 52.2 | | S |

*See new trends developing on pages 72, 86, 143-148.*

# RECENT DOW JONES INDUSTRIALS MARKET PROBABILITY CALENDAR 2023

## THE % CHANCE OF THE MARKET RISING ON ANY TRADING DAY OF THE YEAR*

(Based on the number of times the DJIA rose on a particular trading day during January 2001 to December 2021.**)

| Date | Jan | Feb | Mar | Apr | May | Jun | Jul | Aug | Sep | Oct | Nov | Dec |
|------|-----|-----|-----|-----|-----|-----|-----|-----|-----|-----|-----|-----|
| 1 | S | 81.0 | 61.9 | S | 57.1 | 76.2 | S | 33.3 | 42.9 | S | 66.7 | 42.9 |
| 2 | H | 47.6 | 33.3 | S | 66.7 | 61.9 | S | 52.4 | S | 52.4 | 66.7 | S |
| 3 | 66.7 | 52.4 | 57.1 | 61.9 | 42.9 | S | 76.2 | 52.4 | S | 38.1 | 66.7 | S |
| 4 | 61.9 | S | S | 71.4 | 42.9 | S | H | 52.4 | H | 71.4 | S | 38.1 |
| 5 | 52.4 | S | S | 47.6 | 61.9 | 42.9 | 38.1 | S | 76.2 | 61.9 | S | 61.9 |
| 6 | 52.4 | 61.9 | 47.6 | 66.7 | S | 61.9 | 57.1 | S | 57.1 | 38.1 | 71.4 | 52.4 |
| 7 | S | 47.6 | 52.4 | H | S | 61.9 | 57.1 | 57.1 | 42.9 | S | 66.7 | 61.9 |
| 8 | S | 47.6 | 47.6 | S | 66.7 | 66.7 | S | 52.4 | 52.4 | S | 61.9 | 57.1 |
| 9 | 38.1 | 52.4 | 61.9 | S | 38.1 | 38.1 | S | 47.6 | S | 47.6 | 47.6 | S |
| 10 | 52.4 | 57.1 | 52.4 | 42.9 | 61.9 | S | 57.1 | 33.3 | S | 57.1 | 38.1 | S |
| 11 | 57.1 | S | S | 61.9 | 33.3 | S | 57.1 | 47.6 | 57.1 | 52.4 | S | 47.6 |
| 12 | 47.6 | S | S | 52.4 | 57.1 | 42.9 | 52.4 | S | 71.4 | 38.1 | S | 57.1 |
| 13 | 47.6 | 57.1 | 57.1 | 52.4 | S | 57.1 | 76.2 | S | 66.7 | 61.9 | 61.9 | 57.1 |
| 14 | S | 52.4 | 66.7 | 52.4 | S | 52.4 | 76.2 | 61.9 | 52.4 | S | 47.6 | 52.4 |
| 15 | S | 66.7 | 71.4 | S | 57.1 | 52.4 | S | 57.1 | 61.9 | S | 66.7 | 66.7 |
| 16 | H | 61.9 | 52.4 | S | 52.4 | 61.9 | S | 52.4 | S | 52.4 | 57.1 | S |
| 17 | 52.4 | 42.9 | 66.7 | 71.4 | 38.1 | S | 57.1 | 66.7 | S | 57.1 | 38.1 | S |
| 18 | 57.1 | S | S | 61.9 | 38.1 | S | 47.6 | 47.6 | 81.0 | 52.4 | S | 47.6 |
| 19 | 47.6 | S | S | 61.9 | 47.6 | H | 57.1 | S | 47.6 | 52.4 | S | 33.3 |
| 20 | 42.9 | H | 52.4 | 52.4 | S | 47.6 | 76.2 | S | 52.4 | 33.3 | 42.9 | 47.6 |
| 21 | S | 38.1 | 33.3 | 57.1 | S | 47.6 | 19.0 | 28.6 | 47.6 | S | 42.9 | 71.4 |
| 22 | S | 52.4 | 52.4 | S | 33.3 | 42.9 | S | 61.9 | 28.6 | S | 57.1 | 42.9 |
| 23 | 33.3 | 52.4 | 38.1 | S | 52.4 | 38.1 | S | 52.4 | S | 57.1 | H | S |
| 24 | 42.9 | 57.1 | 33.3 | 42.9 | 47.6 | S | 38.1 | 57.1 | S | 52.4 | 66.7 | S |
| 25 | 57.1 | S | S | 61.9 | 57.1 | S | 61.9 | 47.6 | 42.9 | 47.6 | S | H |
| 26 | 57.1 | S | S | 66.7 | 52.4 | 28.6 | 52.4 | S | 57.1 | 66.7 | S | 71.4 |
| 27 | 52.4 | 42.9 | 61.9 | 66.7 | S | 42.9 | 42.9 | S | 61.9 | 42.9 | 71.4 | 47.6 |
| 28 | S | 28.6 | 47.6 | 28.6 | S | 47.6 | 38.1 | 42.9 | 57.1 | S | 61.9 | 42.9 |
| 29 | S | | 42.9 | S | H | 57.1 | S | 85.7 | 42.9 | S | 66.7 | 42.9 |
| 30 | 47.6 | | 66.7 | S | 61.9 | 52.4 | S | 38.1 | S | 61.9 | 52.4 | S |
| 31 | 42.9 | | 42.9 | | 38.1 | | 38.1 | 52.4 | | 47.6 | | S |

*See new trends developing on pages 72, 86, 143 148. **Based on most recent 21-year period.

124

# S&P 500 MARKET PROBABILITY CALENDAR 2023

## THE % CHANCE OF THE MARKET RISING ON ANY TRADING DAY OF THE YEAR*

(Based on the number of times the S&P 500 rose on a particular trading day during January 1953 to December 2021.)

| Date | Jan | Feb | Mar | Apr | May | Jun | Jul | Aug | Sep | Oct | Nov | Dec |
|------|------|------|------|------|------|------|------|------|------|------|------|------|
| 1 | S | 62.3 | 63.8 | S | 58.0 | 56.5 | S | 46.4 | 59.4 | S | 63.8 | 46.4 |
| 2 | H | 59.4 | 56.5 | S | 65.2 | 63.8 | S | 46.4 | S | 50.7 | 58.0 | S |
| 3 | 49.3 | 49.3 | 60.9 | 62.3 | 55.1 | S | 73.9 | 49.3 | S | 62.3 | 68.1 | S |
| 4 | 68.1 | S | S | 62.3 | 43.5 | S | H | 55.1 | H | 58.0 | S | 52.2 |
| 5 | 53.6 | S | S | 52.2 | 47.8 | 52.2 | 56.5 | S | 55.1 | 60.9 | S | 59.4 |
| 6 | 52.2 | 52.2 | 47.8 | 58.0 | S | 56.5 | 56.5 | S | 58.0 | 46.4 | 58.0 | 58.0 |
| 7 | S | 49.3 | 47.8 | H | S | 47.8 | 59.4 | 56.5 | 44.9 | S | 49.3 | 46.4 |
| 8 | S | 46.4 | 53.6 | S | 52.2 | 47.8 | S | 46.4 | 47.8 | S | 59.4 | 50.7 |
| 9 | 46.4 | 43.5 | 62.3 | S | 47.8 | 39.1 | S | 50.7 | S | 49.3 | 56.5 | S |
| 10 | 52.2 | 62.3 | 52.2 | 52.2 | 52.2 | S | 60.9 | 46.4 | S | 43.5 | 56.5 | S |
| 11 | 53.6 | S | S | 63.8 | 43.5 | S | 56.5 | 47.8 | 53.6 | 46.4 | S | 53.6 |
| 12 | 53.6 | S | S | 60.9 | 52.2 | 53.6 | 53.6 | S | 59.4 | 50.7 | S | 49.3 |
| 13 | 58.0 | 56.5 | 63.8 | 53.6 | S | 62.3 | 52.2 | S | 65.2 | 55.1 | 47.8 | 46.4 |
| 14 | S | 49.3 | 44.9 | 52.2 | S | 58.0 | 72.5 | 62.3 | 49.3 | S | 49.3 | 42.0 |
| 15 | S | 55.1 | 60.9 | S | 55.1 | 55.1 | S | 62.3 | 55.1 | S | 52.2 | 52.2 |
| 16 | H | 39.1 | 62.3 | S | 49.3 | 49.3 | S | 55.1 | S | 52.2 | 52.2 | S |
| 17 | 60.9 | 50.7 | 55.1 | 62.3 | 50.7 | S | 50.7 | 53.6 | S | 59.4 | 50.7 | S |
| 18 | 59.4 | S | S | 60.9 | 40.6 | S | 44.9 | 52.2 | 56.5 | 46.4 | S | 58.0 |
| 19 | 50.7 | S | S | 59.4 | 47.8 | H | 47.8 | S | 47.8 | 65.2 | S | 43.5 |
| 20 | 50.7 | H | 49.3 | 53.6 | S | 55.1 | 55.1 | S | 52.2 | 47.8 | 52.2 | 46.4 |
| 21 | S | 42.0 | 42.0 | 53.6 | S | 43.5 | 39.1 | 44.9 | 44.9 | S | 56.5 | 50.7 |
| 22 | S | 42.0 | 46.4 | S | 50.7 | 52.2 | S | 60.9 | 36.2 | S | 60.9 | 59.4 |
| 23 | 47.8 | 43.5 | 40.6 | S | 43.5 | 46.4 | S | 47.8 | S | 44.9 | H | S |
| 24 | 58.0 | 58.0 | 49.3 | 49.3 | 53.6 | S | 46.4 | 50.7 | S | 47.8 | 60.9 | S |
| 25 | 55.1 | S | S | 58.0 | 49.3 | S | 56.5 | 49.3 | 47.8 | 33.3 | S | H |
| 26 | 52.2 | S | S | 50.7 | 47.8 | 34.8 | 53.6 | S | 50.7 | 58.0 | S | 71.0 |
| 27 | 43.5 | 49.3 | 43.5 | 50.7 | S | 43.5 | 46.4 | S | 58.0 | 55.1 | 68.1 | 53.6 |
| 28 | S | 52.2 | 49.3 | 53.6 | S | 50.7 | 62.3 | 46.4 | 50.7 | S | 59.4 | 59.4 |
| 29 | S | | 53.6 | S | H | 59.4 | S | 63.8 | 43.5 | S | 60.9 | 60.9 |
| 30 | 62.3 | | 40.6 | S | 56.5 | 53.6 | S | 46.4 | S | 60.9 | 49.3 | S |
| 31 | 60.9 | | 42.0 | | 58.0 | | 59.4 | 62.3 | | 53.6 | | S |

*See new trends developing on pages 72, 86, 143-148.

# RECENT S&P 500 MARKET PROBABILITY CALENDAR 2023

## THE % CHANCE OF THE MARKET RISING ON ANY TRADING DAY OF THE YEAR*

(Based on the number of times the S&P 500 rose on a particular trading day during January 2001 to December 2021.**)

| Date | Jan | Feb | Mar | Apr | May | Jun | Jul | Aug | Sep | Oct | Nov | Dec |
|------|------|------|------|------|------|------|------|------|------|------|------|------|
| 1 | S | 76.2 | 71.4 | S | 66.7 | 66.7 | S | 42.9 | 47.6 | S | 66.7 | 38.1 |
| 2 | H | 57.1 | 33.3 | S | 52.4 | 76.2 | S | 57.1 | S | 57.1 | 71.4 | S |
| 3 | 57.1 | 42.9 | 61.9 | 61.9 | 38.1 | S | 85.7 | 47.6 | S | 42.9 | 61.9 | S |
| 4 | 52.4 | S | S | 76.2 | 47.6 | S | H | 57.1 | H | 71.4 | S | 47.6 |
| 5 | 61.9 | S | S | 47.6 | 57.1 | 47.6 | 42.9 | S | 52.4 | 57.1 | S | 52.4 |
| 6 | 57.1 | 61.9 | 52.4 | 66.7 | S | 57.1 | 61.9 | S | 52.4 | 38.1 | 81.0 | 52.4 |
| 7 | S | 47.6 | 52.4 | H | S | 38.1 | 57.1 | 57.1 | 47.6 | S | 57.1 | 57.1 |
| 8 | S | 61.9 | 42.9 | S | 52.4 | 66.7 | S | 57.1 | 47.6 | S | 52.4 | 57.1 |
| 9 | 47.6 | 52.4 | 61.9 | S | 42.9 | 33.3 | S | 47.6 | S | 42.9 | 33.3 | S |
| 10 | 61.9 | 57.1 | 57.1 | 38.1 | 52.4 | S | 57.1 | 42.9 | S | 57.1 | 52.4 | S |
| 11 | 66.7 | S | S | 71.4 | 33.3 | S | 57.1 | 47.6 | 61.9 | 52.4 | S | 52.4 |
| 12 | 47.6 | S | S | 52.4 | 47.6 | 42.9 | 57.1 | S | 71.4 | 47.6 | S | 57.1 |
| 13 | 47.6 | 71.4 | 66.7 | 61.9 | S | 57.1 | 76.2 | S | 71.4 | 61.9 | 57.1 | 47.6 |
| 14 | S | 61.9 | 42.9 | 52.4 | S | 57.1 | 71.4 | 52.4 | 52.4 | S | 47.6 | 47.6 |
| 15 | S | 66.7 | 57.1 | S | 57.1 | 61.9 | S | 66.7 | 57.1 | S | 57.1 | 66.7 |
| 16 | H | 47.6 | 57.1 | S | 57.1 | 57.1 | S | 61.9 | S | 52.4 | 52.4 | S |
| 17 | 52.4 | 42.9 | 66.7 | 61.9 | 38.1 | S | 33.3 | 66.7 | S | 71.4 | 42.9 | S |
| 18 | 71.4 | S | S | 61.9 | 38.1 | S | 47.6 | 47.6 | 71.4 | 61.9 | S | 57.1 |
| 19 | 47.6 | S | S | 71.4 | 47.6 | H | 57.1 | S | 47.6 | 57.1 | S | 38.1 |
| 20 | 52.4 | H | 42.9 | 57.1 | S | 52.4 | 76.2 | S | 47.6 | 42.9 | 47.6 | 47.6 |
| 21 | S | 33.3 | 28.6 | 47.6 | S | 52.4 | 23.8 | 42.9 | 33.3 | S | 47.6 | 71.4 |
| 22 | S | 38.1 | 52.4 | S | 42.9 | 47.6 | S | 71.4 | 28.6 | S | 52.4 | 47.6 |
| 23 | 52.4 | 57.1 | 33.3 | S | 52.4 | 47.6 | S | 47.6 | S | 71.4 | H | S |
| 24 | 52.4 | 57.1 | 42.9 | 47.6 | 57.1 | S | 52.4 | 52.4 | S | 61.9 | 61.9 | S |
| 25 | 61.9 | S | S | 52.4 | 61.9 | S | 57.1 | 57.1 | 42.9 | 42.9 | S | H |
| 26 | 47.6 | S | S | 57.1 | 57.1 | 28.6 | 52.4 | S | 47.6 | 61.9 | S | 71.4 |
| 27 | 42.9 | 47.6 | 57.1 | 66.7 | S | 47.6 | 38.1 | S | 61.9 | 38.1 | 66.7 | 52.4 |
| 28 | S | 28.6 | 47.6 | 33.3 | S | 47.6 | 57.1 | 52.4 | 57.1 | S | 57.1 | 47.6 |
| 29 | S | | 42.9 | S | H | 61.9 | S | 90.5 | 38.1 | S | 76.2 | 38.1 |
| 30 | 52.4 | | 57.1 | S | 61.9 | 52.4 | S | 42.9 | S | 61.9 | 38.1 | S |
| 31 | 47.6 | | 47.6 | | 52.4 | | 42.9 | 57.1 | | 52.4 | | S |

*See new trends developing on pages 72, 86, 143-149. ** Based on most recent 21-year period.

# NASDAQ COMPOSITE MARKET PROBABILITY CALENDAR 2023

## THE % CHANCE OF THE MARKET RISING ON ANY TRADING DAY OF THE YEAR*

(Based on the number of times the NASDAQ rose on a particular trading day during January 1971 to December 2021.)

| Date | Jan | Feb | Mar | Apr | May | Jun | Jul | Aug | Sep | Oct | Nov | Dec |
|------|------|------|------|------|------|------|------|------|------|------|------|------|
| 1 | S | 70.6 | 64.7 | S | 60.8 | 58.8 | S | 54.9 | 56.9 | S | 66.7 | 56.9 |
| 2 | H | 66.7 | 52.9 | S | 66.7 | 74.5 | S | 43.1 | S | 49.0 | 54.9 | S |
| 3 | 56.9 | 54.9 | 66.7 | 47.1 | 54.9 | S | 64.7 | 52.9 | S | 56.9 | 68.6 | S |
| 4 | 62.7 | S | S | 66.7 | 52.9 | S | H | 60.8 | H | 62.7 | S | 58.8 |
| 5 | 58.8 | S | S | 60.8 | 56.9 | 56.9 | 49.0 | S | 60.8 | 60.8 | S | 64.7 |
| 6 | 64.7 | 64.7 | 49.0 | 54.9 | S | 60.8 | 51.0 | S | 58.8 | 56.9 | 58.8 | 60.8 |
| 7 | S | 52.9 | 49.0 | H | S | 52.9 | 54.9 | 54.9 | 56.9 | S | 52.9 | 49.0 |
| 8 | S | 54.9 | 54.9 | S | 62.7 | 51.0 | S | 43.1 | 52.9 | S | 54.9 | 56.9 |
| 9 | 58.8 | 52.9 | 60.8 | S | 54.9 | 41.2 | S | 49.0 | S | 56.9 | 52.9 | S |
| 10 | 60.8 | 64.7 | 49.0 | 45.1 | 43.1 | S | 60.8 | 47.1 | S | 51.0 | 60.8 | S |
| 11 | 58.8 | S | S | 66.7 | 52.9 | S | 68.6 | 58.8 | 49.0 | 51.0 | S | 49.0 |
| 12 | 58.8 | S | S | 60.8 | 58.8 | 52.9 | 62.7 | S | 52.9 | 66.7 | S | 45.1 |
| 13 | 58.8 | 62.7 | 70.6 | 60.8 | S | 60.8 | 66.7 | S | 60.8 | 62.7 | 54.9 | 43.1 |
| 14 | S | 68.6 | 49.0 | 51.0 | S | 62.7 | 74.5 | 60.8 | 56.9 | S | 51.0 | 41.2 |
| 15 | S | 62.7 | 52.9 | S | 54.9 | 54.9 | S | 56.9 | 41.2 | S | 45.1 | 52.9 |
| 16 | H | 49.0 | 66.7 | S | 56.9 | 51.0 | S | 52.9 | S | 51.0 | 51.0 | S |
| 17 | 60.8 | 52.9 | 58.8 | 58.8 | 47.1 | S | 60.8 | 56.9 | S | 52.9 | 49.0 | S |
| 18 | 72.5 | S | S | 52.9 | 43.1 | S | 49.0 | 51.0 | 54.9 | 45.1 | S | 56.9 |
| 19 | 58.8 | S | S | 62.7 | 49.0 | H | 52.9 | S | 51.0 | 62.7 | S | 49.0 |
| 20 | 47.1 | H | 66.7 | 52.9 | S | 54.9 | 62.7 | S | 60.8 | 52.9 | 52.9 | 51.0 |
| 21 | S | 39.2 | 41.2 | 54.9 | S | 49.0 | 35.3 | 35.3 | 49.0 | S | 52.9 | 62.7 |
| 22 | S | 47.1 | 47.1 | S | 51.0 | 49.0 | S | 70.6 | 43.1 | S | 64.7 | 68.6 |
| 23 | 51.0 | 52.9 | 52.9 | S | 49.0 | 51.0 | S | 52.9 | S | 51.0 | H | S |
| 24 | 58.8 | 64.7 | 51.0 | 52.9 | 54.9 | S | 52.9 | 52.9 | S | 49.0 | 58.8 | S |
| 25 | 49.0 | S | S | 47.1 | 54.9 | S | 56.9 | 54.9 | 51.0 | 37.3 | S | H |
| 26 | 64.7 | S | S | 62.7 | 60.8 | 39.2 | 49.0 | S | 47.1 | 45.1 | S | 70.6 |
| 27 | 56.9 | 56.9 | 49.0 | 66.7 | S | 47.1 | 45.1 | S | 49.0 | 54.9 | 62.7 | 49.0 |
| 28 | S | 49.0 | 47.1 | 58.8 | S | 58.8 | 56.9 | 56.9 | 45.1 | S | 68.6 | 60.8 |
| 29 | S | | 51.0 | S | H | 68.6 | S | 66.7 | 51.0 | S | 66.7 | 68.6 |
| 30 | 54.9 | | 56.9 | S | 56.9 | 68.6 | S | 60.8 | S | 60.8 | 60.8 | S |
| 31 | 62.7 | | 64.7 | | 64.7 | | 49.0 | 64.7 | | 62.7 | | S |

* See new trends developing on pages 72, 86, 143-148.

Based on NASDAQ composite, prior to February 5, 1971, based on National Quotation Bureau indices.

# RECENT NASDAQ COMPOSITE MARKET PROBABILITY CALENDAR 2023

## THE % CHANCE OF THE MARKET RISING ON ANY TRADING DAY OF THE YEAR*

(Based on the number of times the NASDAQ rose on a particular trading day during January 2001 to December 2021.**)

| Date | Jan | Feb | Mar | Apr | May | Jun | Jul | Aug | Sep | Oct | Nov | Dec |
|------|-----|-----|-----|-----|-----|-----|-----|-----|-----|-----|-----|-----|
| 1 | S | 76.2 | 66.7 | S | 66.7 | 57.1 | S | 57.1 | 57.1 | S | 66.7 | 47.6 |
| 2 | H | 52.4 | 38.1 | S | 57.1 | 71.4 | S | 47.6 | S | 52.4 | 61.9 | S |
| 3 | 66.7 | 33.3 | 57.1 | 61.9 | 38.1 | S | 76.2 | 52.4 | S | 47.6 | 61.9 | S |
| 4 | 47.6 | S | S | 71.4 | 52.4 | S | H | 52.4 | H | 76.2 | S | 52.4 |
| 5 | 57.1 | S | S | 52.4 | 52.4 | 52.4 | 42.9 | S | 52.4 | 57.1 | S | 61.9 |
| 6 | 57.1 | 61.9 | 42.9 | 57.1 | S | 57.1 | 61.9 | S | 52.4 | 47.6 | 71.4 | 66.7 |
| 7 | S | 47.6 | 38.1 | H | S | 42.9 | 61.9 | 38.1 | 52.4 | S | 66.7 | 52.4 |
| 8 | S | 61.9 | 42.9 | S | 71.4 | 52.4 | S | 47.6 | 52.4 | S | 52.4 | 61.9 |
| 9 | 66.7 | 57.1 | 52.4 | S | 47.6 | 33.3 | S | 42.9 | S | 52.4 | 33.3 | S |
| 10 | 61.9 | 61.9 | 42.9 | 28.6 | 42.9 | S | 57.1 | 38.1 | S | 57.1 | 61.9 | S |
| 11 | 71.4 | S | S | 71.4 | 42.9 | S | 71.4 | 57.1 | 57.1 | 57.1 | S | 61.9 |
| 12 | 52.4 | S | S | 47.6 | 52.4 | 42.9 | 61.9 | S | 61.9 | 57.1 | S | 52.4 |
| 13 | 42.9 | 71.4 | 66.7 | 71.4 | S | 52.4 | 61.9 | S | 61.9 | 66.7 | 66.7 | 42.9 |
| 14 | S | 81.0 | 42.9 | 42.9 | S | 61.9 | 71.4 | 57.1 | 61.9 | S | 42.9 | 52.4 |
| 15 | S | 66.7 | 47.6 | S | 52.4 | 61.9 | S | 57.1 | 42.9 | S | 47.6 | 66.7 |
| 16 | H | 42.9 | 66.7 | S | 61.9 | 52.4 | S | 61.9 | S | 52.4 | 57.1 | S |
| 17 | 38.1 | 42.9 | 71.4 | 47.6 | 42.9 | S | 47.6 | 61.9 | S | 61.9 | 42.9 | S |
| 18 | 71.4 | S | S | 52.4 | 38.1 | S | 52.4 | 47.6 | 81.0 | 57.1 | S | 57.1 |
| 19 | 52.4 | S | S | 71.4 | 57.1 | H | 61.9 | S | 42.9 | 52.4 | S | 33.3 |
| 20 | 42.9 | H | 66.7 | 42.9 | S | 66.7 | 76.2 | S | 47.6 | 38.1 | 52.4 | 42.9 |
| 21 | S | 38.1 | 42.9 | 52.4 | S | 47.6 | 14.3 | 33.3 | 42.9 | S | 52.4 | 61.9 |
| 22 | S | 42.9 | 61.9 | S | 47.6 | 47.6 | S | 81.0 | 38.1 | S | 61.9 | 61.9 |
| 23 | 42.9 | 52.4 | 42.9 | S | 52.4 | 42.9 | S | 47.6 | S | 66.7 | H | S |
| 24 | 66.7 | 71.4 | 47.6 | 52.4 | 52.4 | S | 47.6 | 52.4 | S | 57.1 | 61.9 | S |
| 25 | 52.4 | S | S | 42.9 | 61.9 | S | 57.1 | 57.1 | 47.6 | 52.4 | S | H |
| 26 | 66.7 | S | S | 47.6 | 61.9 | 23.8 | 57.1 | S | 52.4 | 52.4 | S | 66.7 |
| 27 | 57.1 | 57.1 | 66.7 | 76.2 | S | 52.4 | 42.9 | S | 47.6 | 52.4 | 71.4 | 42.9 |
| 28 | S | 28.6 | 38.1 | 33.3 | S | 66.7 | 66.7 | 52.4 | 38.1 | S | 57.1 | 42.9 |
| 29 | S | | 42.9 | S | H | 66.7 | S | 81.0 | 47.6 | S | 71.4 | 28.6 |
| 30 | 47.6 | | 66.7 | S | 66.7 | 57.1 | S | 61.9 | S | 61.9 | 42.9 | S |
| 31 | 47.6 | | 57.1 | | 52.4 | | 38.1 | 52.4 | | 52.4 | | S |

* See new trends developing on page 72, 86, 140-148. ** Based on most recent 21-year period.

# RUSSELL 1000 INDEX MARKET PROBABILITY CALENDAR 2023

## THE % CHANCE OF THE MARKET RISING ON ANY TRADING DAY OF THE YEAR*

(Based on the number of times the Russell 1000 rose on a particular trading day during January 1979 to December 2021.)

| Date | Jan | Feb | Mar | Apr | May | Jun | Jul | Aug | Sep | Oct | Nov | Dec |
|------|------|------|------|------|------|------|------|------|------|------|------|------|
| 1 | S | 67.4 | 62.8 | S | 58.1 | 60.5 | S | 44.2 | 53.5 | S | 74.4 | 48.8 |
| 2 | H | 60.5 | 46.5 | S | 60.5 | 62.8 | S | 44.2 | S | 55.8 | 58.1 | S |
| 3 | 46.5 | 58.1 | 60.5 | 58.1 | 51.2 | S | 76.7 | 48.8 | S | 53.5 | 60.5 | S |
| 4 | 58.1 | S | S | 65.1 | 39.5 | S | H | 53.5 | H | 60.5 | S | 53.5 |
| 5 | 60.5 | S | S | 53.5 | 48.8 | 51.2 | 44.2 | S | 51.2 | 58.1 | S | 60.5 |
| 6 | 55.8 | 55.8 | 41.9 | 60.5 | S | 58.1 | 48.8 | S | 53.5 | 41.9 | 62.8 | 46.5 |
| 7 | S | 53.5 | 44.2 | H | S | 41.9 | 58.1 | 55.8 | 41.9 | S | 48.8 | 48.8 |
| 8 | S | 53.5 | 53.5 | S | 55.8 | 48.8 | S | 55.8 | 46.5 | S | 58.1 | 51.2 |
| 9 | 53.5 | 46.5 | 60.5 | S | 55.8 | 39.5 | S | 44.2 | S | 51.2 | 46.5 | S |
| 10 | 65.1 | 74.4 | 46.5 | 44.2 | 51.2 | S | 58.1 | 46.5 | S | 39.5 | 55.8 | S |
| 11 | 55.8 | S | S | 69.8 | 51.2 | S | 53.5 | 46.5 | 55.8 | 44.2 | S | 51.2 |
| 12 | 55.8 | S | S | 58.1 | 53.5 | 48.8 | 60.5 | S | 65.1 | 58.1 | S | 48.8 |
| 13 | 55.8 | 67.4 | 62.8 | 51.2 | S | 55.8 | 65.1 | S | 69.8 | 62.8 | 55.8 | 44.2 |
| 14 | S | 51.2 | 41.9 | 48.8 | S | 58.1 | 79.1 | 60.5 | 55.8 | S | 55.8 | 39.5 |
| 15 | S | 62.8 | 58.1 | S | 58.1 | 58.1 | S | 65.1 | 53.5 | S | 53.5 | 60.5 |
| 16 | H | 41.9 | 60.5 | S | 55.8 | 53.5 | S | 60.5 | S | 55.8 | 48.8 | S |
| 17 | 65.1 | 44.2 | 55.8 | 55.8 | 48.8 | S | 48.8 | 62.8 | S | 55.8 | 55.8 | S |
| 18 | 67.4 | S | S | 62.8 | 46.5 | S | 51.2 | 62.8 | 51.2 | 48.8 | S | 58.1 |
| 19 | 44.2 | S | S | 60.5 | 51.2 | H | 48.8 | S | 48.8 | 69.8 | S | 46.5 |
| 20 | 41.9 | H | 48.8 | 48.8 | S | 60.5 | 62.8 | S | 46.5 | 48.8 | 48.8 | 44.2 |
| 21 | S | 37.2 | 39.5 | 53.5 | S | 41.9 | 37.2 | 48.8 | 37.2 | S | 53.5 | 60.5 |
| 22 | S | 44.2 | 48.8 | S | 51.2 | 53.5 | S | 69.8 | 37.2 | S | 58.1 | 60.5 |
| 23 | 48.8 | 46.5 | 41.9 | S | 41.9 | 46.5 | S | 48.8 | S | 48.8 | H | S |
| 24 | 48.8 | 58.1 | 41.9 | 48.8 | 62.8 | S | 44.2 | 55.8 | S | 46.5 | 65.1 | S |
| 25 | 55.8 | S | S | 55.8 | 60.5 | S | 72.1 | 48.8 | 39.5 | 34.9 | S | H |
| 26 | 60.5 | S | S | 55.8 | 55.8 | 32.6 | 51.2 | S | 48.8 | 55.8 | S | 69.8 |
| 27 | 48.8 | 53.5 | 51.2 | 58.1 | S | 41.9 | 44.2 | S | 62.8 | 51.2 | 67.4 | 58.1 |
| 28 | S | 48.8 | 44.2 | 51.2 | S | 51.2 | 62.8 | 53.5 | 55.8 | S | 69.8 | 60.5 |
| 29 | S | | 46.5 | S | H | 62.8 | S | 62.8 | 51.2 | S | 67.4 | 51.2 |
| 30 | 58.1 | | 46.5 | S | 55.8 | 58.1 | S | 51.2 | S | 65.1 | 44.2 | S |
| 31 | 55.8 | | 48.8 | | 53.5 | | 55.8 | 58.1 | | 62.8 | | S |

*See new trends developing on pages 72, 86, 143-148.

# RUSSELL 2000 INDEX MARKET PROBABILITY CALENDAR 2023

## THE % CHANCE OF THE MARKET RISING ON ANY TRADING DAY OF THE YEAR*

(Based on the number of times the Russell 2000 rose on a particular trading day during January 1979 to December 2021.)

| Date | Jan | Feb | Mar | Apr | May | Jun | Jul | Aug | Sep | Oct | Nov | Dec |
|------|-----|-----|-----|-----|-----|-----|-----|-----|-----|-----|-----|-----|
| 1 | S | 67.4 | 67.4 | S | 60.5 | 67.4 | S | 46.5 | 51.2 | S | 62.8 | 48.8 |
| 2 | H | 62.8 | 55.8 | S | 65.1 | 72.1 | S | 46.5 | S | 48.8 | 72.1 | S |
| 3 | 46.5 | 55.8 | 62.8 | 48.8 | 55.8 | S | 67.4 | 48.8 | S | 48.8 | 62.8 | S |
| 4 | 62.8 | S | S | 60.5 | 55.8 | S | H | 53.5 | H | 55.8 | S | 60.5 |
| 5 | 60.5 | S | S | 46.5 | 58.1 | 51.2 | 46.5 | S | 60.5 | 62.8 | S | 62.8 |
| 6 | 60.5 | 65.1 | 51.2 | 55.8 | S | 55.8 | 46.5 | S | 53.5 | 41.9 | 60.5 | 62.8 |
| 7 | S | 58.1 | 58.1 | H | S | 60.5 | 55.8 | 51.2 | 58.1 | S | 55.8 | 48.8 |
| 8 | S | 60.5 | 48.8 | S | 53.5 | 46.5 | S | 46.5 | 55.8 | S | 58.1 | 55.8 |
| 9 | 55.8 | 51.2 | 58.1 | S | 60.5 | 44.2 | S | 55.8 | S | 46.5 | 51.2 | S |
| 10 | 62.8 | 69.8 | 46.5 | 46.5 | 48.8 | S | 51.2 | 46.5 | S | 46.5 | 65.1 | S |
| 11 | 55.8 | S | S | 60.5 | 51.2 | S | 60.5 | 46.5 | 58.1 | 51.2 | S | 48.8 |
| 12 | 65.1 | S | S | 60.5 | 48.8 | 51.2 | 55.8 | S | 60.5 | 62.8 | S | 46.5 |
| 13 | 65.1 | 67.4 | 62.8 | 60.5 | S | 58.1 | 58.1 | S | 62.8 | 58.1 | 46.5 | 41.9 |
| 14 | S | 67.4 | 51.2 | 51.2 | S | 60.5 | 65.1 | 69.8 | 55.8 | S | 48.8 | 39.5 |
| 15 | S | 58.1 | 51.2 | S | 51.2 | 58.1 | S | 58.1 | 41.9 | S | 51.2 | 46.5 |
| 16 | H | 55.8 | 62.8 | S | 58.1 | 51.2 | S | 58.1 | S | 60.5 | 30.2 | S |
| 17 | 62.8 | 44.2 | 65.1 | 55.8 | 51.2 | S | 53.5 | 58.1 | S | 46.5 | 58.1 | S |
| 18 | 72.1 | S | S | 60.5 | 55.8 | S | 48.8 | 46.5 | 51.2 | 51.2 | S | 53.5 |
| 19 | 65.1 | S | S | 60.5 | 53.5 | H | 48.8 | S | 44.2 | 65.1 | S | 60.5 |
| 20 | 37.2 | H | 53.5 | 48.8 | S | 44.2 | 55.8 | S | 41.9 | 51.2 | 46.5 | 58.1 |
| 21 | S | 41.9 | 48.8 | 55.8 | S | 46.5 | 37.2 | 46.5 | 44.2 | S | 37.2 | 67.4 |
| 22 | S | 48.8 | 44.2 | S | 51.2 | 48.8 | S | 67.4 | 39.5 | S | 62.8 | 74.4 |
| 23 | 51.2 | 51.2 | 58.1 | S | 55.8 | 51.2 | S | 46.5 | S | 48.8 | H | S |
| 24 | 55.8 | 58.1 | 46.5 | 53.5 | 62.8 | S | 48.8 | 60.5 | S | 46.5 | 65.1 | S |
| 25 | 48.8 | S | S | 60.5 | 53.5 | S | 62.8 | 62.8 | 44.2 | 34.9 | S | H |
| 26 | 65.1 | S | S | 67.4 | 62.8 | 37.2 | 60.5 | S | 39.5 | 39.5 | S | 65.1 |
| 27 | 51.2 | 62.8 | 55.8 | 55.8 | S | 48.8 | 48.8 | S | 53.5 | 53.5 | 62.8 | 53.5 |
| 28 | S | 51.2 | 48.8 | 58.1 | S | 53.5 | 55.8 | 55.8 | 51.2 | S | 62.8 | 60.5 |
| 29 | S | | 48.8 | S | H | 69.8 | S | 69.8 | 62.8 | S | 67.4 | 62.8 |
| 30 | 51.2 | | 58.1 | S | 62.8 | 67.4 | S | 62.8 | S | 55.8 | 62.8 | S |
| 31 | 69.8 | | 81.4 | | 58.1 | | 60.5 | 67.4 | | 67.4 | | S |

* See new trends developing on pages 72, 86, 143-148.

# DECENNIAL CYCLE: A MARKET PHENOMENON

By arranging each year's market gain or loss so that the first and succeeding years of each decade fall into the same column, certain interesting patterns emerge—strong fifth and eighth years; weak first, seventh, and zero years.

This fascinating phenomenon was first presented by Edgar Lawrence Smith in *Common Stocks and Business Cycles* (William-Frederick Press, 1959). Anthony Gaubis co-pioneered the decennial pattern with Smith.

When Smith first cut graphs of market prices into 10-year segments and placed them above one another, he observed that each decade tended to have three bull market cycles and that the longest and strongest bull markets seemed to favor the middle years of a decade.

Don't place too much emphasis on the decennial cycle nowadays, other than the extraordinary fifth and zero years, as the stock market is more influenced by the quadrennial presidential election cycle, shown on page 132. Also, the last half-century, which has been the most prosperous in U.S. history, has distributed the returns among most years of the decade. Interestingly, NASDAQ suffered its worst bear market ever in a zero year.

Third years have the fifth worst record of the decennial cycle. However, this year is also a pre-election year, the best year of the presidential election cycle. The last four years ending in three that were also pre-election years (2003, 1983, 1963 and 1943) averaged 19.1% for the full-year.

## THE 10-YEAR STOCK MARKET CYCLE
### Annual % Change in Dow Jones Industrial Average
### Year of Decade

| DECADES | 1st | 2nd | 3rd | 4th | 5th | 6th | 7th | 8th | 9th | 10th |
|---|---|---|---|---|---|---|---|---|---|---|
| 1881–1890 | 3.0% | −2.9% | −8.5% | −18.8% | 20.1% | 12.4% | −8.4% | 4.8% | 5.5% | −14.1% |
| 1891–1900 | 17.6 | −6.6 | −24.6 | −0.6 | 2.3 | −1.7 | 21.3 | 22.5 | 9.2 | 7.0 |
| 1901–1910 | −8.7 | −0.4 | −23.6 | 41.7 | 38.2 | −1.9 | −37.7 | 46.6 | 15.0 | −17.9 |
| 1911–1920 | 0.4 | 7.6 | −10.3 | −5.4 | 81.7 | −4.2 | −21.7 | 10.5 | 30.5 | −32.9 |
| 1921–1930 | 12.7 | 21.7 | −3.3 | 26.2 | 30.0 | 0.3 | 28.8 | 48.2 | −17.2 | −33.8 |
| 1931–1940 | −52.7 | −23.1 | 66.7 | 4.1 | 38.5 | 24.8 | −32.8 | 28.1 | −2.9 | −12.7 |
| 1941–1950 | −15.4 | 7.6 | 13.8 | 12.1 | 26.6 | −8.1 | 2.2 | −2.1 | 12.9 | 17.6 |
| 1951–1960 | 14.4 | 8.4 | −3.8 | 44.0 | 20.8 | 2.3 | −12.8 | 34.0 | 16.4 | −9.3 |
| 1961–1970 | 18.7 | −10.8 | 17.0 | 14.6 | 10.9 | −18.9 | 15.2 | 4.3 | −15.2 | 4.8 |
| 1971–1980 | 6.1 | 14.6 | −16.6 | −27.6 | 38.3 | 17.9 | −17.3 | −3.1 | 4.2 | 14.9 |
| 1981–1990 | −9.2 | 19.6 | 20.3 | −3.7 | 27.7 | 22.6 | 2.3 | 11.8 | 27.0 | −4.3 |
| 1991–2000 | 20.3 | 4.2 | 13.7 | 2.1 | 33.5 | 26.0 | 22.6 | 16.1 | 25.2 | −6.2 |
| 2001–2010 | −7.1 | −16.8 | 25.3 | 3.1 | −0.6 | 16.3 | 6.4 | −33.8 | 18.8 | 11.0 |
| 2011–2020 | 5.5 | 7.3 | 26.5 | 7.5 | −2.2 | 13.4 | 25.1 | −5.6 | 22.3 | 7.2 |
| 2021–2030 | 18.7 | | | | | | | | | |
| **Total % Change** | 24.3% | 30.4% | 92.6% | 99.3% | 365.8% | 101.2% | −6.8% | 182.3% | 151.7% | −68.7% |
| **Avg % Change** | 1.6% | 2.2% | 6.6% | 7.1% | 26.1% | 7.2% | −0.5% | 13.0% | 10.8% | −4.9% |
| Up Years | 10 | 8 | 7 | 9 | 12 | 9 | 8 | 10 | 11 | 6 |
| Down Years | 5 | 6 | 7 | 5 | 2 | 5 | 6 | 4 | 3 | 8 |

*Based on annual close; Cowles indices 1881–1885; 12 Mixed Stocks, 10 Rails, 2 Inds 1886–1889; 20 Mixed Stocks, 18 Rails, 2 Inds 1890–1896; Railroad average 1897 (First industrial average published May 26, 1896).*

# PRESIDENTIAL ELECTION/STOCK MARKET CYCLE: THE 189-YEAR SAGA CONTINUES

It is no mere coincidence that the last two years (pre-election year and election year) of the 40 administrations since 1833 produced a total net market gain of 772.0%, dwarfing the 345.3% gain of the first two years of these administrations.

Presidential elections every four years have a profound impact on the economy and the stock market. Wars, recessions, and bear markets tend to start or occur in the first half of the term; prosperous times and bull markets, in the latter half. After nine straight annual Dow gains during the millennial bull, the four-year election cycle reasserted its overarching domination of market behavior until 2008. Recovery from the worst recession since the Great Depression produced six straight annual gains, until 2015, when the Dow suffered its first pre-election year loss since 1939.

## STOCK MARKET ACTION SINCE 1833
### Annual % Change In Dow Jones Industrial Average[1]

| 4-Year Cycle Beginning | Elected President | Post-Election Year | Mid-Term Year | Pre-Election Year | Election Year |
|---|---|---|---|---|---|
| 1833 | Jackson (D) | −0.9 | 13.0 | 3.1 | −11.7 |
| 1837 | Van Buren (D) | −11.5 | 1.6 | −12.3 | 5.5 |
| 1841* | W.H. Harrison (W)** | −13.3 | −18.1 | 45.0 | 15.5 |
| 1845* | Polk (D) | 8.1 | −14.5 | 1.2 | −3.6 |
| 1849* | Taylor (W) | N/C | 18.7 | −3.2 | 19.6 |
| 1853* | Pierce (D) | −12.7 | −30.2 | 1.5 | 4.4 |
| 1857 | Buchanan (D) | −31.0 | 14.3 | −10.7 | 14.0 |
| 1861* | Lincoln (R) | −1.8 | 55.4 | 38.0 | 6.4 |
| 1865 | Lincoln (R)** | −8.5 | 3.6 | 1.6 | 10.8 |
| 1869 | Grant (R) | 1.7 | 5.6 | 7.3 | 6.8 |
| 1873 | Grant (R) | −12.7 | 2.8 | −4.1 | −17.9 |
| 1877 | Hayes (R) | −9.4 | 6.1 | 43.0 | 18.7 |
| 1881 | Garfield (R)** | 3.0 | −2.9 | −8.5 | −18.8 |
| 1885* | Cleveland (D) | 20.1 | 12.4 | −8.4 | 4.8 |
| 1889* | B. Harrison (R) | 5.5 | −14.1 | 17.6 | −6.6 |
| 1893* | Cleveland (D) | −24.6 | −0.6 | 2.3 | −1.7 |
| 1897* | McKinley (R) | 21.3 | 22.5 | 9.2 | 7.0 |
| 1901 | McKinley (R)** | −8.7 | −0.4 | −23.6 | 41.7 |
| 1905 | T. Roosevelt (R) | 38.2 | −1.9 | −37.7 | 46.6 |
| 1909 | Taft (R) | 15.0 | −17.9 | 0.4 | 7.6 |
| 1913* | Wilson (D) | −10.3 | −5.4 | 81.7 | −4.2 |
| 1917 | Wilson (D) | −21.7 | 10.5 | 30.5 | −32.9 |
| 1921* | Harding (R)** | 12.7 | 21.7 | −3.3 | 26.2 |
| 1925 | Coolidge (R) | 30.0 | 0.3 | 28.8 | 48.2 |
| 1929 | Hoover (R) | −17.2 | −33.8 | −52.7 | −23.1 |
| 1933* | F. Roosevelt (D) | 66.7 | 4.1 | 38.5 | 24.8 |
| 1937 | F. Roosevelt (D) | −32.8 | 28.1 | −2.9 | −12.7 |
| 1941 | F. Roosevelt (D) | −15.4 | 7.6 | 13.8 | 12.1 |
| 1945 | F. Roosevelt (D)** | 26.6 | −8.1 | 2.2 | −2.1 |
| 1949 | Truman (D) | 12.9 | 17.6 | 14.4 | 8.4 |
| 1953* | Eisenhower (R) | −3.8 | 44.0 | 20.8 | 2.3 |
| 1957 | Eisenhower (R) | −12.8 | 34.0 | 16.4 | −9.3 |
| 1961* | Kennedy (D)** | 18.7 | −10.8 | 17.0 | 14.6 |
| 1965 | Johnson (D) | 10.9 | −18.9 | 15.2 | 4.3 |
| 1969* | Nixon (R) | −15.2 | 4.8 | 6.1 | 14.6 |
| 1973 | Nixon (R)*** | −16.6 | −27.6 | 38.3 | 17.9 |
| 1977* | Carter (D) | −17.3 | −3.1 | 4.2 | 14.9 |
| 1981* | Reagan (R) | −9.2 | 19.6 | 20.3 | −3.7 |
| 1985 | Reagan (R) | 27.7 | 22.6 | 2.3 | 11.8 |
| 1989 | G. H. W. Bush (R) | 27.0 | −4.3 | 20.3 | 4.2 |
| 1993* | Clinton (D) | 13.7 | 2.1 | 33.5 | 26.0 |
| 1997 | Clinton (D) | 22.6 | 16.1 | 25.2 | −6.2 |
| 2001* | G. W. Bush (R) | −7.1 | −16.8 | 25.3 | 3.1 |
| 2005 | G. W. Bush (R) | −0.6 | 16.3 | 6.4 | −33.8 |
| 2009* | Obama (D) | 18.8 | 11.0 | 5.5 | 7.3 |
| 2013 | Obama (D) | 26.5 | 7.5 | −2.2 | 13.4 |
| 2017* | Trump (R) | 25.1 | −5.6 | 22.3 | 7.2 |
| 2021* | Biden (D) | 18.7 | | | |
| **Total % Gain** | | 156.4% | 188.9% | 489.6% | 282.4% |
| **Average % Gain** | | 3.3% | 4.0% | 10.4% | 6.0% |
| # Up | | 23 | 28 | 35 | 32 |
| # Down | | 24 | 19 | 12 | 15 |

*Party in power ousted    **Death in office    ***Resigned    D–Democrat, W–Whig, R–Republican
[1] Based on annual close; Prior to 1886 based on Cowles and other indices; 12 Mixed Stocks, 10 Rails, 2 Inds 1886–1889; 20 Mixed Stocks, 18 Rails, 2 Inds 1890–1896; Railroad average 1897 (First industrial average published May 20, 1896).

# DOW JONES INDUSTRIALS BULL AND BEAR MARKETS SINCE 1900

Bear markets begin at the end of one bull market and end at the start of the next bull market (10/9/07 to 3/9/09 as an example). The longest bull market on record ended on 7/17/98, and the shortest bear market on record ended on 3/23/2020, when the new bull market began. The greatest bull super cycle in history that began 8/12/82 ended in 2000 after the Dow gained 1409% and NASDAQ climbed 3072%. The Dow gained only 497% in the eight-year super bull from 1921 to the top in 1929. NASDAQ suffered its worst loss ever from the 2000 top to the 2002 bottom, down 77.9%, nearly as much as the 89.2% drop in the Dow from the 1929 top to the 1932 bottom. The third-longest Dow bull since 1900 that began 10/9/02 ended on its fifth anniversary. The ensuing bear market was the second worst bear market since 1900, slashing the Dow 53.8%. At press time, the Dow is currently in a bear market, trading around 32,000. Surging inflation has caused the Fed to accelerate raising interest rates. (See page 134 for S&P 500 and NASDAQ bulls and bears.)

## DOW JONES INDUSTRIALS BULL AND BEAR MARKETS SINCE 1900

| — Beginning — | | — Ending — | | Bull | | Bear | |
|---|---|---|---|---|---|---|---|
| Date | DJIA | Date | DJIA | % Gain | Days | % Change | Days |
| 9/24/00 | 38.80 | 6/17/01 | 57.33 | 47.8% | 266 | −46.1% | 875 |
| 11/9/03 | 30.88 | 1/19/06 | 75.45 | 144.3 | 802 | −48.5 | 665 |
| 11/15/07 | 38.83 | 11/19/09 | 73.64 | 89.6 | 735 | −27.4 | 675 |
| 9/25/11 | 53.43 | 9/30/12 | 68.97 | 29.1 | 371 | −24.1 | 668 |
| 7/30/14 | 52.32 | 11/21/16 | 110.15 | 110.5 | 845 | −40.1 | 393 |
| 12/19/17 | 65.95 | 11/3/19 | 119.62 | 81.4 | 684 | −46.6 | 660 |
| 8/24/21 | 63.90 | 3/20/23 | 105.38 | 64.9 | 573 | −18.6 | 221 |
| 10/27/23 | 85.76 | 9/3/29 | 381.17 | 344.5 | 2138 | −47.9 | 71 |
| 11/13/29 | 198.69 | 4/17/30 | 294.07 | 48.0 | 155 | −86.0 | 813 |
| 7/8/32 | 41.22 | 9/7/32 | 79.93 | 93.9 | 61 | −37.2 | 173 |
| 2/27/33 | 50.16 | 2/5/34 | 110.74 | 120.8 | 343 | −22.8 | 171 |
| 7/26/34 | 85.51 | 3/10/37 | 194.40 | 127.3 | 958 | −49.1 | 386 |
| 3/31/38 | 98.95 | 11/12/38 | 158.41 | 60.1 | 226 | −23.3 | 147 |
| 4/8/39 | 121.44 | 9/12/39 | 155.92 | 28.4 | 157 | −40.4 | 959 |
| 4/28/42 | 92.92 | 5/29/46 | 212.50 | 128.7 | 1492 | −23.2 | 353 |
| 5/17/47 | 163.21 | 6/15/48 | 193.16 | 18.4 | 395 | −16.3 | 363 |
| 6/13/49 | 161.60 | 1/5/53 | 293.79 | 81.8 | 1302 | −13.0 | 252 |
| 9/14/53 | 255.49 | 4/6/56 | 521.05 | 103.9 | 935 | −19.4 | 564 |
| 10/22/57 | 419.79 | 1/5/60 | 685.47 | 63.3 | 805 | −17.4 | 294 |
| 10/25/60 | 566.05 | 12/13/61 | 734.91 | 29.8 | 414 | −27.1 | 195 |
| 6/26/62 | 535.76 | 2/9/66 | 995.15 | 85.7 | 1324 | −25.2 | 240 |
| 10/7/66 | 744.32 | 12/3/68 | 985.21 | 32.4 | 788 | −35.9 | 539 |
| 5/26/70 | 631.16 | 4/28/71 | 950.82 | 50.6 | 337 | −16.1 | 209 |
| 11/23/71 | 797.97 | 1/11/73 | 1051.70 | 31.8 | 415 | −45.1 | 694 |
| 12/6/74 | 577.60 | 9/21/76 | 1014.79 | 75.7 | 655 | −26.9 | 525 |
| 2/28/78 | 742.12 | 9/8/78 | 907.74 | 22.3 | 192 | −16.4 | 591 |
| 4/21/80 | 759.13 | 4/27/81 | 1024.05 | 34.9 | 371 | −24.1 | 472 |
| 8/12/82 | 776.92 | 11/29/83 | 1287.20 | 65.7 | 474 | −15.6 | 238 |
| 7/24/84 | 1086.57 | 8/25/87 | 2722.42 | 150.6 | 1127 | −36.1 | 55 |
| 10/19/87 | 1738.74 | 7/17/90 | 2999.75 | 72.5 | 1002 | −21.2 | 86 |
| 10/11/90 | 2365.10 | 7/17/98 | 9337.97 | 294.8 | 2836 | −19.3 | 45 |
| 8/31/98 | 7539.07 | 1/14/00 | 11722.98 | 55.5 | 501 | −29.7 | 616 |
| 9/21/01 | 8235.81 | 3/19/02 | 10635.25 | 29.1 | 179 | −31.5 | 204 |
| 10/9/02 | 7286.27 | 10/9/07 | 14164.53 | 94.4 | 1826 | −53.8 | 517 |
| 3/9/09 | 6547.05 | 4/29/11 | 12810.54 | 95.7 | 781 | −16.8 | 157 |
| 10/3/11 | 10655.30 | 5/19/15 | 18312.39 | 71.9 | 1324 | −14.5 | 268 |
| 2/11/16 | 15660.18 | 2/12/20 | 29551.42 | 88.7 | 1462 | −37.1 | 40 |
| 3/23/20 | 18591.93 | 1/4/22 | 36799.65 | 97.9 | 652 | −18.8* | 164* |
| 6/17/22 | 29888.78 | | | | | | |
| | | | *As of June 30, 2022 – not in averages | | | | |
| | | **Average** | | **86.0%** | **787** | **−30.8%** | **389** |

*Based on Dow Jones industrial average.*
1900–2000 Data: Ned Davis Research
*The NYSE was closed from 7/31/1914 to 12/11/1914 due to World War I.*
*DJIA figures were then adjusted back to reflect the composition change from 12 to 20 stocks in September 1916.*

# STANDARD & POOR'S 500 BULL & BEAR MARKETS SINCE 1929 NASDAQ COMPOSITE SINCE 1971

A constant debate of the definition and timing of bull and bear markets permeates Wall Street like the bell that signals the open and close of every trading day. We have relied on the Ned Davis Research parameters for years to track bulls and bears on the Dow (see page 133). Standard & Poor's 500 index has been a stalwart indicator for decades and at times marched to a slightly different beat than the Dow. The moves of the S&P 500 and NASDAQ have been correlated to the bull and bear dates on page 133. Many dates line up for the three indices, but you will notice quite a lag or lead on several occasions, including NASDAQ's independent cadence from 1975 to 1980.

## STANDARD & POOR'S 500 BULL AND BEAR MARKETS

| — Beginning — | | — Ending — | | Bull | | Bear | |
|---|---|---|---|---|---|---|---|
| Date | S&P 500 | Date | S&P 500 | % Gain | Days | % Change | Days |
| 11/13/29 | 17.66 | 4/10/30 | 25.92 | 46.8% | 148 | −83.0% | 783 |
| 6/1/32 | 4.40 | 9/7/32 | 9.31 | 111.6 | 98 | −40.6 | 173 |
| 2/27/33 | 5.53 | 2/6/34 | 11.82 | 113.7 | 344 | −31.8 | 401 |
| 3/14/35 | 8.06 | 3/6/37 | 18.68 | 131.8 | 723 | −49.0 | 390 |
| 3/31/38 | 8.50 | 11/9/38 | 13.79 | 62.2 | 223 | −26.2 | 150 |
| 4/8/39 | 10.18 | 10/25/39 | 13.21 | 29.8 | 200 | −43.5 | 916 |
| 4/28/42 | 7.47 | 5/29/46 | 19.25 | 157.7 | 1492 | −28.8 | 353 |
| 5/17/47 | 13.71 | 6/15/48 | 17.06 | 24.4 | 395 | −20.6 | 363 |
| 6/13/49 | 13.55 | 1/5/53 | 26.66 | 96.8 | 1302 | −14.8 | 252 |
| 9/14/53 | 22.71 | 8/2/56 | 49.74 | 119.0 | 1053 | −21.6 | 446 |
| 10/22/57 | 38.98 | 8/3/59 | 60.71 | 55.7 | 650 | −13.9 | 449 |
| 10/25/60 | 52.30 | 12/12/61 | 72.64 | 38.9 | 413 | −28.0 | 196 |
| 6/26/62 | 52.32 | 2/9/66 | 94.06 | 79.8 | 1324 | −22.2 | 240 |
| 10/7/66 | 73.20 | 11/29/68 | 108.37 | 48.0 | 784 | −36.1 | 543 |
| 5/26/70 | 69.29 | 4/28/71 | 104.77 | 51.2 | 337 | −13.9 | 209 |
| 11/23/71 | 90.16 | 1/11/73 | 120.24 | 33.4 | 415 | −48.2 | 630 |
| 10/3/74 | 62.28 | 9/21/76 | 107.83 | 73.1 | 719 | −19.4 | 531 |
| 3/6/78 | 86.90 | 9/12/78 | 106.99 | 23.1 | 190 | −8.2 | 562 |
| 3/27/80 | 98.22 | 11/28/80 | 140.52 | 43.1 | 246 | −27.1 | 622 |
| 8/12/82 | 102.42 | 10/10/83 | 172.65 | 68.6 | 424 | −14.4 | 288 |
| 7/24/84 | 147.82 | 8/25/87 | 336.77 | 127.8 | 1127 | −33.5 | 101 |
| 12/4/87 | 223.92 | 7/16/90 | 368.95 | 64.8 | 955 | −19.9 | 87 |
| 10/11/90 | 295.46 | 7/17/98 | 1186.75 | 301.7 | 2836 | −19.3 | 45 |
| 8/31/98 | 957.28 | 3/24/00 | 1527.46 | 59.6 | 571 | −36.8 | 546 |
| 9/21/01 | 965.80 | 1/4/02 | 1172.51 | 21.4 | 105 | −33.8 | 278 |
| 10/9/02 | 776.76 | 10/9/07 | 1565.15 | 101.5 | 1826 | −56.8 | 517 |
| 3/9/09 | 676.53 | 4/29/11 | 1363.61 | 101.6 | 781 | −19.4 | 157 |
| 10/3/11 | 1099.23 | 5/21/15 | 2130.82 | 93.8 | 1326 | −14.2 | 266 |
| 2/11/16 | 1829.08 | 2/19/20 | 3386.15 | 85.1 | 1469 | −33.9 | 33 |
| 3/23/20 | 2237.40 | 1/3/22 | 4796.56 | 114.4 | 651 | −23.6 | 164* |
| 6/16/22 | 3666.77 | | | | | | |
| | | **Average** | | **82.7%** | **771** | **−29.8%** | **363** |

*As of June 30, 2022 – not in averages*

## NASDAQ COMPOSITE BULL AND BEAR MARKETS

| — Beginning — | | — Ending — | | Bull | | Bear | |
|---|---|---|---|---|---|---|---|
| Date | NASDAQ | Date | NASDAQ | % Gain | Days | % Change | Days |
| 11/23/71 | 100.31 | 1/11/73 | 136.84 | 36.4% | 415 | −59.9% | 630 |
| 10/3/74 | 54.87 | 7/15/75 | 88.00 | 60.4 | 285 | −16.2 | 63 |
| 9/16/75 | 73.78 | 9/13/78 | 139.25 | 88.7 | 1093 | −20.4 | 62 |
| 11/14/78 | 110.88 | 2/8/80 | 165.25 | 49.0 | 451 | −24.9 | 48 |
| 3/27/80 | 124.09 | 5/29/81 | 223.47 | 80.1 | 428 | −28.8 | 441 |
| 8/13/82 | 159.14 | 6/24/83 | 328.91 | 106.7 | 315 | −31.5 | 397 |
| 7/25/84 | 225.30 | 8/26/87 | 455.26 | 102.1 | 1127 | −35.9 | 63 |
| 10/28/87 | 291.88 | 10/9/89 | 485.73 | 66.4 | 712 | −33.0 | 372 |
| 10/16/90 | 325.44 | 7/20/98 | 2014.25 | 518.9 | 2834 | −29.5 | 80 |
| 10/8/98 | 1419.12 | 3/10/00 | 5048.62 | 255.8 | 519 | −71.8 | 560 |
| 9/21/01 | 1423.19 | 1/4/02 | 2059.38 | 44.7 | 105 | −45.9 | 278 |
| 10/9/02 | 1114.11 | 10/31/07 | 2859.12 | 156.6 | 1848 | −55.6 | 495 |
| 3/9/09 | 1268.64 | 4/29/11 | 2873.54 | 126.5 | 781 | −18.7 | 157 |
| 10/3/11 | 2335.83 | 7/20/15 | 5218.86 | 123.4 | 1386 | −18.2 | 206 |
| 2/11/16 | 4266.84 | 2/19/20 | 9817.18 | 130.1 | 1469 | −30.1 | 33 |
| 3/23/20 | 6860.67 | 11/19/21 | 16057.44 | 134.1 | 606 | −33.7* | 209* |
| 6/16/22 | 10646.10 | | | | | | |
| | | **Average** | | **130.0%** | **898** | **−34.7%** | **259** |

*As of June 30, 2022 – not in averages*

## JANUARY DAILY POINT CHANGES DOW JONES INDUSTRIALS

| | 2013 | 2014 | 2015 | 2016 | 2017 | 2018 | 2019 | 2020 | 2021 | 2022 |
|---|---|---|---|---|---|---|---|---|---|---|
| Previous Month Close | 13104.14 | 16576.66 | 17823.07 | 17425.03 | 19762.60 | 24719.22 | 23327.46 | 28538.44 | 30606.48 | 36338.30 |
| 1 | H | H | H | H | S | H | H | H | H | S |
| 2 | 308.41 | − 135.31 | 9.92 | S | H | 104.79 | 18.78 | 330.36 | S | S |
| 3 | − 21.19 | 28.64 | S | S | 119.16 | 98.67 | − 660.02 | − 233.92 | S | 246.76 |
| 4 | 43.85 | S | S | − 276.09 | 60.40 | 152.45 | 746.94 | S | − 382.59 | 214.59 |
| 5 | S | S | − 331.34 | 9.72 | − 42.87 | 220.74 | S | S | 167.71 | − 392.54 |
| 6 | S | − 44.89 | − 130.01 | − 252.15 | 64.51 | S | S | 68.50 | 437.80 | − 170.64 |
| 7 | − 50.92 | 105.84 | 212.88 | − 392.41 | S | S | 98.19 | − 119.70 | 211.73 | − 4.81 |
| 8 | − 55.44 | − 68.20 | 323.35 | − 167.65 | S | − 12.87 | 256.10 | 161.41 | 56.84 | S |
| 9 | 61.66 | − 17.98 | − 170.50 | S | − 76.42 | 102.80 | 91.67 | 211.81 | S | S |
| 10 | 80.71 | − 7.71 | S | 52.12 | − 31.85 | − 16.67 | 122.80 | − 133.13 | S | − 162.79 |
| 11 | 17.21 | S | − 96.53 | 117.65 | 98.75 | 205.60 | − 5.97 | S | − 89.28 | 183.15 |
| 12 | S | S | − 96.53 | 117.65 | − 63.28 | 228.46 | S | 60.00 | 38.30 | |
| 13 | S | − 179.11 | − 27.16 | − 364.81 | − 5.27 | S | S | 83.28 | − 8.22 | − 176.70 |
| 14 | 18.89 | 115.92 | − 186.59 | 227.64 | S | S | − 86.11 | 32.62 | − 68.95 | − 201.81 |
| 15 | 27.57 | 108.08 | − 106.38 | − 390.97 | S | H | 155.75 | 90.55 | − 177.26 | S |
| 16 | − 23.66 | − 64.93 | 190.86 | S | H | − 10.33 | 141.57 | 267.42 | S | S |
| 17 | 84.79 | 41.55 | S | S | − 58.96 | 322.79 | 162.94 | 50.46 | S | H |
| 18 | 53.68 | S | S | H | − 22.05 | − 97.84 | 336.25 | S | H | − 543.34 |
| 19 | S | S | H | 27.94 | − 72.32 | 53.91 | S | S | 116.26 | − 339.82 |
| 20 | S | H | 3.66 | − 249.28 | 94.85 | S | S | H | 257.86 | − 313.26 |
| 21 | H | − 44.12 | 39.05 | 115.94 | S | S | H | − 152.06 | − 12.37 | − 450.02 |
| 22 | 62.51 | − 41.10 | 259.70 | 210.83 | S | 142.88 | − 301.87 | − 9.77 | − 179.03 | S |
| 23 | 67.12 | − 175.99 | − 141.38 | S | − 27.40 | − 3.79 | 171.14 | − 26.18 | S | S |
| 24 | 46.00 | − 318.24 | S | S | 112.86 | 41.31 | − 22.38 | − 170.36 | S | 99.13 |
| 25 | 70.65 | S | S | − 208.29 | 155.80 | 140.67 | 183.96 | S | − 36.98 | − 66.77 |
| 26 | S | S | 6.10 | 282.01 | 32.40 | 223.92 | S | S | − 22.96 | − 129.64 |
| 27 | S | − 41.23 | − 291.49 | − 222.77 | − 7.13 | S | S | − 453.93 | − 633.87 | − 7.31 |
| 28 | − 14.05 | 90.68 | − 195.84 | 125.18 | S | S | − 208.98 | 187.05 | 300.19 | 564.69 |
| 29 | 72.49 | − 189.77 | 225.48 | 396.66 | S | − 177.23 | 51.74 | 11.60 | − 620.74 | S |
| 30 | − 44.00 | 109.82 | − 251.90 | S | − 122.65 | − 362.59 | 434.90 | 124.99 | S | S |
| 31 | − 49.84 | − 149.76 | S | S | − 107.04 | 72.50 | − 15.19 | − 603.41 | S | 406.39 |
| Close | 13860.58 | 15698.85 | 17164.95 | 16466.30 | 19864.09 | 26149.39 | 24999.67 | 28256.03 | 29982.62 | 35131.86 |
| Change | 756.44 | − 877.81 | − 658.12 | − 958.73 | 101.49 | 1430.17 | 1672.21 | − 282.41 | − 623.86 | − 1206.44 |

## FEBRUARY DAILY POINT CHANGES DOW JONES INDUSTRIALS

| | 2013 | 2014 | 2015 | 2016 | 2017 | 2018 | 2019 | 2020 | 2021 | 2022 |
|---|---|---|---|---|---|---|---|---|---|---|
| Previous Month Close | 13860.58 | 15698.85 | 17164.95 | 16466.30 | 19864.09 | 26149.39 | 24999.67 | 28256.03 | 29982.62 | 35131.86 |
| 1 | 149.21 | S | S | − 17.12 | 26.85 | 37.32 | 64.22 | S | 229.29 | 273.38 |
| 2 | S | S | 196.09 | − 295.64 | − 6.03 | − 665.75 | S | S | 475.57 | 224.09 |
| 3 | S | − 326.05 | 305.36 | 183.12 | 186.55 | S | S | 143.78 | 36.12 | − 518.17 |
| 4 | − 129.71 | 72.44 | 6.62 | 79.92 | S | S | 175.48 | 407.82 | 332.26 | − 21.42 |
| 5 | 99.22 | − 5.01 | 211.86 | − 211.61 | S | − 1175.21 | 172.15 | 483.22 | 92.38 | S |
| 6 | 7.22 | 188.30 | − 60.59 | S | − 19.04 | 567.02 | − 21.22 | 88.92 | S | S |
| 7 | − 42.47 | 165.55 | S | S | 37.87 | − 19.42 | − 220.77 | − 277.26 | S | 1.39 |
| 8 | 48.92 | S | S | − 177.92 | − 35.95 | − 1032.89 | − 63.20 | S | 237.52 | 371.65 |
| 9 | S | S | − 95.08 | − 12.67 | 118.06 | 330.44 | S | S | − 9.93 | 305.28 |
| 10 | S | 7.71 | 139.55 | − 99.64 | 96.97 | S | 174.31 | 61.97 | − 526.47 | |
| 11 | − 21.73 | 192.98 | − 6.62 | − 254.56 | S | − 53.22 | − 0.48 | − 7.10 | − 503.53 | |
| 12 | 47.46 | − 30.83 | 110.24 | 313.66 | S | 410.37 | 372.65 | 275.08 | 27.70 | S |
| 13 | − 35.79 | 63.65 | 46.97 | S | 142.79 | 39.18 | 117.51 | − 128.11 | S | S |
| 14 | − 9.52 | 126.80 | S | S | 92.25 | 253.04 | − 103.88 | − 25.23 | S | − 171.89 |
| 15 | 8.37 | S | S | H | 107.45 | 306.88 | 443.86 | S | H | 422.67 |
| 16 | S | S | H | 222.57 | 7.91 | 19.01 | S | S | 64.35 | − 54.57 |
| 17 | S | H | 28.23 | 257.42 | 4.28 | S | S | H | 90.27 | − 622.24 |
| 18 | H | − 23.99 | − 17.73 | − 40.40 | S | S | H | − 165.89 | − 119.68 | − 232.85 |
| 19 | 53.91 | − 89.84 | − 44.08 | − 21.44 | S | H | 8.07 | 115.84 | 0.98 | S |
| 20 | − 108.13 | 92.67 | 154.67 | S | H | − 254.63 | 63.12 | − 128.05 | S | S |
| 21 | − 46.92 | − 29.93 | S | S | 118.95 | − 166.97 | − 103.81 | − 227.57 | S | H |
| 22 | 119.95 | S | S | 228.67 | 32.60 | 164.70 | 181.18 | S | 27.37 | − 482.57 |
| 23 | S | S | − 23.60 | − 188.88 | 34.72 | 347.51 | S | S | 15.66 | − 464.85 |
| 24 | S | 103.84 | 92.35 | 53.21 | 11.44 | S | S | − 1031.61 | 424.51 | 92.07 |
| 25 | − 216.40 | − 27.48 | 15.38 | 212.30 | S | S | 60.14 | − 879.44 | − 559.85 | 834.92 |
| 26 | 115.96 | 18.75 | − 10.15 | − 57.32 | S | 399.28 | − 33.97 | − 123.77 | − 469.64 | S |
| 27 | 175.24 | 74.24 | − 81.72 | S | 15.68 | − 299.24 | − 72.82 | − 1190.95 | S | S |
| 28 | − 20.88 | 49.06 | S | S | − 25.20 | − 380.83 | − 69.16 | − 357.28 | S | − 166.15 |
| 29 | — | — | — | − 123.47 | — | — | — | S | — | — |
| Close | 14054.49 | 16321.71 | 18132.70 | 16516.50 | 20812.24 | 25029.20 | 25916.00 | 25409.36 | 30932.37 | 33892.60 |
| Change | 193.91 | 622.86 | 967.75 | 50.20 | 948.15 | − 1120.19 | 916.33 | − 2846.67 | 949.75 | − 1239.26 |

135

# MARCH DAILY POINT CHANGES DOW JONES INDUSTRIALS

| Previous Month Close | 2013 | 2014 | 2015 | 2016 | 2017 | 2018 | 2019 | 2020 | 2021 | 2022 |
|---|---|---|---|---|---|---|---|---|---|---|
|  | 14054.49 | 16321.71 | 18132.70 | 16516.50 | 20812.24 | 25029.20 | 25916.00 | 25409.36 | 30932.37 | 33892.60 |
| 1 | 35.17 | S | S | 348.58 | 303.31 | -420.22 | 110.32 | S | 603.14 | -597.65 |
| 2 | S | S | 155.93 | 34.24 | -112.58 | -70.92 | S | 1293.96 | -143.99 | 596.40 |
| 3 | S | -153.68 | -85.26 | 44.58 | 2.74 | S | S | -785.91 | -121.43 | -96.69 |
| 4 | 38.16 | 227.85 | -106.47 | 62.87 | S | S | -206.67 | 1173.45 | -345.95 | -179.86 |
| 5 | 125.95 | -35.70 | 38.82 | S | S | 336.70 | -13.02 | -969.58 | 572.16 | S |
| 6 | 42.47 | 61.71 | -278.94 | S | -51.37 | 9.36 | -133.17 | -256.50 | S | S |
| 7 | 33.25 | 30.83 | S | 67.18 | -29.58 | -82.76 | -200.23 | S | S | -797.42 |
| 8 | 67.58 | S | S | -109.85 | -69.03 | 93.85 | -22.99 | S | 306.14 | -184.74 |
| 9 | S | S | 138.94 | 36.26 | 2.46 | 440.53 | S | -2013.76 | 30.30 | 653.61 |
| 10 | S | -34.04 | -332.78 | -5.23 | 44.79 | S | S | 1167.14 | 464.28 | -112.18 |
| 11 | 50.22 | -67.43 | -27.55 | 218.18 | S | S | 200.64 | -1464.94 | 188.57 | -229.88 |
| 12 | 2.77 | -11.17 | 259.83 | S | S | -157.13 | -96.22 | -2352.60 | 293.05 | S |
| 13 | 5.22 | -231.19 | -145.91 | S | S | -21.50 | -171.58 | 148.23 | 1985.00 | S |
| 14 | 83.86 | -43.22 | S | 15.82 | -44.11 | -248.91 | 7.05 | S | S | 1.05 |
| 15 | -25.03 | S | S | 22.40 | 112.73 | 115.54 | 138.93 | S | 174.82 | 599.10 |
| 16 | S | S | 228.11 | 74.23 | -15.55 | 72.85 | S | -2997.10 | -127.51 | 518.76 |
| 17 | S | 181.55 | -128.34 | 155.73 | -19.93 | S | S | 1048.86 | 189.42 | 417.66 |
| 18 | -62.05 | 88.97 | 227.11 | 120.81 | S | S | 65.23 | -1338.46 | -153.07 | 274.17 |
| 19 | 3.76 | -114.02 | -117.16 | S | S | -335.60 | -26.72 | 188.27 | -234.33 | S |
| 20 | 55.91 | 108.88 | 168.62 | S | -8.76 | 116.36 | -141.71 | -913.21 | S | S |
| 21 | -90.24 | -28.28 | S | 21.57 | -237.85 | -44.96 | 216.84 | S | S | -201.94 |
| 22 | 90.54 | S | S | -41.30 | -6.71 | -724.42 | -460.19 | S | 103.23 | 254.47 |
| 23 | S | S | -11.61 | -79.98 | -4.72 | -424.69 | S | -582.05 | -308.05 | -448.96 |
| 24 | S | -26.08 | -104.90 | 13.14 | -59.86 | S | S | 2112.98 | -3.09 | 349.44 |
| 25 | -64.28 | 91.19 | -292.60 | H | S | S | 14.51 | 495.64 | 199.42 | 153.30 |
| 26 | 111.90 | -98.89 | -40.31 | S | S | 669.40 | 140.90 | 1351.62 | 453.40 | S |
| 27 | -33.49 | -4.76 | 34.43 | S | -45.74 | -344.89 | -32.14 | -915.39 | S | S |
| 28 | 52.38 | 58.83 | S | 19.66 | 150.52 | -9.29 | 91.87 | S | S | 94.65 |
| 29 | H | S | S | 97.72 | -42.18 | 254.69 | 211.22 | S | 98.49 | 338.30 |
| 30 | S | S | 263.65 | 83.55 | 69.17 | H | S | 690.70 | -104.41 | -65.38 |
| 31 | S | 134.60 | -200.19 | -31.57 | -65.27 | S | S | -410.32 | -85.41 | -550.46 |
| Close | 14578.54 | 16457.66 | 17776.12 | 17685.09 | 20663.22 | 24103.11 | 25928.68 | 21917.16 | 32981.55 | 34678.35 |
| Change | 524.05 | 135.95 | -356.58 | 1168.59 | -149.02 | -926.09 | 12.68 | -3492.20 | 2049.18 | 785.75 |

# APRIL DAILY POINT CHANGES DOW JONES INDUSTRIALS

| Previous Month Close | 2013 | 2014 | 2015 | 2016 | 2017 | 2018 | 2019 | 2020 | 2021 | 2022 |
|---|---|---|---|---|---|---|---|---|---|---|
|  | 14578.54 | 16457.66 | 17776.12 | 17685.09 | 20663.22 | 24103.11 | 25928.68 | 21917.16 | 32981.55 | 34678.35 |
| 1 | -5.69 | 74.95 | -77.94 | 107.66 | S | S | 329.74 | -973.65 | 171.66 | 139.92 |
| 2 | 89.16 | 40.39 | 65.06 | S | S | -458.92 | -79.29 | 469.93 | H | S |
| 3 | -111.66 | -0.45 | H | S | -13.01 | 389.17 | 39.00 | -360.91 | S | S |
| 4 | 55.76 | -159.84 | S | -55.75 | 39.03 | 230.94 | 166.50 | S | S | 103.61 |
| 5 | -40.86 | S | S | -133.68 | -41.09 | 240.92 | 40.36 | S | 373.98 | -280.70 |
| 6 | S | S | 117.61 | 112.73 | 14.80 | -572.46 | S | 1627.46 | -96.95 | -144.67 |
| 7 | S | -166.84 | -5.43 | -174.09 | -6.85 | S | S | -26.13 | 16.02 | 87.06 |
| 8 | 48.23 | 10.27 | 27.09 | 35.00 | S | S | -83.97 | 779.71 | 57.31 | 137.55 |
| 9 | 59.98 | 181.04 | 56.22 | S | S | 46.34 | -190.44 | 285.80 | 297.03 | S |
| 10 | 128.78 | -266.96 | 98.92 | S | 1.92 | 428.90 | 6.58 | H | S | S |
| 11 | 62.90 | -143.47 | S | -20.55 | -6.72 | -218.55 | -14.11 | S | S | -413.04 |
| 12 | -0.08 | S | S | 164.84 | -59.44 | 293.60 | 269.25 | S | -55.20 | -87.72 |
| 13 | S | S | -80.61 | 187.03 | -138.61 | -122.91 | S | -328.60 | -68.13 | 344.23 |
| 14 | S | 146.49 | 59.66 | 18.15 | H | S | S | 558.99 | 53.62 | -113.36 |
| 15 | -265.86 | 89.32 | 75.91 | -28.97 | S | S | -27.53 | -445.41 | 305.10 | H |
| 16 | 157.58 | 162.29 | -6.84 | S | S | 212.90 | 67.89 | 33.33 | 164.68 | S |
| 17 | -138.19 | -16.31 | -279.47 | S | 183.67 | 213.59 | -3.12 | 704.81 | S | S |
| 18 | -81.45 | H | S | 106.70 | -113.64 | -38.56 | 110.00 | S | S | -39.54 |
| 19 | 10.37 | S | S | 49.44 | -118.79 | -83.18 | H | S | -123.04 | 499.51 |
| 20 | S | S | 208.63 | 42.67 | 174.22 | -201.95 | S | -592.05 | -256.33 | 249.59 |
| 21 | S | 40.71 | -85.34 | -113.75 | -30.95 | S | S | -631.56 | 316.01 | -368.03 |
| 22 | 19.66 | 65.12 | 88.68 | 21.23 | S | S | -48.49 | 456.94 | -321.41 | -981.36 |
| 23 | 152.29 | -12.72 | 20.42 | S | S | -14.25 | 145.34 | 39.44 | 227.59 | S |
| 24 | -43.16 | 0.00 | 21.45 | S | 216.13 | -424.56 | -59.34 | 260.01 | S | S |
| 25 | 24.50 | -140.19 | S | -26.51 | 232.23 | 59.70 | -134.97 | S | S | 238.06 |
| 26 | 11.75 | S | S | 13.08 | -21.03 | 238.51 | 81.25 | S | -61.92 | -809.28 |
| 27 | S | S | -42.17 | 51.23 | 6.24 | -11.15 | S | 358.51 | 3.36 | 61.75 |
| 28 | S | 87.28 | 72.17 | -210.79 | -40.82 | S | S | -32.23 | -164.55 | 614.46 |
| 29 | 106.20 | 86.63 | -74.61 | -57.12 | S | S | 11.06 | 532.31 | 239.98 | -939.18 |
| 30 | 21.05 | 45.47 | -195.01 | S | S | -148.04 | 38.52 | -288.14 | -185.51 | S |
| Close | 14839.80 | 16580.84 | 17840.52 | 17773.64 | 20940.51 | 24163.15 | 26592.91 | 24345.72 | 33874.85 | 32977.21 |
| Change | 261.26 | 123.18 | 64.40 | 88.55 | 277.29 | 60.04 | 664.23 | 2428.56 | 893.30 | -1701.14 |

## MAY DAILY POINT CHANGES DOW JONES INDUSTRIALS

| Previous Month | 2012 | 2013 | 2014 | 2015 | 2016 | 2017 | 2018 | 2019 | 2020 | 2021 |
|---|---|---|---|---|---|---|---|---|---|---|
| Close | 13213.63 | 14839.80 | 16580.84 | 17840.52 | 17773.64 | 20940.51 | 24163.15 | 26592.91 | 24345.72 | 33874.85 |
| 1 | 65.69 | -138.85 | -21.97 | 183.54 | S | -27.05 | -64.10 | -162.77 | -622.03 | S |
| 2 | -10.75 | 130.63 | -45.98 | S | 117.52 | 36.43 | -174.07 | -122.35 | S | S |
| 3 | -61.98 | 142.38 | S | S | -140.25 | 8.01 | 5.17 | 197.16 | S | 238.38 |
| 4 | -168.32 | S | S | 46.34 | -99.65 | -6.43 | 332.36 | S | 26.07 | 19.80 |
| 5 | S | S | 17.66 | -142.20 | 9.45 | 55.47 | S | S | 133.33 | 97.31 |
| 6 | S | -5.07 | -129.53 | -86.22 | 79.92 | S | S | -66.47 | -218.45 | 318.19 |
| 7 | -29.74 | 87.31 | 117.52 | 82.08 | S | S | 94.81 | -473.39 | 211.25 | 229.23 |
| 8 | -76.44 | 48.92 | 32.43 | 267.05 | S | 5.34 | 2.89 | 2.24 | 455.43 | S |
| 9 | -97.03 | -22.50 | 32.37 | S | -34.72 | -36.50 | 182.33 | -138.97 | S | S |
| 10 | 19.98 | 35.87 | S | S | 222.44 | -32.67 | 196.99 | 114.01 | S | -34.94 |
| 11 | -34.44 | S | S | -85.94 | -217.23 | -23.69 | 91.64 | S | -109.33 | -473.66 |
| 12 | S | S | 112.13 | -36.94 | 9.38 | -22.81 | S | S | -457.21 | -681.50 |
| 13 | S | -26.81 | 19.97 | -7.74 | -185.18 | S | S | -617.38 | -516.81 | 433.79 |
| 14 | -125.25 | 123.57 | -101.47 | 191.75 | S | S | 68.24 | 207.06 | 377.37 | 360.68 |
| 15 | -63.35 | 60.44 | -167.16 | 20.32 | S | 85.33 | -193.00 | 115.97 | 60.08 | S |
| 16 | -33.45 | -42.47 | 44.50 | S | 175.39 | -2.19 | 62.52 | 214.66 | S | S |
| 17 | -156.06 | 121.18 | S | S | -180.73 | -372.82 | -54.95 | -98.68 | S | -54.34 |
| 18 | -73.11 | S | S | 26.32 | -3.36 | 56.09 | 1.11 | S | 911.95 | -267.13 |
| 19 | S | S | 20.55 | 13.51 | -91.22 | 141.82 | S | S | -390.51 | -164.62 |
| 20 | S | -19.12 | -137.55 | -26.99 | 65.54 | S | S | -84.10 | 369.04 | 188.11 |
| 21 | 135.10 | 52.30 | 158.75 | 0.34 | S | S | 298.20 | 197.43 | -101.78 | 123.69 |
| 22 | -1.67 | -80.41 | 10.02 | -53.72 | S | 89.99 | -178.88 | -100.72 | -8.96 | S |
| 23 | -6.66 | -12.67 | 63.19 | S | -8.01 | 43.08 | 52.40 | -286.14 | S | S |
| 24 | 33.60 | 8.60 | S | S | 213.12 | 74.51 | -75.05 | 95.22 | S | 186.14 |
| 25 | -74.92 | S | S | H | 145.46 | 70.53 | -58.67 | S | H | -81.52 |
| 26 | S | S | H | -190.48 | -23.22 | -2.67 | S | S | 529.95 | 10.59 |
| 27 | S | H | 69.23 | 121.45 | 44.93 | S | S | S | 553.16 | 141.59 |
| 28 | H | 106.29 | -42.32 | -36.87 | S | S | H | -237.92 | -147.63 | 64.81 |
| 29 | 125.86 | -106.59 | 65.56 | -115.44 | S | H | -391.64 | -221.36 | -17.53 | S |
| 30 | -160.83 | 21.73 | 18.43 | S | H | -50.81 | 306.33 | 43.47 | S | S |
| 31 | -26.41 | -208.96 | S | S | -86.02 | -20.82 | -251.94 | -354.84 | S | H |
| Close | 12393.45 | 15115.57 | 16717.17 | 18010.68 | 17787.20 | 21008.65 | 24415.84 | 24815.04 | 25383.11 | 34529.45 |
| Change | -820.18 | 275.77 | 136.33 | 170.16 | 13.56 | 68.14 | 252.69 | -1777.87 | 1037.39 | 654.60 |

## JUNE DAILY POINT CHANGES DOW JONES INDUSTRIALS

| Previous Month | 2012 | 2013 | 2014 | 2015 | 2016 | 2017 | 2018 | 2019 | 2020 | 2021 |
|---|---|---|---|---|---|---|---|---|---|---|
| Close | 12393.45 | 15115.57 | 16717.17 | 18010.68 | 17787.20 | 21008.65 | 24415.84 | 24815.04 | 25383.11 | 34529.45 |
| 1 | -274.88 | S | S | 29.69 | 2.47 | 135.53 | 219.37 | S | 91.91 | 45.86 |
| 2 | S | S | 26.46 | -28.43 | 48.89 | 62.11 | S | S | 267.63 | 25.07 |
| 3 | S | 138.46 | -21.29 | 64.33 | -31.50 | S | S | 4.74 | 527.24 | -23.34 |
| 4 | -17.11 | -76.49 | 15.19 | -170.69 | S | S | 178.48 | 512.40 | 11.93 | 179.35 |
| 5 | 26.49 | -216.95 | 98.58 | -56.12 | S | -22.25 | -13.71 | 207.39 | 829.16 | S |
| 6 | 286.84 | 80.03 | 88.17 | S | 113.27 | -47.81 | 346.41 | 181.09 | S | S |
| 7 | 46.17 | 207.50 | S | S | 17.95 | 37.46 | 95.02 | 263.28 | S | -126.15 |
| 8 | 93.24 | S | S | -82.91 | 66.77 | 8.84 | 75.12 | S | 461.46 | -30.42 |
| 9 | S | S | 18.82 | -2.51 | -19.86 | 89.44 | S | S | -300.14 | -152.68 |
| 10 | S | -9.53 | 2.82 | 236.36 | -119.85 | S | S | 78.74 | -282.31 | 19.10 |
| 11 | -142.97 | -116.57 | -102.04 | 38.97 | S | S | 5.78 | -14.17 | -1861.82 | 13.36 |
| 12 | 162.57 | -126.79 | -109.69 | -140.53 | S | -36.30 | -1.58 | -43.68 | 477.37 | S |
| 13 | -77.42 | 180.85 | 41.55 | S | -132.86 | 92.80 | -119.53 | 101.94 | S | S |
| 14 | 155.53 | -105.90 | S | S | -57.66 | 46.09 | -25.89 | -17.16 | S | -85.85 |
| 15 | 115.26 | S | S | -107.67 | -34.65 | -14.66 | -84.83 | S | 157.62 | -94.42 |
| 16 | S | S | 5.27 | 113.31 | 92.93 | 24.38 | S | S | 526.82 | -265.66 |
| 17 | S | 109.67 | 27.48 | 31.26 | -57.94 | S | S | 22.92 | -170.37 | -210.22 |
| 18 | -25.35 | 138.38 | 98.13 | 180.10 | S | S | -103.01 | 353.01 | -39.51 | -533.37 |
| 19 | 95.51 | -206.04 | 14.84 | -99.89 | S | 144.71 | -287.26 | 38.46 | -208.64 | S |
| 20 | -12.94 | -353.87 | 25.62 | S | 129.71 | -61.85 | -42.41 | 249.17 | S | S |
| 21 | -250.82 | 41.08 | S | S | 24.86 | -57.11 | -196.10 | -34.04 | S | 586.89 |
| 22 | 67.21 | S | S | 103.83 | -48.90 | -12.74 | 119.19 | S | 153.50 | 68.61 |
| 23 | S | S | -9.82 | 24.29 | 230.24 | -2.53 | S | S | 131.14 | -71.34 |
| 24 | S | -139.84 | -119.13 | -178.00 | -610.32 | S | S | 8.41 | -710.16 | 322.58 |
| 25 | -138.12 | 100.75 | 49.38 | -75.71 | S | S | -328.09 | -179.32 | 299.66 | 237.02 |
| 26 | 32.01 | 149.83 | -21.38 | 56.32 | S | 14.79 | 30.31 | -11.40 | -730.05 | S |
| 27 | 92.34 | 114.35 | 5.71 | S | -260.51 | -98.89 | -165.52 | -10.24 | S | S |
| 28 | -24.75 | -114.89 | S | S | 269.48 | 143.95 | 98.46 | 73.38 | S | -150.57 |
| 29 | 277.83 | S | S | -350.33 | 284.96 | -167.58 | 55.36 | S | 580.25 | 9.02 |
| 30 | S | S | -25.24 | 23.16 | 235.31 | 62.60 | S | S | 217.08 | 210.22 |
| Close | 12880.09 | 14909.60 | 16826.60 | 17619.51 | 17929.99 | 21349.63 | 24271.41 | 26599.96 | 25812.88 | 34502.51 |
| Change | 486.64 | -205.97 | 109.43 | -391.17 | 142.79 | 340.98 | -144.43 | 1784.92 | 429.77 | -26.94 |

## JULY DAILY POINT CHANGES DOW JONES INDUSTRIALS

| Previous Month Close | 2012 | 2013 | 2014 | 2015 | 2016 | 2017 | 2018 | 2019 | 2020 | 2021 |
|---|---|---|---|---|---|---|---|---|---|---|
|  | 12880.09 | 14909.60 | 16826.60 | 17619.51 | 17929.99 | 21349.63 | 24271.41 | 26599.96 | 25812.88 | 34502.51 |
| 1 | S | 65.36 | 129.47 | 138.40 | 19.38 | S | S | 117.47 | -77.91 | 131.02 |
| 2 | -8.70 | -42.55 | 20.17 | -27.80 | S | S | 35.77 | 69.25 | 92.39 | 152.82 |
| 3 | 72.43* | 56.14* | 92.02 | H | S | 129.64* | -132.36* | 179.32* | H | S |
| 4 | H | H | H | S | H | H | H | H | S | S |
| 5 | -47.15 | 147.29 | S | S | -108.75 | -1.10 | 181.92 | -43.88 | S | H |
| 6 | -124.20 | S | S | -46.53 | 78.00 | -158.13 | 99.74 | S | 459.67 | -208.98 |
| 7 | S | S | -44.05 | 93.33 | -22.74 | 94.30 | S | S | -396.85 | 104.42 |
| 8 | S | 88.85 | -117.59 | -261.49 | 250.86 | S | S | -115.98 | 177.10 | -259.86 |
| 9 | -36.18 | 75.65 | 78.99 | 33.20 | S | S | 320.11 | -22.65 | -361.19 | 448.23 |
| 10 | -83.17 | -8.68 | -70.54 | 211.79 | S | -5.82 | 143.07 | 76.71 | 369.21 | S |
| 11 | -48.59 | 169.26 | 28.74 | S | 80.19 | 0.55 | -219.21 | 227.88 | S | S |
| 12 | -31.26 | 3.38 | S | S | 120.74 | 123.07 | 224.44 | 243.95 | S | 126.02 |
| 13 | 203.82 | S | S | 217.27 | 24.45 | 20.95 | 94.52 | S | 10.50 | -107.39 |
| 14 | S | S | 111.61 | 75.90 | 134.29 | 84.65 | S | S | 556.79 | 44.44 |
| 15 | S | 19.96 | 5.26 | -3.41 | 10.14 | S | S | 27.13 | 227.51 | 53.79 |
| 16 | -49.88 | -32.41 | 77.52 | 70.08 | S | S | 44.95 | -23.53 | -135.39 | -299.17 |
| 17 | 78.33 | 18.67 | -161.39 | -33.80 | S | -8.02 | 55.53 | -115.78 | -62.76 | S |
| 18 | 103.16 | 78.02 | 123.37 | S | 16.50 | -54.99 | 79.40 | 3.12 | S | S |
| 19 | 34.66 | -4.80 | S | S | 25.96 | 66.02 | -134.79 | -68.77 | S | -725.81 |
| 20 | -120.79 | S | S | 13.96 | 36.02 | -28.97 | -6.38 | S | 8.92 | 549.95 |
| 21 | S | S | -48.45 | -181.12 | -77.80 | -31.71 | S | S | 159.53 | 286.01 |
| 22 | S | 1.81 | 61.81 | -68.25 | 53.62 | S | S | 17.70 | 165.44 | 25.35 |
| 23 | -101.11 | 22.19 | -26.91 | -119.12 | S | S | -13.83 | 177.29 | -353.51 | 238.20 |
| 24 | -104.14 | -25.50 | -2.83 | -163.39 | S | -66.90 | 197.65 | -79.22 | -182.44 | S |
| 25 | 58.73 | 13.37 | -123.23 | S | -77.79 | 100.26 | 172.16 | -128.99 | S | S |
| 26 | 211.88 | 3.22 | S | S | -19.31 | 97.58 | 112.97 | 51.47 | S | 82.76 |
| 27 | 187.73 | S | S | -127.94 | -1.58 | 85.54 | -76.01 | S | 114.88 | -85.79 |
| 28 | S | S | 22.02 | 189.68 | -15.82 | 33.76 | S | S | -205.49 | -127.59 |
| 29 | S | -36.86 | -70.48 | 121.12 | -24.11 | S | S | 28.90 | 160.29 | 153.60 |
| 30 | -2.65 | -1.38 | -31.75 | -5.41 | S | S | -144.23 | -23.33 | -225.92 | -149.06 |
| 31 | -64.33 | -21.05 | -317.06 | -56.12 | S | 60.81 | 108.36 | -333.75 | 114.67 | S |
| **Close** | 13008.68 | 15499.54 | 16563.30 | 17689.86 | 18432.24 | 21891.12 | 25415.19 | 26864.27 | 26428.32 | 34935.47 |
| **Change** | 128.59 | 589.94 | -263.30 | 70.35 | 502.25 | 541.49 | 1143.78 | 264.31 | 615.44 | 432.96 |

* Shortened trading day

## AUGUST DAILY POINT CHANGES DOW JONES INDUSTRIALS

| Previous Month Close | 2012 | 2013 | 2014 | 2015 | 2016 | 2017 | 2018 | 2019 | 2020 | 2021 |
|---|---|---|---|---|---|---|---|---|---|---|
|  | 13008.68 | 15499.54 | 16563.30 | 17689.86 | 18432.24 | 21891.12 | 25415.19 | 26864.27 | 26428.32 | 34935.47 |
| 1 | -37.62 | 128.48 | -69.93 | S | -27.73 | 72.80 | -81.37 | -280.85 | S | S |
| 2 | -92.18 | 30.34 | S | S | -90.74 | 52.32 | -7.66 | -98.41 | S | -97.31 |
| 3 | 217.29 | S | S | -91.66 | 41.23 | 9.86 | 136.42 | S | 236.08 | 278.24 |
| 4 | S | S | 75.91 | -47.51 | -2.95 | 66.71 | S | S | 164.07 | -323.73 |
| 5 | S | -46.23 | -139.81 | -10.22 | 191.48 | S | S | -767.27 | 373.05 | 271.59 |
| 6 | 21.34 | -93.39 | 13.87 | -120.72 | S | S | 39.60 | 311.78 | 185.46 | 144.26 |
| 7 | 51.09 | -48.07 | -75.07 | -46.37 | S | 25.61 | 126.73 | -22.45 | 46.50 | S |
| 8 | 7.04 | 27.65 | 185.66 | S | -14.24 | -33.08 | -45.16 | 371.12 | S | S |
| 9 | -10.45 | -72.81 | S | S | 3.76 | -36.64 | -74.52 | -90.75 | S | -106.66 |
| 10 | 42.76 | S | S | 241.79 | -37.39 | -204.69 | -196.09 | S | 357.96 | 162.82 |
| 11 | S | S | 16.05 | -212.33 | 117.86 | 14.31 | S | S | -104.53 | 220.30 |
| 12 | S | -5.83 | -9.44 | -0.33 | -37.05 | S | S | -380.07 | 289.93 | 14.88 |
| 13 | -38.52 | 31.33 | 91.26 | 5.74 | S | S | -125.44 | 372.54 | -80.12 | 15.53 |
| 14 | 2.71 | -113.35 | 61.78 | 69.15 | S | 135.39 | 112.22 | -800.49 | 34.30 | S |
| 15 | -7.36 | -225.47 | -50.67 | S | 59.58 | 5.28 | -137.51 | 99.97 | S | S |
| 16 | 85.33 | -30.72 | S | S | -84.03 | 25.88 | 396.32 | 306.62 | S | 110.02 |
| 17 | 25.09 | S | S | 67.78 | 21.92 | -274.14 | 110.59 | S | -86.11 | -282.12 |
| 18 | S | S | 175.83 | -33.84 | 23.76 | -76.22 | S | S | -66.84 | -382.59 |
| 19 | S | -70.73 | 80.85 | -162.61 | -45.13 | S | S | 249.78 | -85.19 | -66.57 |
| 20 | -3.56 | -7.75 | 59.54 | -358.04 | S | S | 89.37 | -173.35 | 46.85 | 225.96 |
| 21 | -68.06 | -105.44 | 60.36 | -530.94 | S | 29.24 | 63.60 | 240.29 | 190.60 | S |
| 22 | -30.82 | 66.19 | -38.27 | S | -23.15 | 196.14 | -88.69 | 49.51 | S | S |
| 23 | -115.30 | 46.77 | S | S | 17.88 | -87.80 | -76.62 | -623.34 | S | 215.63 |
| 24 | 100.51 | S | S | -588.40 | -65.82 | -28.69 | 133.37 | S | 378.13 | 30.55 |
| 25 | S | S | 75.65 | -204.91 | -33.07 | 30.27 | S | S | -60.02 | 39.24 |
| 26 | S | -64.05 | 29.83 | 619.07 | -53.01 | S | S | 269.93 | 83.48 | -192.38 |
| 27 | -33.30 | -170.33 | 15.31 | 369.26 | S | S | 259.29 | -120.93 | 160.35 | 242.68 |
| 28 | -21.68 | 48.38 | -42.44 | -11.76 | S | -5.27 | 14.38 | 258.20 | 161.60 | S |
| 29 | 4.49 | 16.44 | 18.88 | S | 107.59 | 56.97 | 60.55 | 326.15 | S | S |
| 30 | -106.77 | -30.64 | S | S | -48.69 | 27.06 | -137.65 | 41.03 | S | -55.96 |
| 31 | 90.13 | S | S | -114.98 | -53.42 | 55.67 | -22.10 | S | -223.82 | -39.11 |
| **Close** | 13090.84 | 14810.31 | 17098.45 | 16528.03 | 18400.88 | 21948.10 | 25964.82 | 26403.28 | 28430.05 | 35360.73 |
| **Change** | 82.16 | -689.23 | 535.15 | -1161.83 | -31.36 | 56.98 | 549.63 | -460.99 | 2001.73 | 425.26 |

| | 2012 | 2013 | 2014 | 2015 | 2016 | 2017 | 2018 | 2019 | 2020 | 2021 |
|---|---|---|---|---|---|---|---|---|---|---|
| Previous Month Close | 13090.84 | 14810.31 | 17098.45 | 16528.03 | 18400.88 | 21948.10 | 25964.82 | 26403.28 | 28430.05 | 35360.73 |
| 1 | S | S | H | -469.68 | 18.42 | 39.46 | S | S | 215.61 | -48.20 |
| 2 | S | H | -30.89 | 293.03 | 72.66 | S | S | H | 454.84 | 131.29 |
| 3 | H | 23.65 | 10.72 | 23.38 | S | S | H | -285.26 | -807.77 | -74.73 |
| 4 | -54.90 | 96.91 | -8.70 | -272.38 | S | H | -12.34 | 237.45 | -159.42 | S |
| 5 | 11.54 | 6.61 | 67.78 | S | H | -234.25 | 22.51 | 372.68 | S | S |
| 6 | 244.52 | -14.98 | S | S | 46.16 | 54.33 | 20.88 | 69.31 | S | H |
| 7 | 14.64 | S | S | H | -11.98 | -22.86 | -79.33 | S | H | -269.09 |
| 8 | S | S | -25.94 | 390.30 | -46.23 | 13.01 | S | S | -632.42 | -68.93 |
| 9 | S | 140.62 | -97.55 | -239.11 | -394.46 | S | S | 38.05 | 439.58 | -151.69 |
| 10 | -52.35 | 127.94 | 54.84 | 76.83 | S | S | -59.47 | 73.92 | -405.89 | -271.66 |
| 11 | 69.07 | 135.54 | -19.71 | 102.69 | S | 259.58 | 113.99 | 227.61 | 131.06 | S |
| 12 | 9.99 | -25.96 | -61.49 | S | 239.62 | 61.49 | 27.86 | 45.41 | S | S |
| 13 | 206.51 | 75.42 | S | S | -258.32 | 39.32 | 147.07 | 37.07 | S | 261.91 |
| 14 | 53.51 | S | S | -62.13 | -31.98 | 45.30 | 8.68 | S | 327.69 | -312.06 |
| 15 | S | S | 43.63 | 228.89 | 177.71 | 64.86 | S | S | 2.27 | 256.82 |
| 16 | S | 118.72 | 100.83 | 140.10 | -88.68 | S | S | -142.70 | 36.78 | -63.07 |
| 17 | -40.27 | 34.95 | 24.88 | -65.21 | S | S | -92.55 | 33.98 | -130.40 | -166.44 |
| 18 | 11.54 | 147.21 | 109.14 | -290.16 | S | 63.01 | 184.84 | 36.28 | -244.56 | S |
| 19 | 13.32 | -40.39 | 13.75 | S | -3.63 | 39.45 | 158.80 | -52.29 | S | S |
| 20 | 18.97 | -185.46 | S | S | 9.79 | 41.79 | 251.22 | -159.72 | S | -614.41 |
| 21 | -17.46 | S | S | 125.61 | 163.74 | -53.36 | 86.52 | S | S | -50.63 |
| 22 | S | S | -107.06 | -179.72 | 98.76 | -9.64 | S | S | 140.48 | 338.48 |
| 23 | S | -49.71 | -116.81 | -50.58 | -131.01 | S | S | 14.92 | -525.05 | 506.50 |
| 24 | -20.55 | -66.79 | 154.19 | -78.57 | S | S | -181.45 | -142.22 | 52.31 | 33.18 |
| 25 | -101.37 | -61.33 | -264.26 | 113.35 | S | -53.50 | -69.84 | 162.94 | 358.52 | S |
| 26 | -44.04 | 55.04 | 167.35 | S | -166.62 | -11.77 | -106.93 | -79.59 | S | S |
| 27 | 72.46 | -70.06 | S | S | 133.47 | 56.39 | 54.65 | -70.87 | S | 71.37 |
| 28 | -48.84 | S | S | -312.78 | 110.94 | 40.49 | 18.38 | S | 410.10 | -569.38 |
| 29 | S | S | -41.93 | 47.24 | -195.79 | 23.89 | S | S | -131.40 | 90.73 |
| 30 | S | -128.57 | -28.32 | 234.87 | 164.70 | S | S | 96.58 | 329.04 | -546.80 |
| Close | 13437.13 | 15129.67 | 17042.90 | 16284.00 | 18308.15 | 22405.09 | 26458.31 | 26916.83 | 27781.70 | 33843.92 |
| Change | 346.29 | 319.36 | -55.55 | -244.03 | -92.73 | 456.99 | 493.49 | 513.55 | -648.35 | -1516.81 |

| | 2012 | 2013 | 2014 | 2015 | 2016 | 2017 | 2018 | 2019 | 2020 | 2021 |
|---|---|---|---|---|---|---|---|---|---|---|
| Previous Month Close | 13437.13 | 15129.67 | 17042.90 | 16284.00 | 18308.15 | 22405.09 | 26458.31 | 26916.83 | 27781.70 | 33843.92 |
| 1 | 77.98 | 62.03 | -238.19 | -11.99 | S | S | 192.90 | -343.79 | 35.20 | 482.54 |
| 2 | -32.75 | -58.56 | -3.66 | 200.36 | S | 152.51 | 122.73 | -494.42 | -134.09 | S |
| 3 | 12.25 | -136.66 | 208.64 | S | -54.30 | 84.07 | 54.45 | 122.42 | S | S |
| 4 | 80.75 | 76.10 | S | S | -85.40 | 19.97 | -200.91 | 372.68 | S | -323.54 |
| 5 | 34.79 | S | S | 304.06 | 112.58 | 113.75 | -180.43 | S | 465.83 | 311.75 |
| 6 | S | S | -17.78 | 13.76 | -12.53 | -1.72 | S | S | -375.88 | 102.32 |
| 7 | S | -136.34 | -272.52 | 122.10 | -28.01 | S | S | -95.70 | 530.70 | 337.95 |
| 8 | -26.50 | -159.71 | 274.83 | 138.46 | S | S | 39.73 | -313.98 | 122.05 | -8.69 |
| 9 | -110.12 | 26.45 | -334.97 | 33.74 | S | -12.60 | -56.21 | 181.97 | 161.39 | S |
| 10 | -128.56 | 323.09 | -115.15 | S | 88.55 | 69.61 | -831.83 | 150.66 | S | S |
| 11 | -18.58 | 111.04 | S | S | -200.38 | 42.21 | -545.91 | 319.92 | S | -250.19 |
| 12 | 2.46 | S | S | 47.37 | 15.54 | -31.88 | 287.16 | S | 250.62 | -117.72 |
| 13 | S | S | -223.03 | -49.97 | -45.26 | 30.71 | S | S | -157.71 | -0.53 |
| 14 | S | 64.15 | -5.88 | -157.14 | 39.44 | S | S | -29.23 | -165.81 | 534.75 |
| 15 | 95.38 | -133.25 | -173.45 | 217.00 | S | S | -89.44 | 237.44 | -19.80 | 382.20 |
| 16 | 127.55 | 205.82 | -24.50 | 74.22 | S | 85.24 | 547.87 | -22.82 | 112.11 | S |
| 17 | 5.22 | -2.18 | 263.17 | S | -51.98 | 40.48 | -91.74 | 23.90 | S | S |
| 18 | -8.06 | 28.00 | S | S | 75.54 | 160.16 | -327.23 | -255.68 | S | -36.15 |
| 19 | -205.43 | S | S | 14.57 | 40.68 | 54.89 | 64.89 | S | -410.89 | 198.70 |
| 20 | S | S | 19.26 | -13.43 | -40.27 | 165.59 | S | S | 113.37 | 152.03 |
| 21 | S | 75.46 | 215.14 | -48.50 | -16.64 | S | S | 57.44 | -97.97 | -6.26 |
| 22 | 2.38 | -7.45 | -153.49 | 320.55 | S | S | -126.93 | -39.54 | 152.84 | 73.94 |
| 23 | -243.36 | -54.33 | 216.58 | 157.54 | S | -54.67 | -125.98 | 45.85 | -28.09 | S |
| 24 | -25.19 | 95.88 | 127.51 | S | 77.32 | 167.80 | -608.01 | -28.42 | S | S |
| 25 | 26.34 | 61.07 | S | S | -53.76 | -112.30 | 401.13 | 152.53 | S | 64.13 |
| 26 | 3.53 | S | S | -23.65 | 30.06 | 71.40 | -296.24 | S | -650.19 | 15.73 |
| 27 | S | S | 12.53 | -41.62 | -29.65 | 33.33 | S | S | -222.19 | -266.19 |
| 28 | H* | -1.35 | 187.81 | 198.09 | -8.49 | S | S | 132.66 | -943.24 | 239.79 |
| 29 | H* | 111.42 | -31.44 | -23.72 | S | S | -245.39 | -19.26 | 139.16 | 89.08 |
| 30 | H* | -61.59 | 221.11 | -92.26 | S | -85.45 | 431.72 | 115.23 | -157.51 | S |
| 31 | -10.75 | -73.01 | 195.10 | S | -18.77 | 28.50 | 241.12 | -140.46 | S | S |
| Close | 13096.46 | 15545.75 | 17390.52 | 17663.54 | 18142.42 | 23377.24 | 25115.76 | 27046.23 | 26501.60 | 35819.56 |
| Change | -340.67 | 416.08 | 347.62 | 1379.54 | -165.73 | 972.15 | -1342.55 | 129.40 | -1280.10 | 1975.64 |

*Hurricane Sandy

| | 2012 | 2013 | 2014 | 2015 | 2016 | 2017 | 2018 | 2019 | 2020 | 2021 |
|---|---|---|---|---|---|---|---|---|---|---|
| Previous Month Close | 13096.46 | 15545.75 | 17390.52 | 17663.54 | 18142.42 | 23377.24 | 25115.76 | 27046.23 | 26501.60 | 35819.56 |
| 1 | 136.16 | 69.80 | S | S | -105.32 | 57.77 | 264.98 | 301.13 | S | 94.28 |
| 2 | -139.46 | S | S | 165.22 | -77.46 | 81.25 | -109.91 | S | 423.45 | 138.79 |
| 3 | S | S | -24.28 | 89.39 | -28.97 | 22.93 | S | S | 554.98 | 104.95 |
| 4 | S | 23.57 | 17.60 | -50.57 | -42.39 | S | S | 114.75 | 367.63 | -33.35 |
| 5 | 19.28 | -20.90 | 100.69 | -4.15 | S | S | 190.87 | 30.52 | 542.52 | 203.72 |
| 6 | 133.24 | 128.66 | 69.94 | 46.90 | S | 9.23 | 173.31 | -0.07 | -66.78 | S |
| 7 | -312.95 | -152.90 | 19.46 | S | 371.32 | 8.81 | 545.29 | 182.24 | S | S |
| 8 | -121.41 | 167.80 | S | S | 73.14 | 6.13 | 10.92 | 6.44 | S | 104.27 |
| 9 | 4.07 | S | S | -179.85 | 256.95 | -101.42 | -201.92 | S | 834.57 | -112.24 |
| 10 | S | S | 39.81 | 27.73 | 218.19 | -39.73 | S | S | 262.95 | -240.04 |
| 11 | S | 21.32 | 1.16 | -55.99 | 39.78 | S | S | 10.25 | -23.29 | -158.71 |
| 12 | -0.31 | -32.43 | -2.70 | -254.15 | S | S | -602.12 | 0.00 | -317.46 | 179.08 |
| 13 | -58.90 | 70.96 | 40.59 | -202.83 | S | 17.49 | -100.69 | 92.10 | 399.64 | S |
| 14 | -185.23 | 54.59 | -18.05 | S | 21.03 | -30.23 | -205.99 | -1.63 | S | -12.86 |
| 15 | -28.57 | 85.48 | S | S | 54.37 | -138.19 | 208.77 | 222.93 | S | 54.77 |
| 16 | 45.93 | S | S | 237.77 | -54.92 | 187.08 | 123.95 | S | 470.63 | -211.17 |
| 17 | S | S | 13.01 | 6.49 | 35.68 | -100.12 | S | 31.33 | -167.09 | -60.10 |
| 18 | S | 14.32 | 40.07 | 247.66 | -35.89 | S | S | 31.33 | -344.93 | -60.10 |
| 19 | 207.65 | -8.99 | -2.09 | -4.41 | S | S | -395.78 | -102.20 | 44.81 | -268.97 |
| 20 | -7.45 | -66.21 | 33.27 | 91.06 | S | 72.09 | -551.80 | -112.93 | -219.75 | S |
| 21 | 48.38 | 109.17 | 91.06 | S | 88.76 | 160.50 | -0.95 | -54.80 | S | S |
| 22 | H | 54.78 | S | S | 67.18 | -64.65 | H | 109.33 | S | 17.27 |
| 23 | 172.79* | S | S | -31.13 | 59.31 | H | -178.74* | S | 327.79 | 194.55 |
| 24 | S | S | 7.84 | 19.51 | H | 31.81* | S | S | 454.97 | -9.42 |
| 25 | S | 7.77 | -2.96 | 1.20 | 68.96* | S | S | 190.85 | -173.77 | H |
| 26 | -42.31 | 0.26 | -2.69 | H | S | S | 354.29 | 55.21 | H | -905.04* |
| 27 | -89.24 | 24.53 | H | -14.9* | S | 22.79 | 108.49 | 42.32 | 37.9* | S |
| 28 | 106.98 | H | 15.99* | S | -54.24 | 255.93 | 617.70 | H | S | S |
| 29 | 36.71 | -10.92* | S | S | 23.70 | 103.97 | -27.59 | -112.59* | S | 236.60 |
| 30 | 3.76 | S | S | -78.57 | 1.98 | 331.67 | 199.62 | S | -271.73 | -652.22 |
| Close | 13025.58 | 16086.41 | 17828.24 | 17719.92 | 19123.58 | 24272.35 | 25538.46 | 28051.41 | 29638.64 | 34483.72 |
| Change | -70.88 | 540.66 | 437.72 | 56.38 | 981.16 | 895.11 | 422.70 | 1005.18 | 3137.04 | -1335.84 |

* Shortened trading day

| | 2012 | 2013 | 2014 | 2015 | 2016 | 2017 | 2018 | 2019 | 2020 | 2021 |
|---|---|---|---|---|---|---|---|---|---|---|
| Previous Month Close | 13025.58 | 16086.41 | 17828.24 | 17719.92 | 19123.58 | 24272.35 | 25538.46 | 28051.41 | 29638.64 | 34483.72 |
| 1 | S | S | -51.44 | 168.43 | 68.35 | -40.76 | S | S | 185.28 | -461.68 |
| 2 | S | -77.64 | 102.75 | -158.67 | -21.51 | S | S | -268.37 | 59.87 | 617.75 |
| 3 | -59.98 | -94.15 | 33.07 | -252.01 | S | S | 287.97 | -280.23 | 85.73 | -59.71 |
| 4 | -13.82 | -24.85 | -12.52 | 369.96 | S | 58.46 | -799.36 | 146.97 | 248.74 | S |
| 5 | 82.71 | -68.26 | 58.69 | S | 45.82 | -109.41 | H** | 28.01 | S | S |
| 6 | 39.55 | 198.69 | S | S | 35.54 | -39.73 | -79.40 | 337.27 | S | 646.95 |
| 7 | 81.09 | S | S | -117.12 | 297.84 | 70.57 | -558.72 | S | -148.47 | 492.40 |
| 8 | S | S | -106.31 | -162.51 | 65.19 | 117.68 | S | S | 104.09 | 35.32 |
| 9 | S | 5.33 | -51.28 | -75.70 | 142.04 | S | S | -105.46 | -105.07 | -0.06 |
| 10 | 14.75 | -52.40 | -268.05 | 82.45 | S | S | 34.31 | -27.88 | -69.55 | 216.30 |
| 11 | 78.56 | -129.60 | 63.19 | -309.54 | S | 56.87 | -53.02 | 29.58 | 47.11 | S |
| 12 | -2.99 | -104.10 | -315.51 | S | 39.58 | 118.77 | 157.03 | 220.75 | S | S |
| 13 | -74.73 | 15.93 | S | 103.29 | 114.78 | 80.63 | 70.11 | 3.33 | S | -320.04 |
| 14 | -35.71 | S | S | 156.41 | -118.68 | -76.77 | -496.87 | S | -184.82 | -106.77 |
| 15 | S | S | -99.99 | 224.18 | 59.71 | 143.08 | S | S | 337.76 | 383.25 |
| 16 | S | 129.21 | -111.97 | -253.25 | -8.83 | S | S | 100.51 | -44.77 | -29.79 |
| 17 | 100.38 | -9.31 | 288.00 | -367.29 | S | S | -507.53 | 31.27 | 148.83 | -532.20 |
| 18 | 115.57 | 292.71 | 421.28 | S | 39.65 | 140.46 | 82.66 | -27.88 | -124.32 | S |
| 19 | -98.99 | 11.11 | 26.65 | S | 91.56 | -37.45 | -351.98 | 137.68 | S | S |
| 20 | 59.75 | 42.06 | S | 123.07 | -32.66 | -28.10 | -464.06 | 78.13 | S | -433.28 |
| 21 | -120.88 | S | S | 165.65 | -23.08 | 55.64 | -414.23 | S | 37.40 | 560.54 |
| 22 | S | S | 154.64 | 185.34 | 14.93 | -28.23 | S | S | -200.94 | 261.19 |
| 23 | S | 73.47 | 64.73 | -50.44* | S | S | S | 96.44 | 114.32 | 196.67 |
| 24 | -51.76* | 62.94* | 6.04* | H | S | S | -653.17* | -36.08* | 70.04* | H |
| 25 | H | H | H | H | S | H | H | H | H | S |
| 26 | -24.49 | 122.33 | 23.50 | S | H | -7.85 | 1086.25 | 105.94 | S | S |
| 27 | -18.28 | -1.47 | S | S | 11.23 | 28.09 | 260.37 | 23.87 | S | 351.82 |
| 28 | -158.20 | S | S | -23.90 | -111.36 | 63.21 | -76.42 | S | 204.10 | 95.83 |
| 29 | S | S | -15.48 | 192.71 | -13.90 | -118.29 | S | S | -68.30 | 90.42 |
| 30 | S | 25.88 | -55.16 | -117.11 | -57.18 | S | S | -183.12 | 73.89 | -90.55 |
| 31 | 166.03 | 72.37 | -160.00 | -178.84 | S | S | 265.06 | 76.30 | 196.92 | -59.78 |
| Close | 13104.14 | 16576.66 | 17823.07 | 17425.03 | 19762.60 | 24719.22 | 23327.46 | 28538.44 | 30606.48 | 36338.30 |
| Change | 78.56 | 490.25 | -5.17 | -294.89 | 639.02 | 446.87 | -2211.00 | 487.03 | 967.84 | 1854.58 |

* Shortened trading day, ** President H.W. Bush Funeral.

# A TYPICAL DAY IN THE MARKET

Half-hourly data became available for the Dow Jones Industrial Average starting in January 1987. The NYSE switched 10:00 a.m. openings to 9:30 a.m. in October 1985. Below is the comparison between half-hourly performance 1987 to May 6, 2022, and hourly November 1963 to June 1985. Stronger openings and closings in a more bullish climate are evident. Morning and afternoon weaknesses appear an hour earlier.

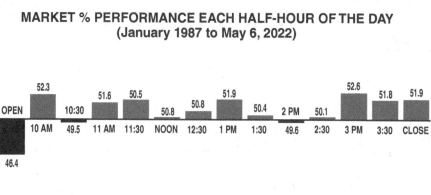

**MARKET % PERFORMANCE EACH HALF-HOUR OF THE DAY**
**(January 1987 to May 6, 2022)**

*Based on the number of times the Dow Jones Industrial Average increased over previous half-hour.*

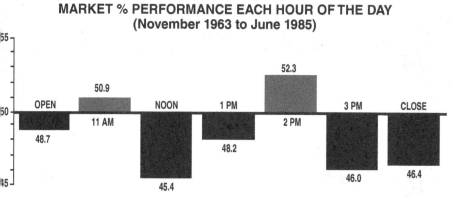

**MARKET % PERFORMANCE EACH HOUR OF THE DAY**
**(November 1963 to June 1985)**

*Based on the number of times the Dow Jones Industrial Average increased over previous hour.*

On the next page, half-hourly movements since January 1987 are separated by day of the week. From 1953 to 1989, Monday was the worst day of the week, especially during long bear markets, but times changed. Monday reversed positions and became the best day of the week and on the plus side eleven years in a row from 1990 to 2000.

During the last 21 years (2001 to May 6, 2022) Friday is the sole net loser. Tuesday and Wednesday are solid gainers, Wednesday the best (page 72). On all days stocks do tend to firm up near the close with weakness early morning and from 2 to 2:30 frequently.

# THROUGH THE WEEK ON A HALF-HOURLY BASIS

From the chart showing the percentage of times the Dow Jones Industrial Average rose over the preceding half-hour (January 1987-May 6, 2022*), the typical week unfolds.

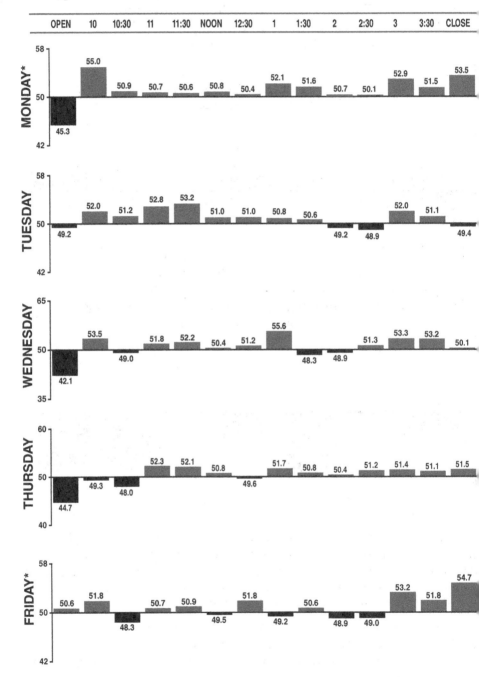

*Monday denotes first trading day of the week, Friday denotes last trading day of the week.

# TUESDAY & WEDNESDAY MOST PROFITABLE DAYS

Between 1952 and 1989, Monday was the worst trading day of the week. The first trading day of the week (including Tuesday, when Monday is a holiday) rose only 44.3% of the time, while the other trading days closed higher 54.8% of the time. (NYSE Saturday trading discontinued June 1952.)

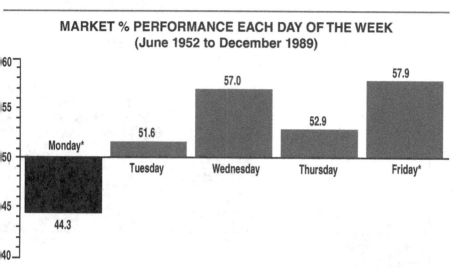

**MARKET % PERFORMANCE EACH DAY OF THE WEEK**
**(June 1952 to December 1989)**

A dramatic reversal occurred in 1990—Monday became the most powerful day of the week. However, during the last 21 and a third years, Tuesday has produced the most gains and Wednesday has been up the most number of times. Since the top in 2000, traders have not been inclined to stay long over the weekend nor buy up equities at the outset of the week. This is not uncommon during uncertain market times. Monday was the worst day during the 2007–2009 bear, and only Tuesday was a net gainer. Since the March 2009 bottom, Monday is best. See pages 72 and 145.

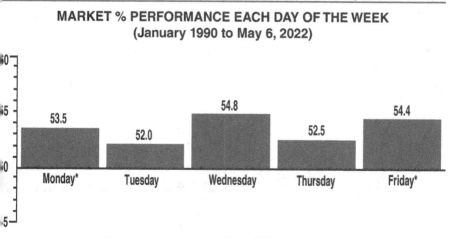

**MARKET % PERFORMANCE EACH DAY OF THE WEEK**
**(January 1990 to May 6, 2022)**

*Charts based on the number of times S&P 500 index closed higher than previous day.*
*\*Monday denotes first trading day of the week, Friday denotes last trading day of the week.*

# NASDAQ STRONGEST LAST THREE DAYS OF WEEK

Despite 20 years less data, daily trading patterns on NASDAQ through 1989 appear to be fairly similar to the S&P on page 143 except for more bullishness on Thursdays. During the mostly flat markets of the 1970s and early 1980s, it would appear that apprehensive investors decided to throw in the towel over the weekends and sell on Mondays and Tuesdays.

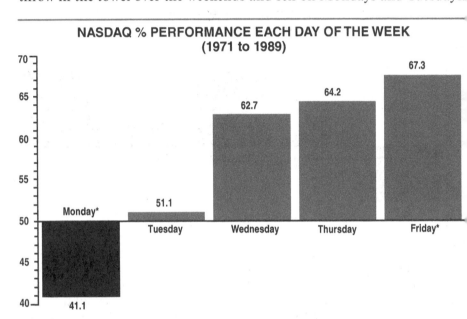

Notice the modest difference in the daily trading pattern between NASDAQ and S&P from January 1, 1990 to recent times. NASDAQ's weekly patterns are beginning to move in step with the rest of the market as technology continues to take an ever-increasing role throughout the economy. Notice the similarities to the S&P since 2001 on pages 145 and 146, Monday and Friday weakness, mid-week strength during periods of uncertainty like 2015 to 2016.

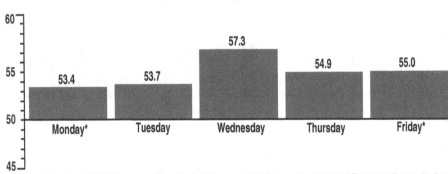

*Based on NASDAQ composite, prior to February 5, 1971, based on National Quotation Bureau indices*
*\*Monday denotes first trading day of the week, Friday denotes last trading day of the week*

# S&P DAILY PERFORMANCE EACH YEAR SINCE 1952

To determine if market trend alters performance of different days of the week, we separated 23 bear years of 1953, '56, '57, '60, '62, '66, '69, '70, '73, '74, '77, '78, '81, '84, '87, '90, '94, 2000, 2001, 2002, 2008, 2011 and 2015 from 47 bull market years. While Tuesday and Thursday did not vary much between bull and bear years, Mondays and Fridays were sharply affected. There was a swing of 10.4 percentage points in Monday's and 9.5 in Friday's performance. Tuesday is the best day of the week based upon total points gained. See page 72.

## PERCENTAGE OF TIMES MARKET CLOSED HIGHER THAN PREVIOUS DAY
### (June 1952 to May 6, 2022)

| | Monday* | Tuesday | Wednesday | Thursday | Friday* |
|---|---|---|---|---|---|
| 1952 | 48.4% | 55.6% | 58.1% | 51.9% | 66.7% |
| 1953 | 32.7 | 50.0 | 54.9 | 57.5 | 56.6 |
| 1954 | 50.0 | 57.5 | 63.5 | 59.2 | 73.1 |
| 1955 | 50.0 | 45.7 | 63.5 | 60.0 | 78.9 |
| 1956 | 36.5 | 39.6 | 46.9 | 50.0 | 59.6 |
| 1957 | 25.0 | 54.0 | 66.7 | 48.9 | 44.2 |
| 1958 | 59.6 | 52.0 | 59.6 | 68.1 | 72.6 |
| 1959 | 42.3 | 53.1 | 55.8 | 48.9 | 69.8 |
| 1960 | 34.6 | 50.0 | 44.2 | 54.0 | 59.6 |
| 1961 | 52.9 | 54.4 | 64.7 | 56.0 | 67.3 |
| 1962 | 28.3 | 52.1 | 54.0 | 51.0 | 50.0 |
| 1963 | 46.2 | 63.3 | 51.0 | 57.5 | 69.2 |
| 1964 | 40.4 | 48.0 | 61.5 | 58.7 | 77.4 |
| 1965 | 44.2 | 57.5 | 55.8 | 51.0 | 71.2 |
| 1966 | 36.5 | 47.8 | 53.9 | 42.0 | 57.7 |
| 1967 | 38.5 | 50.0 | 60.8 | 64.0 | 69.2 |
| 1968† | 49.1 | 57.5 | 64.3 | 42.6 | 54.9 |
| 1969 | 30.8 | 45.8 | 50.0 | 67.4 | 50.0 |
| 1970 | 38.5 | 46.0 | 63.5 | 48.9 | 52.8 |
| 1971 | 44.2 | 64.6 | 57.7 | 55.1 | 51.9 |
| 1972 | 38.5 | 60.9 | 57.7 | 51.0 | 67.3 |
| 1973 | 32.1 | 51.1 | 52.9 | 44.9 | 44.2 |
| 1974 | 32.7 | 57.1 | 51.0 | 36.7 | 30.8 |
| 1975 | 53.9 | 38.8 | 61.5 | 56.3 | 55.8 |
| 1976 | 55.8 | 55.3 | 55.8 | 40.8 | 58.5 |
| 1977 | 40.4 | 40.4 | 46.2 | 53.1 | 53.9 |
| 1978 | 51.9 | 43.5 | 59.6 | 54.0 | 48.1 |
| 1979 | 54.7 | 53.2 | 58.8 | 66.0 | 44.2 |
| 1980 | 55.8 | 54.5 | 71.7 | 35.4 | 59.6 |
| 1981 | 44.2 | 38.6 | 55.8 | 53.2 | 47.2 |
| 1982 | 46.2 | 39.6 | 44.2 | 44.9 | 50.0 |
| 1983 | 55.8 | 46.8 | 61.5 | 52.0 | 55.8 |
| 1984 | 39.6 | 63.8 | 31.4 | 46.0 | 44.2 |
| 1985 | 44.2 | 61.2 | 54.9 | 56.3 | 53.9 |
| 1986 | 51.9 | 44.9 | 67.3 | 58.3 | 55.8 |
| 1987 | 57.1 | 61.7 | 63.5 | 61.7 | 49.1 |
| 1988 | 51.9 | 61.7 | 51.9 | 48.0 | 59.6 |
| 1989 | 51.9 | 47.8 | 69.2 | 58.0 | 69.2 |
| 1990 | 67.9 | 53.2 | 52.9 | 40.0 | 51.9 |
| 1991 | 44.2 | 46.9 | 52.9 | 49.0 | 51.9 |
| 1992 | 51.9 | 49.0 | 53.9 | 56.3 | 45.3 |
| 1993 | 65.4 | 41.7 | 55.8 | 44.9 | 48.1 |
| 1994 | 63.5 | 46.8 | 52.9 | 48.0 | 59.6 |
| 1995 | 54.7 | 56.5 | 63.5 | 62.0 | 63.5 |
| 1996 | 63.5 | 44.9 | 51.0 | 57.1 | 63.5 |
| 1997 | 67.3 | 67.4 | 42.3 | 41.7 | 57.7 |
| 1998 | 57.7 | 62.5 | 57.7 | 38.3 | 60.4 |
| 1999 | 46.2 | 29.8 | 67.3 | 53.1 | 57.7 |
| 2000 | 51.9 | 43.5 | 40.4 | 56.0 | 46.2 |
| 2001 | 45.3 | 51.1 | 44.0 | 59.2 | 43.1 |
| 2002 | 40.4 | 37.5 | 56.9 | 38.8 | 48.1 |
| 2003 | 59.6 | 62.5 | 42.3 | 58.3 | 50.0 |
| 2004 | 51.9 | 61.7 | 59.6 | 52.1 | 52.8 |
| 2005 | 59.6 | 47.8 | 59.6 | 56.0 | 55.8 |
| 2006 | 55.8 | 55.6 | 67.3 | 52.0 | 48.1 |
| 2007 | 47.2 | 50.0 | 64.0 | 50.0 | 61.5 |
| 2008 | 42.3 | 50.0 | 41.5 | 60.4 | 55.8 |
| 2009 | 53.9 | 50.0 | 57.7 | 63.8 | 52.8 |
| 2010 | 61.5 | 57.5 | 55.8 | 53.1 | 57.7 |
| 2011 | 48.1 | 56.5 | 55.8 | 56.0 | 57.7 |
| 2012 | 52.8 | 48.9 | 50.0 | 58.0 | 53.9 |
| 2013 | 51.9 | 60.4 | 54.9 | 59.2 | 65.4 |
| 2014 | 53.9 | 56.3 | 57.7 | 56.3 | 61.5 |
| 2015 | 51.9 | 43.8 | 44.2 | 53.2 | 43.4 |
| 2016 | 50.0 | 58.7 | 55.8 | 50.0 | 46.2 |
| 2017 | 55.8 | 55.6 | 61.5 | 50.0 | 61.5 |
| 2018 | 55.8 | 60.9 | 50.0 | 46.0 | 53.9 |
| 2019 | 50.0 | 54.2 | 60.8 | 65.3 | 67.3 |
| 2020 | 63.5 | 54.2 | 61.5 | 52.1 | 54.7 |
| 2021 | 51.9 | 44.7 | 61.5 | 65.3 | 59.6 |
| 2022‡ | 38.9 | 56.3 | 55.6 | 29.4 | 38.9 |
| **Average** | **48.7%** | **51.7%** | **56.0%** | **53.0%** | **56.5%** |
| **47 Bull Years** | **52.1%** | **53.2%** | **58.2%** | **53.8%** | **59.6%** |
| **23 Bear Years** | **41.7%** | **48.7%** | **51.4%** | **51.3%** | **50.2%** |

*Based on S&P 500*

† Most Wednesdays closed last 7 months of 1968.  ‡ Through 5/6/2022 only, not included in averages.
*Monday denotes first trading day of the week, Friday denotes last trading day of the week.

# NASDAQ DAILY PERFORMANCE EACH YEAR SINCE 1971

After dropping a hefty 77.9% from its 2000 high (versus -37.8% on the Dow and -49.1% on the S&P 500), NASDAQ tech stocks still outpace the blue chips and big caps—but not by nearly as much as they did. From January 1, 1971, through May 6, 2022, NASDAQ moved up an impressive 13453%. The Dow (up 3822%) and the S&P (up 4375%) gained less than a third as much.

Monday's performance on NASDAQ was lackluster during the three-year bear market of 2000-2002. As NASDAQ rebounded (up 50% in 2003) strength returned to Monday during 2003-2006. During the bear market from late 2007 to early 2009, weakness was most consistent on Monday and Friday. At press time, Thursday and Fridays have been most challenging.

## PERCENTAGE OF TIMES NASDAQ CLOSED HIGHER THAN PREVIOUS DAY
### (1971 to MAY 6, 2022)

|  | Monday* | Tuesday | Wednesday | Thursday | Friday* |
|---|---|---|---|---|---|
| 1971 | 51.9% | 52.1% | 59.6% | 65.3% | 71.2% |
| 1972 | 30.8 | 60.9 | 63.5 | 57.1 | 78.9 |
| 1973 | 34.0 | 48.9 | 52.9 | 53.1 | 48.1 |
| 1974 | 30.8 | 44.9 | 52.9 | 51.0 | 42.3 |
| 1975 | 44.2 | 42.9 | 63.5 | 64.6 | 63.5 |
| 1976 | 50.0 | 63.8 | 67.3 | 59.2 | 58.5 |
| 1977 | 51.9 | 40.4 | 53.9 | 63.3 | 73.1 |
| 1978 | 48.1 | 47.8 | 73.1 | 72.0 | 84.6 |
| 1979 | 45.3 | 53.2 | 64.7 | 86.0 | 82.7 |
| 1980 | 46.2 | 64.6 | 84.9 | 52.1 | 73.1 |
| 1981 | 42.3 | 32.7 | 67.3 | 76.6 | 69.8 |
| 1982 | 34.6 | 47.9 | 59.6 | 51.0 | 63.5 |
| 1983 | 42.3 | 44.7 | 67.3 | 68.0 | 73.1 |
| 1984 | 22.6 | 53.2 | 35.3 | 52.0 | 51.9 |
| 1985 | 36.5 | 59.2 | 62.8 | 68.8 | 66.0 |
| 1986 | 38.5 | 55.1 | 65.4 | 72.9 | 75.0 |
| 1987 | 42.3 | 49.0 | 65.4 | 68.1 | 66.0 |
| 1988 | 50.0 | 55.3 | 61.5 | 66.0 | 63.5 |
| 1989 | 38.5 | 54.4 | 71.2 | 72.0 | 75.0 |
| 1990 | 54.7 | 42.6 | 60.8 | 46.0 | 55.8 |
| 1991 | 51.9 | 59.2 | 66.7 | 65.3 | 51.9 |
| 1992 | 44.2 | 53.1 | 59.6 | 60.4 | 45.3 |
| 1993 | 55.8 | 56.3 | 69.2 | 57.1 | 67.3 |
| 1994 | 51.9 | 46.8 | 54.9 | 52.0 | 55.8 |
| 1995 | 50.0 | 52.2 | 63.5 | 64.0 | 63.5 |
| 1996 | 50.9 | 57.1 | 64.7 | 61.2 | 63.5 |
| 1997 | 65.4 | 59.2 | 53.9 | 52.1 | 55.8 |
| 1998 | 59.6 | 58.3 | 65.4 | 44.7 | 58.5 |
| 1999 | 61.5 | 40.4 | 63.5 | 57.1 | 65.4 |
| 2000 | 40.4 | 41.3 | 42.3 | 60.0 | 57.7 |
| 2001 | 41.5 | 57.8 | 52.0 | 55.1 | 47.1 |
| 2002 | 44.2 | 37.5 | 56.9 | 46.9 | 46.2 |
| 2003 | 57.7 | 60.4 | 40.4 | 60.4 | 46.2 |
| 2004 | 57.7 | 59.6 | 53.9 | 50.0 | 50.9 |
| 2005 | 61.5 | 47.8 | 51.9 | 48.0 | 59.6 |
| 2006 | 55.8 | 51.1 | 65.4 | 50.0 | 44.2 |
| 2007 | 47.2 | 63.0 | 66.0 | 56.0 | 57.7 |
| 2008 | 34.6 | 52.1 | 49.1 | 54.2 | 42.3 |
| 2009 | 51.9 | 54.2 | 63.5 | 63.8 | 50.9 |
| 2010 | 61.5 | 53.2 | 61.5 | 55.1 | 61.5 |
| 2011 | 50.0 | 56.5 | 50.0 | 64.0 | 53.9 |
| 2012 | 49.1 | 53.3 | 50.0 | 54.0 | 51.9 |
| 2013 | 57.7 | 60.4 | 52.9 | 59.2 | 67.3 |
| 2014 | 57.7 | 58.3 | 57.7 | 52.1 | 59.6 |
| 2015 | 55.8 | 39.6 | 53.9 | 59.6 | 49.1 |
| 2016 | 51.9 | 52.2 | 55.8 | 50.0 | 57.7 |
| 2017 | 59.6 | 62.2 | 67.3 | 50.0 | 67.3 |
| 2018 | 54.7 | 69.6 | 50.0 | 46.0 | 50.0 |
| 2019 | 50.0 | 58.3 | 62.8 | 59.2 | 59.6 |
| 2020 | 69.2 | 58.3 | 67.3 | 60.4 | 54.7 |
| 2021 | 55.8 | 44.7 | 48.1 | 67.4 | 63.5 |
| 2022† | 50.0 | 56.3 | 50.0 | 29.4 | 33.3 |
| **Average** | **48.9%** | **52.7%** | **59.5%** | **58.8%** | **60.0%** |
| **38 Bull Years** | **51.2%** | **54.9%** | **61.6%** | **59.5%** | **62.5%** |
| **13 Bear Years** | **41.9%** | **46.4%** | **53.4%** | **56.8%** | **52.8%** |

*Based on NASDAQ composite; prior to February 5, 1971, based on National Quotation Bureau indices.*
*† Through 5/6/2022 only, not included in averages.*
*\*Monday denotes first trading day of the week, Friday denotes last trading day of the week.*

# MONTHLY CASH INFLOWS INTO S&P STOCKS

For many years, the last trading day of the month, plus the first four of the following month, were the best market days of the month. This pattern is quite clear in the first chart, showing these five consecutive trading days towering above the other 16 trading days of the average month in the 1953-1981 period. The rationale was that individuals and institutions tended to operate similarly, causing a massive flow of cash into stocks near beginnings of months.

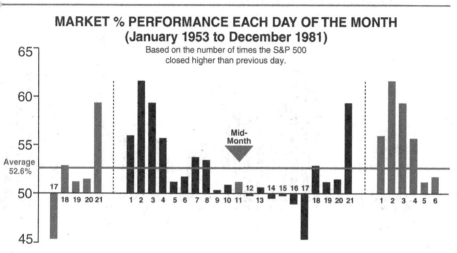

Clearly "front-running" traders took advantage of this phenomenon, drastically altering the previous pattern. The second chart from 1982 onward shows the trading shift caused by these "anticipators" to the last three trading days of the month plus the first two. Another development shows the ninth, tenth, eleventh, and twelveth trading days rising strongly as well. Growth of 401(k) retirement plans, IRAs and similar plans (participants' salaries are usually paid twice monthly) are responsible for this mid-month bulge. First trading days of the month have produced the greatest gains in recent years (see page 90).

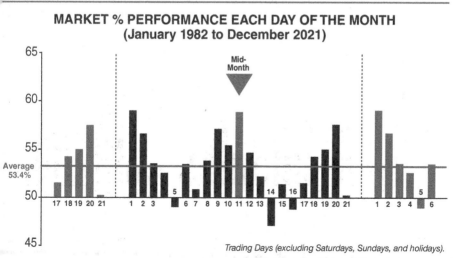

*Trading Days (excluding Saturdays, Sundays, and holidays).*

# MONTHLY CASH INFLOWS INTO NASDAQ STOCKS

NASDAQ stocks moved up 58.1% of the time through 1981 compared to 52.6% for the S&P on page 147. Ends and beginnings of the month are fairly similar, specifically the last plus the first four trading days. But notice how investors piled into NASDAQ stocks until mid-month. NASDAQ rose 118.6% from January 1, 1971, to December 31, 1981, compared to 33.0% for the S&P.

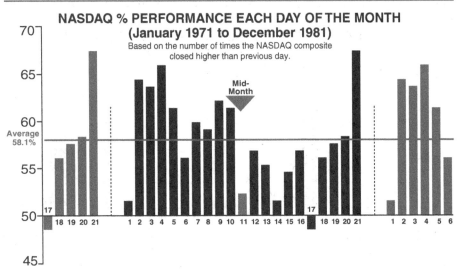

NASDAQ % PERFORMANCE EACH DAY OF THE MONTH
(January 1971 to December 1981)
Based on the number of times the NASDAQ composite closed higher than previous day.

After the air was let out of the tech market 2000-2002, S&P's 3789% gain over the last 40 years is more evenly matched with NASDAQ's 7889% gain. Last three, first four and middle ninth, tenth, eleventh and twelfth days rose the most. Where the S&P has three days of the month that go down more often than up, NASDAQ has none. NASDAQ exhibits the most strength on the first trading day of the month. Over the past 20 years, last days have weakened considerably, down more frequently than not.

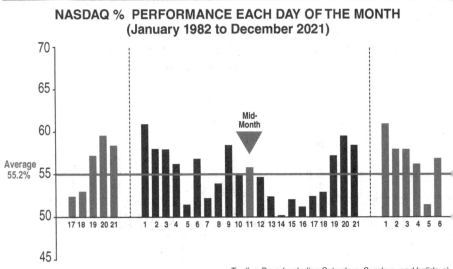

NASDAQ % PERFORMANCE EACH DAY OF THE MONTH
(January 1982 to December 2021)

*Trading Days (excluding Saturdays, Sundays, and holidays).*
*Based on NASDAQ composite, prior to February 5, 1971, based on National Quotation Bureau indices.*

148

# NOVEMBER, DECEMBER, AND JANUARY: YEAR'S BEST THREE-MONTH SPAN

The most important observation to be made from a chart showing the average monthly percent change in market prices since 1950 is that institutions (mutual funds, pension funds, banks, etc.) determine the trading patterns in today's market.

The "investment calendar" reflects the annual, semi-annual and quarterly operations of institutions during January, April and July. October, besides being the last campaign month before elections, is also the time when most bear markets seem to end, as in 1946, 1957, 1960, 1966, 1974, 1987, 1990, 1998 and 2002. (August and September tend to combine to make the worst consecutive two-month period.)

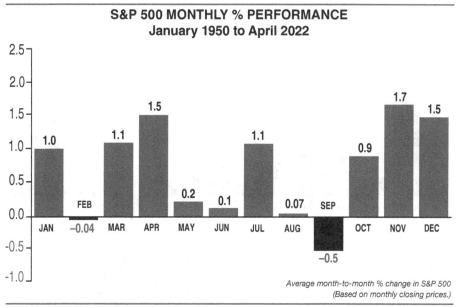

**S&P 500 MONTHLY % PERFORMANCE**
**January 1950 to April 2022**

*Average month-to-month % change in S&P 500*
*(Based on monthly closing prices.)*

Unusual year-end strength comes from corporate and private pension funds, producing a 4.2% gain on average between November 1 and January 31. In 2007-2008 these three months were all down for the fourth time since 1930; previously in 1931-32, 1940-41 and 1969-70, also bear markets. September's dismal performance makes it the worst month of the year. However, in the last 18 years it has been up 11 times after being down five in a row 1999-2003.

In pre-election years since 1950, January is the best month +4.1% (16-2). April is second best with an average 3.5% gain. February, March, June, July August, October, November, and December are also positive. September is the worst month in pre-election years, average loss –0.8% (6-12). May is also a net decliner.

See page 52 for monthly performance tables for the S&P 500 and the Dow Jones Industrials. See pages 54, 56, 62, and 64 for unique switching strategies.

On page 68 you can see how the first month of the first three quarters far outperforms the second and the third months since 1950 and note the improvement in May's and October's performance since 1991.

# NOVEMBER THROUGH JUNE:
# NASDAQ'S EIGHT-MONTH RUN

The two-and-a-half-year plunge of 77.9% in NASDAQ stocks, between March 10, 2000, and October 9, 2002, brought several horrendous monthly losses (the two greatest were November 2000, –22.9%, and February 2001, –22.4%), which trimmed average monthly performance over the 51⅓-year period. Ample Octobers in 16 of the last 24 years, including three huge turnarounds in 2001 (+12.8%), 2002 (+13.5%) and 2011 (+11.1%) have put bear-killing October in the number one spot since 1998. January's 2.5% average gain is still awesome, and more than twice S&P's 1.0% January average since 1971.

**NASDAQ MONTHLY PERFORMANCE**
**January 1971 to April 2022**

*Average month-to-month % change in NASDAQ composite, prior to February 5, 1971, based on National Quotation Bureau indices. (Based on monthly closing prices.)*

Bear in mind when comparing NASDAQ to the S&P on page 149 that there are 23 fewer years of data here. During this 51¼-year (1971-April 2022) period, NASDAQ gained 13665%, while the S&P and the Dow rose only 4384% and 3831%, respectively. On page 60 you can see a statistical monthly comparison between NASDAQ and the Dow.

Year-end strength is even more pronounced in NASDAQ, producing a 6.0% gain on average between November 1 and January 31—nearly 1.5 times greater than that of the S&P 500 on page 149. September is the worst month of the year for the over-the-counter index as well, posting an average loss of –0.7%. These extremes underscore NASDAQ's higher volatility—and moves of greater magnitude.

In pre-election years since 1971, January is best with an average gain of 6.8% (11-2). February, March, April, May, June, July, August, October, November and December are all also positive. September is the only losing month in pre-election years, –0.8% (7-6).

# DOW JONES INDUSTRIALS ANNUAL HIGHS, LOWS, & CLOSES SINCE 1901

| YEAR | HIGH DATE | HIGH CLOSE | LOW DATE | LOW CLOSE | YEAR CLOSE | YEAR | HIGH DATE | HIGH CLOSE | LOW DATE | LOW CLOSE | YEAR CLOSE |
|---|---|---|---|---|---|---|---|---|---|---|---|
| 1901 | 6/17 | 57.33 | 12/24 | 45.07 | 47.29 | 1933 | 7/18 | 108.67 | 2/27 | 50.16 | 99.90 |
| 1902 | 4/24 | 50.14 | 12/15 | 43.64 | 47.10 | 1934 | 2/5 | 110.74 | 7/26 | 85.51 | 104.04 |
| 1903 | 2/16 | 49.59 | 11/9 | 30.88 | 35.98 | 1935 | 11/19 | 148.44 | 3/14 | 96.71 | 144.13 |
| 1904 | 12/5 | 53.65 | 3/12 | 34.00 | 50.99 | 1936 | 11/17 | 184.90 | 1/6 | 143.11 | 179.90 |
| 1905 | 12/29 | 70.74 | 1/25 | 50.37 | 70.47 | 1937 | 3/10 | 194.40 | 11/24 | 113.64 | 120.85 |
| 1906 | 1/19 | 75.45 | 7/13 | 62.40 | 69.12 | 1938 | 11/12 | 158.41 | 3/31 | 98.95 | 154.76 |
| 1907 | 1/7 | 70.60 | 11/15 | 38.83 | 43.04 | 1939 | 9/12 | 155.92 | 4/8 | 121.44 | 150.24 |
| 1908 | 11/13 | 64.74 | 2/13 | 42.94 | 63.11 | 1940 | 1/3 | 152.80 | 6/10 | 111.84 | 131.13 |
| 1909 | 11/19 | 73.64 | 2/23 | 58.54 | 72.56 | 1941 | 1/10 | 133.59 | 12/23 | 106.34 | 110.96 |
| 1910 | 1/3 | 72.04 | 7/26 | 53.93 | 59.60 | 1942 | 12/26 | 119.71 | 4/28 | 92.92 | 119.40 |
| 1911 | 6/19 | 63.78 | 9/25 | 53.43 | 59.84 | 1943 | 7/14 | 145.82 | 1/8 | 119.26 | 135.89 |
| 1912 | 9/30 | 68.97 | 2/10 | 58.72 | 64.37 | 1944 | 12/16 | 152.53 | 2/7 | 134.22 | 152.32 |
| 1913 | 1/9 | 64.88 | 6/11 | 52.83 | 57.71 | 1945 | 12/11 | 195.82 | 1/24 | 151.35 | 192.91 |
| 1914 | 3/20 | 61.12 | 7/30 | 52.32 | 54.58 | 1946 | 5/29 | 212.50 | 10/9 | 163.12 | 177.20 |
| 1915 | 12/27 | 99.21 | 2/24 | 54.22 | 99.15 | 1947 | 7/24 | 186.85 | 5/17 | 163.21 | 181.16 |
| 1916 | 11/21 | 110.15 | 4/22 | 84.96 | 95.00 | 1948 | 6/15 | 193.16 | 3/16 | 165.39 | 177.30 |
| 1917 | 1/3 | 99.18 | 12/19 | 65.95 | 74.38 | 1949 | 12/30 | 200.52 | 6/13 | 161.60 | 200.13 |
| 1918 | 10/18 | 89.07 | 1/15 | 73.38 | 82.20 | 1950 | 11/24 | 235.47 | 1/13 | 196.81 | 235.41 |
| 1919 | 11/3 | 119.62 | 2/8 | 79.15 | 107.23 | 1951 | 9/13 | 276.37 | 1/3 | 238.99 | 269.23 |
| 1920 | 1/3 | 109.88 | 12/21 | 66.75 | 71.95 | 1952 | 12/30 | 292.00 | 5/1 | 256.35 | 291.90 |
| 1921 | 12/15 | 81.50 | 8/24 | 63.90 | 81.10 | 1953 | 1/5 | 293.79 | 9/14 | 255.49 | 280.90 |
| 1922 | 10/14 | 103.43 | 1/10 | 78.59 | 98.73 | 1954 | 12/31 | 404.39 | 1/11 | 279.87 | 404.39 |
| 1923 | 3/20 | 105.38 | 10/27 | 85.76 | 95.52 | 1955 | 12/30 | 488.40 | 1/17 | 388.20 | 488.40 |
| 1924 | 12/31 | 120.51 | 5/20 | 88.33 | 120.51 | 1956 | 4/6 | 521.05 | 1/23 | 462.35 | 499.47 |
| 1925 | 11/6 | 159.39 | 3/30 | 115.00 | 156.66 | 1957 | 7/12 | 520.77 | 10/22 | 419.79 | 435.69 |
| 1926 | 8/14 | 166.64 | 3/30 | 135.20 | 157.20 | 1958 | 12/31 | 583.65 | 2/25 | 436.89 | 583.65 |
| 1927 | 12/31 | 202.40 | 1/25 | 152.73 | 202.40 | 1959 | 12/31 | 679.36 | 2/9 | 574.46 | 679.36 |
| 1928 | 12/31 | 300.00 | 2/20 | 191.33 | 300.00 | 1960 | 1/5 | 685.47 | 10/25 | 566.05 | 615.89 |
| 1929 | 9/3 | 381.17 | 11/13 | 198.69 | 248.48 | 1961 | 12/13 | 734.91 | 1/3 | 610.25 | 731.14 |
| 1930 | 4/17 | 294.07 | 12/16 | 157.51 | 164.58 | 1962 | 1/3 | 726.01 | 6/26 | 535.76 | 652.10 |
| 1931 | 2/24 | 194.36 | 12/17 | 73.79 | 77.90 | 1963 | 12/18 | 767.21 | 1/2 | 646.79 | 762.95 |
| 1932 | 3/8 | 88.78 | 7/8 | 41.22 | 59.93 | 1964 | 11/18 | 891.71 | 1/2 | 766.08 | 874.13 |

*(continued)*

# DOW JONES INDUSTRIALS ANNUAL HIGHS, LOWS, & CLOSES SINCE 1901 (continued)

| YEAR | HIGH DATE | HIGH CLOSE | LOW DATE | LOW CLOSE | YEAR CLOSE | YEAR | HIGH DATE | HIGH CLOSE | LOW DATE | LOW CLOSE | YEAR CLOSE |
|---|---|---|---|---|---|---|---|---|---|---|---|
| 1965 | 12/31 | 969.26 | 6/28 | 840.59 | 969.26 | 1994 | 1/31 | 3978.36 | 4/4 | 3593.35 | 3834.44 |
| 1966 | 2/9 | 995.15 | 10/7 | 744.32 | 785.69 | 1995 | 12/13 | 5216.47 | 1/30 | 3832.08 | 5117.12 |
| 1967 | 9/25 | 943.08 | 1/3 | 786.41 | 905.11 | 1996 | 12/27 | 6560.91 | 1/10 | 5032.94 | 6448.27 |
| 1968 | 12/3 | 985.21 | 3/21 | 825.13 | 943.75 | 1997 | 8/6 | 8259.31 | 4/11 | 6391.69 | 7908.25 |
| 1969 | 5/14 | 968.85 | 12/17 | 769.93 | 800.36 | 1998 | 11/23 | 9374.27 | 8/31 | 7539.07 | 9181.43 |
| 1970 | 12/29 | 842.00 | 5/26 | 631.16 | 838.92 | 1999 | 12/31 | 11497.12 | 1/22 | 9120.67 | 11497.12 |
| 1971 | 4/28 | 950.82 | 11/23 | 797.97 | 890.20 | 2000 | 1/14 | 11722.98 | 3/7 | 9796.03 | 10786.85 |
| 1972 | 12/11 | 1036.27 | 1/26 | 889.15 | 1020.02 | 2001 | 5/21 | 11337.92 | 9/21 | 8235.81 | 10021.50 |
| 1973 | 1/11 | 1051.70 | 12/5 | 788.31 | 850.86 | 2002 | 3/19 | 10635.25 | 10/9 | 7286.27 | 8341.63 |
| 1974 | 3/13 | 891.66 | 12/6 | 577.60 | 616.24 | 2003 | 12/31 | 10453.92 | 3/11 | 7524.06 | 10453.92 |
| 1975 | 7/15 | 881.81 | 1/2 | 632.04 | 852.41 | 2004 | 12/28 | 10854.54 | 10/25 | 9749.99 | 10783.01 |
| 1976 | 9/21 | 1014.79 | 1/2 | 858.71 | 1004.65 | 2005 | 3/4 | 10940.55 | 4/20 | 10012.36 | 10717.50 |
| 1977 | 1/3 | 999.75 | 11/2 | 800.85 | 831.17 | 2006 | 12/27 | 12510.57 | 1/20 | 10667.39 | 12463.15 |
| 1978 | 9/8 | 907.74 | 2/28 | 742.12 | 805.01 | 2007 | 10/9 | 14164.53 | 3/5 | 12050.41 | 13264.82 |
| 1979 | 10/5 | 897.61 | 11/7 | 796.67 | 838.74 | 2008 | 5/2 | 13058.20 | 11/20 | 7552.29 | 8776.39 |
| 1980 | 11/20 | 1000.17 | 4/21 | 759.13 | 963.99 | 2009 | 12/30 | 10548.51 | 3/9 | 6547.05 | 10428.05 |
| 1981 | 4/27 | 1024.05 | 9/25 | 824.01 | 875.00 | 2010 | 12/29 | 11585.38 | 7/2 | 9686.48 | 11577.51 |
| 1982 | 12/27 | 1070.55 | 8/12 | 776.92 | 1046.54 | 2011 | 4/29 | 12810.54 | 10/3 | 10655.30 | 12217.56 |
| 1983 | 11/29 | 1287.20 | 1/3 | 1027.04 | 1258.64 | 2012 | 10/5 | 13610.15 | 6/4 | 12101.46 | 13104.14 |
| 1984 | 1/6 | 1286.64 | 7/24 | 1086.57 | 1211.57 | 2013 | 12/31 | 16576.66 | 1/8 | 13328.85 | 16576.66 |
| 1985 | 12/16 | 1553.10 | 1/4 | 1184.96 | 1546.67 | 2014 | 12/26 | 18053.71 | 2/3 | 15372.80 | 17823.07 |
| 1986 | 12/2 | 1955.57 | 1/22 | 1502.29 | 1895.95 | 2015 | 5/19 | 18312.39 | 8/25 | 15666.44 | 17425.03 |
| 1987 | 8/25 | 2722.42 | 10/19 | 1738.74 | 1938.83 | 2016 | 12/20 | 19974.62 | 2/11 | 15660.18 | 19762.60 |
| 1988 | 10/21 | 2183.50 | 1/20 | 1879.14 | 2168.57 | 2017 | 12/28 | 24837.51 | 1/19 | 19732.40 | 24719.22 |
| 1989 | 10/9 | 2791.41 | 1/3 | 2144.64 | 2753.20 | 2018 | 10/3 | 26828.39 | 12/24 | 21792.20 | 23327.46 |
| 1990 | 7/17 | 2999.75 | 10/11 | 2365.10 | 2633.66 | 2019 | 12/27 | 28645.26 | 1/3 | 22686.22 | 28538.44 |
| 1991 | 12/31 | 3168.83 | 1/9 | 2470.30 | 3168.83 | 2020 | 12/31 | 30606.48 | 3/23 | 18591.93 | 30606.48 |
| 1992 | 6/1 | 3413.21 | 10/9 | 3136.58 | 3301.11 | 2021 | 12/29 | 36488.63 | 1/29 | 29982.62 | 36338.30 |
| 1993 | 12/29 | 3794.33 | 1/20 | 3241.95 | 3754.09 | 2022* | 1/4 | 36799.65 | 6/17 | 29888.78 | At Press Time |

*Through June 30, 2022

# S&P 500 ANNUAL HIGHS, LOWS, & CLOSES SINCE 1930

| YEAR | HIGH DATE | HIGH CLOSE | LOW DATE | LOW CLOSE | YEAR CLOSE | YEAR | HIGH DATE | HIGH CLOSE | LOW DATE | LOW CLOSE | YEAR CLOSE |
|------|------|------|------|------|------|------|------|------|------|------|------|
| 1930 | 4/10 | 25.92 | 12/16 | 14.44 | 15.34 | 1977 | 1/3 | 107.00 | 11/2 | 90.71 | 95.10 |
| 1931 | 2/24 | 18.17 | 12/17 | 7.72 | 8.12 | 1978 | 9/12 | 106.99 | 3/6 | 86.90 | 96.11 |
| 1932 | 9/7 | 9.31 | 6/1 | 4.40 | 6.89 | 1979 | 10/5 | 111.27 | 2/27 | 96.13 | 107.94 |
| 1933 | 7/18 | 12.20 | 2/27 | 5.53 | 10.10 | 1980 | 11/28 | 140.52 | 3/27 | 98.22 | 135.76 |
| 1934 | 2/6 | 11.82 | 7/26 | 8.36 | 9.50 | 1981 | 1/6 | 138.12 | 9/25 | 112.77 | 122.55 |
| 1935 | 11/19 | 13.46 | 3/14 | 8.06 | 13.43 | 1982 | 11/9 | 143.02 | 8/12 | 102.42 | 140.64 |
| 1936 | 11/9 | 17.69 | 1/2 | 13.40 | 17.18 | 1983 | 10/10 | 172.65 | 1/3 | 138.34 | 164.93 |
| 1937 | 3/6 | 18.68 | 11/24 | 10.17 | 10.55 | 1984 | 11/6 | 170.41 | 7/24 | 147.82 | 167.24 |
| 1938 | 11/9 | 13.79 | 3/31 | 8.50 | 13.21 | 1985 | 12/16 | 212.02 | 1/4 | 163.68 | 211.28 |
| 1939 | 1/4 | 13.23 | 4/8 | 10.18 | 12.49 | 1986 | 12/2 | 254.00 | 1/22 | 203.49 | 242.17 |
| 1940 | 1/3 | 12.77 | 6/10 | 8.99 | 10.58 | 1987 | 8/25 | 336.77 | 12/4 | 223.92 | 247.08 |
| 1941 | 1/10 | 10.86 | 12/29 | 8.37 | 8.69 | 1988 | 10/21 | 283.66 | 1/20 | 242.63 | 277.72 |
| 1942 | 12/31 | 9.77 | 4/28 | 7.47 | 9.77 | 1989 | 10/9 | 359.80 | 1/3 | 275.31 | 353.40 |
| 1943 | 7/14 | 12.64 | 1/2 | 9.84 | 11.67 | 1990 | 7/16 | 368.95 | 10/11 | 295.46 | 330.22 |
| 1944 | 12/16 | 13.29 | 2/7 | 11.56 | 13.28 | 1991 | 12/31 | 417.09 | 1/9 | 311.49 | 417.09 |
| 1945 | 12/10 | 17.68 | 1/23 | 13.21 | 17.36 | 1992 | 12/18 | 441.28 | 4/8 | 394.50 | 435.71 |
| 1946 | 5/29 | 19.25 | 10/9 | 14.12 | 15.30 | 1993 | 12/28 | 470.94 | 1/8 | 429.05 | 466.45 |
| 1947 | 2/8 | 16.20 | 5/17 | 13.71 | 15.30 | 1994 | 2/2 | 482.00 | 4/4 | 438.92 | 459.27 |
| 1948 | 6/15 | 17.06 | 2/14 | 13.84 | 15.20 | 1995 | 12/13 | 621.69 | 1/3 | 459.11 | 615.93 |
| 1949 | 12/30 | 16.79 | 6/13 | 13.55 | 16.76 | 1996 | 11/25 | 757.03 | 1/10 | 598.48 | 740.74 |
| 1950 | 12/29 | 20.43 | 1/14 | 16.65 | 20.41 | 1997 | 12/5 | 983.79 | 1/2 | 737.01 | 970.43 |
| 1951 | 10/15 | 23.85 | 1/3 | 20.69 | 23.77 | 1998 | 12/29 | 1241.81 | 1/9 | 927.69 | 1229.23 |
| 1952 | 12/30 | 26.59 | 2/20 | 23.09 | 26.57 | 1999 | 12/31 | 1469.25 | 1/14 | 1212.19 | 1469.25 |
| 1953 | 1/5 | 26.66 | 9/14 | 22.71 | 24.81 | 2000 | 3/24 | 1527.46 | 12/20 | 1264.74 | 1320.28 |
| 1954 | 12/31 | 35.98 | 1/11 | 24.80 | 35.98 | 2001 | 2/1 | 1373.47 | 9/21 | 965.80 | 1148.08 |
| 1955 | 11/14 | 46.41 | 1/17 | 34.58 | 45.48 | 2002 | 1/4 | 1172.51 | 10/9 | 776.76 | 879.82 |
| 1956 | 8/2 | 49.74 | 1/23 | 43.11 | 46.67 | 2003 | 12/31 | 1111.92 | 3/11 | 800.73 | 1111.92 |
| 1957 | 7/15 | 49.13 | 10/22 | 38.98 | 39.99 | 2004 | 12/30 | 1213.55 | 8/12 | 1063.23 | 1211.92 |
| 1958 | 12/31 | 55.21 | 1/2 | 40.33 | 55.21 | 2005 | 12/14 | 1272.74 | 4/20 | 1137.50 | 1248.29 |
| 1959 | 8/3 | 60.71 | 2/9 | 53.58 | 59.89 | 2006 | 12/15 | 1427.09 | 6/13 | 1223.69 | 1418.30 |
| 1960 | 1/5 | 60.39 | 10/25 | 52.30 | 58.11 | 2007 | 10/9 | 1565.15 | 3/5 | 1374.12 | 1468.36 |
| 1961 | 12/12 | 72.64 | 1/3 | 57.57 | 71.55 | 2008 | 1/2 | 1447.16 | 11/20 | 752.44 | 903.25 |
| 1962 | 1/3 | 71.13 | 6/26 | 52.32 | 63.10 | 2009 | 12/28 | 1127.78 | 3/9 | 676.53 | 1115.10 |
| 1963 | 12/31 | 75.02 | 1/2 | 62.69 | 75.02 | 2010 | 12/29 | 1259.78 | 7/2 | 1022.58 | 1257.64 |
| 1964 | 11/20 | 86.28 | 1/2 | 75.43 | 84.75 | 2011 | 4/29 | 1363.61 | 10/3 | 1099.23 | 1257.60 |
| 1965 | 11/15 | 92.63 | 6/28 | 81.60 | 92.43 | 2012 | 9/14 | 1465.77 | 1/3 | 1277.06 | 1426.19 |
| 1966 | 2/9 | 94.06 | 10/7 | 73.20 | 80.33 | 2013 | 12/31 | 1848.36 | 1/8 | 1457.15 | 1848.36 |
| 1967 | 9/25 | 97.59 | 1/3 | 80.38 | 96.47 | 2014 | 12/29 | 2090.57 | 2/3 | 1741.89 | 2058.90 |
| 1968 | 11/29 | 108.37 | 3/5 | 87.72 | 103.86 | 2015 | 5/21 | 2130.82 | 8/25 | 1867.61 | 2043.94 |
| 1969 | 5/14 | 106.16 | 12/17 | 89.20 | 92.06 | 2016 | 12/13 | 2271.72 | 2/11 | 1829.08 | 2238.83 |
| 1970 | 1/5 | 93.46 | 5/26 | 69.29 | 92.15 | 2017 | 12/18 | 2690.16 | 1/3 | 2257.83 | 2673.61 |
| 1971 | 4/28 | 104.77 | 11/23 | 90.16 | 102.09 | 2018 | 9/20 | 2930.75 | 12/24 | 2351.10 | 2506.85 |
| 1972 | 12/11 | 119.12 | 1/3 | 101.67 | 118.05 | 2019 | 12/27 | 3240.02 | 1/3 | 2447.89 | 3230.78 |
| 1973 | 1/11 | 120.24 | 12/5 | 92.16 | 97.55 | 2020 | 12/31 | 3756.07 | 3/23 | 2237.40 | 3756.07 |
| 1974 | 1/3 | 99.80 | 10/3 | 62.28 | 68.56 | 2021 | 12/29 | 4793.06 | 1/4 | 3700.65 | 4766.18 |
| 1975 | 7/15 | 95.61 | 1/8 | 70.04 | 90.19 | 2022* | 1/3 | 4796.56 | 6/16 | 3666.77 | At Press Time |
| 1976 | 9/21 | 107.83 | 1/2 | 90.90 | 107.46 | | | | | | |

*Through June 30, 2022

# NASDAQ ANNUAL HIGHS, LOWS, & CLOSES SINCE 1971

| YEAR | HIGH DATE | HIGH CLOSE | LOW DATE | LOW CLOSE | YEAR CLOSE |
|---|---|---|---|---|---|
| 1971 | 12/31 | 114.12 | 1/5 | 89.06 | 114.12 |
| 1972 | 12/8 | 135.15 | 1/3 | 113.65 | 133.73 |
| 1973 | 1/11 | 136.84 | 12/24 | 88.67 | 92.19 |
| 1974 | 3/15 | 96.53 | 10/3 | 54.87 | 59.82 |
| 1975 | 7/15 | 88.00 | 1/2 | 60.70 | 77.62 |
| 1976 | 12/31 | 97.88 | 1/2 | 78.06 | 97.88 |
| 1977 | 12/30 | 105.05 | 4/5 | 93.66 | 105.05 |
| 1978 | 9/13 | 139.25 | 1/11 | 99.09 | 117.98 |
| 1979 | 10/5 | 152.29 | 1/2 | 117.84 | 151.14 |
| 1980 | 11/28 | 208.15 | 3/27 | 124.09 | 202.34 |
| 1981 | 5/29 | 223.47 | 9/28 | 175.03 | 195.84 |
| 1982 | 12/8 | 240.70 | 8/13 | 159.14 | 232.41 |
| 1983 | 6/24 | 328.91 | 1/3 | 230.59 | 278.60 |
| 1984 | 1/6 | 287.90 | 7/25 | 225.30 | 247.35 |
| 1985 | 12/16 | 325.16 | 1/2 | 245.91 | 324.93 |
| 1986 | 7/3 | 411.16 | 1/9 | 323.01 | 349.33 |
| 1987 | 8/26 | 455.26 | 10/28 | 291.88 | 330.47 |
| 1988 | 7/5 | 396.11 | 1/12 | 331.97 | 381.38 |
| 1989 | 10/9 | 485.73 | 1/3 | 378.56 | 454.82 |
| 1990 | 7/16 | 469.60 | 10/16 | 325.44 | 373.84 |
| 1991 | 12/31 | 586.34 | 1/14 | 355.75 | 586.34 |
| 1992 | 12/31 | 676.95 | 6/26 | 547.84 | 676.95 |
| 1993 | 10/15 | 787.42 | 4/26 | 645.87 | 776.80 |
| 1994 | 3/18 | 803.93 | 6/24 | 693.79 | 751.96 |
| 1995 | 12/4 | 1069.79 | 1/3 | 743.58 | 1052.13 |
| 1996 | 12/9 | 1316.27 | 1/15 | 988.57 | 1291.03 |
| 1997 | 10/9 | 1745.85 | 4/2 | 1201.00 | 1570.35 |
| 1998 | 12/31 | 2192.69 | 10/8 | 1419.12 | 2192.69 |
| 1999 | 12/31 | 4069.31 | 1/4 | 2208.05 | 4069.31 |
| 2000 | 3/10 | 5048.62 | 12/20 | 2332.78 | 2470.52 |
| 2001 | 1/24 | 2859.15 | 9/21 | 1423.19 | 1950.40 |
| 2002 | 1/4 | 2059.38 | 10/9 | 1114.11 | 1335.51 |
| 2003 | 12/30 | 2009.88 | 3/11 | 1271.47 | 2003.37 |
| 2004 | 12/30 | 2178.34 | 8/12 | 1752.49 | 2175.44 |
| 2005 | 12/2 | 2273.37 | 4/28 | 1904.18 | 2205.32 |
| 2006 | 11/22 | 2465.98 | 7/21 | 2020.39 | 2415.29 |
| 2007 | 10/31 | 2859.12 | 3/5 | 2340.68 | 2652.28 |
| 2008 | 1/2 | 2609.63 | 11/20 | 1316.12 | 1577.03 |
| 2009 | 12/30 | 2291.28 | 3/9 | 1268.64 | 2269.15 |
| 2010 | 12/22 | 2671.48 | 7/2 | 2091.79 | 2652.87' |
| 2010 | 12/22 | 2671.48 | 7/2 | 2091.79 | 2652.87 |
| 2011 | 4/29 | 2873.54 | 10/3 | 2335.83 | 2605.15 |
| 2012 | 9/14 | 3183.95 | 1/4 | 2648.36 | 3019.51 |
| 2013 | 12/31 | 4176.59 | 1/8 | 3091.81 | 4176.59 |
| 2014 | 12/29 | 4806.91 | 2/3 | 3996.96 | 4736.05 |
| 2015 | 7/20 | 5218.86 | 8/25 | 4506.49 | 5007.41 |
| 2016 | 12/27 | 5487.44 | 2/11 | 4266.84 | 5383.12 |
| 2017 | 12/18 | 6994.76 | 1/3 | 5429.08 | 6903.39 |
| 2018 | 8/29 | 8109.69 | 12/24 | 6192.92 | 6635.28 |
| 2019 | 12/26 | 9022.39 | 1/3 | 6463.50 | 8972.60 |
| 2020 | 12/28 | 12899.42 | 3/23 | 6860.67 | 12888.28 |
| 2021 | 11/29 | 16057.44 | 3/8 | 12609.16 | 15644.97 |
| 2022* | 1/3 | 15832.80 | 6/16 | 10646.10 | *At Press-time* |

*Through June 30, 2022

# RUSSELL 1000 ANNUAL HIGHS, LOWS, & CLOSES SINCE 1979

| YEAR | HIGH DATE | HIGH CLOSE | LOW DATE | LOW CLOSE | YEAR CLOSE | YEAR | HIGH DATE | HIGH CLOSE | LOW DATE | LOW CLOSE | YEAR CLOSE |
|---|---|---|---|---|---|---|---|---|---|---|---|
| 1979 | 10/5 | 61.18 | 2/27 | 51.83 | 59.87 | 2001 | 1/30 | 727.35 | 9/21 | 507.98 | 604.94 |
| 1980 | 11/28 | 78.26 | 3/27 | 53.68 | 75.20 | 2002 | 3/19 | 618.74 | 10/9 | 410.52 | 466.18 |
| 1981 | 1/6 | 76.34 | 9/25 | 62.03 | 67.93 | 2003 | 12/31 | 594.56 | 3/11 | 425.31 | 594.56 |
| 1982 | 11/9 | 78.47 | 8/12 | 55.98 | 77.24 | 2004 | 12/30 | 651.76 | 8/13 | 566.06 | 650.99 |
| 1983 | 10/10 | 95.07 | 1/3 | 76.04 | 90.38 | 2005 | 12/14 | 692.09 | 4/20 | 613.37 | 679.42 |
| 1984 | 1/6 | 92.80 | 7/24 | 79.49 | 90.31 | 2006 | 12/15 | 775.08 | 6/13 | 665.81 | 770.08 |
| 1985 | 12/16 | 114.97 | 1/4 | 88.61 | 114.39 | 2007 | 10/9 | 852.32 | 3/5 | 749.85 | 799.82 |
| 1986 | 7/2 | 137.87 | 1/22 | 111.14 | 130.00 | 2008 | 1/2 | 788.62 | 11/20 | 402.91 | 487.77 |
| 1987 | 8/25 | 176.22 | 12/4 | 117.65 | 130.02 | 2009 | 12/28 | 619.22 | 3/9 | 367.55 | 612.01 |
| 1988 | 10/21 | 149.94 | 1/20 | 128.35 | 146.99 | 2010 | 12/29 | 698.11 | 7/2 | 562.58 | 696.90 |
| 1989 | 10/9 | 189.93 | 1/3 | 145.78 | 185.11 | 2011 | 4/29 | 758.45 | 10/3 | 604.42 | 693.36 |
| 1990 | 7/16 | 191.56 | 10/11 | 152.36 | 171.22 | 2012 | 9/14 | 809.01 | 1/4 | 703.72 | 789.90 |
| 1991 | 12/31 | 220.61 | 1/9 | 161.94 | 220.61 | 2013 | 12/31 | 1030.36 | 1/8 | 807.95 | 1030.36 |
| 1992 | 12/18 | 235.06 | 4/8 | 208.87 | 233.59 | 2014 | 12/29 | 1161.45 | 2/3 | 972.95 | 1144.37 |
| 1993 | 10/15 | 252.77 | 1/8 | 229.91 | 250.71 | 2015 | 5/21 | 1189.55 | 8/25 | 1042.77 | 1131.88 |
| 1994 | 2/1 | 258.31 | 4/4 | 235.38 | 244.65 | 2016 | 12/13 | 1260.06 | 2/11 | 1005.89 | 1241.66 |
| 1995 | 12/13 | 331.18 | 1/3 | 244.41 | 328.89 | 2017 | 12/18 | 1490.06 | 1/3 | 1252.11 | 1481.81 |
| 1996 | 12/2 | 401.21 | 1/10 | 318.24 | 393.75 | 2018 | 9/20 | 1624.28 | 12/24 | 1298.02 | 1384.26 |
| 1997 | 12/5 | 519.72 | 4/11 | 389.03 | 513.79 | 2019 | 12/26 | 1789.56 | 1/3 | 1351.87 | 1784.21 |
| 1998 | 12/29 | 645.36 | 1/9 | 490.26 | 642.87 | 2020 | 12/31 | 2120.87 | 3/23 | 1224.45 | 2120.87 |
| 1999 | 12/31 | 767.97 | 2/9 | 632.53 | 767.97 | 2021 | 12/27 | 2660.44 | 1/4 | 2089.72 | 2645.91 |
| 2000 | 9/1 | 813.71 | 12/20 | 668.75 | 700.09 | 2022* | 1/3 | 2660.78 | 6/16 | 2009.94 | At Press Time |

# RUSSELL 2000 ANNUAL HIGHS, LOWS, & CLOSES SINCE 1979

| YEAR | HIGH DATE | HIGH CLOSE | LOW DATE | LOW CLOSE | YEAR CLOSE | YEAR | HIGH DATE | HIGH CLOSE | LOW DATE | LOW CLOSE | YEAR CLOSE |
|---|---|---|---|---|---|---|---|---|---|---|---|
| 1979 | 12/31 | 55.91 | 1/2 | 40.81 | 55.91 | 2001 | 5/22 | 517.23 | 9/21 | 378.89 | 488.50 |
| 1980 | 11/28 | 77.70 | 3/27 | 45.36 | 74.80 | 2002 | 4/16 | 522.95 | 10/9 | 327.04 | 383.09 |
| 1981 | 6/15 | 85.16 | 9/25 | 65.37 | 73.67 | 2003 | 12/30 | 565.47 | 3/12 | 345.94 | 556.91 |
| 1982 | 12/8 | 91.01 | 8/12 | 60.33 | 88.90 | 2004 | 12/28 | 654.57 | 8/12 | 517.10 | 651.57 |
| 1983 | 6/24 | 126.99 | 1/3 | 88.29 | 112.27 | 2005 | 12/2 | 690.57 | 4/28 | 575.02 | 673.22 |
| 1984 | 1/12 | 116.69 | 7/25 | 93.95 | 101.49 | 2006 | 12/27 | 797.73 | 7/21 | 671.94 | 787.66 |
| 1985 | 12/31 | 129.87 | 1/2 | 101.21 | 129.87 | 2007 | 7/13 | 855.77 | 11/26 | 735.07 | 766.03 |
| 1986 | 7/3 | 155.30 | 1/9 | 128.23 | 135.00 | 2008 | 6/5 | 763.27 | 11/20 | 385.31 | 499.45 |
| 1987 | 8/25 | 174.44 | 10/28 | 106.08 | 120.42 | 2009 | 12/24 | 634.07 | 3/9 | 343.26 | 625.39 |
| 1988 | 7/15 | 151.42 | 1/12 | 121.23 | 147.37 | 2010 | 12/27 | 792.35 | 2/8 | 586.49 | 783.65 |
| 1989 | 10/9 | 180.78 | 1/3 | 146.79 | 168.30 | 2011 | 4/29 | 865.29 | 10/3 | 609.49 | 740.92 |
| 1990 | 6/15 | 170.90 | 10/30 | 118.82 | 132.16 | 2012 | 9/14 | 864.70 | 6/4 | 737.24 | 849.35 |
| 1991 | 12/31 | 189.94 | 1/15 | 125.25 | 189.94 | 2013 | 12/31 | 1163.64 | 1/3 | 872.60 | 1163.64 |
| 1992 | 12/31 | 221.01 | 7/8 | 185.81 | 221.01 | 2014 | 12/29 | 1219.11 | 10/13 | 1049.30 | 1204.70 |
| 1993 | 11/2 | 260.17 | 2/23 | 217.55 | 258.59 | 2015 | 6/23 | 1295.80 | 9/29 | 1083.91 | 1135.89 |
| 1994 | 3/18 | 271.08 | 12/9 | 235.16 | 250.36 | 2016 | 12/9 | 1388.07 | 2/11 | 953.72 | 1357.13 |
| 1995 | 9/14 | 316.12 | 1/30 | 246.56 | 315.97 | 2017 | 12/28 | 1548.93 | 4/13 | 1345.24 | 1535.51 |
| 1996 | 5/22 | 364.61 | 1/16 | 301.75 | 362.61 | 2018 | 8/31 | 1740.75 | 12/24 | 1266.92 | 1348.56 |
| 1997 | 10/13 | 465.21 | 4/25 | 335.85 | 437.02 | 2019 | 12/24 | 1678.01 | 1/3 | 1330.83 | 1668.47 |
| 1998 | 4/21 | 491.41 | 10/8 | 310.28 | 421.96 | 2020 | 12/23 | 2007.10 | 3/18 | 991.16 | 1974.86 |
| 1999 | 12/31 | 504.75 | 3/23 | 383.37 | 504.75 | 2021 | 11/8 | 2442.74 | 1/4 | 1945.91 | 2245.31 |
| 2000 | 3/9 | 606.05 | 12/20 | 443.80 | 483.53 | 2022* | 1/3 | 2272.56 | 6/16 | 1649.84 | At Press Time |

*Through June 30, 2022*

# DOW JONES INDUSTRIALS MONTHLY PERCENT CHANGES SINCE 1950

| | Jan | Feb | Mar | Apr | May | Jun | Jul | Aug | Sep | Oct | Nov | Dec | Year's Change |
|---|---|---|---|---|---|---|---|---|---|---|---|---|---|
| 1950 | 0.8 | 0.8 | 1.3 | 4.0 | 4.2 | -6.4 | 0.1 | 3.6 | 4.4 | -0.6 | 1.2 | 3.4 | 17.6 |
| 1951 | 5.7 | 1.3 | -1.6 | 4.5 | -3.7 | -2.8 | 6.3 | 4.8 | 0.3 | -3.2 | -0.4 | 3.0 | 14.4 |
| 1952 | 0.5 | -3.9 | 3.6 | -4.4 | 2.1 | 4.3 | 1.9 | -1.6 | -1.6 | -0.5 | 5.4 | 2.9 | 8.4 |
| 1953 | -0.7 | -1.9 | -1.5 | -1.8 | -0.9 | -1.5 | 2.7 | -5.1 | 1.1 | 4.5 | 2.0 | -0.2 | -3.8 |
| 1954 | 4.1 | 0.7 | 3.0 | 5.2 | 2.6 | 1.8 | 4.3 | -3.5 | 7.3 | -2.3 | 9.8 | 4.6 | 44.0 |
| 1955 | 1.1 | 0.7 | -0.5 | 3.9 | -0.2 | 6.2 | 3.2 | 0.5 | -0.3 | -2.5 | 6.2 | 1.1 | 20.8 |
| 1956 | -3.6 | 2.7 | 5.8 | 0.8 | -7.4 | 3.1 | 5.1 | -3.0 | -5.3 | 1.0 | -1.5 | 5.6 | 2.3 |
| 1957 | -4.1 | -3.0 | 2.2 | 4.1 | 2.1 | -0.3 | 1.0 | -4.8 | -5.8 | -3.3 | 2.0 | -3.2 | -12.8 |
| 1958 | 3.3 | -2.2 | 1.6 | 2.0 | 1.5 | 3.3 | 5.2 | 1.1 | 4.6 | 2.1 | 2.6 | 4.7 | 34.0 |
| 1959 | 1.8 | 1.6 | -0.3 | 3.7 | 3.2 | -0.03 | 4.9 | -1.6 | -4.9 | 2.4 | 1.9 | 3.1 | 16.4 |
| 1960 | -8.4 | 1.2 | -2.1 | -2.4 | 4.0 | 2.4 | -3.7 | 1.5 | -7.3 | 0.04 | 2.9 | 3.1 | -9.3 |
| 1961 | 5.2 | 2.1 | 2.2 | 0.3 | 2.7 | -1.8 | 3.1 | 2.1 | -2.6 | 0.4 | 2.5 | 1.3 | 18.7 |
| 1962 | -4.3 | 1.1 | -0.2 | -5.9 | -7.8 | -8.5 | 6.5 | 1.9 | -5.0 | 1.9 | 10.1 | 0.4 | -10.8 |
| 1963 | 4.7 | -2.9 | 3.0 | 5.2 | 1.3 | -2.8 | -1.6 | 4.9 | 0.5 | 3.1 | -0.6 | 1.7 | 17.0 |
| 1964 | 2.9 | 1.9 | 1.6 | -0.3 | 1.2 | 1.3 | 1.2 | -0.3 | 4.4 | -0.3 | 0.3 | -0.1 | 14.6 |
| 1965 | 3.3 | 0.1 | -1.6 | 3.7 | -0.5 | -5.4 | 1.6 | 1.3 | 4.2 | 3.2 | -1.5 | 2.4 | 10.9 |
| 1966 | 1.5 | -3.2 | -2.8 | 1.0 | -5.3 | -1.6 | -2.6 | -7.0 | -1.8 | 4.2 | -1.9 | -0.7 | -18.9 |
| 1967 | 8.2 | -1.2 | 3.2 | 3.6 | -5.0 | 0.9 | 5.1 | -0.3 | 2.8 | -5.1 | -0.4 | 3.3 | 15.2 |
| 1968 | -5.5 | -1.7 | 0.02 | 8.5 | -1.4 | -0.1 | -1.6 | 1.5 | 4.4 | 1.8 | 3.4 | -4.2 | 4.3 |
| 1969 | 0.2 | -4.3 | 3.3 | 1.6 | -1.3 | -6.9 | -6.6 | 2.6 | -2.8 | 5.3 | -5.1 | -1.5 | -15.2 |
| 1970 | -7.0 | 4.5 | 1.0 | -6.3 | -4.8 | -2.4 | 7.4 | 4.1 | -0.5 | -0.7 | 5.1 | 5.6 | 4.8 |
| 1971 | 3.5 | 1.2 | 2.9 | 4.1 | -3.6 | -1.8 | -3.7 | 4.6 | -1.2 | -5.4 | -0.9 | 7.1 | 6.1 |
| 1972 | 1.3 | 2.9 | 1.4 | 1.4 | 0.7 | -3.3 | -0.5 | 4.2 | -1.1 | 0.2 | 6.6 | 0.2 | 14.6 |
| 1973 | -2.1 | -4.4 | -0.4 | -3.1 | -2.2 | -1.1 | 3.9 | -4.2 | 6.7 | 1.0 | -14.0 | 3.5 | -16.6 |
| 1974 | 0.6 | 0.6 | -1.6 | -1.2 | -4.1 | 0.03 | -5.6 | -10.4 | -10.4 | 9.5 | -7.0 | -0.4 | -27.6 |
| 1975 | 14.2 | 5.0 | 3.9 | 6.9 | 1.3 | 5.6 | -5.4 | 0.5 | -5.0 | 5.3 | 2.9 | -1.0 | 38.3 |
| 1976 | 14.4 | -0.3 | 2.8 | -0.3 | -2.2 | 2.8 | -1.8 | -1.1 | 1.7 | -2.6 | -1.8 | 6.1 | 17.9 |
| 1977 | -5.0 | -1.9 | -1.8 | 0.8 | -3.0 | 2.0 | -2.9 | -3.2 | -1.7 | -3.4 | 1.4 | 0.2 | -17.3 |
| 1978 | -7.4 | -3.6 | 2.1 | 10.6 | 0.4 | -2.6 | 5.3 | 1.7 | -1.3 | -8.5 | 0.8 | 0.7 | -3.1 |
| 1979 | 4.2 | -3.6 | 6.6 | -0.8 | -3.8 | 2.4 | 0.5 | 4.9 | -1.0 | -7.2 | 0.8 | 2.0 | 4.2 |
| 1980 | 4.4 | -1.5 | -9.0 | 4.0 | 4.1 | 2.0 | 7.8 | -0.3 | -0.02 | -0.9 | 7.4 | -3.0 | 14.9 |
| 1981 | -1.7 | 2.9 | 3.0 | -0.6 | -0.6 | -1.5 | -2.5 | -7.4 | -3.6 | 0.3 | 4.3 | -1.6 | -9.2 |
| 1982 | -0.4 | -5.4 | -0.2 | 3.1 | -3.4 | -0.9 | -0.4 | 11.5 | -0.6 | 10.7 | 4.8 | 0.7 | 19.6 |
| 1983 | 2.8 | 3.4 | 1.6 | 8.5 | -2.1 | 1.8 | -1.9 | 1.4 | 1.4 | -0.6 | 4.1 | -1.4 | 20.3 |
| 1984 | -3.0 | -5.4 | 0.9 | 0.5 | -5.6 | 2.5 | -1.5 | 9.8 | -1.4 | 0.1 | -1.5 | 1.9 | -3.7 |
| 1985 | 6.2 | -0.2 | -1.3 | -0.7 | 4.6 | 1.5 | 0.9 | -1.0 | -0.4 | 3.4 | 7.1 | 5.1 | 27.7 |
| 1986 | 1.6 | 8.8 | 6.4 | -1.9 | 5.2 | 0.9 | -6.2 | 6.9 | -6.9 | 6.2 | 1.9 | -1.0 | 22.6 |
| 1987 | 13.8 | 3.1 | 3.6 | -0.8 | 0.2 | 5.5 | 6.3 | 3.5 | -2.5 | -23.2 | -8.0 | 5.7 | 2.3 |
| 1988 | 1.0 | 5.8 | -4.0 | 2.2 | -0.1 | 5.4 | -0.6 | -4.6 | 4.0 | 1.7 | -1.6 | 2.6 | 11.8 |

*(continued*

| | Jan | Feb | Mar | Apr | May | Jun | Jul | Aug | Sep | Oct | Nov | Dec | Year's Change |
|---|---|---|---|---|---|---|---|---|---|---|---|---|---|
| 1989 | 8.0 | – 3.6 | 1.6 | 5.5 | 2.5 | – 1.6 | 9.0 | 2.9 | – 1.6 | – 1.8 | 2.3 | 1.7 | 27.0 |
| 1990 | – 5.9 | 1.4 | 3.0 | – 1.9 | 8.3 | 0.1 | 0.9 | –10.0 | – 6.2 | – 0.4 | 4.8 | 2.9 | – 4.3 |
| 1991 | 3.9 | 5.3 | 1.1 | – 0.9 | 4.8 | – 4.0 | 4.1 | 0.6 | – 0.9 | 1.7 | – 5.7 | 9.5 | 20.3 |
| 1992 | 1.7 | 1.4 | – 1.0 | 3.8 | 1.1 | – 2.3 | 2.3 | – 4.0 | 0.4 | – 1.4 | 2.4 | – 0.1 | 4.2 |
| 1993 | 0.3 | 1.8 | 1.9 | – 0.2 | 2.9 | – 0.3 | 0.7 | 3.2 | – 2.6 | 3.5 | 0.1 | 1.9 | 13.7 |
| 1994 | 6.0 | – 3.7 | – 5.1 | 1.3 | 2.1 | – 3.5 | 3.8 | 4.0 | – 1.8 | 1.7 | – 4.3 | 2.5 | 2.1 |
| 1995 | 0.2 | 4.3 | 3.7 | 3.9 | 3.3 | 2.0 | 3.3 | – 2.1 | 3.9 | – 0.7 | 6.7 | 0.8 | 33.5 |
| 1996 | 5.4 | 1.7 | 1.9 | – 0.3 | 1.3 | 0.2 | – 2.2 | 1.6 | 4.7 | 2.5 | 8.2 | – 1.1 | 26.0 |
| 1997 | 5.7 | 0.9 | – 4.3 | 6.5 | 4.6 | 4.7 | 7.2 | – 7.3 | 4.2 | – 6.3 | 5.1 | 1.1 | 22.6 |
| 1998 | – 0.02 | 8.1 | 3.0 | 3.0 | – 1.8 | 0.6 | – 0.8 | –15.1 | 4.0 | 9.6 | 6.1 | 0.7 | 16.1 |
| 1999 | 1.9 | – 0.6 | 5.2 | 10.2 | – 2.1 | 3.9 | – 2.9 | 1.6 | – 4.5 | 3.8 | 1.4 | 5.7 | 25.2 |
| 2000 | – 4.8 | – 7.4 | 7.8 | – 1.7 | – 2.0 | – 0.7 | 0.7 | 6.6 | – 5.0 | 3.0 | – 5.1 | 3.6 | – 6.2 |
| 2001 | 0.9 | – 3.6 | – 5.9 | 8.7 | 1.6 | – 3.8 | 0.2 | – 5.4 | –11.1 | 2.6 | 8.6 | 1.7 | – 7.1 |
| 2002 | – 1.0 | 1.9 | 2.9 | – 4.4 | – 0.2 | – 6.9 | – 5.5 | – 0.8 | –12.4 | 10.6 | 5.9 | – 6.2 | –16.8 |
| 2003 | – 3.5 | – 2.0 | 1.3 | 6.1 | 4.4 | 1.5 | 2.8 | 2.0 | – 1.5 | 5.7 | – 0.2 | 6.9 | 25.3 |
| 2004 | 0.3 | 0.9 | – 2.1 | – 1.3 | – 0.4 | 2.4 | – 2.8 | 0.3 | – 0.9 | – 0.5 | 4.0 | 3.4 | 3.1 |
| 2005 | – 2.7 | 2.6 | – 2.4 | – 3.0 | 2.7 | – 1.8 | 3.6 | – 1.5 | 0.8 | – 1.2 | 3.5 | – 0.8 | – 0.6 |
| 2006 | 1.4 | 1.2 | 1.1 | 2.3 | – 1.7 | – 0.2 | 0.3 | 1.7 | 2.6 | 3.4 | 1.2 | 2.0 | 16.3 |
| 2007 | 1.3 | – 2.8 | 0.7 | 5.7 | 4.3 | – 1.6 | – 1.5 | 1.1 | 4.0 | 0.2 | – 4.0 | – 0.8 | 6.4 |
| 2008 | – 4.6 | – 3.0 | – 0.03 | 4.5 | – 1.4 | – 10.2 | 0.2 | 1.5 | – 6.0 | – 14.1 | – 5.3 | – 0.6 | – 33.8 |
| 2009 | – 8.8 | – 11.7 | 7.7 | 7.3 | 4.1 | – 0.6 | 8.6 | 3.5 | 2.3 | 0.005 | 6.5 | 0.8 | 18.8 |
| 2010 | – 3.5 | 2.6 | 5.1 | 1.4 | – 7.9 | – 3.6 | 7.1 | – 4.3 | 7.7 | 3.1 | – 1.0 | 5.2 | 11.0 |
| 2011 | 2.7 | 2.8 | 0.8 | 4.0 | – 1.9 | – 1.2 | – 2.2 | – 4.4 | – 6.0 | 9.5 | 0.8 | 1.4 | 5.5 |
| 2012 | 3.4 | 2.5 | 2.0 | 0.01 | – 6.2 | 3.9 | 1.0 | 0.6 | 2.6 | – 2.5 | – 0.5 | 0.6 | 7.3 |
| 2013 | 5.8 | 1.4 | 3.7 | 1.8 | 1.9 | –1.4 | 4.0 | – 4.4 | 2.2 | 2.8 | 3.5 | 3.0 | 26.5 |
| 2014 | – 5.3 | 4.0 | 0.8 | 0.7 | 0.8 | 0.7 | –1.6 | 3.2 | – 0.3 | 2.0 | 2.5 | – 0.03 | 7.5 |
| 2015 | – 3.7 | 5.6 | – 2.0 | 0.4 | 1.0 | –2.2 | 0.4 | – 6.6 | – 1.5 | 8.5 | 0.3 | – 1.7 | – 2.2 |
| 2016 | – 5.5 | 0.3 | 7.1 | 0.5 | 0.1 | 0.8 | 2.8 | – 0.2 | – 0.5 | – 0.9 | 5.4 | 3.3 | 13.4 |
| 2017 | 0.5 | 4.8 | – 0.7 | 1.3 | 0.3 | 1.6 | 2.5 | 0.3 | 2.1 | 4.3 | 3.8 | 1.8 | 25.1 |
| 2018 | 5.8 | – 4.3 | – 3.7 | 0.2 | 1.0 | – 0.6 | 4.7 | 2.2 | 1.9 | – 5.1 | 1.7 | – 8.7 | – 5.6 |
| 2019 | 7.2 | 3.7 | 0.1 | 2.6 | – 6.7 | 7.2 | 1.0 | – 1.7 | 1.9 | 0.5 | 3.7 | 1.7 | 22.3 |
| 2020 | – 1.0 | –10.1 | – 13.7 | 11.1 | 4.3 | 1.7 | 2.4 | 7.6 | – 2.3 | – 4.6 | 11.8 | 3.3 | 7.2 |
| 2021 | – 2.0 | 3.2 | 6.6 | 2.7 | 1.9 | – 0.1 | 1.3 | 1.2 | – 4.3 | 5.8 | – 3.7 | 5.4 | 18.7 |
| 2022 | – 3.3 | – 3.5 | 2.3 | – 4.9 | | | | | | | | | |
| TOTALS | 64.9 | 7.9 | 68.5 | 140.6 | – 0.6 | – 11.3 | 90.6 | – 2.6 | – 51.3 | 43.3 | 121.8 | 114.6 | |
| AVG. | 0.9 | 0.1 | 0.9 | 1.9 | – 0.01 | – 0.2 | 1.3 | – 0.04 | – 0.7 | 0.6 | 1.7 | 1.6 | |
| # Up | 45 | 43 | 47 | 50 | 39 | 34 | 47 | 41 | 29 | 43 | 49 | 51 | |
| # Down | 28 | 30 | 26 | 23 | 33 | 38 | 25 | 31 | 43 | 29 | 23 | 21 | |

157

# DOW JONES INDUSTRIALS MONTHLY POINT CHANGES SINCE 1950

| | Jan | Feb | Mar | Apr | May | Jun | Jul | Aug | Sep | Oct | Nov | Dec | Year's Change |
|---|---|---|---|---|---|---|---|---|---|---|---|---|---|
| 1950 | 1.66 | 1.65 | 2.61 | 8.28 | 9.09 | – 14.31 | 0.29 | 7.47 | 9.49 | – 1.35 | 2.59 | 7.81 | 235.41 |
| 1951 | 13.42 | 3.22 | – 4.11 | 11.19 | – 9.48 | – 7.01 | 15.22 | 12.39 | 0.91 | – 8.81 | – 1.08 | 7.96 | 269.23 |
| 1952 | 1.46 | – 10.61 | 9.38 | – 11.83 | 5.31 | 11.32 | 5.30 | – 4.52 | – 4.43 | – 1.38 | 14.43 | 8.24 | 291.90 |
| 1953 | – 2.13 | – 5.50 | – 4.40 | – 5.12 | – 2.47 | – 4.02 | 7.12 | – 14.16 | 2.82 | 11.77 | 5.56 | – 0.47 | 280.90 |
| 1954 | 11.49 | 2.15 | 8.97 | 15.82 | 8.16 | 6.04 | 14.39 | – 12.12 | 24.66 | – 8.32 | 34.63 | 17.62 | 404.39 |
| 1955 | 4.44 | 3.04 | – 2.17 | 15.95 | – 0.79 | 26.52 | 14.47 | 2.33 | – 1.56 | – 11.75 | 28.39 | 5.14 | 488.40 |
| 1956 | – 17.66 | 12.91 | 28.14 | 4.33 | – 38.07 | 14.73 | 25.03 | – 15.77 | – 26.79 | 4.60 | – 7.07 | 26.69 | 499.47 |
| 1957 | – 20.31 | – 14.54 | 10.19 | 19.55 | 10.57 | – 1.64 | 5.23 | – 24.17 | – 28.05 | – 15.26 | 8.83 | – 14.18 | 435.69 |
| 1958 | 14.33 | – 10.10 | 6.84 | 9.10 | 6.84 | 15.48 | 24.81 | 5.64 | 23.46 | 11.13 | 14.24 | 26.19 | 583.65 |
| 1959 | 10.31 | 9.54 | – 1.79 | 22.04 | 20.04 | – 0.19 | 31.28 | – 10.47 | – 32.73 | 14.92 | 12.58 | 20.18 | 679.36 |
| 1960 | – 56.74 | 7.50 | – 13.53 | – 14.89 | 23.80 | 15.12 | – 23.89 | 9.26 | – 45.85 | 0.22 | 16.86 | 18.67 | 615.89 |
| 1961 | 32.31 | 13.88 | 14.55 | 2.08 | 18.01 | – 12.76 | 21.41 | 14.57 | – 18.73 | 2.71 | 17.68 | 9.54 | 731.14 |
| 1962 | – 31.14 | 8.05 | – 1.10 | – 41.62 | – 51.97 | – 52.08 | 36.65 | 11.25 | – 30.20 | 10.79 | 59.53 | 2.80 | 652.10 |
| 1963 | 30.75 | – 19.91 | 19.58 | 35.18 | 9.26 | – 20.08 | – 11.45 | 33.89 | 3.47 | 22.44 | – 4.71 | 12.43 | 762.95 |
| 1964 | 22.39 | 14.80 | 13.15 | – 2.52 | 9.79 | 10.94 | 9.60 | – 2.62 | 36.89 | – 2.29 | 2.35 | – 1.30 | 874.13 |
| 1965 | 28.73 | 0.62 | – 14.43 | 33.26 | – 4.27 | – 50.01 | 13.71 | 11.36 | 37.48 | 30.24 | – 14.11 | 22.55 | 969.26 |
| 1966 | 14.25 | – 31.62 | – 27.12 | 8.91 | – 49.61 | – 13.97 | – 22.72 | – 58.97 | – 14.19 | 32.85 | – 15.48 | – 5.90 | 785.69 |
| 1967 | 64.20 | – 10.52 | 26.61 | 31.07 | – 44.49 | 7.70 | 43.98 | – 2.95 | 25.37 | – 46.92 | – 3.93 | 29.30 | 905.11 |
| 1968 | – 49.64 | – 14.97 | 0.17 | 71.55 | – 13.22 | – 1.20 | – 14.80 | 13.01 | 39.78 | 16.60 | 32.69 | –41.33 | 943.75 |
| 1969 | 2.30 | – 40.84 | 30.27 | 14.70 | – 12.62 | – 64.37 | – 57.72 | 21.25 | – 23.63 | 42.90 | – 43.69 | –11.94 | 800.36 |
| 1970 | – 56.30 | 33.53 | 7.98 | – 49.50 | – 35.63 | – 16.91 | 50.59 | 30.46 | – 3.90 | – 5.07 | 38.48 | 44.83 | 838.92 |
| 1971 | 29.58 | 10.33 | 25.54 | 37.38 | – 33.94 | – 16.67 | – 32.71 | 39.64 | – 10.88 | – 48.19 | – 7.66 | 58.86 | 890.20 |
| 1972 | 11.97 | 25.96 | 12.57 | 13.47 | 6.55 | – 31.69 | – 4.29 | 38.99 | – 10.46 | 2.25 | 62.69 | 1.81 | 1020.02 |
| 1973 | – 21.00 | – 43.95 | – 4.06 | – 29.58 | – 20.02 | – 9.70 | 34.69 | – 38.83 | 59.53 | 9.48 | –134.33 | 28.61 | 850.86 |
| 1974 | 4.69 | 4.98 | – 13.85 | – 9.93 | – 34.58 | 0.24 | – 44.98 | – 78.85 | – 70.71 | 57.65 | – 46.86 | – 2.42 | 616.24 |
| 1975 | 87.45 | 35.36 | 29.10 | 53.19 | 10.95 | 46.70 | – 47.48 | 3.83 | – 41.46 | 42.16 | 24.63 | – 8.26 | 852.41 |
| 1976 | 122.87 | – 2.67 | 26.84 | – 2.60 | – 21.62 | 27.55 | – 18.14 | – 10.90 | 16.45 | – 25.26 | – 17.71 | 57.43 | 1004.65 |
| 1977 | – 50.28 | – 17.95 | – 17.29 | 7.77 | – 28.24 | 17.64 | – 26.23 | – 28.58 | – 14.38 | – 28.76 | 11.35 | 1.47 | 831.17 |
| 1978 | – 61.25 | – 27.80 | 15.24 | 79.96 | 3.29 | – 21.66 | 43.32 | 14.55 | – 11.00 | – 73.37 | 6.58 | 5.98 | 805.01 |
| 1979 | 34.21 | – 30.40 | 53.36 | – 7.28 | – 32.57 | 19.65 | 4.44 | 41.21 | – 9.05 | – 62.88 | 6.65 | 16.39 | 838.74 |
| 1980 | 37.11 | – 12.71 | – 77.39 | 31.31 | 33.79 | 17.07 | 67.40 | – 2.73 | – 0.17 | – 7.93 | 68.85 | –29.35 | 963.99 |
| 1981 | – 16.72 | 27.31 | 29.29 | – 6.12 | – 6.00 | – 14.87 | – 24.54 | – 70.87 | – 31.49 | 2.57 | 36.43 | –13.98 | 875.00 |
| 1982 | – 3.90 | – 46.71 | – 1.62 | 25.59 | – 28.82 | – 7.61 | – 3.33 | 92.71 | – 5.06 | 95.47 | 47.56 | 7.26 | 1046.54 |
| 1983 | 29.16 | 36.92 | 17.41 | 96.17 | – 26.22 | 21.98 | – 22.74 | 16.94 | 16.97 | – 7.93 | 50.82 | –17.38 | 1258.64 |
| 1984 | – 38.06 | – 65.95 | 10.26 | 5.86 | – 65.90 | 27.55 | – 17.12 | 109.10 | – 17.67 | 0.67 | – 18.44 | 22.63 | 1211.57 |
| 1985 | 75.20 | – 2.76 | – 17.23 | – 8.72 | 57.35 | 20.05 | 11.99 | – 13.44 | – 5.38 | 45.68 | 97.82 | 74.54 | 1546.67 |
| 1986 | 24.32 | 138.07 | 109.55 | – 34.63 | 92.73 | 16.01 | –117.41 | 123.03 | –130.76 | 110.23 | 36.42 | –18.28 | 1895.95 |
| 1987 | 262.09 | 65.95 | 80.70 | – 18.33 | 5.21 | 126.96 | 153.54 | 90.88 | – 66.67 | –602.75 | –159.98 | 105.28 | 1938.83 |

*(continued)*

| | Jan | Feb | Mar | Apr | May | Jun | Jul | Aug | Sep | Oct | Nov | Dec | Year's Change |
|---|---|---|---|---|---|---|---|---|---|---|---|---|---|
| 1988 | 19.39 | 113.40 | -83.56 | 44.27 | -1.21 | 110.59 | -12.98 | -97.08 | 81.26 | 35.74 | -34.14 | 54.06 | 2168.57 |
| 1989 | 173.75 | -83.93 | 35.23 | 125.18 | 61.35 | -40.09 | 220.60 | 76.61 | -44.45 | -47.74 | 61.19 | 46.93 | 2753.20 |
| 1990 | -162.66 | 36.71 | 79.96 | -50.45 | 219.90 | 4.03 | 24.51 | -290.84 | -161.88 | -10.15 | 117.32 | 74.01 | 2633.66 |
| 1991 | 102.73 | 145.79 | 31.68 | -25.99 | 139.63 | -120.75 | 118.07 | 18.78 | -26.83 | 52.33 | -174.42 | 274.15 | 3168.83 |
| 1992 | 54.56 | 44.28 | -32.20 | 123.65 | 37.76 | -78.36 | 75.26 | -136.43 | 14.31 | -45.38 | 78.88 | -4.05 | 3301.11 |
| 1993 | 8.92 | 60.78 | 64.30 | -7.56 | 99.88 | -11.35 | 23.39 | 111.78 | -96.13 | 125.47 | 3.36 | 70.14 | 3754.09 |
| 1994 | 224.27 | -146.34 | -196.06 | 45.73 | 76.68 | -133.41 | 139.54 | 148.92 | -70.23 | 64.93 | -168.89 | 95.21 | 3834.44 |
| 1995 | 9.42 | 167.19 | 146.64 | 163.58 | 143.87 | 90.96 | 152.37 | -97.91 | 178.52 | -33.60 | 319.01 | 42.63 | 5117.12 |
| 1996 | 278.18 | 90.32 | 101.52 | -18.06 | 74.10 | 11.45 | -125.72 | 87.30 | 265.96 | 147.21 | 492.32 | -73.43 | 6448.27 |
| 1997 | 364.82 | 64.65 | -294.26 | 425.51 | 322.05 | 341.75 | 549.82 | -600.19 | 322.84 | -503.18 | 381.05 | 85.12 | 7908.25 |
| 1998 | -1.75 | 639.22 | 254.09 | 263.56 | -163.42 | 52.07 | -68.73 | -1344.22 | 303.55 | 749.48 | 524.45 | 64.88 | 9181.43 |
| 1999 | 177.40 | -52.25 | 479.58 | 1002.88 | -229.30 | 411.06 | 315.65 | 174.13 | -492.33 | 392.91 | 147.95 | 619.31 | 11497.12 |
| 2000 | -556.59 | -812.22 | 793.61 | -188.01 | -211.58 | -74.44 | 74.09 | 693.12 | -564.18 | 320.22 | -556.65 | 372.36 | 10786.85 |
| 2001 | 100.51 | -392.08 | -616.50 | 856.19 | 176.97 | -409.54 | 20.41 | -573.06 | -1102.19 | 227.58 | 776.42 | 169.94 | 10021.50 |
| 2002 | -101.50 | 186.13 | 297.81 | -457.72 | -20.97 | -681.99 | 506.67 | -73.09 | -1071.57 | 805.10 | 499.06 | -554.46 | 8341.63 |
| 2003 | -287.82 | -162.73 | 101.05 | 487.96 | 370.17 | 135.18 | 248.36 | 182.02 | -140.76 | 526.06 | -18.66 | 671.46 | 10453.92 |
| 2004 | 34.15 | 95.85 | -226.22 | -132.13 | -37.12 | 247.03 | -295.77 | 34.21 | -93.65 | -52.80 | 400.55 | 354.99 | 10783.01 |
| 2005 | -293.07 | 276.29 | -262.47 | -311.25 | 274.97 | -92.51 | 365.94 | -159.31 | 87.10 | -128.63 | 365.80 | -88.37 | 10717.50 |
| 2006 | 147.36 | 128.55 | 115.91 | 257.82 | -198.83 | -18.09 | 35.46 | 195.47 | 297.92 | 401.66 | 141.20 | 241.22 | 12463.15 |
| 2007 | 158.54 | -353.06 | 85.72 | 708.56 | 564.73 | -219.02 | -196.63 | 145.75 | 537.89 | 34.38 | -558.29 | -106.90 | 13264.82 |
| 2008 | -614.46 | -383.97 | -3.50 | 557.24 | -181.81 | -1288.31 | 28.01 | 165.53 | -692.89 | -1525.65 | -495.97 | -52.65 | 8776.39 |
| 2009 | -775.53 | -937.93 | 545.99 | 559.20 | 332.21 | -53.33 | 724.61 | 324.67 | 216.00 | 0.45 | 632.11 | 83.21 | 10428.05 |
| 2010 | -360.72 | 257.93 | 531.37 | 151.98 | -871.98 | -362.61 | 691.92 | -451.22 | 773.33 | 330.44 | -112.47 | 571.49 | 11577.51 |
| 2011 | 314.42 | 334.41 | 93.39 | 490.81 | -240.75 | -155.45 | -271.10 | -529.71 | -700.15 | 1041.63 | 90.67 | 171.88 | 12217.56 |
| 2012 | 415.35 | 319.16 | 259.97 | 1.59 | -820.18 | 486.64 | 128.59 | 82.16 | 346.29 | -340.67 | -70.88 | 78.56 | 13104.14 |
| 2013 | 756.44 | 193.91 | 524.05 | 261.26 | 275.77 | -205.97 | 589.94 | -689.23 | 319.36 | 416.08 | 540.66 | 490.25 | 16576.66 |
| 2014 | -877.81 | 622.86 | 135.95 | 123.18 | 136.33 | 109.43 | -263.30 | 535.15 | -55.55 | 347.62 | 437.72 | -5.17 | 17823.07 |
| 2015 | -658.12 | 967.75 | -356.58 | 64.40 | 170.16 | -391.17 | 70.35 | -1161.83 | -244.03 | 1379.54 | 56.38 | -294.89 | 17425.03 |
| 2016 | -958.7 | 350.20 | 1168.59 | 88.55 | 13.56 | 142.79 | 502.25 | -31.36 | -92.73 | -165.73 | 981.16 | 639.02 | 19762.60 |
| 2017 | 101.49 | 948.15 | -149.02 | 277.29 | 68.14 | 340.98 | 541.49 | 56.98 | 456.99 | 972.15 | 895.11 | 446.87 | 24719.22 |
| 2018 | 1430.17 | -1120.19 | -926.09 | 60.04 | 252.69 | -144.43 | 1143.78 | 549.63 | 493.49 | -1342.55 | 422.70 | -2211.00 | 23327.46 |
| 2019 | 1672.21 | 916.33 | 12.68 | 664.23 | -1777.87 | 1784.92 | 264.31 | -460.99 | 513.55 | 129.40 | 1005.18 | 487.03 | 28538.44 |
| 2020 | -282.41 | -2846.67 | -3492.20 | 2428.56 | 1037.39 | 429.77 | 615.44 | 2001.73 | -648.35 | -1280.10 | 3137.04 | 967.84 | 30606.48 |
| 2021 | -623.86 | 949.75 | 2049.18 | 893.30 | 654.60 | -26.94 | 432.96 | 425.26 | -1516.81 | 1975.64 | -1335.84 | 1854.58 | 36338.30 |
| 2022 | -1206.44 | -1239.26 | 785.75 | -1701.14 | | | | | | | | | |
| TOTALS | -671.83 | -874.76 | 2443.57 | 8645.25 | 518.10 | 179.39 | 5869.83 | -333.46 | -2964.27 | 4608.95 | 9244.67 | 6111.64 | |
| # Up | 45 | 43 | 47 | 50 | 39 | 34 | 47 | 41 | 29 | 43 | 49 | 51 | |
| # Down | 28 | 30 | 26 | 23 | 33 | 38 | 25 | 31 | 43 | 29 | 23 | 21 | |

159

# DOW JONES INDUSTRIALS MONTHLY CLOSING PRICES SINCE 1950

| | Jan | Feb | Mar | Apr | May | Jun | Jul | Aug | Sep | Oct | Nov | Dec |
|---|---|---|---|---|---|---|---|---|---|---|---|---|
| 1950 | 201.79 | 203.44 | 206.05 | 214.33 | 223.42 | 209.11 | 209.40 | 216.87 | 226.36 | 225.01 | 227.60 | 235.41 |
| 1951 | 248.83 | 252.05 | 247.94 | 259.13 | 249.65 | 242.64 | 257.86 | 270.25 | 271.16 | 262.35 | 261.27 | 269.23 |
| 1952 | 270.69 | 260.08 | 269.46 | 257.63 | 262.94 | 274.26 | 279.56 | 275.04 | 270.61 | 269.23 | 283.66 | 291.90 |
| 1953 | 289.77 | 284.27 | 279.87 | 274.75 | 272.28 | 268.26 | 275.38 | 261.22 | 264.04 | 275.81 | 281.37 | 280.90 |
| 1954 | 292.39 | 294.54 | 303.51 | 319.33 | 327.49 | 333.53 | 347.92 | 335.80 | 360.46 | 352.14 | 386.77 | 404.39 |
| 1955 | 408.83 | 411.87 | 409.70 | 425.65 | 424.86 | 451.38 | 465.85 | 468.18 | 466.62 | 454.87 | 483.26 | 488.40 |
| 1956 | 470.74 | 483.65 | 511.79 | 516.12 | 478.05 | 492.78 | 517.81 | 502.04 | 475.25 | 479.85 | 472.78 | 499.47 |
| 1957 | 479.16 | 464.62 | 474.81 | 494.36 | 504.93 | 503.29 | 508.52 | 484.35 | 456.30 | 441.04 | 449.87 | 435.69 |
| 1958 | 450.02 | 439.92 | 446.76 | 455.86 | 462.70 | 478.18 | 502.99 | 508.63 | 532.09 | 543.22 | 557.46 | 583.65 |
| 1959 | 593.96 | 603.50 | 601.71 | 623.75 | 643.79 | 643.60 | 674.88 | 664.41 | 631.68 | 646.60 | 659.18 | 679.36 |
| 1960 | 622.62 | 630.12 | 616.59 | 601.70 | 625.50 | 640.62 | 616.73 | 625.99 | 580.14 | 580.36 | 597.22 | 615.89 |
| 1961 | 648.20 | 662.08 | 676.63 | 678.71 | 696.72 | 683.96 | 705.37 | 719.94 | 701.21 | 703.92 | 721.60 | 731.14 |
| 1962 | 700.00 | 708.05 | 706.95 | 665.33 | 613.36 | 561.28 | 597.93 | 609.18 | 578.98 | 589.77 | 649.30 | 652.10 |
| 1963 | 682.85 | 662.94 | 682.52 | 717.70 | 726.96 | 706.88 | 695.43 | 729.32 | 732.79 | 755.23 | 750.52 | 762.95 |
| 1964 | 785.34 | 800.14 | 813.29 | 810.77 | 820.56 | 831.50 | 841.10 | 838.48 | 875.37 | 873.08 | 875.43 | 874.13 |
| 1965 | 902.86 | 903.48 | 889.05 | 922.31 | 918.04 | 868.03 | 881.74 | 893.10 | 930.58 | 960.82 | 946.71 | 969.26 |
| 1966 | 983.51 | 951.89 | 924.77 | 933.68 | 884.07 | 870.10 | 847.38 | 788.41 | 774.22 | 807.07 | 791.59 | 785.69 |
| 1967 | 849.89 | 839.37 | 865.98 | 897.05 | 852.56 | 860.26 | 904.24 | 901.29 | 926.66 | 879.74 | 875.81 | 905.11 |
| 1968 | 855.47 | 840.50 | 840.67 | 912.22 | 899.00 | 897.80 | 883.00 | 896.01 | 935.79 | 952.39 | 985.08 | 943.75 |
| 1969 | 946.05 | 905.21 | 935.48 | 950.18 | 937.56 | 873.19 | 815.47 | 836.72 | 813.09 | 855.99 | 812.30 | 800.36 |
| 1970 | 744.06 | 777.59 | 785.57 | 736.07 | 700.44 | 683.53 | 734.12 | 764.58 | 760.68 | 755.61 | 794.09 | 838.92 |
| 1971 | 868.50 | 878.83 | 904.37 | 941.75 | 907.81 | 891.14 | 858.43 | 898.07 | 887.19 | 839.00 | 831.34 | 890.20 |
| 1972 | 902.17 | 928.13 | 940.70 | 954.17 | 960.72 | 929.03 | 924.74 | 963.73 | 953.27 | 955.52 | 1018.21 | 1020.02 |
| 1973 | 999.02 | 955.07 | 951.01 | 921.43 | 901.41 | 891.71 | 926.40 | 887.57 | 947.10 | 956.58 | 822.25 | 850.86 |
| 1974 | 855.55 | 860.53 | 846.68 | 836.75 | 802.17 | 802.41 | 757.43 | 678.58 | 607.87 | 665.52 | 618.66 | 616.24 |
| 1975 | 703.69 | 739.05 | 768.15 | 821.34 | 832.29 | 878.99 | 831.51 | 835.34 | 793.88 | 836.04 | 860.67 | 852.41 |
| 1976 | 975.28 | 972.61 | 999.45 | 996.85 | 975.23 | 1002.78 | 984.64 | 973.74 | 990.19 | 964.93 | 947.22 | 1004.65 |
| 1977 | 954.37 | 936.42 | 919.13 | 926.90 | 898.66 | 916.30 | 890.07 | 861.49 | 847.11 | 818.35 | 829.70 | 831.17 |
| 1978 | 769.92 | 742.12 | 757.36 | 837.32 | 840.61 | 818.95 | 862.27 | 876.82 | 865.82 | 792.45 | 799.03 | 805.01 |
| 1979 | 839.22 | 808.82 | 862.18 | 854.90 | 822.33 | 841.98 | 846.42 | 887.63 | 878.58 | 815.70 | 822.35 | 838.74 |
| 1980 | 875.85 | 863.14 | 785.75 | 817.06 | 850.85 | 867.92 | 935.32 | 932.59 | 932.42 | 924.49 | 993.34 | 963.99 |
| 1981 | 947.27 | 974.58 | 1003.87 | 997.75 | 991.75 | 976.88 | 952.34 | 881.47 | 849.98 | 852.55 | 888.98 | 875.00 |
| 1982 | 871.10 | 824.39 | 822.77 | 848.36 | 819.54 | 811.93 | 808.60 | 901.31 | 896.25 | 991.72 | 1039.28 | 1046.54 |
| 1983 | 1075.70 | 1112.62 | 1130.03 | 1226.20 | 1199.98 | 1221.96 | 1199.22 | 1216.16 | 1233.13 | 1225.20 | 1276.02 | 1258.64 |
| 1984 | 1220.58 | 1154.63 | 1164.89 | 1170.75 | 1104.85 | 1132.40 | 1115.28 | 1224.38 | 1206.71 | 1207.38 | 1188.94 | 1211.57 |
| 1985 | 1286.77 | 1284.01 | 1266.78 | 1258.06 | 1315.41 | 1335.46 | 1347.45 | 1334.01 | 1328.63 | 1374.31 | 1472.13 | 1546.67 |
| 1986 | 1570.99 | 1709.06 | 1818.61 | 1783.98 | 1876.71 | 1892.72 | 1775.31 | 1898.34 | 1767.58 | 1877.81 | 1914.23 | 1895.95 |

*(continued)*

| | Jan | Feb | Mar | Apr | May | Jun | Jul | Aug | Sep | Oct | Nov | Dec |
|---|---|---|---|---|---|---|---|---|---|---|---|---|
| 1987 | 2158.04 | 2223.99 | 2304.69 | 2286.36 | 2291.57 | 2418.53 | 2572.07 | 2662.95 | 2596.28 | 1993.53 | 1833.55 | 1938.83 |
| 1988 | 1958.22 | 2071.62 | 1988.06 | 2032.33 | 2031.12 | 2141.71 | 2128.73 | 2031.65 | 2112.91 | 2148.65 | 2114.51 | 2168.57 |
| 1989 | 2342.32 | 2258.39 | 2293.62 | 2418.80 | 2480.15 | 2440.06 | 2660.66 | 2737.27 | 2692.82 | 2645.08 | 2706.27 | 2753.20 |
| 1990 | 2590.54 | 2627.25 | 2707.21 | 2656.76 | 2876.66 | 2880.69 | 2905.20 | 2614.36 | 2452.48 | 2442.33 | 2559.65 | 2633.66 |
| 1991 | 2736.39 | 2882.18 | 2913.86 | 2887.87 | 3027.50 | 2906.75 | 3024.82 | 3043.60 | 3016.77 | 3069.10 | 2894.68 | 3168.83 |
| 1992 | 3223.39 | 3267.67 | 3235.47 | 3359.12 | 3396.88 | 3318.52 | 3393.78 | 3257.35 | 3271.66 | 3226.28 | 3305.16 | 3301.11 |
| 1993 | 3310.03 | 3370.81 | 3435.11 | 3427.55 | 3527.43 | 3516.08 | 3539.47 | 3651.25 | 3555.12 | 3680.59 | 3683.95 | 3754.09 |
| 1994 | 3978.36 | 3832.02 | 3635.96 | 3681.69 | 3758.37 | 3624.96 | 3764.50 | 3913.42 | 3843.19 | 3908.12 | 3739.23 | 3834.44 |
| 1995 | 3843.86 | 4011.05 | 4157.69 | 4321.27 | 4465.14 | 4556.10 | 4708.47 | 4610.56 | 4789.08 | 4755.48 | 5074.49 | 5117.12 |
| 1996 | 5395.30 | 5485.62 | 5587.14 | 5569.08 | 5643.18 | 5654.63 | 5528.91 | 5616.21 | 5882.17 | 6029.38 | 6521.70 | 6448.27 |
| 1997 | 6813.09 | 6877.74 | 6583.48 | 7008.99 | 7331.04 | 7672.79 | 8222.61 | 7622.42 | 7945.26 | 7442.08 | 7823.13 | 7908.25 |
| 1998 | 7906.50 | 8545.72 | 8799.81 | 9063.37 | 8899.95 | 8952.02 | 8883.29 | 7539.07 | 7842.62 | 8592.10 | 9116.55 | 9181.43 |
| 1999 | 9358.83 | 9306.58 | 9786.16 | 10789.04 | 10559.74 | 10970.80 | 10655.15 | 10829.28 | 10336.95 | 10729.86 | 10877.81 | 11497.12 |
| 2000 | 10940.53 | 10128.31 | 10921.92 | 10733.91 | 10522.33 | 10447.89 | 10521.98 | 11215.10 | 10650.92 | 10971.14 | 10414.49 | 10786.85 |
| 2001 | 10887.36 | 10495.28 | 9878.78 | 10734.97 | 10911.94 | 10502.40 | 10522.81 | 9949.75 | 8847.56 | 9075.14 | 9851.56 | 10021.50 |
| 2002 | 9920.00 | 10106.13 | 10403.94 | 9946.22 | 9925.25 | 9243.26 | 8736.59 | 8663.50 | 7591.93 | 8397.03 | 8896.09 | 8341.63 |
| 2003 | 8053.81 | 7891.08 | 7992.13 | 8480.09 | 8850.26 | 8985.44 | 9233.80 | 9415.82 | 9275.06 | 9801.12 | 9782.46 | 10453.92 |
| 2004 | 10488.07 | 10583.92 | 10357.70 | 10225.57 | 10188.45 | 10435.48 | 10139.71 | 10173.92 | 10080.27 | 10027.47 | 10428.02 | 10783.01 |
| 2005 | 10489.94 | 10766.23 | 10503.76 | 10192.51 | 10467.48 | 10274.97 | 10640.91 | 10481.60 | 10568.70 | 10440.07 | 10805.87 | 10717.50 |
| 2006 | 10864.86 | 10993.41 | 11109.32 | 11367.14 | 11168.31 | 11150.22 | 11185.68 | 11381.15 | 11679.07 | 12080.73 | 12221.93 | 12463.15 |
| 2007 | 12621.69 | 12268.63 | 12354.35 | 13062.91 | 13627.64 | 13408.62 | 13211.99 | 13357.74 | 13895.63 | 13930.01 | 13371.72 | 13264.82 |
| 2008 | 12650.36 | 12266.39 | 12262.89 | 12820.13 | 12638.32 | 11350.01 | 11378.02 | 11543.55 | 10850.66 | 9325.01 | 8829.04 | 8776.39 |
| 2009 | 8000.86 | 7062.93 | 7608.92 | 8168.12 | 8500.33 | 8447.00 | 9171.61 | 9496.28 | 9712.28 | 9712.73 | 10344.84 | 10428.05 |
| 2010 | 10067.33 | 10325.26 | 10856.63 | 11008.61 | 10136.63 | 9774.02 | 10465.94 | 10014.72 | 10788.05 | 11118.49 | 11006.02 | 11577.51 |
| 2011 | 11891.93 | 12226.34 | 12319.73 | 12810.54 | 12569.79 | 12414.34 | 12143.24 | 11613.53 | 10913.38 | 11955.01 | 12045.68 | 12217.56 |
| 2012 | 12632.91 | 12952.07 | 13212.04 | 13213.63 | 12393.45 | 12880.09 | 13008.68 | 13090.84 | 13437.13 | 13096.46 | 13025.58 | 13104.14 |
| 2013 | 13860.58 | 14054.49 | 14578.54 | 14839.80 | 15115.57 | 14909.60 | 15499.54 | 14810.31 | 15129.67 | 15545.75 | 16086.41 | 16576.66 |
| 2014 | 15698.85 | 16321.71 | 16457.66 | 16580.84 | 16717.17 | 16826.60 | 16563.30 | 17098.45 | 17042.90 | 17390.52 | 17828.24 | 17823.07 |
| 2015 | 17164.95 | 18132.70 | 17776.12 | 17840.52 | 18010.68 | 17619.51 | 17689.86 | 16528.03 | 16284.00 | 17663.54 | 17719.92 | 17425.03 |
| 2016 | 16466.30 | 16516.50 | 17685.09 | 17773.64 | 17787.20 | 17929.99 | 18432.24 | 18400.88 | 18308.15 | 18142.42 | 19123.58 | 19762.60 |
| 2017 | 19864.09 | 20812.24 | 20663.22 | 20940.51 | 21008.65 | 21349.63 | 21891.12 | 21948.10 | 22405.09 | 23377.24 | 24272.35 | 24719.22 |
| 2018 | 26149.39 | 25029.20 | 24103.11 | 24163.15 | 24415.84 | 24271.41 | 25415.19 | 25964.82 | 26458.31 | 25115.76 | 25538.46 | 23327.46 |
| 2019 | 24999.67 | 25916.00 | 25928.68 | 26592.91 | 24815.04 | 26599.96 | 26864.27 | 26403.28 | 26916.83 | 27046.23 | 28051.41 | 28538.44 |
| 2020 | 28256.03 | 25409.36 | 21917.16 | 24345.72 | 25383.11 | 25812.88 | 26428.32 | 28430.05 | 27781.70 | 26501.60 | 29638.64 | 30606.48 |
| 2021 | 29982.62 | 30932.37 | 32981.55 | 33874.85 | 34529.45 | 34502.51 | 34935.47 | 35360.73 | 33843.92 | 35819.56 | 34483.72 | 36338.30 |
| 2022 | 35131.86 | 33892.60 | 34678.35 | 32977.21 | | | | | | | | |

# STANDARD & POOR'S 500 MONTHLY PERCENT CHANGES SINCE 1950

| | Jan | Feb | Mar | Apr | May | Jun | Jul | Aug | Sep | Oct | Nov | Dec | Year's Change |
|---|---|---|---|---|---|---|---|---|---|---|---|---|---|
| 1950 | 1.7 | 1.0 | 0.4 | 4.5 | 3.9 | – 5.8 | 0.8 | 3.3 | 5.6 | 0.4 | – 0.1 | 4.6 | 21.8 |
| 1951 | 6.1 | 0.6 | – 1.8 | 4.8 | – 4.1 | – 2.6 | 6.9 | 3.9 | – 0.1 | – 1.4 | – 0.3 | 3.9 | 16.5 |
| 1952 | 1.6 | – 3.6 | 4.8 | – 4.3 | 2.3 | 4.6 | 1.8 | – 1.5 | – 2.0 | – 0.1 | 4.6 | 3.5 | 11.8 |
| 1953 | – 0.7 | – 1.8 | – 2.4 | – 2.6 | – 0.3 | – 1.6 | 2.5 | – 5.8 | 0.1 | 5.1 | 0.9 | 0.2 | – 6.6 |
| 1954 | 5.1 | 0.3 | 3.0 | 4.9 | 3.3 | 0.1 | 5.7 | – 3.4 | 8.3 | – 1.9 | 8.1 | 5.1 | 45.0 |
| 1955 | 1.8 | 0.4 | – 0.5 | 3.8 | – 0.1 | 8.2 | 6.1 | – 0.8 | 1.1 | – 3.0 | 7.5 | – 0.1 | 26.4 |
| 1956 | – 3.6 | 3.5 | 6.9 | – 0.2 | – 6.6 | 3.9 | 5.2 | – 3.8 | – 4.5 | 0.5 | – 1.1 | 3.5 | 2.6 |
| 1957 | – 4.2 | – 3.3 | 2.0 | 3.7 | 3.7 | – 0.1 | 1.1 | – 5.6 | – 6.2 | – 3.2 | 1.6 | – 4.1 | – 14.3 |
| 1958 | 4.3 | – 2.1 | 3.1 | 3.2 | 1.5 | 2.6 | 4.3 | 1.2 | 4.8 | 2.5 | 2.2 | 5.2 | 38.1 |
| 1959 | 0.4 | – 0.02 | 0.1 | 3.9 | 1.9 | – 0.4 | 3.5 | – 1.5 | – 4.6 | 1.1 | 1.3 | 2.8 | 8.5 |
| 1960 | – 7.1 | 0.9 | – 1.4 | – 1.8 | 2.7 | 2.0 | – 2.5 | 2.6 | – 6.0 | – 0.2 | 4.0 | 4.6 | – 3.0 |
| 1961 | 6.3 | 2.7 | 2.6 | 0.4 | 1.9 | – 2.9 | 3.3 | 2.0 | – 2.0 | 2.8 | 3.9 | 0.3 | 23.1 |
| 1962 | – 3.8 | 1.6 | – 0.6 | – 6.2 | – 8.6 | – 8.2 | 6.4 | 1.5 | – 4.8 | 0.4 | 10.2 | 1.3 | – 11.8 |
| 1963 | 4.9 | – 2.9 | 3.5 | 4.9 | 1.4 | – 2.0 | – 0.3 | 4.9 | – 1.1 | 3.2 | – 1.1 | 2.4 | 18.9 |
| 1964 | 2.7 | 1.0 | 1.5 | 0.6 | 1.1 | 1.6 | 1.8 | – 1.6 | 2.9 | 0.8 | – 0.5 | 0.4 | 13.0 |
| 1965 | 3.3 | – 0.1 | – 1.5 | 3.4 | – 0.8 | – 4.9 | 1.3 | 2.3 | 3.2 | 2.7 | – 0.9 | 0.9 | 9.1 |
| 1966 | 0.5 | – 1.8 | – 2.2 | 2.1 | – 5.4 | – 1.6 | – 1.3 | – 7.8 | – 0.7 | 4.8 | 0.3 | – 0.1 | – 13.1 |
| 1967 | 7.8 | 0.2 | 3.9 | 4.2 | – 5.2 | 1.8 | 4.5 | – 1.2 | 3.3 | – 2.9 | 0.1 | 2.6 | 20.1 |
| 1968 | – 4.4 | – 3.1 | 0.9 | 8.2 | 1.1 | 0.9 | – 1.8 | 1.1 | 3.9 | 0.7 | 4.8 | – 4.2 | 7.7 |
| 1969 | – 0.8 | – 4.7 | 3.4 | 2.1 | – 0.2 | – 5.6 | – 1.8 | 1.1 | 3.9 | 0.7 | 4.8 | – 4.2 | 7.7 |
| 1970 | – 7.6 | 5.3 | 0.1 | – 9.0 | – 6.1 | – 5.0 | 7.3 | 4.4 | 3.3 | – 1.1 | 4.7 | 5.7 | 0.1 |
| 1971 | 4.0 | 0.9 | 3.7 | 3.6 | – 4.2 | 0.1 | 7.3 | 4.4 | 3.3 | – 1.1 | 4.7 | 5.7 | 0.1 |
| 1972 | 1.8 | 2.5 | 0.6 | 0.4 | 1.7 | – 2.2 | 0.2 | 3.4 | – 0.5 | 0.9 | 4.6 | 1.2 | 15.6 |
| 1973 | – 1.7 | – 3.7 | – 0.1 | – 4.1 | – 1.9 | – 0.7 | 3.8 | – 3.7 | 4.0 | – 0.1 | –11.4 | 1.7 | – 17.4 |
| 1974 | – 1.0 | – 0.4 | – 2.3 | – 3.9 | – 3.4 | – 1.5 | – 7.8 | – 9.0 | –11.9 | 16.3 | – 5.3 | – 2.0 | – 29.7 |
| 1975 | 12.3 | 6.0 | 2.2 | 4.7 | 4.4 | 4.4 | – 6.8 | – 2.1 | – 3.5 | 6.2 | 2.5 | – 1.2 | 31.5 |
| 1976 | 11.8 | – 1.1 | 3.1 | – 1.1 | – 1.4 | 4.1 | – 0.8 | – 0.5 | 2.3 | – 2.2 | – 0.8 | 5.2 | 19.1 |
| 1977 | – 5.1 | – 2.2 | – 1.4 | 0.02 | – 2.4 | 4.5 | – 1.6 | – 2.1 | – 0.2 | – 4.3 | 2.7 | 0.3 | – 11.5 |
| 1978 | – 6.2 | – 2.5 | 2.5 | 8.5 | 0.4 | – 1.8 | 5.4 | 2.6 | – 0.7 | – 9.2 | 1.7 | 1.5 | 1.1 |
| 1979 | 4.0 | – 3.7 | 5.5 | 0.2 | – 2.6 | 3.9 | 0.9 | 5.3 | NC | – 6.9 | 4.3 | 1.7 | 12.3 |
| 1980 | 5.8 | – 0.4 | –10.2 | 4.1 | 4.7 | 2.7 | 6.5 | 0.6 | 2.5 | 1.6 | 10.2 | – 3.4 | 25.8 |
| 1981 | – 4.6 | 1.3 | 3.6 | – 2.3 | – 0.2 | – 1.0 | – 0.2 | – 6.2 | – 5.4 | 4.9 | 3.7 | – 3.0 | – 9.7 |
| 1982 | – 1.8 | – 6.1 | – 1.0 | 4.0 | – 3.9 | – 2.0 | – 2.3 | 11.6 | 0.8 | 11.0 | 3.6 | 1.5 | 14.8 |
| 1983 | 3.3 | 1.9 | 3.3 | 7.5 | – 1.2 | 3.5 | – 3.3 | 1.1 | 1.0 | – 1.5 | 1.7 | – 0.9 | 17.3 |
| 1984 | – 0.9 | – 3.9 | 1.3 | 0.5 | – 5.9 | 1.7 | – 1.6 | 10.6 | – 0.3 | – 0.01 | – 1.5 | 2.2 | 1.4 |
| 1985 | 7.4 | 0.9 | – 0.3 | – 0.5 | 5.4 | 1.2 | – 0.5 | – 1.2 | – 3.5 | 4.3 | 6.5 | 4.5 | 26.3 |
| 1986 | 0.2 | 7.1 | 5.3 | – 1.4 | 5.0 | 1.4 | – 5.9 | 7.1 | – 8.5 | 5.5 | 2.1 | – 2.8 | 14.6 |
| 1987 | 13.2 | 3.7 | 2.6 | – 1.1 | 0.6 | 4.8 | 4.8 | 3.5 | – 2.4 | –21.8 | – 8.5 | 7.3 | 2.0 |
| 1988 | 4.0 | 4.2 | – 3.3 | 0.9 | 0.3 | 4.3 | – 0.5 | – 3.9 | 4.0 | 2.6 | – 1.9 | 1.5 | 12.4 |

*(continued)*

162

| | Jan | Feb | Mar | Apr | May | Jun | Jul | Aug | Sep | Oct | Nov | Dec | Year's Change |
|---|---|---|---|---|---|---|---|---|---|---|---|---|---|
| 1989 | 7.1 | – 2.9 | 2.1 | 5.0 | 3.5 | – 0.8 | 8.8 | 1.6 | – 0.7 | – 2.5 | 1.7 | 2.1 | 27.3 |
| 1990 | – 6.9 | 0.9 | 2.4 | – 2.7 | 9.2 | – 0.9 | 8.8 | 1.6 | – 0.7 | – 2.5 | 1.7 | 2.1 | 27.3 |
| 1991 | 4.2 | 6.7 | 2.2 | 0.03 | 3.9 | – 4.8 | 4.5 | 2.0 | – 1.9 | 1.2 | – 4.4 | 11.2 | 26.3 |
| 1992 | – 2.0 | 1.0 | – 2.2 | 2.8 | 0.1 | – 1.7 | 3.9 | – 2.4 | 0.9 | 0.2 | 3.0 | 1.0 | 4.5 |
| 1993 | 0.7 | 1.0 | 1.9 | – 2.5 | 2.3 | 0.1 | – 0.5 | 3.4 | – 1.0 | 1.9 | – 1.3 | 1.0 | 7.1 |
| 1994 | 3.3 | – 3.0 | – 4.6 | 1.2 | 1.2 | – 2.7 | 3.1 | 3.8 | – 2.7 | 2.1 | – 4.0 | 1.2 | – 1.5 |
| 1995 | 2.4 | 3.6 | 2.7 | 2.8 | 3.6 | 2.1 | 3.2 | – 0.03 | 4.0 | – 0.5 | 4.1 | 1.7 | 34.1 |
| 1996 | 3.3 | 0.7 | 0.8 | 1.3 | 2.3 | 0.2 | – 4.6 | 1.9 | 5.4 | 2.6 | 7.3 | – 2.2 | 20.3 |
| 1997 | 6.1 | 0.6 | – 4.3 | 5.8 | 5.9 | 4.3 | 7.8 | – 5.7 | 5.3 | – 3.4 | 4.5 | 1.6 | 31.0 |
| 1998 | 1.0 | 7.0 | 5.0 | 0.9 | – 1.9 | 3.9 | – 1.2 | –14.6 | 6.2 | 8.0 | 5.9 | 5.6 | 26.7 |
| 1999 | 4.1 | – 3.2 | 3.9 | 3.8 | – 2.5 | 5.4 | – 3.2 | – 0.6 | – 2.9 | 6.3 | 1.9 | 5.8 | 19.5 |
| 2000 | – 5.1 | – 2.0 | 9.7 | – 3.1 | – 2.2 | 2.4 | – 1.6 | 6.1 | – 5.3 | – 0.5 | – 8.0 | 0.4 | – 10.1 |
| 2001 | 3.5 | – 9.2 | – 6.4 | 7.7 | 0.5 | – 2.5 | – 1.1 | – 6.4 | – 8.2 | 1.8 | 7.5 | 0.8 | – 13.0 |
| 2002 | – 1.6 | – 2.1 | 3.7 | – 6.1 | – 0.9 | – 7.2 | – 7.9 | 0.5 | –11.0 | 8.6 | 5.7 | – 6.0 | – 23.4 |
| 2003 | – 2.7 | – 1.7 | 1.0 | 8.0 | 5.1 | 1.1 | 1.6 | 1.8 | – 1.2 | 5.5 | 0.7 | 5.1 | 26.4 |
| 2004 | 1.7 | 1.2 | – 1.6 | – 1.7 | 1.2 | 1.8 | – 3.4 | 0.2 | 0.9 | 1.4 | 3.9 | 3.2 | 9.0 |
| 2005 | – 2.5 | 1.9 | – 1.9 | – 2.0 | 3.0 | – 0.01 | 3.6 | – 1.1 | 0.7 | – 1.8 | 3.5 | – 0.1 | 3.0 |
| 2006 | 2.5 | 0.1 | 1.1 | 1.2 | – 3.1 | 0.01 | 0.5 | 2.1 | 2.5 | 3.2 | 1.6 | 1.3 | 13.6 |
| 2007 | 1.4 | – 2.2 | 1.0 | 4.3 | 3.3 | – 1.8 | – 3.2 | 1.3 | 3.6 | 1.5 | – 4.4 | – 0.9 | 3.5 |
| 2008 | – 6.1 | – 3.5 | – 0.6 | 4.8 | 1.1 | – 8.6 | – 1.0 | 1.2 | – 9.1 | – 16.9 | – 7.5 | 0.8 | – 38.5 |
| 2009 | – 8.6 | – 11.0 | 8.5 | 9.4 | 5.3 | 0.02 | 7.4 | 3.4 | 3.6 | – 2.0 | 5.7 | 1.8 | 23.5 |
| 2010 | – 3.7 | 2.9 | 5.9 | 1.5 | – 8.2 | – 5.4 | 6.9 | – 4.7 | 8.8 | 3.7 | – 0.2 | 6.5 | 12.8 |
| 2011 | 2.3 | 3.2 | – 0.1 | 2.8 | – 1.4 | – 1.8 | – 2.1 | – 5.7 | – 7.2 | 10.8 | – 0.5 | 0.9 | – 0.003 |
| 2012 | 4.4 | 4.1 | 3.1 | – 0.7 | – 6.3 | 4.0 | 1.3 | 2.0 | 2.4 | – 2.0 | 0.3 | 0.7 | 13.4 |
| 2013 | 5.0 | 1.1 | 3.6 | 1.8 | 2.1 | – 1.5 | 4.9 | – 3.1 | 3.0 | 4.5 | 2.8 | 2.4 | 29.6 |
| 2014 | – 3.6 | 4.3 | 0.7 | 0.6 | 2.1 | 1.9 | – 1.5 | 3.8 | – 1.6 | 2.3 | 2.5 | – 0.4 | 11.4 |
| 2015 | – 3.1 | 5.5 | – 1.7 | 0.9 | 1.0 | – 2.1 | 2.0 | – 6.3 | – 2.6 | 8.3 | 0.1 | – 1.8 | – 0.7 |
| 2016 | – 5.1 | – 0.4 | 6.6 | 0.3 | 1.5 | 0.1 | 3.6 | – 0.1 | – 0.1 | – 1.9 | 3.4 | 1.8 | 9.5 |
| 2017 | 1.8 | 3.7 | – 0.04 | 0.9 | 1.2 | 0.5 | 1.9 | 0.1 | 1.9 | 2.2 | 2.8 | 1.0 | 19.4 |
| 2018 | 5.6 | – 3.9 | – 2.7 | 0.3 | 2.2 | 0.5 | 3.6 | 3.0 | 0.4 | – 6.9 | 1.8 | – 9.2 | – 6.2 |
| 2019 | 7.9 | 3.0 | 1.8 | 3.9 | – 6.6 | 6.9 | 1.3 | – 1.8 | 1.7 | 2.0 | 3.4 | 2.9 | 28.9 |
| 2020 | – 0.2 | – 8.4 | – 12.5 | 12.7 | 4.5 | 1.8 | 5.5 | 7.0 | – 3.9 | – 2.8 | 10.8 | 3.7 | 16.3 |
| 2021 | – 1.1 | 2.6 | 4.2 | 5.2 | 0.5 | 2.2 | 2.3 | 2.9 | – 4.8 | 6.9 | – 0.8 | 4.4 | 26.9 |
| 2022 | – 5.3 | – 3.1 | 3.6 | – 8.8 | | | | | | | | | |
| TOTALS | 71.5 | – 3.0 | 77.8 | 113.0 | 16.3 | 9.8 | 82.7 | 5.1 | – 39.0 | 61.8 | 120.4 | 111.3 | |
| AVG. | 1.0 | – 0.04 | 1.1 | 1.5 | 0.2 | 0.1 | 1.1 | 0.07 | – 0.5 | 0.9 | 1.7 | 1.5 | |
| # Up | 43 | 40 | 47 | 52 | 43 | 40 | 42 | 40 | 32 | 43 | 49 | 54 | |
| # Down | 30 | 33 | 26 | 21 | 29 | 32 | 30 | 32 | 39 | 29 | 23 | 18 | |

# STANDARD & POOR'S 500 MONTHLY CLOSING PRICES SINCE 1950

|      | Jan | Feb | Mar | Apr | May | Jun | Jul | Aug | Sep | Oct | Nov | Dec |
|------|------|------|------|------|------|------|------|------|------|------|------|------|
| 1950 | 17.05 | 17.22 | 17.29 | 18.07 | 18.78 | 17.69 | 17.84 | 18.42 | 19.45 | 19.53 | 19.51 | 20.41 |
| 1951 | 21.66 | 21.80 | 21.40 | 22.43 | 21.52 | 20.96 | 22.40 | 23.28 | 23.20 | 22.94 | 22.88 | 23.77 |
| 1952 | 24.14 | 23.26 | 24.37 | 23.32 | 23.86 | 24.96 | 25.40 | 25.03 | 24.54 | 24.52 | 25.66 | 26.57 |
| 1953 | 26.38 | 25.90 | 25.29 | 24.62 | 24.54 | 24.14 | 24.75 | 23.32 | 23.35 | 24.54 | 24.76 | 24.81 |
| 1954 | 26.08 | 26.15 | 26.94 | 28.26 | 29.19 | 29.21 | 30.88 | 29.83 | 32.31 | 31.68 | 34.24 | 35.98 |
| 1955 | 36.63 | 36.76 | 36.58 | 37.96 | 37.91 | 41.03 | 43.52 | 43.18 | 43.67 | 42.34 | 45.51 | 45.48 |
| 1956 | 43.82 | 45.34 | 48.48 | 48.38 | 45.20 | 46.97 | 49.39 | 47.51 | 45.35 | 45.58 | 45.08 | 46.67 |
| 1957 | 44.72 | 43.26 | 44.11 | 45.74 | 47.43 | 47.37 | 47.91 | 45.22 | 42.42 | 41.06 | 41.72 | 39.99 |
| 1958 | 41.70 | 40.84 | 42.10 | 43.44 | 44.09 | 45.24 | 47.19 | 47.75 | 50.06 | 51.33 | 52.48 | 55.21 |
| 1959 | 55.42 | 55.41 | 55.44 | 57.59 | 58.68 | 58.47 | 60.51 | 59.60 | 56.88 | 57.52 | 58.28 | 59.89 |
| 1960 | 55.61 | 56.12 | 55.34 | 54.37 | 55.83 | 56.92 | 55.51 | 56.96 | 53.52 | 53.39 | 55.54 | 58.11 |
| 1961 | 61.78 | 63.44 | 65.06 | 65.31 | 66.56 | 64.64 | 66.76 | 68.07 | 66.73 | 68.62 | 71.32 | 71.55 |
| 1962 | 68.84 | 69.96 | 69.55 | 65.24 | 59.63 | 54.75 | 58.23 | 59.12 | 56.27 | 56.52 | 62.26 | 63.10 |
| 1963 | 66.20 | 64.29 | 66.57 | 69.80 | 70.80 | 69.37 | 69.13 | 72.50 | 71.70 | 74.01 | 73.23 | 75.02 |
| 1964 | 77.04 | 77.80 | 78.98 | 79.46 | 80.37 | 81.69 | 83.18 | 81.83 | 84.18 | 84.86 | 84.42 | 84.75 |
| 1965 | 87.56 | 87.43 | 86.16 | 89.11 | 88.42 | 84.12 | 85.25 | 87.17 | 89.96 | 92.42 | 91.61 | 92.43 |
| 1966 | 92.88 | 91.22 | 89.23 | 91.06 | 86.13 | 84.74 | 83.60 | 77.10 | 76.56 | 80.20 | 80.45 | 80.33 |
| 1967 | 86.61 | 86.78 | 90.20 | 94.01 | 89.08 | 90.64 | 94.75 | 93.64 | 96.71 | 93.90 | 94.00 | 96.47 |
| 1968 | 92.24 | 89.36 | 90.20 | 97.59 | 98.68 | 99.58 | 97.74 | 98.86 | 102.67 | 103.41 | 108.37 | 103.86 |
| 1969 | 103.01 | 98.13 | 101.51 | 103.69 | 103.46 | 97.71 | 91.83 | 95.51 | 93.12 | 97.24 | 93.81 | 92.06 |
| 1970 | 85.02 | 89.50 | 89.63 | 81.52 | 76.55 | 72.72 | 78.05 | 81.52 | 84.21 | 83.25 | 87.20 | 92.15 |
| 1971 | 95.88 | 96.75 | 100.31 | 103.95 | 99.63 | 99.70 | 95.58 | 99.03 | 98.34 | 94.23 | 93.99 | 102.09 |
| 1972 | 103.94 | 106.57 | 107.20 | 107.67 | 109.53 | 107.14 | 107.39 | 111.09 | 110.55 | 111.58 | 116.67 | 118.05 |
| 1973 | 116.03 | 111.68 | 111.52 | 106.97 | 104.95 | 104.26 | 108.22 | 104.25 | 108.43 | 108.29 | 95.96 | 97.55 |
| 1974 | 96.57 | 96.22 | 93.98 | 90.31 | 87.28 | 86.00 | 79.31 | 72.15 | 63.54 | 73.90 | 69.97 | 68.56 |
| 1975 | 76.98 | 81.59 | 83.36 | 87.30 | 91.15 | 95.19 | 88.75 | 86.88 | 83.87 | 89.04 | 91.24 | 90.19 |
| 1976 | 100.86 | 99.71 | 102.77 | 101.64 | 100.18 | 104.28 | 103.44 | 102.91 | 105.24 | 102.90 | 102.10 | 107.46 |
| 1977 | 102.03 | 99.82 | 98.42 | 98.44 | 96.12 | 100.48 | 98.85 | 96.77 | 96.53 | 92.34 | 94.83 | 95.10 |
| 1978 | 89.25 | 87.04 | 89.21 | 96.83 | 97.24 | 95.53 | 100.68 | 103.29 | 102.54 | 93.15 | 94.70 | 96.11 |
| 1979 | 99.93 | 96.28 | 101.59 | 101.76 | 99.08 | 102.91 | 103.81 | 109.32 | 109.32 | 101.82 | 106.16 | 107.94 |
| 1980 | 114.16 | 113.66 | 102.09 | 106.29 | 111.24 | 114.24 | 121.67 | 122.38 | 125.46 | 127.47 | 140.52 | 135.76 |
| 1981 | 129.55 | 131.27 | 136.00 | 132.81 | 132.59 | 131.21 | 130.92 | 122.79 | 116.18 | 121.89 | 126.35 | 122.55 |
| 1982 | 120.40 | 113.11 | 111.96 | 116.44 | 111.88 | 109.61 | 107.09 | 119.51 | 120.42 | 133.71 | 138.54 | 140.64 |
| 1983 | 145.30 | 148.06 | 152.96 | 164.42 | 162.39 | 168.11 | 162.56 | 164.40 | 166.07 | 163.55 | 166.40 | 164.93 |
| 1984 | 163.41 | 157.06 | 159.18 | 160.05 | 150.55 | 153.18 | 150.66 | 166.68 | 166.10 | 166.09 | 163.58 | 167.24 |
| 1985 | 179.63 | 181.18 | 180.66 | 179.83 | 189.55 | 191.85 | 190.92 | 188.63 | 182.08 | 189.82 | 202.17 | 211.28 |
| 1986 | 211.78 | 226.92 | 238.90 | 235.52 | 247.35 | 250.84 | 236.12 | 252.93 | 231.32 | 243.98 | 249.22 | 242.17 |

*(continued)*

164

| | Jan | Feb | Mar | Apr | May | Jun | Jul | Aug | Sep | Oct | Nov | Dec |
|---|---|---|---|---|---|---|---|---|---|---|---|---|
| 1987 | 274.08 | 284.20 | 291.70 | 288.36 | 290.10 | 304.00 | 318.66 | 329.80 | 321.83 | 251.79 | 230.30 | 247.08 |
| 1988 | 257.07 | 267.82 | 258.89 | 261.33 | 262.16 | 273.50 | 272.02 | 261.52 | 271.91 | 278.97 | 273.70 | 277.72 |
| 1989 | 297.47 | 288.86 | 294.87 | 309.64 | 320.52 | 317.98 | 346.08 | 351.45 | 349.15 | 340.36 | 345.99 | 353.40 |
| 1990 | 329.08 | 331.89 | 339.94 | 330.80 | 361.23 | 358.02 | 356.15 | 322.56 | 306.05 | 304.00 | 322.22 | 330.22 |
| 1991 | 343.93 | 367.07 | 375.22 | 375.35 | 389.83 | 371.16 | 387.81 | 395.43 | 387.86 | 392.46 | 375.22 | 417.09 |
| 1992 | 408.79 | 412.70 | 403.69 | 414.95 | 415.35 | 408.14 | 424.21 | 414.03 | 417.80 | 418.68 | 431.35 | 435.71 |
| 1993 | 438.78 | 443.38 | 451.67 | 440.19 | 450.19 | 450.53 | 448.13 | 463.56 | 458.93 | 467.83 | 461.79 | 466.45 |
| 1994 | 481.61 | 467.14 | 445.77 | 450.91 | 456.50 | 444.27 | 458.26 | 475.49 | 462.69 | 472.35 | 453.69 | 459.27 |
| 1995 | 470.42 | 487.39 | 500.71 | 514.71 | 533.40 | 544.75 | 562.06 | 561.88 | 584.41 | 581.50 | 605.37 | 615.93 |
| 1996 | 636.02 | 640.43 | 645.50 | 654.17 | 669.12 | 670.63 | 639.95 | 651.99 | 687.31 | 705.27 | 757.02 | 740.74 |
| 1997 | 786.16 | 790.82 | 757.12 | 801.34 | 848.28 | 885.14 | 954.29 | 899.47 | 947.28 | 914.62 | 955.40 | 970.43 |
| 1998 | 980.28 | 1049.34 | 1101.75 | 1111.75 | 1090.82 | 1133.84 | 1120.67 | 957.28 | 1017.01 | 1098.67 | 1163.63 | 1229.23 |
| 1999 | 1279.64 | 1238.33 | 1286.37 | 1335.18 | 1301.84 | 1372.71 | 1328.72 | 1320.41 | 1282.71 | 1362.93 | 1388.91 | 1469.25 |
| 2000 | 1394.46 | 1366.42 | 1498.58 | 1452.43 | 1420.60 | 1454.60 | 1430.83 | 1517.68 | 1436.51 | 1429.40 | 1314.95 | 1320.28 |
| 2001 | 1366.01 | 1239.94 | 1160.33 | 1249.46 | 1255.82 | 1224.42 | 1211.23 | 1133.58 | 1040.94 | 1059.78 | 1139.45 | 1148.08 |
| 2002 | 1130.20 | 1106.73 | 1147.39 | 1076.92 | 1067.14 | 989.82 | 911.62 | 916.07 | 815.28 | 885.76 | 936.31 | 879.82 |
| 2003 | 855.70 | 841.15 | 849.18 | 916.92 | 963.59 | 974.50 | 990.31 | 1008.01 | 995.97 | 1050.71 | 1058.20 | 1111.92 |
| 2004 | 1131.13 | 1144.94 | 1126.21 | 1107.30 | 1120.68 | 1140.84 | 1101.72 | 1104.24 | 1114.58 | 1130.20 | 1173.82 | 1211.92 |
| 2005 | 1181.27 | 1203.60 | 1180.59 | 1156.85 | 1191.50 | 1191.33 | 1234.18 | 1220.33 | 1228.81 | 1207.01 | 1249.48 | 1248.29 |
| 2006 | 1280.08 | 1280.66 | 1294.83 | 1310.61 | 1270.09 | 1270.20 | 1276.66 | 1303.82 | 1335.85 | 1377.94 | 1400.63 | 1418.30 |
| 2007 | 1438.24 | 1406.82 | 1420.86 | 1482.37 | 1530.62 | 1503.35 | 1455.27 | 1473.99 | 1526.75 | 1549.38 | 1481.14 | 1468.36 |
| 2008 | 1378.55 | 1330.63 | 1322.70 | 1385.59 | 1400.38 | 1280.00 | 1267.38 | 1282.83 | 1166.36 | 968.75 | 896.24 | 903.25 |
| 2009 | 825.88 | 735.09 | 797.87 | 872.81 | 919.14 | 919.32 | 987.48 | 1020.62 | 1057.08 | 1036.19 | 1095.63 | 1115.10 |
| 2010 | 1073.87 | 1104.49 | 1169.43 | 1186.69 | 1089.41 | 1030.71 | 1101.60 | 1049.33 | 1141.20 | 1183.26 | 1180.55 | 1257.64 |
| 2011 | 1286.12 | 1327.22 | 1325.83 | 1363.61 | 1345.20 | 1320.64 | 1292.28 | 1218.89 | 1131.42 | 1253.30 | 1246.96 | 1257.60 |
| 2012 | 1312.41 | 1365.68 | 1408.47 | 1397.91 | 1310.33 | 1362.16 | 1379.32 | 1406.58 | 1440.67 | 1412.16 | 1416.18 | 1426.19 |
| 2013 | 1498.11 | 1514.68 | 1569.19 | 1597.57 | 1630.74 | 1606.28 | 1685.73 | 1632.97 | 1681.55 | 1756.54 | 1805.81 | 1848.36 |
| 2014 | 1782.59 | 1859.45 | 1872.34 | 1883.95 | 1923.57 | 1960.23 | 1930.67 | 2003.37 | 1972.29 | 2018.05 | 2067.56 | 2058.90 |
| 2015 | 1994.99 | 2104.50 | 2067.89 | 2085.51 | 2107.39 | 2063.11 | 2103.84 | 1972.18 | 1920.03 | 2079.36 | 2080.41 | 2043.94 |
| 2016 | 1940.24 | 1932.23 | 2059.74 | 2065.30 | 2096.96 | 2098.86 | 2173.60 | 2170.95 | 2168.27 | 2126.15 | 2198.81 | 2238.83 |
| 2017 | 2278.87 | 2363.64 | 2362.72 | 2384.20 | 2411.80 | 2423.41 | 2470.30 | 2471.65 | 2519.36 | 2575.26 | 2647.58 | 2673.61 |
| 2018 | 2823.81 | 2713.83 | 2640.87 | 2648.05 | 2705.27 | 2718.37 | 2816.29 | 2901.52 | 2913.98 | 2711.74 | 2760.16 | 2506.85 |
| 2019 | 2704.10 | 2784.49 | 2834.40 | 2945.83 | 2752.06 | 2941.76 | 2980.38 | 2926.46 | 2976.74 | 3037.56 | 3140.98 | 3230.78 |
| 2020 | 3225.52 | 2954.22 | 2584.59 | 2912.43 | 3044.31 | 3100.29 | 3271.12 | 3500.31 | 3363.00 | 3269.96 | 3621.63 | 3756.07 |
| 2021 | 3714.24 | 3811.15 | 3972.89 | 4181.17 | 4204.11 | 4297.50 | 4395.26 | 4522.68 | 4307.54 | 4605.38 | 4567.00 | 4766.18 |
| 2022 | 4515.55 | 4373.94 | 4530.41 | 4131.93 | | | | | | | | |

| | Jan | Feb | Mar | Apr | May | Jun | Jul | Aug | Sep | Oct | Nov | Dec | Year's Change |
|---|---|---|---|---|---|---|---|---|---|---|---|---|---|
| 1971 | 10.2 | 2.6 | 4.6 | 6.0 | −3.6 | −0.4 | −2.3 | 3.0 | 0.6 | −3.6 | −1.1 | 9.8 | 27.4 |
| 1972 | 4.2 | 5.5 | 2.2 | 2.5 | 0.9 | −1.8 | −1.8 | 1.7 | −0.3 | 0.5 | 2.1 | 0.6 | 17.2 |
| 1973 | −4.0 | −6.2 | −2.4 | −8.2 | −4.8 | −1.6 | 7.6 | −3.5 | 6.0 | −0.9 | −15.1 | −1.4 | −31.1 |
| 1974 | 3.0 | −0.6 | −2.2 | −5.9 | −7.7 | −5.3 | −7.9 | −10.9 | −0.7 | 17.2 | −3.5 | −5.0 | −35.1 |
| 1975 | 16.6 | 4.6 | 3.6 | 3.8 | 5.8 | 4.7 | −4.4 | −5.0 | −5.9 | 3.6 | 2.4 | −1.5 | 29.8 |
| 1976 | 12.1 | 3.7 | 0.4 | −0.6 | −2.3 | 2.6 | 1.1 | −1.7 | 1.7 | −1.0 | 0.9 | 7.4 | 26.1 |
| 1977 | −2.4 | −1.0 | −0.5 | 1.4 | 0.1 | 4.3 | 0.9 | −0.5 | 0.7 | −3.3 | 5.8 | 1.8 | 7.3 |
| 1978 | −4.0 | 0.6 | 4.7 | 8.5 | 4.4 | 0.05 | 5.0 | 6.9 | −1.6 | −16.4 | 3.2 | 2.9 | 12.3 |
| 1979 | 6.6 | −2.6 | 7.5 | 1.6 | −1.8 | 5.1 | 2.3 | 6.4 | −0.3 | −9.6 | 6.4 | 4.8 | 28.1 |
| 1980 | 7.0 | −2.3 | −17.1 | 6.9 | 7.5 | 4.9 | 8.9 | 5.7 | 3.4 | 2.7 | 8.0 | −2.8 | 33.9 |
| 1981 | −2.2 | 0.1 | 6.1 | 3.1 | 3.1 | −3.5 | −1.9 | −7.5 | −8.0 | 8.4 | 3.1 | −2.7 | −3.2 |
| 1982 | −3.8 | −4.8 | −2.1 | 5.2 | −3.3 | −4.1 | −2.3 | 6.2 | 5.6 | 13.3 | 9.3 | 0.04 | 18.7 |
| 1983 | 6.9 | 5.0 | 3.9 | 8.2 | 5.3 | 3.2 | −4.6 | −3.8 | 1.4 | −7.4 | 4.1 | −2.5 | 19.9 |
| 1984 | −3.7 | −5.9 | −0.7 | −1.3 | −5.9 | 2.9 | −4.2 | 10.9 | −1.8 | −1.2 | −1.8 | 2.0 | −11.2 |
| 1985 | 12.7 | 2.0 | −1.7 | 0.5 | 3.6 | 1.9 | 1.7 | −1.2 | −5.8 | 4.4 | 7.3 | 3.5 | 31.4 |
| 1986 | 3.3 | 7.1 | 4.2 | 2.3 | 4.4 | 1.3 | −8.4 | 3.1 | −8.4 | 2.9 | −0.3 | −2.8 | 7.5 |
| 1987 | 12.2 | 8.4 | 1.2 | −2.8 | −0.3 | 2.0 | 2.4 | 4.6 | −2.3 | −27.2 | −5.6 | 8.3 | −5.4 |
| 1988 | 4.3 | 6.5 | 2.1 | 1.2 | −2.3 | 6.6 | −1.9 | −2.8 | 3.0 | −1.4 | −2.9 | 2.7 | 15.4 |
| 1989 | 5.2 | −0.4 | 1.8 | 5.1 | 4.4 | −2.4 | 4.3 | 3.4 | 0.8 | −3.7 | 0.1 | −0.3 | 19.3 |
| 1990 | −8.6 | 2.4 | 2.3 | −3.6 | 9.3 | 0.7 | −5.2 | −13.0 | −9.6 | −4.3 | 8.9 | 4.1 | −17.8 |
| 1991 | 10.8 | 9.4 | 6.5 | 0.5 | 4.4 | −6.0 | 5.5 | 4.7 | 0.2 | 3.1 | −3.5 | 11.9 | 56.8 |
| 1992 | 5.8 | 2.1 | −4.7 | −4.2 | 1.1 | −3.7 | 3.1 | −3.0 | 3.6 | 3.8 | 7.9 | 3.7 | 15.5 |
| 1993 | 2.9 | −3.7 | 2.9 | −4.2 | 5.9 | 0.5 | 0.1 | 5.4 | 2.7 | 2.2 | −3.2 | 3.0 | 14.7 |
| 1994 | 3.0 | −1.0 | −6.2 | −1.3 | 0.2 | −4.0 | 2.3 | 6.0 | −0.2 | 1.7 | −3.5 | 0.2 | −3.2 |
| 1995 | 0.4 | 5.1 | 3.0 | 3.3 | 2.4 | 8.0 | 7.3 | 1.9 | 2.3 | −0.7 | 2.2 | −0.7 | 39.9 |
| 1996 | 0.7 | 3.8 | 0.1 | 8.1 | 4.4 | −4.7 | −8.8 | 5.6 | 7.5 | −0.4 | 5.8 | −0.1 | 22.7 |
| 1997 | 6.9 | −5.1 | −6.7 | 3.2 | 11.1 | 3.0 | 10.5 | −0.4 | 6.2 | −5.5 | 0.4 | −1.9 | 21.6 |
| 1998 | 3.1 | 9.3 | 3.7 | 1.8 | −4.8 | 6.5 | −1.2 | −19.9 | 13.0 | 4.6 | 10.1 | 12.5 | 39.6 |

*(continued)*

*Based on NASDAQ composite, prior to February 5, 1971, based on National Quotation Bureau indices.*

# NASDAQ COMPOSITE MONTHLY PERCENT CHANGES SINCE 1971 (continued)

| | Jan | Feb | Mar | Apr | May | Jun | Jul | Aug | Sep | Oct | Nov | Dec | Year's Change |
|---|---|---|---|---|---|---|---|---|---|---|---|---|---|
| 1999 | 14.3 | –8.7 | 7.6 | 3.3 | –2.8 | 8.7 | –1.8 | 3.8 | 0.2 | 8.0 | 12.5 | 22.0 | 85.6 |
| 2000 | –3.2 | 19.2 | –2.6 | –15.6 | –11.9 | 16.6 | –5.0 | 11.7 | –12.7 | –8.3 | –22.9 | –4.9 | –39.3 |
| 2001 | 12.2 | –22.4 | –14.5 | 15.0 | –0.3 | 2.4 | –6.2 | –10.9 | –17.0 | 12.8 | 14.2 | 1.0 | –21.1 |
| 2002 | –0.8 | –10.5 | 6.6 | –8.5 | –4.3 | –9.4 | –9.2 | –1.0 | –10.9 | 13.5 | 11.2 | –9.7 | –31.5 |
| 2003 | –1.1 | 1.3 | 0.3 | 9.2 | 9.0 | 1.7 | 6.9 | 4.3 | –1.3 | 8.1 | 1.5 | 2.2 | 50.0 |
| 2004 | 3.1 | –1.8 | –1.8 | –3.7 | 3.5 | 3.1 | –7.8 | –2.6 | 3.2 | 4.1 | 6.2 | 3.7 | 8.6 |
| 2005 | –5.2 | –0.5 | –2.6 | –3.9 | 7.6 | –0.5 | 6.2 | –1.5 | –0.02 | –1.5 | 5.3 | –1.2 | 1.4 |
| 2006 | 4.6 | –1.1 | 2.6 | –0.7 | –6.2 | –0.3 | –3.7 | 4.4 | 3.4 | 4.8 | 2.7 | –0.7 | 9.5 |
| 2007 | 2.0 | –1.9 | 0.2 | 4.3 | 3.1 | –0.05 | –2.2 | 2.0 | 4.0 | 5.8 | –6.9 | –0.3 | 9.8 |
| 2008 | –9.9 | –5.0 | 0.3 | 5.9 | 4.6 | –9.1 | 1.4 | 1.8 | –11.6 | –17.7 | –10.8 | 2.7 | –40.5 |
| 2009 | –6.4 | –6.7 | 10.9 | 12.3 | 3.3 | 3.4 | 7.8 | 1.5 | 5.6 | –3.6 | 4.9 | 5.8 | 43.9 |
| 2010 | –5.4 | 4.2 | 7.1 | 2.6 | –8.3 | –6.5 | 6.9 | –6.2 | 12.0 | 5.9 | –0.4 | 6.2 | 16.9 |
| 2011 | 1.8 | 3.0 | –0.04 | 3.3 | –1.3 | –2.2 | –0.6 | –6.4 | –6.4 | 11.1 | –2.4 | –0.6 | –1.8 |
| 2012 | 8.0 | 5.4 | 4.2 | –1.5 | –7.2 | 3.8 | 0.2 | 4.3 | 1.6 | –4.5 | 1.1 | 0.3 | 15.9 |
| 2013 | 4.1 | 0.6 | 3.4 | 1.9 | 3.8 | –1.5 | 6.6 | –1.0 | 5.1 | 3.9 | 3.6 | 2.9 | 38.3 |
| 2014 | –1.7 | 5.0 | –2.5 | –2.0 | 3.1 | 3.9 | –0.9 | 4.8 | –1.9 | 3.1 | 3.5 | –1.2 | 13.4 |
| 2015 | –2.1 | 7.1 | –1.3 | 0.8 | 2.6 | –1.6 | 2.8 | –6.9 | –3.3 | 9.4 | 1.1 | –2.0 | 5.7 |
| 2016 | –7.9 | –1.2 | 6.8 | –1.9 | 3.6 | –2.1 | 6.6 | 1.0 | 1.9 | –2.3 | 2.6 | 1.1 | 7.5 |
| 2017 | 4.3 | 3.8 | 1.5 | 2.3 | 2.5 | –0.9 | 3.4 | 1.3 | 1.0 | 3.6 | 2.2 | 0.4 | 28.2 |
| 2018 | 7.4 | –1.9 | –2.9 | 0.04 | 5.3 | 0.9 | 2.2 | 5.7 | –0.8 | –9.2 | 0.3 | –9.5 | –3.9 |
| 2019 | 9.7 | 3.4 | 2.6 | 4.7 | –7.9 | 7.4 | 2.1 | –2.6 | 0.5 | 3.7 | 4.5 | 3.5 | 35.2 |
| 2020 | 2.0 | –6.4 | –10.1 | 15.4 | 6.8 | 6.0 | 6.8 | 9.6 | –5.2 | –2.3 | 11.8 | 5.7 | 43.6 |
| 2021 | 1.4 | 0.9 | 0.4 | 5.4 | –1.5 | 5.5 | 1.2 | 4.0 | –5.3 | 7.3 | 0.3 | 0.7 | |
| 2022 | –9.0 | –3.4 | 3.4 | –13.3 | | | | | | | | | |
| TOTALS | 131.4 | 27.0 | 36.1 | 76.4 | 48.6 | 50.0 | 31.8 | 23.4 | –34.1 | 37.5 | 93.6 | 85.6 | |
| AVG. | 2.5 | 0.5 | 0.7 | 1.5 | 1.0 | 1.0 | 0.6 | 0.5 | –0.7 | 0.7 | 1.8 | 1.7 | |
| # Up | 34 | 28 | 33 | 34 | 31 | 29 | 29 | 29 | 27 | 28 | 36 | 31 | |
| # Down | 18 | 24 | 19 | 18 | 20 | 22 | 22 | 22 | 24 | 23 | 15 | 20 | |

Based on NASDAQ composite, prior to February 5, 1971, based on National Quotation Bureau indices.

# NASDAQ COMPOSITE MONTHLY CLOSING PRICES SINCE 1971

| | Jan | Feb | Mar | Apr | May | Jun | Jul | Aug | Sep | Oct | Nov | Dec |
|---|---|---|---|---|---|---|---|---|---|---|---|---|
| 1971 | 98.77 | 101.34 | 105.97 | 112.30 | 108.25 | 107.80 | 105.27 | 108.42 | 109.03 | 105.10 | 103.97 | 114.12 |
| 1972 | 118.87 | 125.38 | 128.14 | 131.33 | 132.53 | 130.08 | 127.75 | 129.95 | 129.61 | 130.24 | 132.96 | 133.73 |
| 1973 | 128.40 | 120.41 | 117.46 | 107.85 | 102.64 | 100.98 | 108.64 | 104.87 | 111.20 | 110.17 | 93.51 | 92.19 |
| 1974 | 94.93 | 94.35 | 92.27 | 86.86 | 80.20 | 75.96 | 9.99 | 62.37 | 55.67 | 65.23 | 62.95 | 59.82 |
| 1975 | 69.78 | 73.00 | 75.66 | 78.54 | 83.10 | 87.02 | 83.19 | 79.01 | 74.33 | 76.99 | 78.80 | 77.62 |
| 1976 | 87.05 | 90.26 | 90.62 | 90.08 | 88.04 | 90.32 | 91.29 | 89.70 | 91.26 | 90.35 | 91.12 | 97.88 |
| 1977 | 95.54 | 94.57 | 94.13 | 95.48 | 95.59 | 99.73 | 100.65 | 100.10 | 100.85 | 97.52 | 103.15 | 105.05 |
| 1978 | 100.84 | 101.47 | 106.20 | 115.18 | 120.24 | 120.30 | 126.32 | 135.01 | 132.89 | 111.12 | 114.69 | 117.98 |
| 1979 | 125.82 | 122.56 | 131.76 | 133.82 | 131.42 | 138.13 | 141.33 | 150.44 | 149.98 | 135.53 | 144.26 | 151.14 |
| 1980 | 161.75 | 158.03 | 131.00 | 139.99 | 150.45 | 157.78 | 171.81 | 181.52 | 187.76 | 192.78 | 208.15 | 202.34 |
| 1981 | 197.81 | 198.01 | 210.18 | 216.74 | 223.47 | 215.75 | 211.63 | 195.75 | 180.03 | 195.24 | 201.37 | 195.84 |
| 1982 | 188.39 | 179.43 | 175.65 | 184.70 | 178.54 | 171.30 | 167.35 | 177.71 | 187.65 | 212.63 | 232.31 | 232.41 |
| 1983 | 248.35 | 260.67 | 270.80 | 293.06 | 308.73 | 318.70 | 303.96 | 292.42 | 296.65 | 274.55 | 285.67 | 278.60 |
| 1984 | 268.43 | 252.57 | 250.78 | 247.44 | 232.82 | 239.65 | 229.70 | 254.64 | 249.94 | 247.03 | 242.53 | 247.35 |
| 1985 | 278.70 | 284.17 | 279.20 | 280.56 | 290.80 | 296.20 | 229.70 | 254.64 | 249.94 | 247.03 | 242.53 | 247.35 |
| 1986 | 335.77 | 359.53 | 374.72 | 383.24 | 400.16 | 405.51 | 371.37 | 382.86 | 350.67 | 360.77 | 359.57 | 349.33 |
| 1987 | 392.06 | 424.97 | 430.05 | 417.81 | 416.54 | 424.67 | 434.93 | 454.97 | 444.29 | 323.30 | 305.16 | 330.47 |
| 1988 | 344.66 | 366.95 | 374.64 | 379.23 | 370.34 | 394.66 | 387.33 | 376.55 | 387.71 | 382.46 | 371.45 | 381.38 |
| 1989 | 401.30 | 399.71 | 406.73 | 427.55 | 446.17 | 435.29 | 453.84 | 469.33 | 472.92 | 455.63 | 456.09 | 454.82 |
| 1990 | 415.81 | 425.83 | 435.54 | 420.07 | 458.97 | 462.29 | 438.24 | 381.21 | 344.51 | 329.84 | 359.06 | 373.84 |
| 1991 | 414.20 | 453.05 | 482.30 | 484.72 | 506.11 | 475.92 | 502.04 | 525.68 | 526.88 | 542.98 | 523.90 | 586.34 |
| 1992 | 620.21 | 633.47 | 603.77 | 578.68 | 585.31 | 563.60 | 580.83 | 563.12 | 583.27 | 605.17 | 652.73 | 676.95 |
| 1993 | 696.34 | 670.77 | 690.13 | 661.42 | 700.53 | 703.95 | 704.70 | 742.84 | 762.78 | 779.26 | 754.39 | 776.80 |
| 1994 | 800.47 | 792.50 | 743.46 | 733.84 | 735.19 | 705.96 | 722.16 | 765.62 | 764.29 | 777.49 | 750.32 | 751.96 |
| 1995 | 755.20 | 793.73 | 817.21 | 843.98 | 864.58 | 933.45 | 1001.21 | 1020.11 | 1043.54 | 1036.06 | 1059.20 | 1052.13 |
| 1996 | 1059.79 | 1100.05 | 1101.40 | 1190.52 | 1243.43 | 1185.02 | 1080.59 | 1141.50 | 1226.92 | 1221.51 | 1292.61 | 1291.03 |

Based on NASDAQ composite, prior to February 5, 1971, based on National Quotation Bureau indices.

168

| | Jan | Feb | Mar | Apr | May | Jun | Jul | Aug | Sep | Oct | Nov | Dec |
|---|---|---|---|---|---|---|---|---|---|---|---|---|
| 1997 | 1379.85 | 1309.00 | 1221.70 | 1260.76 | 1400.32 | 1442.07 | 1593.81 | 1587.32 | 1685.69 | 1593.61 | 1600.55 | 1570.35 |
| 1998 | 1619.36 | 1770.51 | 1835.68 | 1868.41 | 1778.87 | 1894.74 | 1872.39 | 1499.25 | 1693.84 | 1771.39 | 1949.54 | 2192.69 |
| 1999 | 2505.89 | 2288.03 | 2461.40 | 2542.85 | 2470.52 | 2686.12 | 2638.49 | 2739.35 | 2746.16 | 2966.43 | 3336.16 | 4069.31 |
| 2000 | 3940.35 | 4696.69 | 4572.83 | 3860.66 | 3400.91 | 3966.11 | 3766.99 | 4206.35 | 3672.82 | 3369.63 | 2597.93 | 2470.52 |
| 2001 | 2772.73 | 2151.83 | 1840.26 | 2116.24 | 2110.49 | 2160.54 | 2027.13 | 1805.43 | 1498.80 | 1690.20 | 1930.58 | 1950.40 |
| 2002 | 1934.03 | 1731.49 | 1845.35 | 1688.23 | 1615.73 | 1463.21 | 1328.26 | 1314.85 | 1172.06 | 1329.75 | 1478.78 | 1335.51 |
| 2003 | 1320.91 | 1337.52 | 1341.17 | 1464.31 | 1595.91 | 1622.80 | 1735.02 | 1810.45 | 1786.94 | 1932.21 | 1960.26 | 2003.37 |
| 2004 | 2066.15 | 2029.82 | 1994.22 | 1920.15 | 1986.74 | 2047.79 | 1887.36 | 1838.10 | 1896.84 | 1974.99 | 2096.81 | 2175.44 |
| 2005 | 2062.41 | 2051.72 | 1999.23 | 1921.65 | 2068.22 | 2056.96 | 2184.83 | 2152.09 | 2151.69 | 2120.30 | 2232.82 | 2205.32 |
| 2006 | 2305.82 | 2281.39 | 2339.79 | 2322.57 | 2178.88 | 2172.09 | 2091.47 | 2183.75 | 2258.43 | 2366.71 | 2431.77 | 2415.29 |
| 2007 | 2463.93 | 2416.15 | 2421.64 | 2525.09 | 2604.52 | 2603.23 | 2545.57 | 2596.36 | 2701.50 | 2859.12 | 2660.96 | 2652.28 |
| 2008 | 2389.86 | 2271.48 | 2279.10 | 2412.80 | 2522.66 | 2292.98 | 2325.55 | 2367.52 | 2091.88 | 1720.95 | 1535.57 | 1577.03 |
| 2009 | 1476.42 | 1377.84 | 1528.59 | 1717.30 | 1774.33 | 1835.04 | 1978.50 | 2009.06 | 2122.42 | 2045.11 | 2144.60 | 2269.15 |
| 2010 | 2147.35 | 2238.26 | 2397.96 | 2461.19 | 2257.04 | 2109.24 | 2254.70 | 2114.03 | 2368.62 | 2507.41 | 2498.23 | 2652.87 |
| 2011 | 2700.08 | 2782.27 | 2781.07 | 2873.54 | 2835.30 | 2773.52 | 2756.38 | 2579.46 | 2415.40 | 2684.41 | 2620.34 | 2605.15 |
| 2012 | 2813.84 | 2966.89 | 3091.57 | 3046.36 | 2827.34 | 2935.05 | 2939.52 | 3066.96 | 3116.23 | 2977.23 | 3010.24 | 3019.51 |
| 2013 | 3142.13 | 3160.19 | 3267.52 | 3328.79 | 3455.91 | 3403.25 | 3626.37 | 3589.87 | 3771.48 | 3919.71 | 4059.89 | 4176.59 |
| 2014 | 4103.88 | 4308.12 | 4198.99 | 4114.56 | 4242.62 | 4408.18 | 4369.77 | 4580.27 | 4493.39 | 4630.74 | 4791.63 | 4736.05 |
| 2015 | 4635.24 | 4963.53 | 4900.88 | 4941.42 | 5070.03 | 4986.87 | 5128.28 | 4776.51 | 4620.16 | 5053.75 | 5108.67 | 5007.41 |
| 2016 | 4613.95 | 4557.95 | 4869.85 | 4775.36 | 4948.05 | 4842.67 | 5162.13 | 5213.22 | 5312.00 | 5189.13 | 5323.68 | 5383.12 |
| 2017 | 5614.79 | 5825.44 | 5911.74 | 6047.61 | 6198.52 | 6140.42 | 6348.12 | 6428.66 | 6495.96 | 6727.67 | 6873.97 | 6903.39 |
| 2018 | 7411.48 | 7273.01 | 7063.44 | 7066.27 | 7442.12 | 7510.30 | 7671.79 | 8109.54 | 8046.35 | 7305.90 | 7330.54 | 6635.28 |
| 2019 | 7281.74 | 7532.53 | 7729.32 | 8095.39 | 7453.15 | 8006.24 | 8175.42 | 7962.88 | 7999.34 | 8292.36 | 8665.47 | 8972.60 |
| 2020 | 9150.94 | 8567.37 | 7700.10 | 8889.55 | 9489.87 | 10058.77 | 10745.27 | 11775.46 | 11167.51 | 10911.59 | 12198.74 | 12888.28 |
| 2021 | 13070.69 | 13192.35 | 13246.87 | 13962.68 | 13748.74 | 14503.95 | 14672.68 | 15259.24 | 14448.58 | 15498.39 | 15537.69 | 15644.97 |
| 2022 | 14239.88 | 13751.40 | 14220.52 | 12334.64 | | | | | | | | |

Based on NASDAQ composite, prior to February 5, 1971, based on National Quotation Bureau indices.

# RUSSELL 1000 INDEX MONTHLY PERCENT CHANGES SINCE 1979

| | Jan | Feb | Mar | Apr | May | Jun | Jul | Aug | Sep | Oct | Nov | Dec | Year's Change |
|---|---|---|---|---|---|---|---|---|---|---|---|---|---|
| 1979 | 4.2 | −3.5 | 6.0 | 0.3 | −2.2 | 4.3 | 1.1 | 5.6 | 0.02 | −7.1 | 5.1 | 2.1 | 16.1 |
| 1980 | 5.9 | −0.5 | −11.5 | 4.6 | 5.0 | 3.2 | 6.4 | 1.1 | 2.6 | 1.8 | 10.1 | −3.9 | 25.6 |
| 1981 | −4.6 | 1.0 | 3.8 | −1.9 | 0.2 | −1.2 | −0.1 | −6.2 | −6.4 | 5.4 | 4.0 | −3.3 | −9.7 |
| 1982 | −2.7 | −5.9 | −1.3 | 3.9 | −3.6 | −2.6 | −2.3 | 11.3 | 1.2 | 11.3 | 4.0 | 1.3 | 13.7 |
| 1983 | 3.2 | 2.1 | 3.2 | 7.1 | −0.2 | 3.7 | −3.2 | 0.5 | 1.3 | −2.4 | 2.0 | −1.2 | 17.0 |
| 1984 | −1.9 | −4.4 | 1.1 | 0.3 | −5.9 | 2.1 | −1.8 | 10.8 | −0.2 | −0.1 | −1.4 | 2.2 | −0.1 |
| 1985 | 7.8 | 1.1 | −0.4 | −0.3 | 5.4 | 1.6 | −0.8 | −1.0 | −3.9 | 4.5 | 6.5 | 4.1 | 26.7 |
| 1986 | 0.9 | 7.2 | 5.1 | −1.3 | 5.0 | 1.4 | −5.9 | 6.8 | −8.5 | 5.1 | 1.4 | −3.0 | 13.6 |
| 1987 | 12.7 | 4.0 | 1.9 | −1.8 | 0.4 | 4.5 | 4.2 | 3.8 | −2.4 | −21.9 | −8.0 | 7.2 | 0.02 |
| 1988 | 4.3 | 4.4 | −2.9 | 0.7 | 0.2 | 4.8 | −0.9 | −3.3 | 3.9 | 2.0 | −2.0 | 1.7 | 13.1 |
| 1989 | 6.8 | −2.5 | 2.0 | 4.9 | 3.8 | −0.8 | 8.2 | 1.7 | −0.5 | −2.8 | 1.5 | 1.8 | 25.9 |
| 1990 | −7.4 | 1.2 | 2.2 | −2.8 | 8.9 | −0.7 | −1.1 | −9.6 | −5.3 | −0.8 | 6.4 | 2.7 | −7.5 |
| 1991 | 4.5 | 6.9 | 2.5 | −0.1 | 3.8 | −4.7 | 4.6 | 2.2 | −1.5 | 1.4 | −4.1 | 11.2 | 28.8 |
| 1992 | −1.4 | 0.9 | −2.4 | 2.3 | 0.3 | −1.9 | 4.1 | −2.5 | 1.0 | 0.7 | 3.5 | 1.4 | 5.9 |
| 1993 | 0.7 | 0.6 | 2.2 | −2.8 | 2.4 | 0.4 | −0.4 | 3.5 | −0.5 | 1.2 | −1.7 | 1.6 | 7.3 |
| 1994 | 2.9 | −2.9 | −4.5 | 1.1 | 1.0 | −2.9 | 3.1 | 3.9 | −2.6 | 1.7 | −3.9 | 1.2 | −2.4 |
| 1995 | 2.4 | 3.8 | 2.3 | 2.5 | 3.5 | 2.4 | 3.7 | 0.5 | 3.9 | −0.6 | 4.2 | 1.4 | 34.4 |
| 1996 | 3.1 | 1.1 | 0.7 | 1.4 | 2.1 | −0.1 | −4.9 | 2.5 | 5.5 | 2.1 | 7.1 | −1.8 | 19.7 |
| 1997 | 5.8 | 0.2 | −4.6 | 5.3 | 6.2 | 4.0 | 8.0 | −4.9 | 5.4 | −3.4 | 4.2 | 1.9 | 30.5 |
| 1998 | 0.6 | 7.0 | 4.9 | 0.9 | −2.3 | 3.6 | −1.3 | −15.1 | 6.5 | 7.8 | 6.1 | 6.2 | 25.1 |
| 1999 | 3.5 | −3.3 | 3.7 | 4.2 | −2.3 | 5.1 | −3.2 | −1.0 | −2.8 | 6.5 | 2.5 | 6.0 | 19.5 |
| 2000 | −4.2 | −0.4 | 8.9 | −3.3 | −2.7 | 2.5 | −1.8 | 7.4 | −4.8 | −1.2 | −9.3 | 1.1 | −8.8 |
| 2001 | 3.2 | −9.5 | −6.7 | 8.0 | 0.5 | −2.4 | −1.4 | −6.2 | −8.6 | 2.0 | 7.5 | 0.9 | −13.6 |
| 2002 | −1.4 | −2.1 | 4.0 | −5.8 | −1.0 | −7.5 | −7.5 | 0.3 | −10.9 | 8.1 | 5.7 | −5.8 | −22.9 |
| 2003 | −2.5 | −1.7 | 0.9 | 7.9 | 5.5 | 1.2 | 1.8 | 1.9 | −1.2 | 5.7 | 1.0 | 4.6 | 27.5 |
| 2004 | 1.8 | 1.2 | −1.5 | −1.9 | 1.3 | 1.7 | −3.6 | 0.3 | 1.1 | 1.5 | 4.1 | 3.5 | 9.5 |
| 2005 | −2.6 | 2.0 | −1.7 | −2.0 | 3.4 | 0.3 | 3.8 | −1.1 | 0.8 | −1.9 | 3.5 | 0.01 | 4.4 |
| 2006 | 2.7 | 0.01 | 1.3 | 1.1 | −3.2 | 0.003 | 0.1 | 2.2 | 2.3 | 3.3 | 1.9 | 1.1 | 13.3 |
| 2007 | 1.8 | −1.9 | 0.9 | 4.1 | 3.4 | −2.0 | −3.2 | 1.2 | 3.7 | 1.6 | −4.5 | −0.8 | 3.9 |
| 2008 | −6.1 | −3.3 | −0.8 | 5.0 | 1.6 | −8.5 | −1.3 | 1.2 | −9.7 | −17.6 | −7.9 | 1.3 | −39.0 |
| 2009 | −8.3 | −10.7 | 8.5 | 10.0 | 5.3 | 0.1 | 7.5 | 3.4 | 3.9 | −2.3 | 5.6 | 2.3 | 25.5 |
| 2010 | −3.7 | 3.1 | 6.0 | 1.8 | −8.1 | −5.7 | 6.8 | −4.7 | 9.0 | 3.8 | 0.1 | 6.5 | 13.9 |
| 2011 | 2.3 | 3.3 | 0.1 | 2.9 | −1.3 | −1.9 | −2.3 | −6.0 | −7.6 | 11.1 | −0.5 | 0.7 | −0.5 |
| 2012 | 4.8 | 4.1 | 3.0 | −0.7 | −6.4 | 3.7 | 1.1 | 2.2 | 2.4 | −1.8 | 0.5 | 0.8 | 13.9 |
| 2013 | 5.3 | 1.1 | 3.7 | 1.7 | 2.0 | −1.5 | 5.2 | −3.0 | 3.3 | 4.3 | 2.6 | 2.5 | 30.4 |
| 2014 | −3.3 | 4.5 | 0.5 | 0.4 | 2.1 | 2.1 | −1.7 | 3.9 | −1.9 | 2.3 | 2.4 | −0.4 | 11.1 |
| 2015 | −2.8 | 5.5 | −1.4 | 0.6 | 1.1 | −2.0 | 1.8 | −6.2 | −2.9 | 8.0 | 0.1 | −2.0 | −1.1 |
| 2016 | −5.5 | −0.3 | 6.8 | 0.4 | 1.5 | 0.1 | 3.7 | −0.1 | −0.1 | −2.1 | 3.7 | 1.7 | 9.7 |
| 2017 | 1.9 | 3.6 | −0.1 | 0.9 | 1.0 | 0.5 | 1.9 | 0.1 | 2.0 | 2.2 | 2.8 | 1.0 | 19.3 |
| 2018 | 5.4 | −3.9 | −2.4 | 0.2 | 2.3 | 0.5 | 3.3 | 3.2 | 0.2 | −7.2 | 1.8 | −9.3 | −6.6 |
| 2019 | 8.2 | 3.2 | 1.6 | 3.9 | −6.6 | 6.9 | 1.4 | −2.0 | 1.6 | 2.0 | 3.6 | 2.7 | 28.9 |
| 2020 | −0.01 | −8.3 | −13.4 | 13.1 | 5.1 | 2.1 | 5.7 | 7.2 | −3.8 | −2.5 | 11.6 | 4.1 | 18.9 |
| 2021 | −0.9 | 2.8 | 3.7 | 5.3 | 0.3 | 2.4 | 2.0 | 2.8 | −4.7 | 6.9 | −1.5 | 3.9 | 24.8 |
| 2022 | −5.7 | −2.9 | 3.2 | −9.0 | | | | | | | | | |
| TOTALS | 41.7 | 7.9 | 39.1 | 73.1 | 38.8 | 18.8 | 40.8 | 18.6 | −29.2 | 38.6 | 82.3 | 61.2 | |
| AVG. | 0.9 | 0.2 | 0.9 | 1.7 | 0.9 | 0.4 | 0.9 | 0.4 | −0.7 | 0.9 | 1.9 | 1.4 | |
| # Up | 26 | 26 | 29 | 31 | 30 | 27 | 23 | 27 | 21 | 27 | 32 | 33 | |
| # Down | 18 | 18 | 15 | 13 | 13 | 16 | 20 | 16 | 22 | 16 | 11 | 10 | |

| | Jan | Feb | Mar | Apr | May | Jun | Jul | Aug | Sep | Oct | Nov | Dec |
|---|---|---|---|---|---|---|---|---|---|---|---|---|
| 1979 | 53.76 | 51.88 | 54.97 | 55.15 | 53.92 | 56.25 | 56.86 | 60.04 | 60.05 | 55.78 | 58.65 | 59.87 |
| 1980 | 63.40 | 63.07 | 55.79 | 58.38 | 61.31 | 63.27 | 67.30 | 68.05 | 69.84 | 71.08 | 78.26 | 75.20 |
| 1981 | 71.75 | 72.49 | 75.21 | 73.77 | 73.90 | 73.01 | 72.92 | 68.42 | 64.06 | 67.54 | 70.23 | 67.93 |
| 1982 | 66.12 | 62.21 | 61.43 | 63.85 | 61.53 | 59.92 | 58.54 | 65.14 | 65.89 | 73.34 | 76.28 | 77.24 |
| 1983 | 79.75 | 81.45 | 84.06 | 90.04 | 89.89 | 93.18 | 90.18 | 90.65 | 91.85 | 89.69 | 91.50 | 90.38 |
| 1984 | 88.69 | 84.76 | 85.73 | 86.00 | 80.94 | 82.61 | 81.13 | 89.87 | 89.67 | 89.62 | 88.36 | 90.31 |
| 1985 | 97.31 | 98.38 | 98.03 | 97.72 | 103.02 | 104.65 | 103.78 | 102.76 | 98.75 | 103.16 | 109.91 | 114.39 |
| 1986 | 115.39 | 123.71 | 130.07 | 128.44 | 134.82 | 136.75 | 128.74 | 137.43 | 125.70 | 132.11 | 133.97 | 130.00 |
| 1987 | 146.48 | 152.29 | 155.20 | 152.39 | 152.94 | 159.84 | 166.57 | 172.95 | 168.83 | 131.89 | 121.28 | 130.02 |
| 1988 | 135.55 | 141.54 | 137.45 | 138.37 | 138.66 | 145.31 | 143.99 | 139.26 | 144.68 | 147.55 | 144.59 | 146.99 |
| 1989 | 156.93 | 152.98 | 155.99 | 163.63 | 169.85 | 168.49 | 182.27 | 185.33 | 184.40 | 179.17 | 181.85 | 185.11 |
| 1990 | 171.44 | 173.43 | 177.28 | 172.32 | 187.66 | 186.29 | 184.32 | 166.69 | 157.83 | 156.62 | 166.69 | 171.22 |
| 1991 | 179.00 | 191.34 | 196.15 | 195.94 | 203.32 | 193.78 | 202.67 | 207.18 | 204.02 | 206.96 | 198.46 | 220.61 |
| 1992 | 217.52 | 219.50 | 214.29 | 219.13 | 219.71 | 215.60 | 224.37 | 218.86 | 221.15 | 222.65 | 230.44 | 233.59 |
| 1993 | 235.25 | 236.67 | 241.80 | 235.13 | 240.80 | 241.78 | 240.78 | 249.20 | 247.95 | 250.97 | 246.70 | 250.71 |
| 1994 | 258.08 | 250.52 | 239.19 | 241.71 | 244.13 | 237.11 | 244.44 | 254.04 | 247.49 | 251.62 | 241.82 | 244.65 |
| 1995 | 250.52 | 260.08 | 266.11 | 272.81 | 282.48 | 289.29 | 299.98 | 301.40 | 313.28 | 311.37 | 324.36 | 328.89 |
| 1996 | 338.97 | 342.56 | 345.01 | 349.84 | 357.35 | 357.10 | 339.44 | 347.79 | 366.77 | 374.38 | 401.05 | 393.75 |
| 1997 | 416.77 | 417.46 | 398.19 | 419.15 | 445.06 | 462.95 | 499.89 | 475.33 | 500.78 | 483.86 | 504.25 | 513.79 |
| 1998 | 517.02 | 553.14 | 580.31 | 585.46 | 572.46 | 592.57 | 584.97 | 496.66 | 529.11 | 570.63 | 605.31 | 642.87 |
| 1999 | 665.64 | 643.67 | 667.49 | 695.25 | 679.10 | 713.61 | 690.51 | 683.27 | 663.83 | 707.19 | 724.66 | 767.97 |
| 2000 | 736.08 | 733.04 | 797.99 | 771.58 | 750.98 | 769.68 | 755.57 | 811.17 | 772.60 | 763.06 | 692.40 | 700.09 |
| 2001 | 722.55 | 654.25 | 610.36 | 658.90 | 662.39 | 646.64 | 637.43 | 597.67 | 546.46 | 557.29 | 599.32 | 604.94 |
| 2002 | 596.66 | 583.88 | 607.35 | 572.04 | 566.18 | 523.72 | 484.39 | 486.08 | 433.22 | 468.51 | 495.00 | 466.18 |
| 2003 | 454.30 | 446.37 | 450.35 | 486.09 | 512.92 | 518.94 | 528.53 | 538.40 | 532.15 | 562.51 | 568.32 | 594.56 |
| 2004 | 605.21 | 612.58 | 603.42 | 591.83 | 599.40 | 609.31 | 587.21 | 589.09 | 595.66 | 604.51 | 629.26 | 650.99 |
| 2005 | 633.99 | 646.93 | 635.78 | 623.32 | 644.28 | 645.92 | 670.26 | 663.13 | 668.53 | 656.09 | 679.35 | 679.42 |
| 2006 | 697.79 | 697.83 | 706.74 | 714.37 | 691.78 | 691.80 | 692.59 | 707.55 | 723.48 | 747.30 | 761.43 | 770.08 |
| 2007 | 784.11 | 768.92 | 775.97 | 807.82 | 835.14 | 818.17 | 792.11 | 801.22 | 830.59 | 844.20 | 806.44 | 799.82 |
| 2008 | 750.97 | 726.42 | 720.32 | 756.03 | 768.28 | 703.22 | 694.07 | 702.17 | 634.08 | 522.47 | 481.43 | 487.77 |
| 2009 | 447.32 | 399.61 | 433.67 | 476.84 | 501.95 | 502.27 | 539.88 | 558.21 | 579.97 | 566.50 | 598.41 | 612.01 |
| 2010 | 589.41 | 607.45 | 643.79 | 655.06 | 601.79 | 567.37 | 606.09 | 577.68 | 629.78 | 653.57 | 654.24 | 696.90 |
| 2011 | 712.97 | 736.24 | 737.07 | 758.45 | 748.75 | 734.48 | 717.77 | 674.79 | 623.45 | 692.41 | 688.77 | 693.36 |
| 2012 | 726.33 | 756.42 | 778.92 | 773.50 | 724.12 | 750.61 | 758.60 | 775.07 | 793.74 | 779.35 | 783.37 | 789.90 |
| 2013 | 831.74 | 840.97 | 872.11 | 886.89 | 904.44 | 890.67 | 937.16 | 909.28 | 939.50 | 979.68 | 1004.97 | 1030.36 |
| 2014 | 996.48 | 1041.36 | 1046.42 | 1050.20 | 1071.96 | 1094.59 | 1075.60 | 1117.71 | 1096.43 | 1121.98 | 1148.90 | 1144.37 |
| 2015 | 1111.85 | 1173.46 | 1156.95 | 1164.03 | 1176.67 | 1152.64 | 1173.55 | 1100.51 | 1068.46 | 1153.55 | 1154.66 | 1131.88 |
| 2016 | 1069.78 | 1066.58 | 1138.84 | 1143.76 | 1160.95 | 1161.57 | 1204.43 | 1203.05 | 1202.25 | 1177.22 | 1220.68 | 1241.66 |
| 2017 | 1265.35 | 1311.34 | 1310.06 | 1322.44 | 1336.18 | 1343.52 | 1368.57 | 1369.61 | 1396.90 | 1427.43 | 1467.42 | 1481.81 |
| 2018 | 1561.66 | 1501.23 | 1464.87 | 1468.28 | 1502.31 | 1509.96 | 1560.36 | 1610.70 | 1614.54 | 1498.65 | 1525.56 | 1384.26 |
| 2019 | 1498.36 | 1545.73 | 1570.23 | 1631.87 | 1524.42 | 1629.02 | 1652.40 | 1618.61 | 1644.18 | 1677.08 | 1736.85 | 1784.21 |
| 2020 | 1784.03 | 1635.21 | 1416.49 | 1601.82 | 1682.75 | 1717.47 | 1815.99 | 1946.15 | 1872.70 | 1825.67 | 2037.36 | 2120.87 |
| 2021 | 2101.36 | 2159.32 | 2238.17 | 2356.67 | 2364.53 | 2421.14 | 2469.17 | 2537.31 | 2418.16 | 2583.83 | 2545.78 | 2645.91 |
| 2022 | 2494.64 | 2422.79 | 2501.29 | 2276.45 | | | | | | | | |

| | Jan | Feb | Mar | Apr | May | Jun | Jul | Aug | Sep | Oct | Nov | Dec | Year's Change |
|---|---|---|---|---|---|---|---|---|---|---|---|---|---|
| 1979 | 9.0 | -3.2 | 9.7 | 2.3 | -1.8 | 5.3 | 2.9 | 7.8 | -0.7 | -11.3 | 8.1 | 6.6 | 38.0 |
| 1980 | 8.2 | 2.1 | 18.5 | 6.0 | 8.0 | 4.0 | 11.0 | 0.5 | 2.9 | 3.9 | 7.0 | -3.7 | 33.8 |
| 1981 | -0.6 | 0.3 | 7.7 | 2.5 | 3.0 | -2.5 | -2.6 | -8.0 | -8.6 | 8.2 | 2.8 | -2.0 | -1.5 |
| 1982 | -3.7 | -5.3 | -1.5 | 5.1 | -3.2 | -4.0 | -1.7 | 7.5 | 3.6 | 14.1 | 8.8 | 1.1 | 20.7 |
| 1983 | 7.5 | 6.0 | 2.5 | 7.2 | 7.0 | 4.4 | -3.0 | -4.0 | 1.6 | -7.0 | 5.0 | -2.1 | 26.3 |
| 1984 | -1.8 | -5.9 | 0.4 | -0.7 | -5.4 | 2.6 | -5.0 | 11.5 | -1.0 | -2.0 | -2.9 | 1.4 | -9.6 |
| 1985 | 13.1 | 2.4 | -2.2 | -1.4 | 3.4 | 1.0 | 2.7 | -1.2 | -6.2 | 3.6 | 6.8 | 4.2 | 28.0 |
| 1986 | 1.5 | 7.0 | 4.7 | 1.4 | 3.3 | -0.2 | -9.5 | 3.0 | -6.3 | 3.9 | -0.5 | -3.1 | 4.0 |
| 1987 | 11.5 | 8.2 | 2.4 | -3.0 | -0.5 | 2.3 | 2.8 | 2.9 | -2.0 | -30.8 | -5.5 | 7.8 | -10.8 |
| 1988 | 4.0 | 8.7 | 4.4 | 2.0 | -2.5 | 7.0 | -0.9 | -2.8 | 2.3 | -1.2 | -3.6 | 3.8 | 22.4 |
| 1989 | 4.4 | 0.5 | 2.2 | 4.3 | 4.2 | -2.4 | 4.2 | 2.1 | 0.01 | -6.0 | 0.4 | 0.1 | 14.2 |
| 1990 | -8.9 | 2.9 | 3.7 | -3.4 | 6.8 | 0.1 | -4.5 | -13.6 | -9.2 | -6.2 | 7.3 | 3.7 | -21.5 |
| 1991 | 9.1 | 11.0 | 6.9 | -0.2 | 4.5 | -6.0 | 3.1 | 3.7 | 0.6 | 2.7 | -4.7 | 7.7 | 43.7 |
| 1992 | 8.0 | 2.9 | -3.5 | -3.7 | 1.2 | -5.0 | 3.2 | -3.1 | 2.2 | 3.1 | 7.5 | 3.4 | 16.4 |
| 1993 | 3.2 | -2.5 | 3.1 | -2.8 | 4.3 | 0.5 | 1.3 | 4.1 | 2.7 | 2.5 | -3.4 | 3.3 | 17.0 |
| 1994 | 3.1 | -0.4 | -5.4 | 0.6 | -1.3 | -3.6 | 1.6 | 5.4 | -0.5 | -0.4 | -4.2 | 2.5 | -3.2 |
| 1995 | -1.4 | 3.9 | 1.6 | 2.1 | 1.5 | 5.0 | 5.7 | 1.9 | 1.7 | -4.6 | 4.2 | 2.4 | 26.2 |
| 1996 | -0.2 | 3.0 | 1.8 | 5.3 | 3.9 | -4.2 | -8.8 | 5.7 | 3.7 | -1.7 | 4.0 | 2.4 | 14.8 |
| 1997 | 1.9 | -2.5 | -4.9 | 0.1 | 11.0 | 4.1 | 4.6 | 2.2 | 7.2 | -4.5 | -0.8 | 1.7 | 20.5 |
| 1998 | -1.6 | 7.4 | 4.1 | 0.5 | -5.4 | 0.2 | -8.2 | -19.5 | 7.6 | 4.0 | 5.2 | 6.1 | -3.4 |
| 1999 | 1.2 | -8.2 | 1.4 | 8.8 | 1.4 | 4.3 | -2.8 | -3.8 | -0.1 | 0.3 | 5.9 | 11.2 | 19.6 |
| 2000 | -1.7 | 16.4 | -6.7 | -6.1 | -5.9 | 8.6 | -3.2 | 7.4 | -3.1 | -4.5 | -10.4 | 8.4 | -4.2 |
| 2001 | 5.1 | -6.7 | -5.0 | 7.7 | 2.3 | 3.3 | -5.4 | -3.3 | -13.6 | 5.8 | 7.6 | 6.0 | 1.0 |
| 2002 | -1.1 | -2.8 | 7.9 | 0.8 | -4.5 | -5.1 | -15.2 | -0.4 | -7.3 | 3.1 | 8.8 | -5.7 | -21.6 |
| 2003 | -2.9 | -3.1 | 1.1 | 9.4 | 10.6 | 1.7 | 6.2 | 4.5 | -2.0 | 8.3 | 3.5 | 1.9 | 45.4 |
| 2004 | 4.3 | 0.8 | 0.8 | -5.2 | 1.5 | 4.1 | -6.8 | -0.6 | 4.6 | 1.9 | 8.6 | 2.8 | 17.0 |
| 2005 | -4.2 | 1.6 | -3.0 | -5.8 | 6.4 | 3.7 | 6.3 | -1.9 | 0.2 | -3.2 | 4.7 | -0.6 | 3.3 |
| 2006 | 8.9 | -0.3 | 4.7 | -0.1 | -5.7 | 0.5 | -3.3 | 2.9 | 0.7 | 5.7 | 2.5 | 0.2 | 17.0 |
| 2007 | 1.6 | -0.9 | 0.9 | 1.7 | 4.0 | -1.6 | -6.9 | 2.2 | 1.6 | 2.8 | -7.3 | -0.2 | -2.7 |
| 2008 | -6.9 | -3.8 | 0.3 | 4.1 | 4.5 | -7.8 | 3.6 | 3.5 | -8.1 | -20.9 | -12.0 | 5.6 | -34.8 |
| 2009 | -11.2 | -12.3 | 8.7 | 15.3 | 2.9 | 1.3 | 9.5 | 2.8 | 5.6 | -6.9 | 3.0 | 7.9 | 25.2 |
| 2010 | -3.7 | 4.4 | 8.0 | 5.6 | -7.7 | -7.9 | 6.8 | -7.5 | 12.3 | 4.0 | 3.4 | 7.8 | 25.3 |
| 2011 | -0.3 | 5.4 | 2.4 | 2.6 | -2.0 | -2.5 | -3.7 | -8.8 | -11.4 | 15.0 | -0.5 | 0.5 | -5.5 |
| 2012 | 7.0 | 2.3 | 2.4 | -1.6 | -6.7 | 4.8 | -1.4 | 3.2 | 3.1 | -2.2 | 0.4 | 3.3 | 14.6 |
| 2013 | 6.2 | 1.0 | 4.4 | -0.4 | 3.9 | -0.7 | 6.9 | -3.3 | 6.2 | 2.5 | 3.9 | 1.8 | 37.0 |
| 2014 | -2.8 | 4.6 | -0.8 | -3.9 | 0.7 | 5.2 | -6.1 | 4.8 | -6.2 | 6.5 | -0.02 | 2.7 | 3.5 |
| 2015 | -3.3 | 5.8 | 1.6 | -2.6 | 2.2 | 0.6 | -1.2 | -6.4 | -5.1 | 5.6 | 3.1 | -5.2 | -5.7 |
| 2016 | -8.8 | -0.1 | 7.8 | 1.5 | 2.1 | -0.2 | 5.9 | 1.6 | 0.9 | -4.8 | 11.0 | 2.6 | 19.5 |
| 2017 | 0.3 | 1.8 | -0.1 | 1.0 | -2.2 | 3.3 | 0.7 | -1.4 | 6.1 | 0.8 | 2.8 | -0.6 | 13.1 |
| 2018 | 2.6 | -4.0 | 1.1 | 0.8 | 5.9 | 0.6 | 1.7 | 4.2 | -2.5 | -10.9 | 1.4 | -12.0 | -12.2 |
| 2019 | 11.2 | 5.1 | -2.3 | 3.3 | -7.9 | 6.9 | 0.5 | -5.1 | 1.9 | 2.6 | 4.0 | 2.7 | 23.7 |
| 2020 | -3.3 | -8.5 | -21.9 | 13.7 | 6.4 | 3.4 | 2.7 | 5.5 | -3.5 | 2.0 | 18.3 | 8.5 | 18.4 |
| 2021 | 5.0 | 6.1 | 0.9 | 2.1 | 0.1 | 1.8 | -3.6 | 2.1 | -3.1 | 4.2 | -4.3 | 2.1 | 13.7 |
| 2022 | -9.7 | 1.0 | 1.1 | -10.0 | | | | | | | | | |
| TOTALS | 59.8 | 47.9 | 34.9 | 66.9 | 54.3 | 36.9 | -9.9 | 14.3 | -21.2 | -12.0 | 99.9 | 99.0 | |
| AVG. | 1.4 | 1.1 | 0.8 | 1.5 | 1.3 | 0.9 | -0.2 | 0.3 | -0.5 | -0.3 | 2.3 | 2.3 | |
| # Up | 24 | 26 | 31 | 28 | 28 | 28 | 22 | 25 | 23 | 25 | 29 | 33 | |
| # Down | 20 | 18 | 13 | 16 | 15 | 15 | 21 | 18 | 20 | 18 | 14 | 10 | |

# RUSSELL 2000 INDEX MONTHLY CLOSING PRICES SINCE 1979

| | Jan | Feb | Mar | Apr | May | Jun | Jul | Aug | Sep | Oct | Nov | Dec |
|---|---|---|---|---|---|---|---|---|---|---|---|---|
| 1979 | 44.18 | 42.78 | 46.94 | 48.00 | 47.13 | 49.62 | 51.08 | 55.05 | 54.68 | 48.51 | 52.43 | 55.91 |
| 1980 | 60.50 | 59.22 | 48.27 | 51.18 | 55.26 | 57.47 | 63.81 | 67.97 | 69.94 | 72.64 | 77.70 | 74.80 |
| 1981 | 74.33 | 74.52 | 80.25 | 82.25 | 84.72 | 82.56 | 80.41 | 73.94 | 67.55 | 73.06 | 75.14 | 73.67 |
| 1982 | 70.96 | 67.21 | 66.21 | 69.59 | 67.39 | 64.67 | 63.59 | 68.38 | 70.84 | 80.86 | 87.96 | 88.90 |
| 1983 | 95.53 | 101.23 | 103.77 | 111.20 | 118.94 | 124.17 | 120.43 | 115.60 | 117.43 | 109.17 | 114.66 | 112.27 |
| 1984 | 110.21 | 103.72 | 104.10 | 103.34 | 97.75 | 100.30 | 95.25 | 106.21 | 105.17 | 103.07 | 100.11 | 101.49 |
| 1985 | 114.77 | 117.54 | 114.92 | 113.35 | 117.26 | 118.38 | 121.56 | 120.10 | 112.65 | 116.73 | 124.62 | 129.87 |
| 1986 | 131.78 | 141.00 | 147.63 | 149.66 | 154.61 | 154.23 | 139.65 | 143.83 | 134.73 | 139.95 | 139.26 | 135.00 |
| 1987 | 150.48 | 162.84 | 166.79 | 161.82 | 161.02 | 164.75 | 169.42 | 174.25 | 170.81 | 118.26 | 111.70 | 120.42 |
| 1988 | 125.24 | 136.10 | 142.15 | 145.01 | 141.37 | 151.30 | 149.89 | 145.74 | 149.08 | 147.25 | 142.01 | 147.37 |
| 1989 | 153.84 | 154.56 | 157.89 | 164.68 | 171.53 | 167.42 | 174.50 | 178.20 | 178.21 | 167.47 | 168.17 | 168.30 |
| 1990 | 153.27 | 157.72 | 163.63 | 158.09 | 168.91 | 169.04 | 161.51 | 139.52 | 126.70 | 118.83 | 127.50 | 132.16 |
| 1991 | 144.17 | 160.00 | 171.01 | 170.61 | 178.34 | 167.61 | 172.76 | 179.11 | 180.16 | 185.00 | 176.37 | 189.94 |
| 1992 | 205.16 | 211.15 | 203.69 | 196.25 | 198.52 | 188.64 | 194.74 | 188.79 | 192.92 | 198.90 | 213.81 | 221.01 |
| 1993 | 228.10 | 222.41 | 229.21 | 222.68 | 232.19 | 233.35 | 236.46 | 246.19 | 252.95 | 259.18 | 250.41 | 258.59 |
| 1994 | 266.52 | 265.53 | 251.06 | 252.55 | 249.28 | 240.29 | 244.06 | 257.32 | 256.12 | 255.02 | 244.25 | 250.36 |
| 1995 | 246.85 | 256.57 | 260.77 | 266.17 | 270.25 | 283.63 | 299.72 | 305.31 | 310.38 | 296.25 | 308.58 | 315.97 |
| 1996 | 315.38 | 324.93 | 330.77 | 348.28 | 361.85 | 346.61 | 316.00 | 333.88 | 346.39 | 340.57 | 354.11 | 362.61 |
| 1997 | 369.45 | 360.05 | 342.56 | 343.00 | 380.76 | 396.37 | 414.48 | 423.43 | 453.82 | 433.26 | 429.92 | 437.02 |
| 1998 | 430.05 | 461.83 | 480.68 | 482.89 | 456.62 | 457.39 | 419.75 | 337.95 | 363.59 | 378.16 | 397.75 | 421.96 |
| 1999 | 427.22 | 392.26 | 397.63 | 432.81 | 438.68 | 457.68 | 444.77 | 427.83 | 427.30 | 428.64 | 454.08 | 504.75 |
| 2000 | 496.23 | 577.71 | 539.09 | 506.25 | 476.18 | 517.23 | 500.64 | 537.89 | 521.37 | 497.68 | 445.94 | 483.53 |
| 2001 | 508.34 | 474.37 | 450.53 | 485.32 | 496.50 | 512.64 | 484.78 | 468.56 | 404.87 | 428.17 | 460.78 | 488.50 |
| 2002 | 483.10 | 469.36 | 506.46 | 510.67 | 487.47 | 462.64 | 392.42 | 390.96 | 362.27 | 373.50 | 406.35 | 383.09 |
| 2003 | 372.17 | 360.52 | 364.54 | 398.68 | 441.00 | 448.37 | 476.02 | 497.42 | 487.68 | 528.22 | 546.51 | 556.91 |
| 2004 | 580.76 | 585.56 | 590.31 | 559.80 | 568.28 | 591.52 | 551.29 | 547.93 | 572.94 | 583.79 | 633.77 | 651.57 |
| 2005 | 624.02 | 634.06 | 615.07 | 579.38 | 616.71 | 639.66 | 679.75 | 666.51 | 667.80 | 646.61 | 677.29 | 673.22 |
| 2006 | 733.20 | 730.64 | 765.14 | 764.54 | 721.01 | 724.67 | 700.56 | 720.53 | 725.59 | 766.84 | 786.12 | 787.66 |
| 2007 | 800.34 | 793.30 | 800.71 | 814.57 | 847.19 | 833.69 | 776.13 | 792.86 | 805.45 | 828.02 | 767.77 | 766.03 |
| 2008 | 713.30 | 686.18 | 687.97 | 716.18 | 748.28 | 689.66 | 714.52 | 739.50 | 679.58 | 537.52 | 473.14 | 499.45 |
| 2009 | 443.53 | 389.02 | 422.75 | 487.56 | 501.58 | 508.28 | 556.71 | 572.07 | 604.28 | 562.77 | 579.73 | 625.39 |
| 2010 | 602.04 | 628.56 | 678.64 | 716.60 | 661.61 | 609.49 | 650.89 | 602.06 | 676.14 | 703.35 | 727.01 | 783.65 |
| 2011 | 781.25 | 823.45 | 843.55 | 865.29 | 848.30 | 827.43 | 797.03 | 726.81 | 644.16 | 741.06 | 737.42 | 740.92 |
| 2012 | 792.82 | 810.94 | 830.30 | 816.88 | 761.82 | 798.49 | 786.94 | 812.09 | 837.45 | 818.73 | 821.92 | 849.35 |
| 2013 | 902.09 | 911.11 | 951.54 | 947.46 | 984.14 | 977.48 | 1045.26 | 1010.90 | 1073.79 | 1100.15 | 1142.89 | 1163.64 |
| 2014 | 1130.88 | 1183.03 | 1173.04 | 1126.86 | 1134.50 | 1192.96 | 1120.07 | 1174.35 | 1101.68 | 1173.51 | 1173.23 | 1204.70 |
| 2015 | 1165.39 | 1233.37 | 1252.77 | 1220.13 | 1246.53 | 1253.95 | 1238.68 | 1159.45 | 1100.69 | 1161.86 | 1198.11 | 1135.89 |
| 2016 | 1035.38 | 1033.90 | 1114.03 | 1130.84 | 1154.79 | 1151.92 | 1219.94 | 1239.91 | 1251.65 | 1191.39 | 1322.34 | 1357.13 |
| 2017 | 1361.82 | 1386.68 | 1385.92 | 1400.43 | 1370.21 | 1415.36 | 1425.14 | 1405.28 | 1490.86 | 1502.77 | 1544.14 | 1535.51 |
| 2018 | 1574.98 | 1512.45 | 1529.43 | 1541.88 | 1633.61 | 1643.07 | 1670.80 | 1740.75 | 1696.57 | 1511.41 | 1533.27 | 1348.56 |
| 2019 | 1499.42 | 1575.55 | 1539.74 | 1591.21 | 1465.49 | 1566.57 | 1574.61 | 1494.84 | 1523.37 | 1562.45 | 1624.50 | 1668.47 |
| 2020 | 1614.06 | 1476.43 | 1153.10 | 1310.66 | 1394.04 | 1441.37 | 1480.43 | 1561.88 | 1507.69 | 1538.48 | 1819.82 | 1974.86 |
| 2021 | 2073.64 | 2201.05 | 2220.52 | 2266.45 | 2268.97 | 2310.55 | 2226.25 | 2273.77 | 2204.37 | 2297.19 | 2198.91 | 2245.31 |
| 2022 | 2028.45 | 2048.09 | 2070.13 | 1864.10 | | | | | | | | |

# 10 BEST DAYS BY PERCENT AND POINT

| | BY PERCENT CHANGE | | | | BY POINT CHANGE | | |
|---|---|---|---|---|---|---|---|
| DAY | CLOSE | PNT CHANGE | % CHANGE | DAY | CLOSE | PNT CHANGE | % CHANGE |
| | | | DJIA 1901 to 1949 | | | | |
| 3/15/33 | 62.10 | 8.26 | 15.3 | 10/30/29 | 258.47 | 28.40 | 12.3 |
| 10/6/31 | 99.34 | 12.86 | 14.9 | 11/14/29 | 217.28 | 18.59 | 9.4 |
| 10/30/29 | 258.47 | 28.40 | 12.3 | 10/5/29 | 341.36 | 16.19 | 5.0 |
| 9/21/32 | 75.16 | 7.67 | 11.4 | 10/31/29 | 273.51 | 15.04 | 5.8 |
| 8/3/32 | 58.22 | 5.06 | 9.5 | 10/6/31 | 99.34 | 12.86 | 14.9 |
| 2/11/32 | 78.60 | 6.80 | 9.5 | 11/15/29 | 228.73 | 11.45 | 5.3 |
| 11/14/29 | 217.28 | 18.59 | 9.4 | 6/19/30 | 228.97 | 10.13 | 4.6 |
| 12/18/31 | 80.69 | 6.90 | 9.4 | 9/5/39 | 148.12 | 10.03 | 7.3 |
| 2/13/32 | 85.82 | 7.22 | 9.2 | 11/22/28 | 290.34 | 9.81 | 3.5 |
| 5/6/32 | 59.01 | 4.91 | 9.1 | 10/1/30 | 214.14 | 9.24 | 4.5 |
| | | | DJIA 1950 to MAY 6, 2022 | | | | |
| 3/24/20 | 20704.91 | 2112.98 | 11.4 | 3/24/20 | 20704.91 | 2112.98 | 11.4 |
| 10/13/08 | 9387.61 | 936.42 | 11.1 | 3/13/20 | 23185.62 | 1985.00 | 9.4 |
| 10/28/08 | 9065.12 | 889.35 | 10.9 | 4/6/20 | 22679.99 | 1627.46 | 7.7 |
| 10/21/87 | 2027.85 | 186.84 | 10.2 | 3/26/20 | 22552.17 | 1351.62 | 6.4 |
| 3/13/20 | 23185.62 | 1985.00 | 9.4 | 3/2/20 | 26703.32 | 1293.96 | 5.1 |
| 4/6/20 | 22679.99 | 1627.46 | 7.7 | 3/4/20 | 27090.86 | 1173.45 | 4.5 |
| 3/23/09 | 7775.86 | 497.48 | 6.8 | 3/10/20 | 25018.16 | 1167.14 | 4.9 |
| 11/13/08 | 8835.25 | 552.59 | 6.7 | 12/26/18 | 22878.45 | 1086.25 | 5.0 |
| 11/21/08 | 8046.42 | 494.13 | 6.5 | 3/17/20 | 21237.38 | 1048.86 | 5.2 |
| 3/26/20 | 22552.17 | 1351.62 | 6.4 | 10/13/08 | 9387.61 | 936.42 | 11.1 |
| | | | S&P 500 1930 to MAY 6, 2022 | | | | |
| 3/15/33 | 6.81 | 0.97 | 16.6 | 3/13/20 | 2711.02 | 230.38 | 9.3 |
| 10/6/31 | 9.91 | 1.09 | 12.4 | 3/24/20 | 2447.33 | 209.93 | 9.4 |
| 9/21/32 | 8.52 | 0.90 | 11.8 | 4/6/20 | 2663.68 | 175.03 | 7.0 |
| 10/13/08 | 1003.35 | 104.13 | 11.6 | 3/26/20 | 2630.07 | 154.51 | 6.2 |
| 10/28/08 | 940.51 | 91.59 | 10.8 | 3/17/20 | 2529.19 | 143.06 | 6.0 |
| 2/16/35 | 10.00 | 0.94 | 10.4 | 3/2/20 | 3090.23 | 136.01 | 4.6 |
| 8/17/35 | 11.70 | 1.08 | 10.2 | 3/10/20 | 2882.23 | 135.67 | 4.9 |
| 3/16/35 | 9.05 | 0.82 | 10.0 | 3/4/20 | 3130.12 | 126.75 | 4.2 |
| 9/12/38 | 12.06 | 1.06 | 9.6 | 5/4/22 | 4300.17 | 124.69 | 3.0 |
| 9/5/39 | 12.64 | 1.11 | 9.6 | 12/26/18 | 2467.70 | 116.60 | 5.0 |
| | | | NASDAQ 1971 to MAY 6, 2022 | | | | |
| 1/3/01 | 2616.69 | 324.83 | 14.2 | 3/13/20 | 7874.88 | 673.08 | 9.4 |
| 10/13/08 | 1844.25 | 194.74 | 11.8 | 3/24/20 | 7417.86 | 557.19 | 8.1 |
| 12/5/00 | 2889.80 | 274.05 | 10.5 | 4/6/20 | 7913.24 | 540.16 | 7.3 |
| 10/28/08 | 1649.47 | 143.57 | 9.5 | 3/16/22 | 13436.55 | 487.93 | 3.8 |
| 3/13/20 | 7874.88 | 673.08 | 9.4 | 1/31/22 | 14239.88 | 469.31 | 3.4 |
| 4/5/01 | 1785.00 | 146.20 | 8.9 | 3/9/21 | 13073.82 | 464.66 | 3.7 |
| 3/24/20 | 7417.86 | 557.19 | 8.1 | 12/7/21 | 15686.92 | 461.77 | 3.0 |
| 4/18/01 | 2079.44 | 156.22 | 8.1 | 3/9/22 | 13255.55 | 460.00 | 3.6 |
| 5/30/00 | 3459.48 | 254.37 | 7.9 | 2/24/22 | 13473.59 | 436.10 | 3.3 |
| 10/13/00 | 3316.77 | 242.09 | 7.9 | 11/4/20 | 11590.78 | 430.21 | 3.9 |
| | | | RUSSELL 1000 1979 to MAY 6, 2022 | | | | |
| 10/13/08 | 542.98 | 56.75 | 11.7 | 3/13/20 | 1488.04 | 123.38 | 9.0 |
| 10/28/08 | 503.74 | 47.68 | 10.5 | 3/24/20 | 1340.32 | 115.87 | 9.5 |
| 3/24/20 | 1340.32 | 115.87 | 9.5 | 4/6/20 | 1455.56 | 96.55 | 7.1 |
| 3/13/20 | 1488.04 | 123.38 | 9.0 | 3/26/20 | 1442.70 | 83.87 | 6.2 |
| 10/21/87 | 135.85 | 11.15 | 8.9 | 3/17/20 | 1381.49 | 74.98 | 5.7 |
| 4/6/20 | 1455.56 | 96.55 | 7.1 | 3/10/20 | 1588.36 | 73.59 | 4.9 |
| 3/23/09 | 446.90 | 29.36 | 7.0 | 3/2/20 | 1708.13 | 72.92 | 4.5 |
| 11/13/08 | 489.83 | 31.99 | 7.0 | 3/4/20 | 1729.80 | 68.44 | 4.1 |
| 11/24/08 | 456.14 | 28.26 | 6.6 | 5/4/22 | 2368.74 | 67.67 | 2.9 |
| 3/10/09 | 391.01 | 23.46 | 6.4 | 12/26/18 | 1362.48 | 64.46 | 5.0 |
| | | | RUSSELL 2000 1979 to MAY 6, 2022 | | | | |
| 3/24/20 | 1096.54 | 94.14 | 9.4 | 3/24/20 | 1096.54 | 94.14 | 9.4 |
| 10/13/08 | 570.89 | 48.41 | 9.3 | 3/13/20 | 1210.13 | 87.20 | 7.8 |
| 11/13/08 | 491.23 | 38.43 | 8.5 | 4/6/20 | 1138.78 | 86.73 | 8.2 |
| 3/23/09 | 433.72 | 33.61 | 8.4 | 1/6/21 | 2057.92 | 78.81 | 4.0 |
| 4/6/20 | 1138.78 | 86.73 | 8.2 | 5/18/20 | 1333.69 | 76.70 | 6.1 |
| 3/13/20 | 1210.13 | 87.20 | 7.8 | 3/1/21 | 2275.32 | 74.27 | 3.4 |
| 10/21/87 | 130.65 | 9.26 | 7.6 | 3/26/20 | 1180.32 | 69.95 | 6.3 |
| 10/28/08 | 482.55 | 34.15 | 7.6 | 3/17/20 | 1106.51 | 69.09 | 6.7 |
| 11/24/08 | 436.80 | 30.26 | 7.4 | 3/19/20 | 1058.75 | 67.59 | 6.8 |
| 3/10/09 | 367.75 | 24.49 | 7.1 | 7/20/21 | 2194.30 | 63.62 | 3.0 |

# 10 <u>WORST</u> DAYS BY PERCENT AND POINT

| BY PERCENT CHANGE | | | | BY POINT CHANGE | | | |
|---|---|---|---|---|---|---|---|
| DAY | CLOSE | PNT CHANGE | % CHANGE | DAY | CLOSE | PNT CHANGE | % CHANGE |
| **DJIA 1901 to 1949** | | | | | | | |
| 10/28/29 | 260.64 | −38.33 | −12.8 | 10/28/29 | 260.64 | −38.33 | −12.8 |
| 10/29/29 | 230.07 | −30.57 | −11.7 | 10/29/29 | 230.07 | −30.57 | −11.7 |
| 11/6/29 | 232.13 | −25.55 | −9.9 | 11/6/29 | 232.13 | −25.55 | −9.9 |
| 8/12/32 | 63.11 | −5.79 | −8.4 | 10/23/29 | 305.85 | −20.66 | −6.3 |
| 3/14/07 | 55.84 | −5.05 | −8.3 | 11/11/29 | 220.39 | −16.14 | −6.8 |
| 7/21/33 | 88.71 | −7.55 | −7.8 | 11/4/29 | 257.68 | −15.83 | −5.8 |
| 10/18/37 | 125.73 | −10.57 | −7.8 | 12/12/29 | 243.14 | −15.30 | −5.9 |
| 2/1/17 | 88.52 | −6.91 | −7.2 | 10/3/29 | 329.95 | −14.55 | −4.2 |
| 10/5/32 | 66.07 | −5.09 | −7.2 | 6/16/30 | 230.05 | −14.20 | −5.8 |
| 9/24/31 | 107.79 | −8.20 | −7.1 | 8/9/29 | 337.99 | −14.11 | −4.0 |
| **DJIA 1950 to MAY 6, 2022** | | | | | | | |
| 10/19/87 | 1738.74 | −508.00 | −22.6 | 3/16/20 | 20188.52 | −2997.10 | −12.9 |
| 3/16/20 | 20188.52 | −2997.10 | −12.9 | 3/12/20 | 21200.62 | −2352.60 | −10.0 |
| 3/12/20 | 21200.62 | −2352.60 | −10.0 | 3/9/20 | 23851.02 | −2013.76 | −7.8 |
| 10/26/87 | 1793.93 | −156.83 | −8.0 | 6/11/20 | 25128.17 | −1861.82 | −6.9 |
| 10/15/08 | 8577.91 | −733.08 | −7.9 | 3/11/20 | 23553.22 | −1464.94 | −5.9 |
| 3/9/20 | 23851.02 | −2013.76 | −7.8 | 3/18/20 | 19898.92 | −1338.46 | −6.3 |
| 12/1/08 | 8149.09 | −679.95 | −7.7 | 2/27/20 | 25766.64 | −1190.95 | −4.4 |
| 10/9/08 | 8579.19 | −678.91 | −7.3 | 2/5/18 | 24345.75 | −1175.21 | −4.6 |
| 10/27/97 | 7161.15 | −554.26 | −7.2 | 5/5/22 | 32997.97 | −1063.09 | −3.1 |
| 9/17/01 | 8920.70 | −684.81 | −7.1 | 2/8/18 | 23860.46 | −1032.89 | −4.2 |
| **S&P 500 1930 to MAY 6, 2022** | | | | | | | |
| 10/19/87 | 224.84 | −57.86 | −20.5 | 3/16/20 | 2386.13 | −324.89 | −12.0 |
| 3/16/20 | 2386.13 | −324.89 | −12.0 | 3/12/20 | 2480.64 | −260.74 | −9.5 |
| 3/18/35 | 8.14 | −0.91 | −10.1 | 3/9/20 | 2746.56 | −225.81 | −7.6 |
| 4/16/35 | 8.22 | −0.91 | −10.0 | 6/11/20 | 3002.10 | −188.04 | −5.9 |
| 9/3/46 | 15.00 | −1.65 | −9.9 | 4/29/22 | 4131.93 | −155.57 | −3.6 |
| 3/12/20 | 2480.64 | −260.74 | −9.5 | 5/5/22 | 4146.87 | −153.30 | −3.6 |
| 10/18/37 | 10.76 | −1.10 | −9.3 | 3/11/20 | 2741.38 | −140.85 | −4.9 |
| 10/15/08 | 907.84 | −90.17 | −9.0 | 2/27/20 | 2978.76 | −137.63 | −4.4 |
| 12/1/08 | 816.21 | −80.03 | −8.9 | 3/18/20 | 2398.10 | −131.09 | −5.2 |
| 7/20/33 | 10.57 | −1.03 | −8.9 | 3/7/22 | 4201.09 | −127.78 | −3.0 |
| **NASDAQ 1971 to MAY 6, 2022** | | | | | | | |
| 3/16/20 | 6904.59 | −970.29 | −12.3 | 3/16/20 | 6904.59 | −970.29 | −12.3 |
| 10/19/87 | 360.21 | −46.12 | −11.4 | 3/12/20 | 7201.80 | −750.25 | −9.4 |
| 4/14/00 | 3321.29 | −355.49 | −9.7 | 5/5/22 | 12317.69 | −647.17 | −5.0 |
| 3/12/20 | 7201.80 | −750.25 | −9.4 | 3/9/20 | 7950.68 | −624.94 | −7.3 |
| 9/29/08 | 1983.73 | −199.61 | −9.1 | 9/3/20 | 11458.10 | −598.34 | −5.0 |
| 10/26/87 | 298.90 | −29.55 | −9.0 | 2/3/22 | 13878.82 | −538.73 | −3.7 |
| 10/20/87 | 327.79 | −32.42 | −9.0 | 4/29/22 | 12334.64 | −536.89 | −4.2 |
| 12/1/08 | 1398.07 | −137.50 | −9.0 | 6/11/20 | 9492.73 | −527.62 | −5.3 |
| 8/31/98 | 1499.25 | −140.43 | −8.6 | 1/5/22 | 15100.17 | −522.55 | −3.3 |
| 10/15/08 | 1628.33 | −150.68 | −8.5 | 4/26/22 | 12490.74 | −514.11 | −4.0 |
| **RUSSELL 1000 1979 to MAY 6, 2022** | | | | | | | |
| 10/19/87 | 121.04 | −28.40 | −19.0 | 3/16/20 | 1306.51 | −181.53 | −12.2 |
| 3/16/20 | 1306.51 | −181.53 | −12.2 | 3/12/20 | 1364.66 | −144.34 | −9.6 |
| 3/12/20 | 1364.66 | −144.34 | −9.6 | 3/9/20 | 1514.77 | −127.21 | −7.8 |
| 10/15/08 | 489.71 | −49.11 | −9.1 | 6/11/20 | 1660.70 | −104.50 | −5.9 |
| 12/1/08 | 437.75 | −43.68 | −9.1 | 5/5/22 | 2281.85 | −86.89 | −3.7 |
| 9/29/08 | 602.34 | −57.35 | −8.7 | 4/29/22 | 2276.45 | −85.24 | −3.6 |
| 10/26/87 | 119.45 | −10.74 | −8.3 | 3/11/20 | 1509.00 | −79.36 | −5.0 |
| 3/9/20 | 1514.77 | −127.21 | −7.8 | 3/18/20 | 1304.56 | −76.93 | −5.6 |
| 10/9/08 | 492.13 | −40.05 | −7.5 | 2/27/20 | 1649.14 | −75.62 | −4.4 |
| 8/8/11 | 617.28 | −45.56 | −6.9 | 3/7/22 | 2315.76 | −73.92 | −3.1 |
| **RUSSELL 2000 1979 to MAY 6, 2022** | | | | | | | |
| 3/16/20 | 1037.42 | −172.71 | −14.3 | 3/16/20 | 1037.42 | −172.71 | −14.3 |
| 10/19/87 | 133.60 | −19.14 | −12.5 | 3/12/20 | 1122.93 | −141.37 | −11.2 |
| 12/1/08 | 417.07 | −56.07 | −11.9 | 3/9/20 | 1313.44 | −135.78 | −9.4 |
| 3/12/20 | 1122.93 | −141.37 | −11.2 | 3/18/20 | 991.16 | −115.35 | −10.4 |
| 3/18/20 | 991.16 | −115.35 | −10.4 | 6/11/20 | 1356.22 | −111.17 | −7.6 |
| 10/15/08 | 502.11 | −52.54 | −9.5 | 3/11/20 | 1264.30 | −86.60 | −6.4 |
| 3/9/20 | 1313.44 | −135.78 | −9.4 | 11/26/21 | 2245.94 | −85.52 | −3.7 |
| 10/26/87 | 110.33 | −11.26 | −9.3 | 2/25/21 | 2200.17 | −84.21 | −3.7 |
| 10/20/87 | 121.39 | −12.21 | −9.1 | 3/23/21 | 2185.69 | −81.15 | −3.6 |
| 8/8/11 | 650.96 | −63.67 | −8.9 | 4/1/20 | 1071.99 | −81.11 | −7.0 |

175

# 10 BEST WEEKS BY PERCENT AND POINT

| | BY PERCENT CHANGE | | | | BY POINT CHANGE | | |
|---|---|---|---|---|---|---|---|
| WEEK ENDS | CLOSE | PNT CHANGE | % CHANGE | WEEK ENDS | CLOSE | PNT CHANGE | % CHANGE |
| **DJIA 1901 to 1949** | | | | | | | |
| 8/6/32 | 66.56 | 12.30 | 22.7 | 12/7/29 | 263.46 | 24.51 | 10.3 |
| 6/25/38 | 131.94 | 18.71 | 16.5 | 6/25/38 | 131.94 | 18.71 | 16.5 |
| 2/13/32 | 85.82 | 11.37 | 15.3 | 6/27/31 | 156.93 | 17.97 | 12.9 |
| 4/22/33 | 72.24 | 9.36 | 14.9 | 11/22/29 | 245.74 | 17.01 | 7.4 |
| 10/10/31 | 105.61 | 12.84 | 13.8 | 8/17/29 | 360.70 | 15.86 | 4.6 |
| 7/30/32 | 54.26 | 6.42 | 13.4 | 12/22/28 | 285.94 | 15.22 | 5.6 |
| 6/27/31 | 156.93 | 17.97 | 12.9 | 8/24/29 | 375.44 | 14.74 | 4.1 |
| 9/24/32 | 74.83 | 8.39 | 12.6 | 2/21/29 | 310.06 | 14.21 | 4.8 |
| 8/27/32 | 75.61 | 8.43 | 12.6 | 5/10/30 | 272.01 | 13.70 | 5.3 |
| 3/18/33 | 60.56 | 6.72 | 12.5 | 11/15/30 | 186.68 | 13.54 | 7.8 |
| **DJIA 1950 to MAY 6, 2022** | | | | | | | |
| 3/27/20 | 21636.78 | 2462.80 | 12.8 | 4/9/20 | 23719.37 | 2666.84 | 12.7 |
| 4/9/20 | 23719.37 | 2666.84 | 12.7 | 3/27/20 | 21636.78 | 2462.80 | 12.8 |
| 10/11/74 | 658.17 | 73.61 | 12.6 | 11/6/20 | 28323.40 | 1821.80 | 6.9 |
| 10/31/08 | 9325.01 | 946.06 | 11.3 | 3/18/22 | 34754.93 | 1810.74 | 5.5 |
| 8/20/82 | 869.29 | 81.24 | 10.3 | 6/5/20 | 27110.98 | 1727.87 | 6.8 |
| 11/28/08 | 8829.04 | 782.62 | 9.7 | 12/10/21 | 35970.99 | 1390.91 | 4.0 |
| 3/13/09 | 7223.98 | 597.04 | 9.0 | 3/12/21 | 32778.64 | 1282.34 | 4.1 |
| 10/8/82 | 986.85 | 79.11 | 8.7 | 11/30/18 | 25538.46 | 1252.51 | 5.2 |
| 3/21/03 | 8521.97 | 662.26 | 8.4 | 6/7/19 | 25983.94 | 1168.90 | 4.7 |
| 8/3/84 | 1202.08 | 87.46 | 7.9 | 2/5/21 | 31148.24 | 1165.62 | 3.9 |
| **S&P 500 1930 to MAY 6, 2022** | | | | | | | |
| 8/6/32 | 7.22 | 1.12 | 18.4 | 4/9/20 | 2789.82 | 301.17 | 12.1 |
| 6/25/38 | 11.39 | 1.72 | 17.8 | 3/18/22 | 4463.12 | 258.81 | 6.2 |
| 7/30/32 | 6.10 | 0.89 | 17.1 | 11/6/20 | 3509.44 | 239.48 | 7.3 |
| 4/22/33 | 7.75 | 1.09 | 16.4 | 3/27/20 | 2541.47 | 236.55 | 10.3 |
| 10/11/74 | 71.14 | 8.80 | 14.1 | 12/10/21 | 4712.02 | 173.59 | 3.8 |
| 2/13/32 | 8.80 | 1.08 | 14.0 | 2/5/21 | 3886.83 | 172.59 | 4.7 |
| 9/24/32 | 8.52 | 1.02 | 13.6 | 6/5/20 | 3193.93 | 149.62 | 4.9 |
| 10/10/31 | 10.64 | 1.27 | 13.6 | 10/9/20 | 3477.13 | 128.69 | 3.8 |
| 8/27/32 | 8.57 | 1.01 | 13.4 | 11/30/18 | 2760.16 | 127.60 | 4.9 |
| 3/18/33 | 6.61 | 0.77 | 13.2 | 6/7/19 | 2873.34 | 121.28 | 4.4 |
| **NASDAQ 1971 to MAY 6, 2022** | | | | | | | |
| 6/2/00 | 3813.38 | 608.27 | 19.0 | 3/18/22 | 13893.84 | 1050.03 | 8.2 |
| 4/12/01 | 1961.43 | 241.07 | 14.0 | 11/6/20 | 11895.23 | 983.64 | 9.0 |
| 11/28/08 | 1535.57 | 151.22 | 10.9 | 2/5/21 | 13856.30 | 785.61 | 6.0 |
| 10/31/08 | 1720.95 | 168.92 | 10.9 | 4/9/20 | 8153.58 | 780.50 | 10.6 |
| 3/13/09 | 1431.50 | 137.65 | 10.6 | 3/27/20 | 7502.38 | 622.86 | 9.1 |
| 4/9/20 | 8153.58 | 780.50 | 10.6 | 6/2/00 | 3813.38 | 608.27 | 19.0 |
| 4/20/01 | 2163.41 | 201.98 | 10.3 | 12/10/21 | 15630.60 | 545.13 | 3.6 |
| 12/8/00 | 2917.43 | 272.14 | 10.3 | 1/22/21 | 13543.06 | 544.56 | 4.2 |
| 4/20/00 | 3643.88 | 322.59 | 9.7 | 5/8/20 | 9121.32 | 516.37 | 6.0 |
| 10/11/74 | 60.42 | 5.26 | 9.5 | 10/9/20 | 11579.94 | 504.92 | 4.6 |
| **RUSSELL 1000 1979 to MAY 6, 2022** | | | | | | | |
| 4/9/20 | 1530.05 | 171.04 | 12.6 | 4/9/20 | 1530.05 | 171.04 | 12.6 |
| 11/28/08 | 481.43 | 53.55 | 12.5 | 3/18/22 | 2466.14 | 146.57 | 6.3 |
| 10/31/08 | 522.47 | 50.94 | 10.8 | 11/6/20 | 1962.60 | 136.93 | 7.5 |
| 3/13/09 | 411.10 | 39.88 | 10.7 | 3/27/20 | 1394.65 | 133.96 | 10.6 |
| 3/27/20 | 1394.65 | 133.96 | 10.6 | 2/5/21 | 2204.27 | 102.91 | 4.9 |
| 8/20/82 | 61.51 | 4.83 | 8.5 | 12/10/21 | 2615.38 | 92.35 | 3.7 |
| 6/2/00 | 785.02 | 57.93 | 8.0 | 6/5/20 | 1767.94 | 85.19 | 5.1 |
| 9/28/01 | 546.46 | 38.48 | 7.6 | 10/9/20 | 1943.01 | 74.39 | 4.0 |
| 10/16/98 | 546.09 | 38.45 | 7.6 | 11/30/18 | 1525.56 | 69.33 | 4.8 |
| 8/3/84 | 87.43 | 6.13 | 7.5 | 7/2/20 | 1735.01 | 67.76 | 4.1 |
| **RUSSELL 2000 1979 to MAY 6, 2022** | | | | | | | |
| 4/9/20 | 1246.73 | 194.68 | 18.5 | 4/9/20 | 1246.73 | 194.68 | 18.5 |
| 11/28/08 | 473.14 | 66.60 | 16.4 | 3/12/21 | 2352.79 | 160.58 | 7.3 |
| 10/31/08 | 537.52 | 66.40 | 14.1 | 2/5/21 | 2233.33 | 159.69 | 7.7 |
| 6/2/00 | 513.03 | 55.66 | 12.2 | 11/5/21 | 2437.08 | 139.89 | 6.1 |
| 3/13/09 | 393.09 | 42.04 | 12.0 | 11/11/16 | 1282.38 | 118.94 | 10.2 |
| 3/27/20 | 1131.99 | 118.10 | 11.7 | 3/27/20 | 1131.99 | 118.10 | 11.7 |
| 12/2/11 | 735.02 | 68.86 | 10.3 | 1/8/21 | 2091.66 | 116.80 | 5.9 |
| 11/11/16 | 1282.38 | 118.94 | 10.2 | 6/5/20 | 1507.15 | 113.11 | 8.1 |
| 10/14/11 | 712.46 | 56.25 | 8.6 | 8/27/21 | 2277.15 | 109.55 | 5.1 |
| 6/5/20 | 1507.15 | 113.11 | 8.1 | 3/18/22 | 2086.14 | 106.47 | 5.4 |

# 10 WORST WEEKS BY PERCENT AND POINT

| BY PERCENT CHANGE | | | | BY POINT CHANGE | | | |
|---|---|---|---|---|---|---|---|
| WEEK ENDS | CLOSE | PNT CHANGE | % CHANGE | WEEK ENDS | CLOSE | PNT CHANGE | % CHANGE |
| DJIA 1901 to 1949 | | | | | | | |
| 7/22/33 | 88.42 | −17.68 | −16.7 | 11/8/29 | 236.53 | −36.98 | −13.5 |
| 5/18/40 | 122.43 | −22.42 | −15.5 | 12/8/28 | 257.33 | −33.47 | −11.5 |
| 10/8/32 | 61.17 | −10.92 | −15.2 | 6/21/30 | 215.30 | −28.95 | −11.9 |
| 10/3/31 | 92.77 | −14.59 | −13.6 | 10/19/29 | 323.87 | −28.82 | −8.2 |
| 11/8/29 | 236.53 | −36.98 | −13.5 | 5/3/30 | 258.31 | −27.15 | −9.5 |
| 9/17/32 | 66.44 | −10.10 | −13.2 | 10/31/29 | 273.51 | −25.46 | −8.5 |
| 10/21/33 | 83.64 | −11.95 | −12.5 | 10/26/29 | 298.97 | −24.90 | −7.7 |
| 12/12/31 | 78.93 | −11.21 | −12.4 | 5/18/40 | 122.43 | −22.42 | −15.5 |
| 5/8/15 | 62.77 | −8.74 | −12.2 | 2/8/29 | 301.53 | −18.23 | −5.7 |
| 6/21/30 | 215.30 | −28.95 | −11.9 | 10/11/30 | 193.05 | −18.05 | −8.6 |
| DJIA 1950 to MAY 6, 2022 | | | | | | | |
| 10/10/08 | 8451.19 | −1874.19 | −18.2 | 3/20/20 | 19173.98 | −4011.64 | −17.3 |
| 3/20/20 | 19173.98 | −4011.64 | −17.3 | 2/28/20 | 25409.36 | −3583.05 | −12.4 |
| 9/21/01 | 8235.81 | −1369.70 | −14.3 | 3/13/20 | 23185.62 | −2679.16 | −10.4 |
| 10/23/87 | 1950.76 | −295.98 | −13.2 | 10/10/08 | 8451.19 | −1874.19 | −18.2 |
| 2/28/20 | 25409.36 | −3583.05 | −12.4 | 10/30/20 | 26501.60 | −1833.97 | −6.5 |
| 3/13/20 | 23185.62 | −2679.16 | −10.4 | 12/21/18 | 22445.37 | −1655.14 | −6.9 |
| 10/16/87 | 2246.74 | −235.47 | −9.5 | 1/21/22 | 34265.37 | −1646.44 | −4.6 |
| 10/13/89 | 2569.26 | −216.26 | −7.8 | 6/12/20 | 25605.54 | −1505.44 | −5.6 |
| 3/16/01 | 9823.41 | −821.21 | −7.7 | 3/23/18 | 23533.20 | −1413.31 | −5.7 |
| 7/19/02 | 8019.26 | −665.27 | −7.7 | 9/21/01 | 8235.81 | −1369.70 | −14.3 |
| S&P 500 1930 to MAY 6, 2022 | | | | | | | |
| 7/22/33 | 9.71 | −2.20 | −18.5 | 3/20/20 | 2304.92 | −406.10 | −15.0 |
| 10/10/08 | 899.22 | −200.01 | −18.2 | 2/28/20 | 2954.22 | −383.53 | −11.5 |
| 5/18/40 | 9.75 | −2.05 | −17.4 | 1/21/22 | 4397.94 | −264.91 | −5.7 |
| 10/8/32 | 6.77 | −1.38 | −16.9 | 3/13/20 | 2711.02 | −261.35 | −8.8 |
| 3/20/20 | 2304.92 | −406.10 | −15.0 | 10/10/08 | 899.22 | −200.01 | −18.2 |
| 9/17/32 | 7.50 | −1.28 | −14.6 | 10/30/20 | 3269.96 | −195.43 | −5.6 |
| 10/21/33 | 8.57 | −1.31 | −13.3 | 12/21/18 | 2416.62 | −183.33 | −7.1 |
| 10/3/31 | 9.37 | −1.36 | −12.7 | 3/23/18 | 2588.26 | −163.75 | −6.0 |
| 10/23/87 | 248.22 | −34.48 | −12.2 | 4/14/00 | 1356.56 | −159.79 | −10.5 |
| 12/12/31 | 8.20 | −1.13 | −12.1 | 6/12/20 | 3041.31 | −152.62 | −4.8 |
| NASDAQ 1971 to MAY 6, 2022 | | | | | | | |
| 4/14/00 | 3321.29 | −1125.16 | −25.3 | 4/14/00 | 3321.29 | −1125.16 | −25.3 |
| 10/23/87 | 328.45 | −77.88 | −19.2 | 1/21/22 | 13768.92 | −1124.83 | −7.6 |
| 9/21/01 | 1423.19 | −272.19 | −16.1 | 2/28/20 | 8567.37 | −1009.22 | −10.5 |
| 10/10/08 | 1649.51 | −297.88 | −15.3 | 3/20/20 | 6879.52 | −995.36 | −12.6 |
| 3/20/20 | 6879.52 | −995.36 | −12.6 | 1/7/22 | 14935.90 | −709.07 | −4.5 |
| 11/10/00 | 3028.99 | −422.59 | −12.2 | 3/13/20 | 7874.88 | −700.74 | −8.2 |
| 10/3/08 | 1947.39 | −235.95 | −10.8 | 2/26/21 | 13192.35 | −682.11 | −4.9 |
| 7/28/00 | 3663.00 | −431.45 | −10.5 | 10/30/20 | 10911.59 | −636.69 | −5.5 |
| 2/28/20 | 8567.37 | −1009.22 | −10.5 | 12/21/18 | 6332.99 | −577.67 | −8.4 |
| 10/24/08 | 1552.03 | −159.26 | −9.3 | 11/26/21 | 15491.66 | −565.78 | −3.5 |
| RUSSELL 1000 1979 to MAY 6, 2022 | | | | | | | |
| 10/10/08 | 486.23 | −108.31 | −18.2 | 3/20/20 | 1260.69 | −227.35 | −15.3 |
| 3/20/20 | 1260.69 | −227.35 | −15.3 | 2/28/20 | 1635.21 | −214.22 | −11.6 |
| 10/23/87 | 130.19 | −19.25 | −12.9 | 3/13/20 | 1488.04 | −153.94 | −9.4 |
| 9/21/01 | 507.98 | −67.59 | −11.7 | 1/21/22 | 2427.56 | −149.96 | −5.8 |
| 2/28/20 | 1635.21 | −214.22 | −11.6 | 10/30/20 | 1825.67 | −110.60 | −5.7 |
| 4/14/00 | 715.20 | −90.39 | −11.2 | 10/10/08 | 486.23 | −108.31 | −18.2 |
| 10/3/08 | 594.54 | −65.15 | −9.9 | 12/21/18 | 1333.95 | −102.36 | −7.1 |
| 3/13/20 | 1488.04 | −153.94 | −9.4 | 4/14/00 | 715.20 | −90.39 | −11.2 |
| 10/16/87 | 149.44 | −14.42 | −8.8 | 3/23/18 | 1436.72 | −88.62 | −5.8 |
| 11/21/08 | 427.88 | −41.15 | −8.8 | 6/12/20 | 1682.92 | −85.02 | −4.8 |
| RUSSELL 2000 1979 to MAY 6, 2022 | | | | | | | |
| 10/23/87 | 121.59 | −31.15 | −20.4 | 3/13/20 | 1210.13 | −239.09 | −16.5 |
| 3/13/20 | 1210.13 | −239.09 | −16.5 | 2/28/20 | 1476.43 | −202.18 | −12.0 |
| 4/14/00 | 453.72 | −89.27 | −16.4 | 3/20/20 | 1013.89 | −196.24 | −16.2 |
| 3/20/20 | 1013.89 | −196.24 | −16.2 | 1/21/22 | 1987.92 | −174.54 | −8.1 |
| 10/10/08 | 522.48 | −96.92 | −15.7 | 6/12/20 | 1387.68 | −119.47 | −7.9 |
| 9/21/01 | 378.89 | −61.84 | −14.0 | 12/21/18 | 1292.09 | −118.72 | −8.4 |
| 10/3/08 | 619.40 | −85.39 | −12.1 | 7/16/21 | 2163.24 | −116.76 | −5.1 |
| 2/28/20 | 1476.43 | −202.18 | −12.0 | 10/30/20 | 1538.48 | −102.02 | −6.2 |
| 11/21/08 | 406.54 | −49.98 | −11.0 | 6/18/21 | 2237.75 | −98.06 | −4.2 |
| 10/24/08 | 471.12 | −55.31 | −10.5 | 11/26/21 | 2245.94 | −97.22 | −4.2 |

# 10 BEST MONTHS BY PERCENT AND POINT

| | BY PERCENT CHANGE | | | | BY POINT CHANGE | | |
|---|---|---|---|---|---|---|---|
| MONTH | CLOSE | PNT CHANGE | % CHANGE | MONTH | CLOSE | PNT CHANGE | % CHANGE |
| **DJIA 1901 to 1949** | | | | | | | |
| Apr-1933 | 77.66 | 22.26 | 40.2 | Nov-1928 | 293.38 | 41.22 | 16.3 |
| Aug-1932 | 73.16 | 18.90 | 34.8 | Jun-1929 | 333.79 | 36.38 | 12.2 |
| Jul-1932 | 54.26 | 11.42 | 26.7 | Aug-1929 | 380.33 | 32.63 | 9.4 |
| Jun-1938 | 133.88 | 26.14 | 24.3 | Jun-1938 | 133.88 | 26.14 | 24.3 |
| Apr-1915 | 71.78 | 10.95 | 18.0 | Aug-1928 | 240.41 | 24.41 | 11.3 |
| Jun-1931 | 150.18 | 21.72 | 16.9 | Apr-1933 | 77.66 | 22.26 | 40.2 |
| Nov-1928 | 293.38 | 41.22 | 16.3 | Feb-1931 | 189.66 | 22.11 | 13.2 |
| Nov-1904 | 52.76 | 6.59 | 14.3 | Jun-1931 | 150.18 | 21.72 | 16.9 |
| May-1919 | 105.50 | 12.62 | 13.6 | Aug-1932 | 73.16 | 18.90 | 34.8 |
| Sep-1939 | 152.54 | 18.13 | 13.5 | Jan-1930 | 267.14 | 18.66 | 7.5 |
| **DJIA 1950 to APRIL 2022** | | | | | | | |
| Jan-1976 | 975.28 | 122.87 | 14.4 | Nov-2020 | 29638.64 | 3137.04 | 11.8 |
| Jan-1975 | 703.69 | 87.45 | 14.2 | Apr-2020 | 24345.72 | 2428.56 | 11.1 |
| Jan-1987 | 2158.04 | 262.09 | 13.8 | Mar-2021 | 32981.55 | 2049.18 | 6.6 |
| Nov-2020 | 29638.64 | 3137.04 | 11.8 | Aug-2020 | 28430.05 | 2001.73 | 7.6 |
| Aug-1982 | 901.31 | 92.71 | 11.5 | Oct-2021 | 35819.56 | 1975.64 | 5.8 |
| Apr-2020 | 24345.72 | 2428.56 | 11.1 | Dec-2021 | 36338.30 | 1854.58 | 5.4 |
| Oct-1982 | 991.72 | 95.47 | 10.7 | Jun-2019 | 26599.96 | 1784.92 | 7.2 |
| Oct-2002 | 8397.03 | 805.10 | 10.6 | Jan-2019 | 24999.67 | 1672.21 | 7.2 |
| Apr-1978 | 837.32 | 79.96 | 10.6 | Jan-2018 | 26149.39 | 1430.17 | 5.8 |
| Apr-1999 | 10789.04 | 1002.88 | 10.3 | Oct-2015 | 17663.54 | 1379.54 | 8.5 |
| **S&P 500 1930 to APRIL 2022** | | | | | | | |
| Apr-1933 | 8.32 | 2.47 | 42.2 | Nov-2020 | 3621.63 | 351.67 | 10.8 |
| Jul-1932 | 6.10 | 1.67 | 37.7 | Apr-2020 | 2912.43 | 327.84 | 12.7 |
| Aug-1932 | 8.39 | 2.29 | 37.5 | Oct-2021 | 4605.38 | 297.84 | 6.9 |
| Jun-1938 | 11.56 | 2.29 | 24.7 | Aug-2020 | 3500.31 | 229.19 | 7.0 |
| Sep-1939 | 13.02 | 1.84 | 16.5 | Apr-2021 | 4181.17 | 208.28 | 5.2 |
| Oct-1974 | 73.90 | 10.36 | 16.3 | Dec-2021 | 4766.18 | 199.18 | 4.4 |
| May-1933 | 9.64 | 1.32 | 15.9 | Jan-2019 | 2704.10 | 197.25 | 7.9 |
| Apr-1938 | 9.70 | 1.20 | 14.1 | Jun-2019 | 2941.76 | 189.70 | 6.9 |
| Jun-1931 | 14.83 | 1.81 | 13.9 | Jul-2020 | 3271.12 | 170.83 | 5.5 |
| Jan-1987 | 274.08 | 31.91 | 13.2 | Mar-2021 | 3972.89 | 161.74 | 4.2 |
| **NASDAQ 1971 to APRIL 2022** | | | | | | | |
| Dec-1999 | 4069.31 | 733.15 | 22.0 | Nov-2020 | 12198.74 | 1287.15 | 11.8 |
| Feb-2000 | 4696.69 | 756.34 | 19.2 | Apr-2020 | 8889.55 | 1189.45 | 15.5 |
| Oct-1974 | 65.23 | 9.56 | 17.2 | Oct-2021 | 15498.39 | 1049.81 | 7.3 |
| Jan-1975 | 69.78 | 9.96 | 16.7 | Aug-2020 | 11775.46 | 1030.19 | 9.6 |
| Jun-2000 | 3966.11 | 565.20 | 16.6 | Feb-2000 | 4696.69 | 756.34 | 19.2 |
| Apr-2020 | 8889.55 | 1189.45 | 15.5 | Jun-2021 | 14503.95 | 755.21 | 5.5 |
| Apr-2001 | 2116.24 | 275.98 | 15.0 | Dec-1999 | 4069.31 | 733.15 | 22.0 |
| Jan-1999 | 2505.89 | 313.20 | 14.3 | Apr-2021 | 13962.68 | 715.81 | 5.4 |
| Nov-2001 | 1930.58 | 240.38 | 14.2 | Dec-2020 | 12888.28 | 689.54 | 5.7 |
| Oct-2002 | 1329.75 | 157.69 | 13.5 | Jul-2020 | 10745.27 | 686.50 | 6.8 |
| **RUSSELL 1000 1979 to APRIL 2022** | | | | | | | |
| Apr-2020 | 1601.82 | 185.33 | 13.1 | Nov-2020 | 2037.36 | 211.69 | 11.6 |
| Jan-1987 | 146.48 | 16.48 | 12.7 | Apr-2020 | 1601.82 | 185.33 | 13.1 |
| Nov-2020 | 2037.36 | 211.69 | 11.6 | Oct-2021 | 2583.83 | 165.67 | 6.9 |
| Oct-1982 | 73.34 | 7.45 | 11.3 | Aug-2020 | 1946.15 | 130.16 | 7.2 |
| Aug-1982 | 65.14 | 6.60 | 11.3 | Apr-2021 | 2356.67 | 118.50 | 5.3 |
| Dec-1991 | 220.61 | 22.15 | 11.2 | Jan-2019 | 1498.36 | 114.10 | 8.2 |
| Oct-2011 | 692.41 | 68.96 | 11.1 | Jun-2019 | 1629.02 | 104.60 | 6.9 |
| Aug-1984 | 89.87 | 8.74 | 10.8 | Dec-2021 | 2645.91 | 100.13 | 3.9 |
| Nov-1980 | 78.26 | 7.18 | 10.1 | Jul-2020 | 1815.99 | 98.52 | 5.7 |
| Apr-2009 | 476.84 | 43.17 | 10.0 | Oct-2015 | 1153.55 | 85.09 | 8.0 |
| **RUSSELL 2000 1979 to APRIL 2022** | | | | | | | |
| Nov-2020 | 1819.82 | 281.34 | 18.3 | Nov-2020 | 1819.82 | 281.34 | 18.3 |
| Feb-2000 | 577.71 | 81.48 | 16.4 | Apr-2020 | 1310.66 | 157.56 | 13.7 |
| Apr-2009 | 487.56 | 64.81 | 15.3 | Dec-2020 | 1974.86 | 155.04 | 8.5 |
| Oct-2011 | 741.06 | 96.90 | 15.0 | Jan-2019 | 1499.42 | 150.86 | 11.2 |
| Oct-1982 | 80.86 | 10.02 | 14.1 | Nov-2016 | 1322.34 | 130.95 | 11.0 |
| Apr-2020 | 1310.66 | 157.56 | 13.7 | Feb-2021 | 2201.05 | 127.41 | 6.1 |
| Jan-1985 | 114.77 | 13.28 | 13.1 | Jun-2019 | 1566.57 | 101.08 | 6.9 |
| Sep-2010 | 676.14 | 74.08 | 12.3 | Jan-2021 | 2073.64 | 98.78 | 5.0 |
| Aug-1984 | 106.21 | 10.96 | 11.5 | Oct-2011 | 741.06 | 96.90 | 15.0 |
| Jan-1987 | 150.48 | 15.48 | 11.5 | Oct-2021 | 2297.19 | 92.82 | 4.2 |

# 10 WORST MONTHS BY PERCENT AND POINT

| | BY PERCENT CHANGE | | | | BY POINT CHANGE | | |
|---|---|---|---|---|---|---|---|
| MONTH | CLOSE | PNT CHANGE | % CHANGE | MONTH | CLOSE | PNT CHANGE | % CHANGE |
| **DJIA 1901 to 1949** | | | | | | | |
| Sep-1931 | 96.61 | −42.80 | −30.7 | Oct-1929 | 273.51 | −69.94 | −20.4 |
| Mar-1938 | 98.95 | −30.69 | −23.7 | Jun-1930 | 226.34 | −48.73 | −17.7 |
| Apr-1932 | 56.11 | −17.17 | −23.4 | Sep-1931 | 96.61 | −42.80 | −30.7 |
| May-1940 | 116.22 | −32.21 | −21.7 | Sep-1929 | 343.45 | −36.88 | −9.7 |
| Oct-1929 | 273.51 | −69.94 | −20.4 | Sep-1930 | 204.90 | −35.52 | −14.8 |
| May-1932 | 44.74 | −11.37 | −20.3 | Nov-1929 | 238.95 | −34.56 | −12.6 |
| Jun-1930 | 226.34 | −48.73 | −17.7 | May-1940 | 116.22 | −32.21 | −21.7 |
| Dec-1931 | 77.90 | −15.97 | −17.0 | Mar-1938 | 98.95 | −30.69 | −23.7 |
| Feb-1933 | 51.39 | −9.51 | −15.6 | Sep-1937 | 154.57 | −22.84 | −12.9 |
| May-1931 | 128.46 | −22.73 | −15.0 | May-1931 | 128.46 | −22.73 | −15.0 |
| **DJIA 1950 to APRIL 2022** | | | | | | | |
| Oct-1987 | 1993.53 | −602.75 | −23.2 | Mar-2020 | 21917.16 | −3492.20 | −13.7 |
| Aug-1998 | 7539.07 | −1344.22 | −15.1 | Feb-2020 | 25409.36 | −2846.67 | −10.1 |
| Oct-2008 | 9325.01 | −1525.65 | −14.1 | Dec-2018 | 23327.46 | −2211.00 | −8.7 |
| Nov-1973 | 822.25 | −134.33 | −14.0 | May-2019 | 24815.04 | −1777.87 | −6.7 |
| Mar-2020 | 21917.16 | −3492.20 | −13.7 | Apr-2022 | 32977.21 | −1701.14 | −4.9 |
| Sep-2002 | 7591.93 | −1071.57 | −12.4 | Oct-2008 | 9325.01 | −1525.65 | −14.1 |
| Feb-2009 | 7062.93 | −937.93 | −11.7 | Sep-2021 | 33843.92 | −1516.81 | −4.3 |
| Sep-2001 | 8847.56 | −1102.19 | −11.1 | Aug-1998 | 7539.07 | −1344.22 | −15.1 |
| Sep-1974 | 607.87 | −70.71 | −10.4 | Oct-2018 | 25115.76 | −1342.55 | −5.1 |
| Aug-1974 | 678.58 | −78.85 | −10.4 | Nov-2021 | 34483.72 | −1335.84 | −3.7 |
| **S&P 500 1930 to APRIL 2022** | | | | | | | |
| Sep-1931 | 9.71 | −4.15 | −29.9 | Apr-2022 | 4131.93 | −398.48 | −8.8 |
| Mar-1938 | 8.50 | −2.84 | −25.0 | Mar-2020 | 2584.59 | −369.63 | −12.5 |
| May-1940 | 9.27 | −2.92 | −24.0 | Feb-2020 | 2954.22 | −271.30 | −8.4 |
| May-1932 | 4.47 | −1.36 | −23.3 | Dec-2018 | 2506.85 | −253.31 | −9.2 |
| Oct-1987 | 251.79 | −70.04 | −21.8 | Jan-2022 | 4515.55 | −250.63 | −5.3 |
| Apr-1932 | 5.83 | −1.48 | −20.2 | Sep-2021 | 4307.54 | −215.14 | −4.8 |
| Feb-1933 | 5.66 | −1.28 | −18.4 | Oct-2018 | 2711.74 | −202.24 | −6.9 |
| Oct-2008 | 968.75 | −197.61 | −16.9 | Oct-2008 | 968.75 | −197.61 | −16.9 |
| Jun-1930 | 20.46 | −4.03 | −16.5 | May-2019 | 2752.06 | −193.77 | −6.6 |
| Aug-1998 | 957.28 | −163.39 | −14.6 | Aug-1998 | 957.28 | −163.39 | −14.6 |
| **NASDAQ 1971 to APRIL 2022** | | | | | | | |
| Oct-1987 | 323.30 | −120.99 | −27.2 | Apr-2022 | 12334.64 | −1885.88 | −13.3 |
| Nov-2000 | 2597.93 | −771.70 | −22.9 | Jan-2022 | 14239.88 | −1405.09 | −9.0 |
| Feb-2001 | 2151.83 | −620.90 | −22.4 | Mar-2020 | 7700.10 | −867.27 | −10.1 |
| Aug-1998 | 1499.25 | −373.14 | −19.9 | Sep-2021 | 14448.58 | −810.66 | −5.3 |
| Oct-2008 | 1720.95 | −370.93 | −17.7 | Nov-2000 | 2597.93 | −771.70 | −22.9 |
| Mar-1980 | 131.00 | −27.03 | −17.1 | Oct-2018 | 7305.90 | −740.45 | −9.2 |
| Sep-2001 | 1498.80 | −306.63 | −17.0 | Apr-2000 | 3860.66 | −712.17 | −15.6 |
| Oct-1978 | 111.12 | −21.77 | −16.4 | Dec-2018 | 6635.28 | −695.26 | −9.5 |
| Apr-2000 | 3860.66 | −712.17 | −15.6 | May-2019 | 7453.15 | −642.24 | −7.9 |
| Nov-1973 | 93.51 | −16.66 | −15.1 | Feb-2001 | 2151.83 | −620.90 | −22.4 |
| **RUSSELL 1000 1979 to APRIL 2022** | | | | | | | |
| Oct-1987 | 131.89 | −36.94 | −21.9 | Apr-2022 | 2276.45 | −224.84 | −9.0 |
| Oct-2008 | 522.47 | −111.61 | −17.6 | Mar-2020 | 1416.49 | −218.72 | −13.4 |
| Aug-1998 | 496.66 | −88.31 | −15.1 | Jan-2022 | 2494.64 | −151.27 | −5.7 |
| Mar-2020 | 1416.49 | −218.72 | −13.4 | Feb-2020 | 1635.21 | −148.82 | −8.3 |
| Mar-1980 | 55.79 | −7.28 | −11.5 | Dec-2018 | 1384.26 | −141.30 | −9.3 |
| Sep-2002 | 433.22 | −52.86 | −10.9 | Sep-2021 | 2418.16 | −119.15 | −4.7 |
| Feb-2009 | 399.61 | −47.71 | −10.7 | Oct-2018 | 1498.65 | −115.89 | −7.2 |
| Sep-2008 | 634.08 | −68.09 | −9.7 | Oct-2008 | 522.47 | −111.61 | −17.6 |
| Aug-1990 | 166.69 | −17.63 | −9.6 | May-2019 | 1524.42 | −107.45 | −6.6 |
| Feb-2001 | 654.25 | −68.30 | −9.5 | Aug-1998 | 496.66 | −88.31 | −15.1 |
| **RUSSELL 2000 1979 to APRIL 2022** | | | | | | | |
| Oct-1987 | 118.26 | −52.55 | −30.8 | Mar-2020 | 1153.10 | −323.33 | −21.9 |
| Mar-2020 | 1153.10 | −323.33 | −21.9 | Jan-2022 | 2028.45 | −216.86 | −9.7 |
| Oct-2008 | 537.52 | −142.06 | −20.9 | Apr-2022 | 1864.10 | −206.03 | −10.0 |
| Aug-1998 | 337.95 | −81.80 | −19.5 | Oct-2018 | 1511.41 | −185.16 | −10.9 |
| Mar-1980 | 48.27 | −10.95 | −18.5 | Dec-2018 | 1348.56 | −184.71 | −12.0 |
| Jul-2002 | 392.42 | −70.22 | −15.2 | Oct-2008 | 537.52 | −142.06 | −20.9 |
| Aug-1990 | 139.52 | −21.99 | −13.6 | Feb-2020 | 1476.43 | −137.63 | −8.5 |
| Sep-2001 | 404.87 | −63.69 | −13.6 | May-2019 | 1465.49 | −125.72 | −7.9 |
| Feb-2009 | 389.02 | −54.51 | −12.3 | Jan-2016 | 1035.38 | −100.51 | −8.8 |
| Dec-2018 | 1348.56 | −184.71 | −12.0 | Nov-2021 | 2198.91 | −98.28 | −4.3 |

# 10 <u>BEST</u> QUARTERS BY PERCENT AND POINT

| | BY PERCENT CHANGE | | | | BY POINT CHANGE | | |
|---|---|---|---|---|---|---|---|
| QUARTER | CLOSE | PNT CHANGE | % CHANGE | QUARTER | CLOSE | PNT CHANGE | % CHANGE |
| | | | **DJIA 1901 to 1949** | | | | |
| Jun-1933 | 98.14 | 42.74 | 77.1 | Dec-1928 | 300.00 | 60.57 | 25.3 |
| Sep-1932 | 71.56 | 28.72 | 67.0 | Jun-1933 | 98.14 | 42.74 | 77.1 |
| Jun-1938 | 133.88 | 34.93 | 35.3 | Mar-1930 | 286.10 | 37.62 | 15.1 |
| Sep-1915 | 90.58 | 20.52 | 29.3 | Jun-1938 | 133.88 | 34.93 | 35.3 |
| Dec-1928 | 300.00 | 60.57 | 25.3 | Sep-1927 | 197.59 | 31.36 | 18.9 |
| Dec-1904 | 50.99 | 8.80 | 20.9 | Sep-1928 | 239.43 | 28.88 | 13.7 |
| Jun-1919 | 106.98 | 18.13 | 20.4 | Sep-1932 | 71.56 | 28.72 | 67.0 |
| Sep-1927 | 197.59 | 31.36 | 18.9 | Jun-1929 | 333.79 | 24.94 | 8.1 |
| Dec-1905 | 70.47 | 10.47 | 17.4 | Sep-1939 | 152.54 | 21.91 | 16.8 |
| Jun-1935 | 118.21 | 17.40 | 17.3 | Sep-1915 | 90.58 | 20.52 | 29.3 |
| | | | **DJIA 1950 to APRIL 2022** | | | | |
| Mar-1975 | 768.15 | 151.91 | 24.7 | Jun-2020 | 25812.88 | 3895.72 | 17.8 |
| Mar-1987 | 2304.69 | 408.74 | 21.6 | Dec-2020 | 30606.48 | 2824.78 | 10.2 |
| Jun-2020 | 25812.88 | 3895.72 | 17.8 | Mar-2019 | 25928.68 | 2601.22 | 11.2 |
| Mar-1986 | 1818.61 | 271.94 | 17.6 | Dec-2021 | 36338.30 | 2494.38 | 7.4 |
| Mar-1976 | 999.45 | 147.04 | 17.3 | Mar-2021 | 32981.55 | 2375.07 | 7.8 |
| Dec-1998 | 9181.43 | 1338.81 | 17.1 | Dec-2017 | 24719.22 | 2314.13 | 10.3 |
| Dec-1982 | 1046.54 | 150.29 | 16.8 | Sep-2018 | 26458.31 | 2186.90 | 9.0 |
| Jun-1997 | 7672.79 | 1089.31 | 16.6 | Sep-2020 | 27781.70 | 1968.82 | 7.6 |
| Dec-1985 | 1546.67 | 218.04 | 16.4 | Dec-2019 | 28538.44 | 1621.61 | 6.0 |
| Sep-2009 | 9712.28 | 1265.28 | 15.0 | Jun-2021 | 34502.51 | 1520.96 | 4.6 |
| | | | **S&P 500 1930 to APRIL 2022** | | | | |
| Jun-1933 | 10.91 | 5.06 | 86.5 | Jun-2020 | 3100.29 | 515.70 | 20.0 |
| Sep-1932 | 8.08 | 3.65 | 82.4 | Dec-2021 | 4766.18 | 458.64 | 10.7 |
| Jun-1938 | 11.56 | 3.06 | 36.0 | Dec-2020 | 3756.07 | 393.07 | 11.7 |
| Mar-1975 | 83.36 | 14.80 | 21.6 | Mar-2019 | 2834.40 | 327.55 | 13.1 |
| Dec-1998 | 1229.23 | 212.22 | 20.9 | Jun-2021 | 4297.50 | 324.61 | 8.2 |
| Jun-1935 | 10.23 | 1.76 | 20.8 | Sep-2020 | 3363.00 | 262.71 | 8.5 |
| Mar-1987 | 291.70 | 49.53 | 20.5 | Dec-2019 | 3230.78 | 254.04 | 8.5 |
| Jun-2020 | 3100.29 | 515.70 | 20.0 | Mar-2021 | 3972.89 | 216.82 | 5.8 |
| Sep-1939 | 13.02 | 2.16 | 19.9 | Dec-1998 | 1229.23 | 212.22 | 20.9 |
| MAR-1943 | 11.58 | 1.81 | 18.5 | SEP-2018 | 2913.98 | 195.61 | 7.2 |
| | | | **NASDAQ 1971 to APRIL 2022** | | | | |
| Dec-1999 | 4069.31 | 1323.15 | 48.2 | Jun-2020 | 10058.77 | 2358.67 | 30.6 |
| Jun-2020 | 10058.77 | 2358.67 | 30.6 | Dec-2020 | 12888.28 | 1720.77 | 15.4 |
| Dec-2001 | 1950.40 | 451.60 | 30.1 | Dec-1999 | 4069.31 | 1323.15 | 48.2 |
| Dec-1998 | 2192.69 | 498.85 | 29.5 | Jun-2021 | 14503.95 | 1257.08 | 9.5 |
| Mar-1991 | 482.30 | 108.46 | 29.0 | Dec-2021 | 15644.97 | 1196.39 | 8.3 |
| Mar-1975 | 75.66 | 15.84 | 26.5 | Sep-2020 | 11167.51 | 1108.74 | 11.0 |
| Dec-1982 | 232.41 | 44.76 | 23.9 | Mar-2019 | 7729.32 | 1094.04 | 16.5 |
| Mar-1987 | 430.05 | 80.72 | 23.1 | Dec-2019 | 8972.60 | 973.26 | 12.2 |
| Jun-2003 | 1622.80 | 281.63 | 21.0 | Sep-2018 | 8046.35 | 536.05 | 7.1 |
| Jun-1980 | 157.78 | 26.78 | 20.4 | Mar-2017 | 5911.74 | 528.62 | 9.8 |
| | | | **RUSSELL 1000 1979 to APRIL 2022** | | | | |
| Dec-1998 | 642.87 | 113.76 | 21.5 | Jun-2020 | 1717.47 | 300.98 | 21.3 |
| Jun-2020 | 1717.47 | 300.98 | 21.3 | Dec-2020 | 2120.87 | 248.17 | 13.3 |
| Mar-1987 | 155.20 | 25.20 | 19.4 | Dec-2021 | 2645.91 | 227.75 | 9.4 |
| Dec-1982 | 77.24 | 11.35 | 17.2 | Mar-2019 | 1570.23 | 185.97 | 13.4 |
| Jun-1997 | 462.95 | 64.76 | 16.3 | Jun-2021 | 2421.14 | 182.97 | 8.2 |
| Dec-1985 | 114.39 | 15.64 | 15.8 | Sep-2020 | 1872.70 | 155.23 | 9.0 |
| Jun-2009 | 502.27 | 68.60 | 15.8 | Dec-2019 | 1784.21 | 140.03 | 8.5 |
| Dec-1999 | 767.97 | 104.14 | 15.7 | Mar-2021 | 2238.17 | 117.30 | 5.5 |
| Sep-2009 | 579.97 | 77.70 | 15.5 | Dec-1998 | 642.87 | 113.76 | 21.5 |
| Jun-2003 | 518.94 | 68.59 | 15.2 | Sep-2018 | 1614.54 | 104.58 | 6.9 |
| | | | **RUSSELL 2000 1979 to APRIL 2022** | | | | |
| Dec-2020 | 1974.86 | 467.17 | 31.0 | Dec-2020 | 1974.86 | 467.17 | 31.0 |
| Mar-1991 | 171.01 | 38.85 | 29.4 | Jun-2020 | 1441.37 | 288.27 | 25.0 |
| Dec-1982 | 88.90 | 18.06 | 25.5 | Mar-2021 | 2220.52 | 245.66 | 12.4 |
| Jun-2020 | 1441.37 | 288.27 | 25.0 | Mar-2019 | 1539.74 | 191.18 | 14.2 |
| Mar-1979 | 166.79 | 31.79 | 23.6 | Dec-2019 | 1668.47 | 145.10 | 9.5 |
| Jun-2003 | 448.37 | 83.83 | 23.0 | Jun-2018 | 1643.07 | 113.64 | 7.4 |
| Sep-1980 | 69.94 | 12.47 | 21.7 | Dec-2010 | 783.65 | 107.51 | 15.9 |
| Dec-2001 | 488.50 | 83.63 | 20.7 | Dec-2016 | 1357.13 | 105.48 | 8.4 |
| Jun-2009 | 508.28 | 85.53 | 20.2 | Dec-2014 | 1204.70 | 103.02 | 9.4 |
| Jun-1983 | 124.17 | 20.40 | 19.7 | Mar-2013 | 951.54 | 102.19 | 12.0 |

# 10 <u>WORST</u> QUARTERS BY PERCENT AND POINT

| BY PERCENT CHANGE | | | | BY POINT CHANGE | | | |
|---|---|---|---|---|---|---|---|
| QUARTER | CLOSE | PNT CHANGE | % CHANGE | QUARTER | CLOSE | PNT CHANGE | % CHANGE |
| **DJIA 1901 to 1949** | | | | | | | |
| Jun-1932 | 42.84 | −30.44 | −41.5 | Dec-1929 | 248.48 | −94.97 | −27.7 |
| Sep-1931 | 96.61 | −53.57 | −35.7 | Jun-1930 | 226.34 | −59.76 | −20.9 |
| Dec-1929 | 248.48 | −94.97 | −27.7 | Sep-1931 | 96.61 | −53.57 | −35.7 |
| Sep-1903 | 33.55 | −9.73 | −22.5 | Dec-1930 | 164.58 | −40.32 | −19.7 |
| Dec-1937 | 120.85 | −33.72 | −21.8 | Dec-1937 | 120.85 | −33.72 | −21.8 |
| Jun-1930 | 226.34 | −59.76 | −20.9 | Sep-1946 | 172.42 | −33.20 | −16.1 |
| Dec-1930 | 164.58 | −40.32 | −19.7 | Jun-1932 | 42.84 | −30.44 | −41.5 |
| Dec-1931 | 77.90 | −18.71 | −19.4 | Jun-1940 | 121.87 | −26.08 | −17.6 |
| Mar-1938 | 98.95 | −21.90 | −18.1 | Mar-1939 | 131.84 | −22.92 | −14.8 |
| Jun-1940 | 121.87 | −26.08 | −17.6 | Jun-1931 | 150.18 | −22.18 | −12.9 |
| **DJIA 1950 to MARCH 2022** | | | | | | | |
| Dec-1987 | 1938.83 | −657.45 | −25.3 | Mar-2020 | 21917.16 | −6621.28 | −23.2 |
| Sep-1974 | 607.87 | −194.54 | −24.2 | Dec-2018 | 23327.46 | −3130.85 | −11.8 |
| Mar-2020 | 21917.16 | −6621.28 | −23.2 | Dec-2008 | 8776.39 | −2074.27 | −19.1 |
| Jun-1962 | 561.28 | −145.62 | −20.6 | Mar-2022 | 34678.35 | −1659.95 | −4.6 |
| Dec-2008 | 8776.39 | −2074.27 | −19.1 | Sep-2001 | 8847.56 | −1654.84 | −15.8 |
| Sep-2002 | 7591.93 | −1651.33 | −17.9 | Sep-2002 | 7591.93 | −1651.33 | −17.9 |
| Sep-2001 | 8847.56 | −1654.84 | −15.8 | Sep-2011 | 10913.38 | −1500.96 | −12.1 |
| Sep-1990 | 2452.48 | −428.21 | −14.9 | Sep-2015 | 16284.00 | −1335.51 | −7.6 |
| Mar-2009 | 7608.92 | −1167.47 | −13.3 | Mar-2009 | 7608.92 | −1167.47 | −13.3 |
| Sep-1981 | 849.98 | −126.90 | −13.0 | Jun-2002 | 9243.26 | −1160.68 | −11.2 |
| **S&P 500 1930 to MARCH 2022** | | | | | | | |
| Jun-1932 | 4.43 | −2.88 | −39.4 | Mar-2020 | 2584.59 | −646.19 | −20.0 |
| Sep-1931 | 9.71 | −5.12 | −34.5 | Dec-2018 | 2506.85 | −407.13 | −14.0 |
| Sep-1974 | 63.54 | −22.46 | −26.1 | Dec-2008 | 903.25 | −263.11 | −22.6 |
| Dec-1937 | 10.55 | −3.21 | −23.3 | Mar-2022 | 4530.41 | −235.77 | −4.9 |
| Dec-1987 | 247.08 | −74.75 | −23.2 | Sep-2011 | 1131.42 | −189.22 | −14.3 |
| Dec-2008 | 903.25 | −263.11 | −22.6 | Sep-2001 | 1040.94 | −183.48 | −15.0 |
| Jun-1962 | 54.75 | −14.80 | −21.3 | Sep-2002 | 815.28 | −174.54 | −17.6 |
| Mar-2020 | 2584.59 | −646.19 | −20.0 | Mar-2001 | 1160.33 | −159.95 | −12.1 |
| Mar-1938 | 8.50 | −2.05 | −19.4 | Jun-2002 | 989.82 | −157.57 | −13.7 |
| Jun-1970 | 72.72 | −16.91 | −18.9 | Mar-2008 | 1322.70 | −145.66 | −9.9 |
| **NASDAQ 1971 to MARCH 2022** | | | | | | | |
| Dec-2000 | 2470.52 | −1202.30 | −32.7 | Mar-2022 | 14220.52 | −1424.45 | −9.1 |
| Sep-2001 | 1498.80 | −661.74 | −30.6 | Dec-2018 | 6635.28 | −1411.07 | −17.5 |
| Sep-1974 | 55.67 | −20.29 | −26.7 | Mar-2020 | 7700.10 | −1272.50 | −14.2 |
| Dec-1987 | 330.47 | −113.82 | −25.6 | Dec-2000 | 2470.52 | −1202.30 | −32.7 |
| Mar-2001 | 1840.26 | −630.26 | −25.5 | Sep-2001 | 1498.80 | −661.74 | −30.6 |
| Sep-1990 | 344.51 | −117.78 | −25.5 | Mar-2001 | 1840.26 | −630.26 | −25.5 |
| Dec-2008 | 1577.03 | −514.85 | −24.6 | Jun-2000 | 3966.11 | −606.72 | −13.3 |
| Jun-2002 | 1463.21 | −382.14 | −20.7 | Dec-2008 | 1577.03 | −514.85 | −24.6 |
| Sep-2002 | 1172.06 | −291.15 | −19.9 | Jun-2002 | 1463.21 | −382.14 | −20.7 |
| Jun-1974 | 75.96 | −16.31 | −17.7 | Mar-2008 | 2279.10 | −373.18 | −14.1 |
| **RUSSELL 1000 1979 to MARCH 2022** | | | | | | | |
| Dec-2008 | 487.77 | −146.31 | −23.1 | Mar-2020 | 1416.49 | −367.72 | −20.6 |
| Dec-1987 | 130.02 | −38.81 | −23.0 | Dec-2018 | 1384.26 | −230.28 | −14.3 |
| Mar-2020 | 1416.49 | −367.72 | −20.6 | Dec-2008 | 487.77 | −146.31 | −23.1 |
| Sep-2002 | 433.22 | −90.50 | −17.3 | Mar-2022 | 2501.29 | −144.62 | −5.5 |
| Sep-2001 | 546.46 | −100.18 | −15.5 | Sep-2011 | 623.45 | −111.03 | −15.1 |
| Sep-1990 | 157.83 | −28.46 | −15.3 | Sep-2001 | 546.46 | −100.18 | −15.5 |
| Sep-2011 | 623.45 | −111.03 | −15.1 | Sep-2002 | 433.22 | −90.50 | −17.3 |
| Dec-2018 | 1384.26 | −230.28 | −14.3 | Mar-2001 | 610.36 | −89.73 | −12.8 |
| Jun-2002 | 523.72 | −83.63 | −13.8 | Sep-2015 | 1068.46 | −84.18 | −7.3 |
| Mar-2001 | 610.36 | −89.73 | −12.8 | Jun-2002 | 523.72 | −83.63 | −13.8 |
| **RUSSELL 2000 1979 to MARCH 2022** | | | | | | | |
| Mar-2020 | 1153.10 | −515.37 | −30.9 | Mar-2020 | 1153.10 | −515.37 | −30.9 |
| Dec-1987 | 120.42 | −50.39 | −29.5 | Dec-2018 | 1348.56 | −348.01 | −20.5 |
| Dec-2008 | 499.45 | −180.13 | −26.5 | Sep-2011 | 644.16 | −183.27 | −22.1 |
| Sep-1990 | 126.70 | −42.34 | −25.0 | Dec-2008 | 499.45 | −180.13 | −26.5 |
| Sep-2011 | 644.16 | −183.27 | −22.1 | Mar-2022 | 2070.13 | −175.18 | −7.8 |
| Sep-2002 | 362.27 | −100.37 | −21.7 | Sep-2015 | 1100.69 | −153.26 | −12.2 |
| Sep-2001 | 404.87 | −107.77 | −21.0 | Sep-2001 | 404.87 | −107.77 | −21.0 |
| Dec-2018 | 1348.56 | −348.01 | −20.5 | Sep-2021 | 2204.37 | −106.18 | −4.6 |
| Sep-1998 | 363.59 | −93.80 | −20.5 | Sep-2002 | 362.27 | −100.37 | −21.7 |
| Sep-1981 | 67.55 | −15.01 | −18.2 | Sep-1998 | 363.59 | −93.80 | −20.5 |

# 10 BEST YEARS BY PERCENT AND POINT

| | BY PERCENT CHANGE | | | | BY POINT CHANGE | | |
|---|---|---|---|---|---|---|---|
| YEAR | CLOSE | PNT CHANGE | % CHANGE | YEAR | CLOSE | PNT CHANGE | % CHANGE |
| **DJIA 1901 to 1949** | | | | | | | |
| 1915 | 99.15 | 44.57 | 81.7 | 1928 | 300.00 | 97.60 | 48.2 |
| 1933 | 99.90 | 39.97 | 66.7 | 1927 | 202.40 | 45.20 | 28.8 |
| 1928 | 300.00 | 97.60 | 48.2 | 1915 | 99.15 | 44.57 | 81.7 |
| 1908 | 63.11 | 20.07 | 46.6 | 1945 | 192.91 | 40.59 | 26.6 |
| 1904 | 50.99 | 15.01 | 41.7 | 1935 | 144.13 | 40.09 | 38.5 |
| 1935 | 144.13 | 40.09 | 38.5 | 1933 | 99.90 | 39.97 | 66.7 |
| 1905 | 70.47 | 19.48 | 38.2 | 1925 | 156.66 | 36.15 | 30.0 |
| 1919 | 107.23 | 25.03 | 30.5 | 1936 | 179.90 | 35.77 | 24.8 |
| 1925 | 156.66 | 36.15 | 30.0 | 1938 | 154.76 | 33.91 | 28.1 |
| 1927 | 202.40 | 45.20 | 28.8 | 1919 | 107.23 | 25.03 | 30.5 |
| **DJIA 1950 to 2021** | | | | | | | |
| 1954 | 404.39 | 123.49 | 44.0 | 2021 | 36338.30 | 5731.82 | 18.7 |
| 1975 | 852.41 | 236.17 | 38.3 | 2019 | 28538.44 | 5210.98 | 22.3 |
| 1958 | 583.65 | 147.96 | 34.0 | 2017 | 24719.22 | 4956.62 | 25.1 |
| 1995 | 5117.12 | 1282.68 | 33.5 | 2013 | 16576.66 | 3472.52 | 26.5 |
| 1985 | 1546.67 | 335.10 | 27.7 | 2016 | 19762.60 | 2337.57 | 13.4 |
| 1989 | 2753.20 | 584.63 | 27.0 | 1999 | 11497.12 | 2315.69 | 25.2 |
| 2013 | 16576.66 | 3472.52 | 26.5 | 2003 | 10453.92 | 2112.29 | 25.3 |
| 1996 | 6448.27 | 1331.15 | 26.0 | 2020 | 30606.48 | 2068.04 | 7.3 |
| 2003 | 10453.92 | 2112.29 | 25.3 | 2006 | 12463.15 | 1745.65 | 16.3 |
| 1999 | 11497.12 | 2315.69 | 25.2 | 2009 | 10428.05 | 1651.66 | 18.8 |
| **S&P 500 1930 to 2021** | | | | | | | |
| 1933 | 10.10 | 3.21 | 46.6 | 2021 | 4766.18 | 1010.11 | 26.9 |
| 1954 | 35.98 | 11.17 | 45.0 | 2019 | 3230.78 | 723.93 | 28.9 |
| 1935 | 13.43 | 3.93 | 41.4 | 2020 | 3756.07 | 525.29 | 16.3 |
| 1958 | 55.21 | 15.22 | 38.1 | 2017 | 2673.61 | 434.78 | 19.4 |
| 1995 | 615.93 | 156.66 | 34.1 | 2013 | 1848.36 | 422.17 | 29.6 |
| 1975 | 90.19 | 21.63 | 31.5 | 1998 | 1229.23 | 258.80 | 26.7 |
| 1997 | 970.43 | 229.69 | 31.0 | 1999 | 1469.25 | 240.02 | 19.5 |
| 1945 | 17.36 | 4.08 | 30.7 | 2003 | 1111.92 | 232.10 | 26.4 |
| 2013 | 1848.36 | 422.17 | 29.6 | 1997 | 970.43 | 229.69 | 31.0 |
| 2019 | 3230.78 | 723.93 | 28.9 | 2009 | 1115.10 | 211.85 | 23.5 |
| **NASDAQ 1971 to 2021** | | | | | | | |
| 1999 | 4069.31 | 1876.62 | 85.6 | 2020 | 12888.28 | 3915.68 | 43.6 |
| 1991 | 586.34 | 212.50 | 56.8 | 2021 | 15644.97 | 2756.69 | 21.4 |
| 2003 | 2003.37 | 667.86 | 50.0 | 2019 | 8972.60 | 2337.32 | 35.2 |
| 2009 | 2269.15 | 692.12 | 43.9 | 1999 | 4069.31 | 1876.62 | 85.6 |
| 2020 | 12888.28 | 3915.68 | 43.6 | 2017 | 6903.39 | 1520.27 | 28.2 |
| 1995 | 1052.13 | 300.17 | 39.9 | 2013 | 4176.59 | 1157.08 | 38.3 |
| 1998 | 2192.69 | 622.34 | 39.6 | 2009 | 2269.15 | 692.12 | 43.9 |
| 2013 | 4176.59 | 1157.08 | 38.3 | 2003 | 2003.37 | 667.86 | 50.0 |
| 2019 | 8972.60 | 2337.32 | 35.2 | 1998 | 2192.69 | 622.34 | 39.6 |
| 1980 | 202.34 | 51.20 | 33.9 | 2014 | 4736.05 | 559.46 | 13.4 |
| **RUSSELL 1000 1979 to 2021** | | | | | | | |
| 1995 | 328.89 | 84.24 | 34.4 | 2021 | 2645.91 | 525.04 | 24.8 |
| 1997 | 513.79 | 120.04 | 30.5 | 2019 | 1784.21 | 399.95 | 28.9 |
| 2013 | 1030.36 | 240.46 | 30.4 | 2020 | 2120.87 | 336.66 | 18.9 |
| 2019 | 1784.21 | 399.95 | 28.9 | 2013 | 1030.36 | 240.46 | 30.4 |
| 1991 | 220.61 | 49.39 | 28.9 | 2017 | 1481.81 | 240.15 | 19.3 |
| 2003 | 594.56 | 128.38 | 27.5 | 1998 | 642.87 | 129.08 | 25.1 |
| 1985 | 114.39 | 24.08 | 26.7 | 2003 | 594.56 | 128.38 | 27.5 |
| 1989 | 185.11 | 38.12 | 25.9 | 1999 | 767.97 | 125.10 | 19.5 |
| 1980 | 75.20 | 15.33 | 25.6 | 2009 | 612.01 | 124.24 | 25.5 |
| 2009 | 612.01 | 124.24 | 25.5 | 1997 | 513.79 | 120.04 | 30.5 |
| **RUSSELL 2000 1979 to 2021** | | | | | | | |
| 2003 | 556.91 | 173.82 | 45.4 | 2019 | 1668.47 | 319.91 | 23.7 |
| 1991 | 189.94 | 57.78 | 43.7 | 2013 | 1163.64 | 314.29 | 37.0 |
| 1979 | 55.91 | 15.39 | 38.0 | 2020 | 1974.86 | 306.39 | 18.4 |
| 2013 | 1163.64 | 314.29 | 37.0 | 2021 | 2245.31 | 270.45 | 13.7 |
| 1980 | 74.80 | 18.89 | 33.8 | 2016 | 1357.13 | 221.24 | 19.5 |
| 1985 | 129.87 | 28.38 | 28.0 | 2017 | 1535.51 | 178.38 | 13.1 |
| 1983 | 112.27 | 23.37 | 26.3 | 2003 | 556.91 | 173.82 | 45.4 |
| 1995 | 315.97 | 65.61 | 26.2 | 2010 | 783.65 | 158.26 | 25.3 |
| 2010 | 783.65 | 158.26 | 25.3 | 2009 | 625.39 | 125.94 | 25.2 |
| 2009 | 625.39 | 125.94 | 25.2 | 2006 | 787.66 | 114.44 | 17.0 |

182

# 10 WORST YEARS BY PERCENT AND POINT

| | BY PERCENT CHANGE | | | | BY POINT CHANGE | | |
|---|---|---|---|---|---|---|---|
| YEAR | CLOSE | PNT CHANGE | % CHANGE | YEAR | CLOSE | PNT CHANGE | % CHANGE |
| | | | **DJIA 1901 to 1949** | | | | |
| 1931 | 77.90 | −86.68 | −52.7 | 1931 | 77.90 | −86.68 | −52.7 |
| 1907 | 43.04 | −26.08 | −37.7 | 1930 | 164.58 | −83.90 | −33.8 |
| 1930 | 164.58 | −83.90 | −33.8 | 1937 | 120.85 | −59.05 | −32.8 |
| 1920 | 71.95 | −35.28 | −32.9 | 1929 | 248.48 | −51.52 | −17.2 |
| 1937 | 120.85 | −59.05 | −32.8 | 1920 | 71.95 | −35.28 | −32.9 |
| 1903 | 35.98 | −11.12 | −23.6 | 1907 | 43.04 | −26.08 | −37.7 |
| 1932 | 59.93 | −17.97 | −23.1 | 1917 | 74.38 | −20.62 | −21.7 |
| 1917 | 74.38 | −20.62 | −21.7 | 1941 | 110.96 | −20.17 | −15.4 |
| 1910 | 59.60 | −12.96 | −17.9 | 1940 | 131.13 | −19.11 | −12.7 |
| 1929 | 248.48 | −51.52 | −17.2 | 1932 | 59.93 | −17.97 | −23.1 |
| | | | **DJIA 1950 to 2021** | | | | |
| 2008 | 8776.39 | −4488.43 | −33.8 | 2008 | 8776.39 | −4488.43 | −33.8 |
| 1974 | 616.24 | −234.62 | −27.6 | 2002 | 8341.63 | −1679.87 | −16.8 |
| 1966 | 785.69 | −183.57 | −18.9 | 2018 | 23327.46 | −1391.76 | −5.6 |
| 1977 | 831.17 | −173.48 | −17.3 | 2001 | 10021.50 | −765.35 | −7.1 |
| 2002 | 8341.63 | −1679.87 | −16.8 | 2000 | 10786.85 | −710.27 | −6.2 |
| 1973 | 850.86 | −169.16 | −16.6 | 2015 | 17425.03 | −398.04 | −2.2 |
| 1969 | 800.36 | −143.39 | −15.2 | 1974 | 616.24 | −234.62 | −27.6 |
| 1957 | 435.69 | −63.78 | −12.8 | 1966 | 785.69 | −183.57 | −18.9 |
| 1962 | 652.10 | −79.04 | −10.8 | 1977 | 831.17 | −173.48 | −17.3 |
| 1960 | 615.89 | −63.47 | −9.3 | 1973 | 850.86 | −169.16 | −16.6 |
| | | | **S&P 500 1930 to 2021** | | | | |
| 1931 | 8.12 | −7.22 | −47.1 | 2008 | 903.25 | −565.11 | −38.5 |
| 1937 | 10.55 | −6.63 | −38.6 | 2002 | 879.82 | −268.26 | −23.4 |
| 2008 | 903.25 | −565.11 | −38.5 | 2001 | 1148.08 | −172.20 | −13.0 |
| 1974 | 68.56 | −28.99 | −29.7 | 2018 | 2506.85 | −166.76 | −6.2 |
| 1930 | 15.34 | −6.11 | −28.5 | 2000 | 1320.28 | −148.97 | −10.1 |
| 2002 | 879.82 | −268.26 | −23.4 | 1974 | 68.56 | −28.99 | −29.7 |
| 1941 | 8.69 | −1.89 | −17.9 | 1990 | 330.22 | −23.18 | −6.6 |
| 1973 | 97.55 | −20.50 | −17.4 | 1973 | 97.55 | −20.50 | −17.4 |
| 1940 | 10.58 | −1.91 | −15.3 | 2015 | 2043.94 | −14.96 | −0.7 |
| 1932 | 6.89 | −1.23 | −15.1 | 1981 | 122.55 | −13.21 | −9.7 |
| | | | **NASDAQ 1971 to 2021** | | | | |
| 2008 | 1577.03 | −1075.25 | −40.5 | 2000 | 2470.52 | −1598.79 | −39.3 |
| 2000 | 2470.52 | −1598.79 | −39.3 | 2008 | 1577.03 | −1075.25 | −40.5 |
| 1974 | 59.82 | −32.37 | −35.1 | 2002 | 1335.51 | −614.89 | −31.5 |
| 2002 | 1335.51 | −614.89 | −31.5 | 2001 | 1950.40 | −520.12 | −21.1 |
| 1973 | 92.19 | −41.54 | −31.1 | 2018 | 6635.28 | −268.11 | −3.9 |
| 2001 | 1950.40 | −520.12 | −21.1 | 1990 | 373.84 | −80.98 | −17.8 |
| 1990 | 373.84 | −80.98 | −17.8 | 2011 | 2605.15 | −47.72 | −1.8 |
| 1984 | 247.35 | −31.25 | −11.2 | 1973 | 92.19 | −41.54 | −31.1 |
| 1987 | 330.47 | −18.86 | −5.4 | 1974 | 59.82 | −32.37 | −35.1 |
| 2018 | 6635.28 | −268.11 | −3.9 | 1984 | 247.35 | −31.25 | −11.2 |
| | | | **RUSSELL 1000 1979 to 2021** | | | | |
| 2008 | 487.77 | −312.05 | −39.0 | 2008 | 487.77 | −312.05 | −39.0 |
| 2002 | 466.18 | −138.76 | −22.9 | 2002 | 466.18 | −138.76 | −22.9 |
| 2001 | 604.94 | −95.15 | −13.6 | 2018 | 1384.26 | −97.55 | −6.6 |
| 1981 | 67.93 | −7.27 | −9.7 | 2001 | 604.94 | −95.15 | −13.6 |
| 2000 | 700.09 | −67.88 | −8.8 | 2000 | 700.09 | −67.88 | −8.8 |
| 1990 | 171.22 | −13.89 | −7.5 | 1990 | 171.22 | −13.89 | −7.5 |
| 2018 | 1384.26 | −97.55 | −6.6 | 2015 | 1131.88 | −12.49 | −1.1 |
| 1994 | 244.65 | −6.06 | −2.4 | 1981 | 67.93 | −7.27 | −9.7 |
| 2015 | 1131.88 | −12.49 | −1.1 | 1994 | 244.65 | −6.06 | −2.4 |
| 2011 | 693.36 | −3.54 | −0.5 | 2011 | 693.36 | −3.54 | −0.5 |
| | | | **RUSSELL 2000 1979 to 2021** | | | | |
| 2008 | 499.45 | −266.58 | −34.8 | 2008 | 499.45 | −266.58 | −34.8 |
| 2002 | 383.09 | −105.41 | −21.6 | 2018 | 1348.56 | −186.95 | −12.2 |
| 1990 | 132.16 | −36.14 | −21.5 | 2002 | 383.09 | −105.41 | −21.6 |
| 2018 | 1348.56 | −186.95 | −12.2 | 2015 | 1135.89 | −68.81 | −5.7 |
| 1987 | 120.42 | −14.58 | −10.8 | 2011 | 740.92 | −42.73 | −5.5 |
| 1984 | 101.49 | −10.78 | −9.6 | 1990 | 132.16 | −36.14 | −21.5 |
| 2015 | 1135.89 | −68.81 | −5.7 | 2007 | 766.03 | −21.63 | −2.7 |
| 2011 | 740.92 | −42.73 | −5.5 | 2000 | 483.53 | −21.22 | −4.2 |
| 2000 | 483.53 | −21.22 | −4.2 | 1998 | 421.96 | −15.06 | −3.4 |
| 1998 | 421.96 | −15.06 | −3.4 | 1987 | 120.42 | −14.58 | −10.8 |

# STRATEGY PLANNING AND RECORD SECTION

## CONTENTS

*These forms are available at our website, www.stocktradersalmanac.com under "Forms" located at the bottom of the homepage.*

# PORTFOLIO AT START OF 2023

| DATE ACQUIRED | NO. OF SHARES | SECURITY | PRICE | TOTAL COST | PAPER PROFITS | PAPER LOSSES |
|---|---|---|---|---|---|---|
| | | | | | | |
| | | | | | | |
| | | | | | | |
| | | | | | | |
| | | | | | | |
| | | | | | | |
| | | | | | | |
| | | | | | | |
| | | | | | | |
| | | | | | | |
| | | | | | | |
| | | | | | | |
| | | | | | | |
| | | | | | | |
| | | | | | | |
| | | | | | | |
| | | | | | | |
| | | | | | | |
| | | | | | | |
| | | | | | | |
| | | | | | | |
| | | | | | | |
| | | | | | | |
| | | | | | | |
| | | | | | | |
| | | | | | | |

# ADDITIONAL PURCHASES

| DATE ACQUIRED | NO. OF SHARES | SECURITY | PRICE | TOTAL COST | REASON FOR PURCHASE PRIME OBJECTIVE, ETC. |
|---|---|---|---|---|---|
| | | | | | |
| | | | | | |
| | | | | | |
| | | | | | |
| | | | | | |
| | | | | | |
| | | | | | |
| | | | | | |
| | | | | | |
| | | | | | |
| | | | | | |
| | | | | | |
| | | | | | |
| | | | | | |
| | | | | | |
| | | | | | |
| | | | | | |
| | | | | | |
| | | | | | |
| | | | | | |
| | | | | | |
| | | | | | |
| | | | | | |
| | | | | | |
| | | | | | |
| | | | | | |
| | | | | | |

# ADDITIONAL PURCHASES

| DATE ACQUIRED | NO. OF SHARES | SECURITY | PRICE | TOTAL COST | REASON FOR PURCHASE PRIME OBJECTIVE, ETC. |
|---|---|---|---|---|---|
| | | | | | |
| | | | | | |
| | | | | | |
| | | | | | |
| | | | | | |
| | | | | | |
| | | | | | |
| | | | | | |
| | | | | | |
| | | | | | |
| | | | | | |
| | | | | | |
| | | | | | |
| | | | | | |
| | | | | | |
| | | | | | |
| | | | | | |
| | | | | | |
| | | | | | |
| | | | | | |
| | | | | | |
| | | | | | |
| | | | | | |
| | | | | | |
| | | | | | |
| | | | | | |
| | | | | | |
| | | | | | |
| | | | | | |
| | | | | | |
| | | | | | |

# SHORT-TERM TRANSACTIONS

Pages 188-191 can accompany next year's income tax return (Schedule D). Enter transactions as completed to avoid last-minute pressures.

| NO. OF SHARES | SECURITY | DATE ACQUIRED | DATE SOLD | SALE PRICE | COST | LOSS | GAIN |
|---|---|---|---|---|---|---|---|
| | | | | | | | |
| | | | | | | | |
| | | | | | | | |
| | | | | | | | |
| | | | | | | | |
| | | | | | | | |
| | | | | | | | |
| | | | | | | | |
| | | | | | | | |
| | | | | | | | |
| | | | | | | | |
| | | | | | | | |
| | | | | | | | |
| | | | | | | | |
| | | | | | | | |

**TOTALS:** Carry over to next page

188

| NO. OF SHARES | SECURITY | DATE ACQUIRED | DATE SOLD | SALE PRICE | COST | LOSS | GAIN |
|---|---|---|---|---|---|---|---|
| | | | | | | | |
| | | | | | | | |
| | | | | | | | |
| | | | | | | | |
| | | | | | | | |
| | | | | | | | |
| | | | | | | | |
| | | | | | | | |
| | | | | | | | |
| | | | | | | | |
| | | | | | | | |
| | | | | | | | |
| | | | | | | | |
| | | | | | | | |
| | | | | | | | |
| | | | | | | | |
| | | | | | | | |

TOTALS:

# LONG-TERM TRANSACTIONS

Pages 188-191 can accompany next year's income tax return (Schedule D). Enter transactions as completed to avoid last-minute pressures.

| NO. OF SHARES | SECURITY | DATE ACQUIRED | DATE SOLD | SALE PRICE | COST | LOSS | GAIN |
|---|---|---|---|---|---|---|---|
| | | | | | | | |
| | | | | | | | |
| | | | | | | | |
| | | | | | | | |
| | | | | | | | |
| | | | | | | | |
| | | | | | | | |
| | | | | | | | |
| | | | | | | | |
| | | | | | | | |
| | | | | | | | |
| | | | | | | | |
| | | | | | | | |

**TOTALS:** Carry over to next page

# LONG-TERM TRANSACTIONS (continued)

| NO. OF SHARES | SECURITY | DATE ACQUIRED | DATE SOLD | SALE PRICE | COST | LOSS | GAIN |
|---|---|---|---|---|---|---|---|
| | | | | | | | |
| | | | | | | | |
| | | | | | | | |
| | | | | | | | |
| | | | | | | | |
| | | | | | | | |
| | | | | | | | |
| | | | | | | | |
| | | | | | | | |
| | | | | | | | |
| | | | | | | | |
| | | | | | | | |
| | | | | | | | |
| | | | | | | | |
| | | | | | | | |

TOTALS:

191

# INTEREST/DIVIDENDS RECEIVED DURING 2023

| SHARES | STOCK/BOND | FIRST QUARTER | | SECOND QUARTER | | THIRD QUARTER | | FOURTH QUARTER | |
|--------|-----------|---------------|--|----------------|--|---------------|--|----------------|--|
| | | $ | | $ | | $ | | $ | |
| | | | | | | | | | |
| | | | | | | | | | |
| | | | | | | | | | |
| | | | | | | | | | |
| | | | | | | | | | |
| | | | | | | | | | |
| | | | | | | | | | |
| | | | | | | | | | |
| | | | | | | | | | |
| | | | | | | | | | |

# BROKERAGE ACCOUNT DATA 2023

| | MARGIN INTEREST | TRANSFER TAXES | CAPITAL ADDED | CAPITAL WITHDRAWN |
|-----|-----------------|----------------|---------------|-------------------|
| JAN | | | | |
| FEB | | | | |
| MAR | | | | |
| APR | | | | |
| MAY | | | | |
| JUN | | | | |
| JUL | | | | |
| AUG | | | | |
| SEP | | | | |
| OCT | | | | |
| NOV | | | | |
| DEC | | | | |

# PORTFOLIO PRICE RECORD 2023 (FIRST HALF)

Place purchase price above stock name and weekly closes below.

| STOCKS / Week ending | 1 | 2 | 3 | 4 | 5 | 6 | 7 | 8 | 9 | 10 |
|---|---|---|---|---|---|---|---|---|---|---|
| 6 | | | | | | | | | | |
| 13 | | | | | | | | | | |
| 20 | | | | | | | | | | |
| 27 | | | | | | | | | | |
| 3 | | | | | | | | | | |
| 10 | | | | | | | | | | |
| 17 | | | | | | | | | | |
| 24 | | | | | | | | | | |
| 3 | | | | | | | | | | |
| 10 | | | | | | | | | | |
| 17 | | | | | | | | | | |
| 24 | | | | | | | | | | |
| 31 | | | | | | | | | | |
| 7 | | | | | | | | | | |
| 14 | | | | | | | | | | |
| 21 | | | | | | | | | | |
| 28 | | | | | | | | | | |
| 5 | | | | | | | | | | |
| 12 | | | | | | | | | | |
| 19 | | | | | | | | | | |
| 26 | | | | | | | | | | |
| 2 | | | | | | | | | | |
| 9 | | | | | | | | | | |
| 16 | | | | | | | | | | |
| 23 | | | | | | | | | | |
| 30 | | | | | | | | | | |

# PORTFOLIO PRICE RECORD 2023 (SECOND HALF)

Place purchase price above stock name and weekly closes below.

| STOCKS | | | | | | | | | | |
|---|---|---|---|---|---|---|---|---|---|---|
| Week Ending | 1 | 2 | 3 | 4 | 5 | 6 | 7 | 8 | 9 | 10 |
| **JULY** | | | | | | | | | | |
| 7 | | | | | | | | | | |
| 14 | | | | | | | | | | |
| 21 | | | | | | | | | | |
| 28 | | | | | | | | | | |
| **AUGUST** | | | | | | | | | | |
| 4 | | | | | | | | | | |
| 11 | | | | | | | | | | |
| 18 | | | | | | | | | | |
| 25 | | | | | | | | | | |
| **SEPTEMBER** | | | | | | | | | | |
| 1 | | | | | | | | | | |
| 8 | | | | | | | | | | |
| 15 | | | | | | | | | | |
| 22 | | | | | | | | | | |
| 29 | | | | | | | | | | |
| **OCTOBER** | | | | | | | | | | |
| 6 | | | | | | | | | | |
| 13 | | | | | | | | | | |
| 20 | | | | | | | | | | |
| 27 | | | | | | | | | | |
| **NOVEMBER** | | | | | | | | | | |
| 3 | | | | | | | | | | |
| 10 | | | | | | | | | | |
| 17 | | | | | | | | | | |
| 24 | | | | | | | | | | |
| **DECEMBER** | | | | | | | | | | |
| 1 | | | | | | | | | | |
| 8 | | | | | | | | | | |
| 15 | | | | | | | | | | |
| 22 | | | | | | | | | | |
| 29 | | | | | | | | | | |

# WEEKLY INDICATOR DATA 2023 (FIRST HALF)

| Week Ending | Dow Jones Industrial Average | Net Change for Week | Net Change on Friday | Net Change Next Monday | S&P or NASDAQ | NYSE Ad-vances | NYSE De-clines | New Highs | New Lows | CBOE Put/Call Ratio | 90-Day Treas. Rate | Moody's AAA Rate |
|---|---|---|---|---|---|---|---|---|---|---|---|---|
| 6 | | | | | | | | | | | | |
| 13 | | | | | | | | | | | | |
| 20 | | | | | | | | | | | | |
| 27 | | | | | | | | | | | | |
| 3 | | | | | | | | | | | | |
| 10 | | | | | | | | | | | | |
| 17 | | | | | | | | | | | | |
| 24 | | | | | | | | | | | | |
| 3 | | | | | | | | | | | | |
| 10 | | | | | | | | | | | | |
| 17 | | | | | | | | | | | | |
| 24 | | | | | | | | | | | | |
| 31 | | | | | | | | | | | | |
| 7 | | | | | | | | | | | | |
| 14 | | | | | | | | | | | | |
| 21 | | | | | | | | | | | | |
| 28 | | | | | | | | | | | | |
| 5 | | | | | | | | | | | | |
| 12 | | | | | | | | | | | | |
| 19 | | | | | | | | | | | | |
| 26 | | | | | | | | | | | | |
| 2 | | | | | | | | | | | | |
| 9 | | | | | | | | | | | | |
| 16 | | | | | | | | | | | | |
| 23 | | | | | | | | | | | | |
| 30 | | | | | | | | | | | | |

# WEEKLY INDICATOR DATA 2023 (SECOND HALF)

| | Week Ending | Dow Jones Industrial Average | Net Change for Week | Net Change on Friday | Net Change Next Monday | S&P or NASDAQ | NYSE Advances | NYSE Declines | New Highs | New Lows | CBOE Put/Call Ratio | 90-Day Treas. Rate | Moody's AAA Rate |
|---|---|---|---|---|---|---|---|---|---|---|---|---|---|
| JULY | 7 | | | | | | | | | | | | |
| | 14 | | | | | | | | | | | | |
| | 21 | | | | | | | | | | | | |
| | 28 | | | | | | | | | | | | |
| AUGUST | 4 | | | | | | | | | | | | |
| | 11 | | | | | | | | | | | | |
| | 18 | | | | | | | | | | | | |
| | 25 | | | | | | | | | | | | |
| SEPTEMBER | 1 | | | | | | | | | | | | |
| | 8 | | | | | | | | | | | | |
| | 15 | | | | | | | | | | | | |
| | 22 | | | | | | | | | | | | |
| | 29 | | | | | | | | | | | | |
| OCTOBER | 6 | | | | | | | | | | | | |
| | 13 | | | | | | | | | | | | |
| | 20 | | | | | | | | | | | | |
| | 27 | | | | | | | | | | | | |
| NOVEMBER | 3 | | | | | | | | | | | | |
| | 10 | | | | | | | | | | | | |
| | 17 | | | | | | | | | | | | |
| | 24 | | | | | | | | | | | | |
| DECEMBER | 1 | | | | | | | | | | | | |
| | 8 | | | | | | | | | | | | |
| | 15 | | | | | | | | | | | | |
| | 22 | | | | | | | | | | | | |
| | 29 | | | | | | | | | | | | |

# MONTHLY INDICATOR DATA 2023

| | DJIA% Last 3 + 1st 2 Days | DJIA% 9th to 11th Trading Days | DJIA% Change Rest of Month | DJIA% Change Whole Month | % Change Your Stocks | Gross Domestic Product | Prime Rate | Trade Deficit $ Billion | CPI % Change | % Unem- ployment Rate |
|-----|---|---|---|---|---|---|---|---|---|---|
| JAN | | | | | | | | | | |
| FEB | | | | | | | | | | |
| MAR | | | | | | | | | | |
| APR | | | | | | | | | | |
| MAY | | | | | | | | | | |
| JUN | | | | | | | | | | |
| JUL | | | | | | | | | | |
| AUG | | | | | | | | | | |
| SEP | | | | | | | | | | |
| OCT | | | | | | | | | | |
| NOV | | | | | | | | | | |
| DEC | | | | | | | | | | |

## INSTRUCTIONS:

**Weekly Indicator Data** (pages 195-196). Keeping data on several indicators may give you a better feel for the market. In addition to the closing DJIA and its net change for the week, post the net change for Friday's Dow and also the following Monday's. A series of "down Fridays" followed by "down Mondays" often precedes a downswing (see page 78). Tracking either the S&P or NASDAQ composite, and advances and declines, will help prevent the Dow from misleading you. New highs and lows and put/call ratios (www.cboe.com) are also useful indicators. Many of these weekly figures appear in weekend papers or Barron's (https://www.barrons.com/market-data/market-lab). Data for the 90-day Treasury Rate and Moody's AAA Bond Rate are quite important for tracking short- and long-term interest rates. These figures are available from:

Weekly U.S. Financial Data
Federal Reserve Bank of St. Louis
P.O. Box 442
St. Louis MO 63166
**https://fred.stlouisfed.org/**

**Monthly Indicator Data.** The purpose of the first three columns is to enable you to track the market's bullish bias near the end, beginning and middle of the month, which has been shifting lately (see pages 86, 147 and 148). Market direction, performance of your stocks, gross domestic product, prime rate, trade deficit, Consumer Price Index, and unemployment rate are worthwhile indicators to follow. Or, readers may wish to gauge other data.

# PORTFOLIO AT END OF 2023

| DATE ACQUIRED | NO. OF SHARES | SECURITY | PRICE | TOTAL COST | PAPER PROFITS | PAPER LOSSES |
|---|---|---|---|---|---|---|
| | | | | | | |
| | | | | | | |
| | | | | | | |
| | | | | | | |
| | | | | | | |
| | | | | | | |
| | | | | | | |
| | | | | | | |
| | | | | | | |
| | | | | | | |
| | | | | | | |
| | | | | | | |
| | | | | | | |
| | | | | | | |
| | | | | | | |
| | | | | | | |
| | | | | | | |
| | | | | | | |
| | | | | | | |
| | | | | | | |
| | | | | | | |
| | | | | | | |
| | | | | | | |
| | | | | | | |
| | | | | | | |

# IF YOU DON'T PROFIT FROM YOUR
# INVESTMENT MISTAKES, SOMEONE ELSE WILL

No matter how much we may deny it, almost every successful person in Wall Street pays a great deal of attention to trading suggestions—especially when they come from "the right sources."

One of the hardest things to learn is to distinguish between good tips and bad ones. Usually, the best tips have a logical reason in back of them, which accompanies the tip. Poor tips usually have no reason to support them.

The important thing to remember is that the market discounts. It does not review, it does not reflect. The Street's real interest in "tips," inside information, buying and selling suggestions, and everything else of this kind emanates from a desire to find out just what the market has on hand to discount. The process of finding out involves separating the wheat from the chaff—and there is plenty of chaff.

---

### HOW TO MAKE USE OF STOCK "TIPS"

- The source should be **reliable**. (By listing all "tips" and suggestions on a Performance Record of Recommendations, such as the form below, and then periodically evaluating the outcomes, you will soon know the "batting average" of your sources.)

- The story should make sense. Would the merger violate antitrust laws? Are there too many computers on the market already? How many years will it take to become profitable?

- The stock should not have had a recent sharp run-up. Otherwise, the story may already be discounted, and confirmation or denial in the press would most likely be accompanied by a sell-off in the stock.

---

## PERFORMANCE RECORD OF RECOMMENDATIONS

| STOCK RECOMMENDED | BY WHOM | DATE | PRICE | REASON FOR RECOMMENDATION | SUBSEQUENT ACTION OF STOCK |
|---|---|---|---|---|---|
|  |  |  |  |  |  |
|  |  |  |  |  |  |
|  |  |  |  |  |  |
|  |  |  |  |  |  |
|  |  |  |  |  |  |
|  |  |  |  |  |  |
|  |  |  |  |  |  |
|  |  |  |  |  |  |

# INDIVIDUAL RETIREMENT ACCOUNTS: MOST AWESOME INVESTMENT INCENTIVE EVER DEVISED

MAX IRA INVESTMENTS OF $6,000* A YEAR COMPOUNDED AT VARIOUS INTEREST RATES OF RETURN FOR DIFFERENT PERIODS

| Annual Rate | 5 Yrs | 10 Yrs | 15 Yrs | 20 Yrs | 25 Yrs | 30 Yrs | 35 Yrs | 40 Yrs | 45 Yrs | 50 Yrs |
|---|---|---|---|---|---|---|---|---|---|---|
| 1% | $30,912 | $63,401 | $97,547 | $133,435 | $171,154 | $210,796 | $252,461 | $296,251 | $342,275 | $390,647 |
| 2% | 31,849 | 67,012 | 105,836 | 148,700 | 196,025 | 248,277 | 305,966 | 369,660 | 439,983 | 517,626 |
| 3% | 32,810 | 70,847 | 114,941 | 166,059 | 225,318 | 294,016 | 373,656 | 465,980 | 573,009 | 697,085 |
| 4% | 33,798 | 74,918 | 124,947 | 185,815 | 259,870 | 349,970 | 459,590 | 592,959 | 755,223 | 952,643 |
| 5% | 34,811 | 79,241 | 135,945 | 208,316 | 300,681 | 418,565 | 569,018 | 761,039 | 1,006,111 | 1,318,892 |
| 6% | 35,852 | 83,830 | 148,035 | 233,956 | 348,938 | 502,810 | 708,725 | 984,286 | 1,353,049 | 1,846,536 |
| 7% | 36,920 | 88,702 | 161,328 | 263,191 | 406,059 | 606,438 | 887,481 | 1,281,657 | 1,834,511 | 2,609,916 |
| 8% | 38,016 | 93,873 | 175,946 | 296,538 | 473,726 | 734,075 | 1,116,613 | 1,678,686 | 2,504,556 | 3,718,031 |
| 9% | 39,140 | 99,362 | 192,020 | 334,587 | 553,944 | 891,451 | 1,410,748 | 2,209,751 | 3,439,116 | 5,330,646 |
| 10% | 40,294 | 105,187 | 209,698 | 378,015 | 649,091 | 1,085,661 | 1,788,761 | 2,921,111 | 4,744,772 | 7,681,796 |
| 11% | 41,477 | 111,369 | 229,140 | 427,591 | 761,993 | 1,325,479 | 2,274,986 | 3,874,962 | 6,571,013 | 11,114,016 |
| 12% | 42,691 | 117,927 | 250,520 | 484,192 | 896,004 | 1,621,756 | 2,900,779 | 5,154,854 | 9,127,306 | 16,128,123 |
| 13% | 43,936 | 124,886 | 274,030 | 548,820 | 1,055,101 | 1,987,891 | 3,706,496 | 6,872,915 | 12,706,836 | 23,455,458 |
| 14% | 45,213 | 132,267 | 299,882 | 622,611 | 1,243,996 | 2,440,422 | 4,744,037 | 9,179,452 | 17,719,463 | 34,162,526 |
| 15% | 46,522 | 140,096 | 328,305 | 706,861 | 1,468,272 | 2,999,742 | 6,080,074 | 12,275,723 | 24,737,386 | 49,802,242 |
| 16% | 47,865 | 148,397 | 359,550 | 803,043 | 1,734,530 | 3,690,970 | 7,800,162 | 16,430,870 | 34,558,306 | 72,632,115 |
| 17% | 49,241 | 157,200 | 393,893 | 912,831 | 2,050,576 | 4,545,023 | 10,013,967 | 22,004,343 | 48,292,620 | 105,928,302 |
| 18% | 50,652 | 166,531 | 431,634 | 1,038,126 | 2,425,633 | 5,599,912 | 12,861,893 | 29,475,548 | 67,483,566 | 154,436,703 |
| 19% | 52,098 | 176,421 | 473,101 | 1,181,085 | 2,870,583 | 6,902,325 | 16,523,486 | 39,482,979 | 94,272,449 | 225,019,501 |
| 20% | 53,580 | 186,903 | 518,653 | 1,344,154 | 3,398,264 | 8,509,547 | 21,228,056 | 52,875,776 | 131,625,432 | 327,579,773 |

* At some time, 2023 Contribution Limit will be indexed to inflation.

# G. M. LOEB'S "BATTLE PLAN" FOR INVESTMENT SURVIVAL

**LIFE IS CHANGE**: Nothing can ever be the same a minute from now as it was a minute ago. Everything you own is changing in price and value. You can find that last price of an active security on the stock ticker, but you cannot find the next price anywhere. The value of your money is changing. Even the value of your home is changing, though no one walks in front of it with a sandwich board consistently posting the changes.

**RECOGNIZE CHANGE**: Your basic objective should be to profit from change. The art of investing is being able to recognize change and to adjust investment goals accordingly.

**WRITE THINGS DOWN**: You will score more investment success and avoid more investment failures if you write things down. Very few investors have the drive and inclination to do this.

**KEEP A CHECKLIST**: If you aim to improve your investment results, get into the habit of keeping a checklist on every issue you consider buying. Before making a commitment, it will pay you to write down the answers to at least some of the basic questions—How much am I investing in this company? How much do I think I can make? How much do I have to risk? How long do I expect to take to reach my goal?

**HAVE A SINGLE RULING REASON**: Above all, writing things down is the best way to find "the ruling reason." When all is said and done, there is invariably a single reason that stands out above all others, why a particular security transaction can be expected to show a profit. All too often, many relatively unimportant statistics are allowed to obscure this single important point.

Any one of a dozen factors may be the point of a particular purchase or sale. It could be a technical reason—an increase in earnings or dividend not yet discounted in the market price—a change of management—a promising new product—an expected improvement in the market's valuation of earnings—or many others. But, in any given case, one of these factors will almost certainly be more important than all the rest put together.

**CLOSING OUT A COMMITMENT**: If you have a loss, the solution is automatic, provided you decide what to do at the time you buy. Otherwise, the question divides itself into two parts. Are we in a bull or bear market? Few of us really know until it is too late. For the sake of the record, if you think it is a bear market, just put that consideration first and sell as much as your conviction suggests and your nature allows.

If you think it is a bull market, or at least a market where some stocks move up, some mark time, and only a few decline, do not sell unless:

✓ You see a bear market ahead.

✓ You see trouble for a particular company in which you own shares.

✓ Time and circumstances have turned up a new and seemingly far better buy than the issue you like least in your list.

✓ Your shares stop going up and start going down.

A subsidiary question is: Which stock to sell first? Two further observations may help:

✓ Do not sell solely because you think a stock is "overvalued."

✓ If you want to sell some of your stocks and not all, in most cases it is better to go against your emotional inclinations and sell first the issues with losses, small profits, or none at all, the weakest, the most disappointing, etc.

Mr. Loeb is the author of *The Battle for Investment Survival*, John Wiley & Sons.

# G. M. LOEB'S INVESTMENT SURVIVAL CHECKLIST

## OBJECTIVES AND RISKS

| Security | | Price | Shares | Date |
|---|---|---|---|---|
| | | | | |

"Ruling reason" for commitment

Amount of commitment

$ _____

% of my investment capital

_____ %

| Price objective | Est. time to achieve it | I will risk _____ points | Which would be $ _____ |
|---|---|---|---|

## TECHNICAL POSITION

Price action of stock:

❏ Hitting new highs                    ❏ In a trading range

❏ Pausing in an uptrend            ❏ Moving up from low ground

❏ Acting stronger than market    ❏ _____

Dow Jones Industrial Average

Trend of market

## SELECTED YARDSTICKS

| | Price Range | | Earnings Per Share Actual or Projected | Price/Earnings Ratio Actual or Projected |
|---|---|---|---|---|
| | High | Low | | |
| Current year | | | | |
| Previous year | | | | |
| Merger possibilities | | | Years for earnings to double in past | |
| Comment on future | | | Years for market price to double in past | |

## PERIODIC RE-CHECKS

| Date | Stock Price | DJIA | Comment | Action taken, if any |
|---|---|---|---|---|
| | | | | |
| | | | | |

## COMPLETED TRANSACTIONS

| Date closed | Period of time held | Profit or loss |
|---|---|---|

Reason for profit or loss

# NOTES

# NOTES